This edition published in 2010

Copyright © Carlton Books Limited 2010

Carlton Books Limited
20 Mortimer Street
London W1T 3JW

A CIP catalogue record for this book is available from the
British Library

10 9 8 7 6 5 4 3 2 1

ISBN: 978-1-84732-635-5

Editor: Martin Corteel
Designer: Paul Chattaway
Picture research: Paul Langan
Production: Rachel Burgess

Manufactured under licence by Carlton Books

Printed in Dubai

OVERLEAF: Stars of world
football: Top: Xavi (Spain);
Upper (left to right): Wayne
Rooney (England), Patrice Evra
(France), Birgit Prinz (Germany); Lower
(left to right): Cristiano Ronaldo (Portugal),
Lionel Messi (Argentina), Obafemi Martins
(Nigeria); Bottom: Iker Casillas (Spain, with
FIFA World Cup Trophy).

WORLD FOOTBALL RECORDS 2011

KEIR RADNEDGE

FIFA OFFICIAL LICENSED PRODUCT

© 2005 FIFA

CONTENTS

⚽ **Introduction** 6

⚽ **PART 1: FIFA WORLD CUP™** 8

2010 FIFA World Cup South Africa™ 10

Team Records 12   Player Records 14   Other Records 16

⚽ **FIFA World Cup™: All-Time Records** 18

FIFA World Cup: Qualifiers 20   FIFA World Cup: Team Records 26

FIFA World Cup: Goalscoring 30   FIFA World Cup: Appearances 36

FIFA World Cup: Goalkeeping 40   FIFA World Cup: Managers 44

FIFA World Cup: Refereeing 46   FIFA World Cup: Discipline 48

FIFA World Cup: Attendances 50   FIFA World Cup: Stadiums & Hosts 52

FIFA World Cup: Penalties 54

⚽ **PART 2: THE COUNTRIES** 56

Europe 58   **England** 60   **France** 66   **Germany** 72

Netherlands 78   **Italy** 84   **Spain** 90   **Belgium** 96   **Bulgaria** 98

Croatia 100   **Czech Republic** 102   **Denmark** 104   **Greece** 106

Hungary 108   **Northern Ireland** 110   **Norway** 112   **Poland** 114

Portugal 116   **Republic of Ireland** 118   **Romania** 120   **Russia** 122

Scotland 124   **Serbia** 126   **Sweden** 128   **Switzerland** 130   **Turkey** 132

Ukraine 134   **Wales** 136   **Other Teams Europe** 138

⚽ **South America** 144

Argentina 146   **Brazil** 150   **Uruguay** 154

Other Teams South America 156

⚽ **Africa** 160

North Africa: FIFA World Cup Records 162

North Africa: National Records 164

Sub-Saharan Africa: FIFA World Cup Records 166

Sub-Saharan Africa: National Records 168

⚽ **Asia & Oceania** 170

Australia 172

Other Asian Countries 174

Oceania 180

⚽ **CONCACAF** 182

Mexico 184

United States 186

CONCACAF Other Teams 188

⚽ **PART 3: EUROPEAN CHAMPIONSHIP** 190

European Championship: Qualifiers 192   European Championship: Team Records 194

European Championship: Player Records 196   European Championship: Other Records 198

⚽ PART 4: COPA AMERICA 200

Copa America: Team Records 202   Copa America: Player Records 204

Copa America: Other Records 206

⚽ PART 5: AFRICA CUP OF NATIONS 208

Africa Cup of Nations: Team Records 210

Africa Cup of Nations: Player Records 212   Africa Cup of Nations: Other Records 214

⚽ PART 6: OTHER FIFA TOURNAMENTS 216

FIFA U-20 World Cup 218   FIFA U-17 World Cup 220

FIFA Confederations Cup 222   FIFA Club World Cup 224

Men's Olympic Football Tournament 226

Blue Stars/FIFA Youth Cup 230   FIFA Futsal World Cup 231

FIFA Beach Soccer World Cup 232   FIFA Interactive World Cup 233

⚽ PART 7: WOMEN'S FOOTBALL 234

FIFA Women's World Cup 236

Other Women's Tournaments 240

⚽ APPENDIX 1: FIFA AWARDS 242

FIFA Player of the Year 2009 244

FIFA Women's Player of the Year 2009 245

Other FIFA Awards 246

⚽ APPENDIX 2:

FIFA/Coca-Cola World
Rankings 2010 248

⚽ INDEX 252

AFRICA'S historic first staging of the FIFA World Cup in 2010 is the focus of the comprehensively revised second edition of *FIFA World Football Records 2011*. South Africa provided a unique backdrop for the four-yearly showcase of the world game – a host nation whose unified efforts provided both the best possible facilities as well as joyous welcome to the players, officials, fans and journalists who descended on the country.

South Africa, in even its short life back in the international fold, had staged other world sports events. But nothing compared with the impact on national life of the FIFA World Cup, not only through events between 11 June and 11 July of 2010 but also through significant social and infrastructural legacies. The value of the FIFA World Cup will thus live on – just as images of the games, the goals and the drama will live on in the minds of those who witnessed them live in the stadiums or via the medium of television.

This volume maintains its own mission to explore, explain and intrigue the reader with the people and places and competitions that have made association football the No.1 sport around the globe. The FIFA World Cup is the cornerstone of the international game and events at the finals define the direction of the game over the subsequent four years. Thus this volume focuses on key events and people from the FIFA World Cup, the finalist nations and then on all those other events which link the football family from Albania to Zimbabwe.

Pioneers introduced here such as Charles Alcock and Lord Kinnaird could never have dreamed, when they constructed the original laws of the game in the 19th century, how they would one day be interpreted by the likes of Leo Messi, Diego Forlan, Cristiano Ronaldo and the ever-refreshing wave of new heroes such as Germany's Thomas Muller and Ghana's Andre Ayew.

Special thanks are due to Jolene Kieu at Global Brands, and to the editorial writers and researchers on the project, in particular to Aidan Radnedge, as well as Kevin Connolly, David Ballheimer, Mary Morton and Fred Morton.

The pace of change and development in the world game creates an insoluble challenge for any statistician. The game never stands still; records from only yesterday are being superseded not merely year by year or month by month but day by day and match by match. Thus a cut-off point of the 2010 FIFA World Cup final was established for the statistical information contained here.

The nature of the game's development within the modern nation-state framework means many of the older official records are at variance. This applied particularly in the cross-over years between amateur and professional football. But the majority of fixed points remain incontrovertible ever since the original challenge matches between Scotland and England in the late 19th century.

Since then football has accumulated many labels: as the simplest game, as the game of the people and as the beautiful game. It is also a game whose passion encircles the world ... just like the 2010 FIFA World Cup South Africa.

When almost all – bar the final – had been said and done on the pitch at Soccer City, the 2010 FIFA World Cup closing ceremony featured Colombian singer Shakira performing the tournament song "Waka Waka".

PART 1:
FIFA WORLD CUP™

THE thrill and passion of victory and defeat, that soaring dynamic of delight and depression which envelops millions, is the key to the amazing success of the FIFA World Cup. Its progression to world sports event domination has been reflected in the steady expansion of the finals tournament. Initially 13 nations competed, and the number varied until it became formalized at 16 in 1954, then, in 1982, came an increase to 24 and – since 1998 – the focus has been on 32 finalists.

But football fans all around the world, not merely those of the lucky 32, devour the multi-platform coverage in the media to follow the fortunes – good and bad – of the heroes of Spain, Holland, Germany, Brazil, Italy, England, Argentina and their global rivals.

The FIFA World Cup was launched in 1930 in Uruguay, its inspiration being derived from the persuasive powers of FIFA's then-president, Frenchman Jules Rimet. Uruguay had been Olympic champions in 1924 and 1928, but the advent of professionalism meant that the supposedly all-amateur Olympic Games could no longer claim to represent a footballing pinnacle of excellence. Only four European nations dared send teams on the long sea crossing to Montevideo for the first finals – though it was Frenchman Lucien Laurent who made history by scoring the first-ever goal in the FIFA World Cup. Since then, however, Europe has more than made amends for its initial reluctance. It outstrips South America with 10 FIFA World Cup wins to nine and has played host to the tournament on 10 occasions (Italy, France and Germany, twice each, plus once in Switzerland, Sweden, England and Spain) – far ahead of the four held in South America (Uruguay, Brazil, Chile and Argentina all one apiece), three in Central and North America (Mexico, twice, and the United States) and one each in Asia (Japan and South Korea as co-hosts) and, of course, Africa (South Africa in 2010).

The party will return in 2014, back in Brazil – a nation which treats football with an almost religious fervour.

As a mist of ticker-tape envelops them, excited Spanish players pass around the FIFA World Cup Trophy following their dramatic 1-0 extra-time victory over Holland in the 2010 final at Soccer City, Johannesburg.

2010 FIFA WORLD CUP SOUTH AFRICA™

South Africa hosted a remarkable 2010 FIFA World Cup™ between 11 June and 11 July: the combined attendance of more than three million at the 64 matches was the third-largest in the history of the tournament. And the global television audience for the final between Spain and Holland was recorded at more than 700 million. This first-ever African hosting of the finals was staged in 10 venues in nine cities spread across the nation.

Fireworks light up the night sky around the Soccer City Stadium in Johannesburg at the start of the closing ceremony of the 2010 FIFA World Cup.

TEAM RECORDS

HOME DISCOMFORT

Uruguay's 3-0 victory over South Africa in Pretoria on 16 June 2010 equalled the highest losing margin suffered by a FIFA World Cup host, following Brazil's 5-2 win over Sweden in the 1958 final and Italy's 4-1 trouncing of Mexico in their 1970 quarter-final.

KIWI HAPPY THREE

Only one team finished the 2010 FIFA World Cup unbeaten – and it wasn't eventual champions Spain. Instead an unblemished record rested with minnows New Zealand alone. They drew all three of their Group F games – against Slovakia, Italy (**Shane Smeltz** scoring in a 1-1 stalemate) and Paraguay but failed to reach the second round on goal difference.

COMEBACK KINGS

After a shock 1-0 defeat to Switzerland in their opening game of the 2010 FIFA World Cup, **Iker Casillas**, Spain's captain, became the first man to lift the trophy after his team had lost their first match.

THREE AND OUT

Holland, coached by **Bert van Marwijk** in 2010, are the only country to have reached the final of three FIFA World Cups without managing to lift the trophy even once. Their six victories en route to the 2010 final are also more than any other team has managed in one tournament without going on to claim the main prize.

CONSOLING KOMANO

When Paraguay beat Japan on penalties in the second round in 2010, it was the first of 21 FIFA World Cup shoot-outs not to involve at least one European team. Japan full-back **Yuichi Komano** was the only player to miss, hitting the bar as Paraguay won 5-3. But the distraught defender was promised sympathy – and a special commemorative World Cup medal – on his return home to Japan.

FIRST ELEVEN

In an age of squad numbers, Brazil may have pleased some traditionalists when fielding players wearing shirt numbers one to 11 in their starting line-ups for their first two games of the 2010 FIFA World Cup, against North Korea and the Ivory Coast. Kicking off for Dunga on each occasion were: 1 Julio Cesar, 2 Maicon, 3 Lucio, 4 Juan, 5 Felipe Melo, 6 Michel Bastos, 7 Elano, 8 Gilberto Silva, 9 Luis Fabiano, 10 Kaka and 11 Robinho. Holland managed a similar starting structure for not only their second-round tie against Slovakia, but the final against Spain: 1 Maarten Stekelenburg, 2 Gregory van der Wiel, 3 John Heitinga, 4 Joris Mathijsen, 5 Giovanni van Bronckhorst, 6 Mark van Bommel, 7 Dirk Kuyt, 8 Nigel de Jong, 9 Robin van Persie, 10 Wesley Sneijder and 11 Arjen Robben. Both Brazil and Holland came close to the same feat when they met in the quarter-finals, though both featured a number 13 – Brazil's Dani Alves, in place of 7 Elano, and Holland's Andre Ooijer instead of 4 Joris Mathijsen (Elano and Mathijsen were unavailable through injury).

SAFE EUROPEAN HOME

Europe edged ahead of South America in FIFA World Cup wins thanks to Spain's 2010 glory, making it 10-9 to Europe since the first tournament in 1930. This was also the first time a European team had won the trophy outside their own continent, and – after Italy's success in 2006 – the first time the prize has gone to different European nations twice in succession.

2010 FIFA WORLD CUP™ RANKINGS

These are the tournament rankings of the 32 finalists. They should not be confused with the FIFA/Coca-Cola World Rankings on pp250–51,

1 Spain
2 Netherlands
3 Germany
4 Uruguay
5 Argentina
6 Brazil
7 Ghana
8 Paraguay
9 Japan
10 Chile
11 Portugal
12 USA
13 England
14 Mexico
15 South Korea
16 Slovakia
17 Ivory Coast
18 Slovenia
19 Switzerland
20 South Africa
21 Australia
22 New Zealand
23 Serbia
24 Denmark
25 Greece
26 Italy
27 Nigeria
28 Algeria
29 France
30 Honduras
31 Cameroon
32 North Korea

DO YOU COME HERE OFTEN?

Germany or West Germany have now played Yugoslavia/Serbia a record-equalling seven times at FIFA World Cup finals, after **Milan Jovanovic**'s (red shirt) goal gave Serbia a 1-0 win in Port Elizabeth in the 2010 tournament. Germany enjoyed victories in 1954, 1958, 1974 and 1990, while Yugoslavia won in 1962 and the countries drew in 1998. There have also been seven FIFA World Cup clashes between Brazil and Sweden, though the latter have yet to taste success. Brazil won in 1938, 1950, 1958, 1990 and twice in 1994, but they drew in 1978.

2010 FIFA WORLD CUP™ BY THE NUMBERS

Most goals scored:	Germany (16)
Most goals conceded:	North Korea (12)
Fewest goals scored:	Algeria, Honduras (0)
Fewest goals conceded:	Spain (2)
Most wins:	Spain, Netherlands (6)
Fewest wins:	Algeria, Cameroon, France, Honduras, Italy, New Zealand, Nigeria, North Korea (0)
Most defeats:	Cameroon, North Korea (3)
Fewest defeats:	New Zealand (0)
Most yellow cards:	Netherlands (25)
Fewest yellow cards:	North Korea (2)
Most red cards:	Australia, Algeria, Brazil, Uruguay (2)
Fewest red cards:	Argentina, Cameroon, Denmark, England, Ghana, Greece, Honduras, Italy, Ivory Coast, Japan, Mexico, New Zealand, North Korea, Paraguay, Slovakia, Slovenia, South Korea, Spain, USA (0)
Fair play award:	Spain

SPAIN GAIN

The FIFA World Cup trophy has a new name engraved on it for the first time since 1998 after **Spain** beat Holland 1-0 in the 2010 final, in Johannesburg's Soccer City stadium on 11 July. The match was the first final in 32 years to feature two teams who had never won the competition before. The only previous finals featuring two non-former winners were when Argentina beat the Dutch in 1978, Brazil beat Sweden in 1958, West Germany beat Hungary in 1954, Italy beat Czechoslovakia in 1934 and, of course, Uruguay beat Argentina in the inaugural 1930 tournament.

GOLDEN YEARS FOR URUGUAY

While his Uruguay team finished fourth at the 2010 FIFA World Cup, forward Diego Forlan did win the Golden Ball after being voted the best player of the competition. Dutch playmaker Wesley Sneijder finished second and Spanish striker David Villa third. Forlan became Uruguay's second Golden Ball winner, though the honour granted to 1930 captain Jose Nasazzi was a retrospective one. FIFA decisions on who deserved the prizes for the 1930–1978 tournaments were devised only after the award was first presented in 1982. In 2010, Forlan received 23.4 per cent of the vote to Sneijder's 21.8 per cent and Villa's 16.9 per cent.

INDIVIDUAL AWARDS/ACHIEVEMENTS

Golden Ball (best player)	Diego Forlan (Uruguay)
Silver Ball (second-best player)	Wesley Sneijder (Netherlands)
Bronze Ball (third-best player)	David Villa (Spain)
Golden Boot (top scorer)	Thomas Muller (Germany), five goals, three assists
Silver Boot (second-top scorer)	David Villa (Spain), five goals, one assist (634 minutes)
Bronze Boot (third-top scorer)	Wesley Sneijder (Holland), five goals, one assist (652 mins)
Golden Glove (best goalkeeper)	Iker Casillas (Spain)
Hyundai young player	Thomas Muller
Most yellow cards	John Heitinga (Holland), Kaka (Brazil), Aleksandar Lukovic (Serbia), 3
Oldest scorer	Cuauhtemoc Blanco (37 years, 151 days), Mexico v France
Youngest scorer	Thomas Muller (20 years, 273 days), Germany v Australia
Fastest goal	Thomas Muller (2 minutes, 38 seconds), Germany v Argentina
Most assists	Kaka (Brazil), Dirk Kuyt (Holland), Thomas Muller, Mesut Ozil (Germany), Bastian Schweinsteiger (Germany), 3
Most man of the match awards	Wesley Sneijder (Holland) 4

JAMES THE FIRST

England goalkeeper **David James** was the oldest player at the 2010 FIFA World Cup and played in three of his side's four games, after missing the first against the United States when Robert Green was preferred. James was 39 years and 330 days old for his final appearance of the summer, a 4-1 second-round defeat to Germany. After being an unused reserve goalkeeper in 2002 and 2006, James's inclusion in Fabio Capello's 2010 starting line-ups spared him from becoming the first player to go to three different FIFA World Cup finals without seeing any action.

DIFFERENT DRUMS

Dutch playmaker **Wesley Sneijder** won four Budweiser man of the match prizes, more than any other player. The prize was designed by South African graduate Jonathan Fundudis and based on the design of the traditional African "djembe" drum. Four more players received the prize three times apiece: Japan's Keisuke Honda, Portugal's Cristiano Ronaldo, Uruguay's Diego Forlan, and Spain's Andres Iniesta, who was voted best player of the final against Holland.

GOING FOR GOLD

Four different players were tied as top scorer at the 2010 FIFA World Cup, but for the first time, the adidas Golden Boot prize was awarded to only one after being decided on goals set up as well as goals scored. Uruguay's Diego Forlan, Spain's David Villa and Holland's Wesley Sneijder missed out on the award, which went to Germany's 20-year-old Thomas Muller. Like them, he had scored five times, but he had also contributed more assists – three, compared with one apiece for Villa, Sneijder and Forlan. Villa received the adidas Silver Boot, because he made his contributions in fewer minutes on the pitch (634) than adidas Bronze Boot recipient Sneijder (652) or Forlan (654).

TROUBLE TWENTY

Uruguay's defensive midfielder Diego Perez committed more fouls than any other player at the 2010 FIFA World Cup. His tally of 20 offences was one more than Holland's Mark van Bommel and Japanese playmaker Keisuke Honda.

ANDRES THE GIANT

Spain's hero in the 2010 FIFA World Cup final was **Andres Iniesta**, whose 116th-minute goal was also the latest trophy-winning goal in the tournament's history. Iniesta celebrated by taking off his Spain shirt and revealing a T-shirt bearing a message in honour of former Espanyol defender Dani Jarque, who died of a heart attack aged 26 in August 2009. Iniesta was booked for taking off his shirt but later said it was a worthwhile sacrifice to pay tribute to his old friend and Spain U21s team-mate. After the game, two more members of the victorious Spain squad – Sergio Ramos and Jesus Navas – wore T-shirts paying similar tribute to former Sevilla and Spain team-mate Antonio Puerta, who died of a cardiac arrest at the age of 22 in August 2007.

SCORING SKIPPERS

Both captains scored when Holland beat Uruguay in their Cape Town semi-final – **Giovanni van Bronckhorst** for the Dutch, **Diego Forlan** for Uruguay. This had happened only four times before in FIFA World Cup history.

WOE FOR ASAMOAH

Ghana striker **Asamoah Gyan** is the only player to have missed two penalties, during match time, at FIFA World Cups. He hit the post with a spot-kick against the Czech Republic during a group game at the 2006 tournament, then struck a shot against the bar with the final kick of extra-time in Ghana's 2010 quarter-final versus Uruguay. Had he scored then, Gyan would have given Ghana a 2-1 win – following Luis Suarez's goal-stopping handball on the goal-line – and a first African place in a FIFA World Cup semi-final. Despite such a traumatic miss, Gyan did then step up to take Ghana's first penalty in the shoot-out, again striking it high – but this time into the back of the net. His team still lost, though, 4-2 on penalties. Gyan did at least end the tournament as Africa's second-top scorer in FIFA World Cup matches, on four goals – beaten only by Cameroon's five-goal Roger Milla.

DOUBLE DEUTSCH

Germany enjoyed double success when it came to players' prizes, in both 2006 and 2010. On home turf in 2006, German striker Miroslav Klose won the Golden Boot as leading scorer while team-mate Lukas Podolski was named Hyundai Young Player of the Tournament, ahead of Portugal's Cristiano Ronaldo and Ecuador's Luis Antonio Valencia. Four years later, 20-year-old **Thomas Muller** won not only the Golden Boot but also the young player prize – ahead of Ghana's Andre Ayew and Mexico's Giovani dos Santos, who were also nominated.

INDIVIDUAL AWARDS/ACHIEVEMENTS

Goalkeeper: Iker Casillas (Spain)
Defenders: Maicon (Brazil), Sergio Ramos (Spain), Carles Puyol (Spain), Philipp Lahm (Germany)
Midfielders: Andres Iniesta (Spain), Xavi (Spain), Bastian Schweinsteiger (Germany), Wesley Sneijder (Holland)
Attackers: Diego Forlan (Uruguay), David Villa (Spain)
Coach: Vicente del Bosque (Spain)

2010 FIFA WORLD CUP STADIUMS

Stadium	City	Capacity	Goals	Matches
Soccer City	Johannesburg	84,490	21	8
Green Point Stadium	Cape Town	64,100	22	8
Moses Mabhida Stadium	Durban	62,760	14	7
Ellis Park Stadium	Johannesburg	55,686	19	7
Loftus Versfeld Stadium	Pretoria	42,858	11	6
Nelson Mandela Bay Stadium	Port Elizabeth	42,486	16	8
Peter Mokaba Stadium	Polokwane	41,733	5	4
Mbombela Stadium	Nelspruit	40,929	9	4
Free State Stadium	Bloemfontein	40,911	14	6
Royal Bafokeng Stadium	Rustenburg	38,646	14	6

PRIZE MONEY (teams listed in post-finals FIFA ranking order)

$30 million: Spain (champions)

$24 million: Netherlands (runners-up)

$20 million: Germany (third)

$18 million: Uruguay (fourth)

$14 million: Argentina, Brazil, Ghana, Paraguay (quarter-finals losers)

$9 million: Japan, Chile, Portugal, United States, England, Mexico, South Korea, Slovakia (second round losers)

$8 million: Ivory Coast, Slovenia, Switzerland, South Africa, Australia, New Zealand, Serbia, Denmark, Greece, Italy, Nigeria, Algeria, France, Honduras, Cameroon, North Korea (knocked out in the first round)

VERY EARLY BATHS

Quickfire offenders at the 2010 FIFA World Cup included Algerian striker **Abdelkader Ghezzal**, booked within a minute of coming on as a substitute against Slovakia and sent off after 15 minutes for his second yellow. Uruguay's young playmaker **Nicolas Lodeiro** lasted just 16 minutes as a substitute against France before becoming the first dismissal of the tournament – receiving one booking for kicking the ball away and a second for a late lunge on Bacary Sagna. But it was Brazilian superstar Kaka who left the least time between his first and second yellow cards in one match – receiving his first booking after 85 minutes of his first-round match against the Ivory Coast, before a second yellow, and inevitable red, just three minutes later.

FINE HOST

Siphiwe Tshabalala's goal for South Africa at Soccer City, Johannesburg, in the opening match of FIFA World Cup 2010 not only gave his team the lead against Mexico – it was also the fifth time the hosts had scored the first goal of a FIFA World Cup. Previous examples were: Ademir, for Brazil in a 4-0 win over Mexico in 1950; Agne Simonsson, for Sweden in a 3-0 win, also against Mexico, in 1958; Paul Breitner, West Germany's only and winning goal, against Chile in 1974 (though it was in the second game – Brazil and Yugoslavia having played out a goalless draw); and Philipp Lahm, for Germany in a 4-2 defeat of Costa Rica in 2006. It was the fourth time Mexico conceded the first goal of a FIFA World Cup. As well as Ademir and Simonsson, Mexico conceded the first ever goal in a FIFA World Cup, scored by France's Lucien Laurent in 1930.

THIS IS ENGLAND

The English Premier League was the best-represented domestic league at the 2010 FIFA World Cup, providing the base for 117 of the 32 squads' 736 players. Next came Germany's Bundesliga with 84, Italy's Serie A with 80, Spain's La Liga with 59, France's Ligue 1 with 45, Holland's Eredivisie with 34 and Japan's J-League with 25. Spanish champions Barcelona had more players at the 2010 FIFA World Cup than any other club, with 14 – eight for Spain, including new signing David Villa, though reserve goalkeeper Victor Valdes was the only one not to play. English clubs Chelsea and Liverpool had 12 each, followed by 11 from Germany's Bayern Munich.

NUMBER 73

The goals that proved to be decisive in the two 2010 semi-finals were both scored in the 73rd minute: Arjen Robben's header in Holland's 3-2 win over Uruguay, and Carles Puyol's header – the only goal of the game – for Spain against Germany the following evening.

ALL'S FAIR

FIFA World Cup organizers hailed an improvement in fair play between the 2006 tournament in Germany and the 2010 event in South Africa. Not only were red cards down from 28 to 17, but also injuries which could be blamed on fouls were reduced from 40 per cent to 16 per cent. There were 260 yellow cards shown, and eight of those were second yellow cards. Three of those eight (Aleksandar Lukovic of Serbia, Kaka of Brazil and Johnny Heitinga of Holland) also received a yellow card in one other match they played.

PLAYER MANAGERS

Eight managers at the 2010 FIFA World Cup had previous World Cup experience as a player: Mexico's Javier Aguirre, Brazil's **Dunga**, New Zealand's Ricki Herbert, Denmark's Morten Olsen, South Korea's Huh Jung-Moo, Argentina's **Diego Maradona**, Slovakia's former Czechoslovakia international Vladimir Weiss and England's Italian coach Fabio Capello. Both Maradona and Dunga won the trophy, not just as players but as captains, while Maradona and Aguirre had both been red-carded at a FIFA World Cup – Maradona against Brazil in 1982, Aguirre against West Germany four years later.

FINAL FEVER

No FIFA World Cup final has had more cards shown to players than in 2010, when referee **Howard Webb** flourished 13 – seven yellows and a red for Holland and five yellows for Spain. The Dutch were shown more cards than any other FIFA World Cup finalist, and their twice-booked centre-back Johnny Heitinga became the fifth man sent off in a FIFA World Cup final. Webb was still booed and criticized by fans from both sides, and found himself variously accused of either being too harsh or too lenient. Before receiving five yellow cards against Holland, Spain had accumulated just three yellow cards in the six games en route to the final.

SQUID ARMY

One of the most-hyped personalities of the 2010 FIFA World Cup wasn't a footballer on two legs, but an octopus of eight tentacles. German zoo-based **Paul the Octopus** "predicted" seven correct results out of seven. Paul chose by entering one of two identical boxes with the countries' flags, each containing the same piece of food. Despite being based in Oberhausen, he rightly went against Germany twice – ahead of their first-round defeat to Serbia and semi-final loss to Spain. He also correctly chose Germany to beat Australia, Ghana, England, Argentina and Uruguay, while also calling Spain's final victory over Holland. His only – known – wrong decision came two years earlier, when he suggested Germany would beat Spain in the 2008 UEFA European Championship final.

Spain became only the eighth winners of the FIFA World Cup™ when they triumphed in South Africa in 2010. However, Brazil remain the record-holders, with five victories inspired by superstars from Pele and Garrincha to Ronaldo and Ronaldinho. Argentina and Uruguay are the other South American winners, with past European champions being England, France, Germany and Italy.

FIFA WORLD CUP™ QUALIFIERS

OCEANIA ADVENTURES

After completing their qualification rounds in Oceania for the 2010 FIFA World Cup, **New Zealand** had to wait 11 months before finally taking on Bahrain – Asia's fifth-best-placed team – in a two-legged play-off for a place in South Africa. The "All Whites" triumphed 1-0 on aggregate in November 2009, but it was another Oceanian team that boasted the best goals-per-game ratio of any country taking part in 2010 qualifiers. The Solomon Islands scored an average of 3.8 times per match, their record boosted by a 12-1 win over American Samoa. England were the next most prolific, managing 3.4 goals per game – and, unlike the unfortunate Solomon Islands, they secured a berth at the finals to boot.

UAE IN A SQUEEZE

The **United Arab Emirates** reached the finals in 1990 by recording just one win and scoring only four goals in the Asian final round. They drew four of their five matches, but beat China 2-1 to qualify in second place behind South Korea.

T&T AT FULL STRETCH

Trinidad and Tobago share the record for the most games played to qualify for a FIFA World Cup finals. They played 20 in reaching the 2006 finals, beginning with 2-0 away and 4-0 home wins over the Dominican Republic in the preliminaries. T&T then finished second behind Mexico at the four-team first group stage to reach the six-team final group. After finishing fourth, they had to play off against Bahrain and won 2-1 on aggregate. Uruguay matched that figure in 2010, with 18 South America group matches and a two-legged play-off.

FIFA OPENS WORLD CUP TO THE WORLD

FIFA has enlarged the World Cup finals twice since 1978, to take account of the rising football nations of Africa and Asia. The rise in interest is reflected in the massive number of sides entering the qualifying competition – 204 for the 2010 event. **Joao Havelange**, the Brazilian who was president of FIFA from 1974 to 1998, enlarged the organization both to take advantage of commercial opportunities and to give smaller nations a chance. The number of teams in the finals was first increased from 16 to 24 for the 1982 finals in Spain, with an extra place given for Africa and Asia and a chance for a nation from Oceania to reach the finals. The number of finalists was further increased to 32 for the 1998 tournament in France. This decision offered five places to African teams, four to sides from Asia and Oceania and three from North/Central America and the Caribbean. The formula for the 2010 finals in South Africa offered 13 places to Europe, four to South America, five to Africa, plus the hosts; four for Asia, with another for the winners of an Asia v Oceania play-off, in which Oceania's New Zealand beat Asia's Bahrain. CONCACAF (the North and Central American and Caribbean federation) had three spots. The other place was decided by a play-off in which Uruguay, the fifth-placed South American team, saw off Costa Rica, the fourth-placed team in the CONCACAF qualifiers.

EGYPT POINT THE WAY

African teams, such as Cameroon, Tunisia, South Africa and Nigeria, make frequent appearances in the modern FIFA World Cup finals, but for many years, Egypt were the only African nation to have played in the finals. They qualified in 1934, by beating Palestine 7-1 at home and 4-1 away. The next African qualifiers were Morocco, who reached the finals in Mexico 36 years later.

ALL-TIME QUALIFICATIONS BY REGIONAL CONFEDERATION

1	Europe	218
2	South America	74
3	North/Central America & Caribbean	35
4	Africa	34
5	Asia	28
6	Oceania	4

THE FIRST SHOOT-OUT

The first penalty shoot-out in qualifying history came on 9 January 1977 when Tunisia beat Morocco 4-2 on spot-kicks after a 1-1 draw in Tunis. The first game, in Casablanca, had also finished 1-1. Tunisia went on to qualify for the finals.

SPANISH INVINCIBLES

Several countries have qualified for a FIFA World Cup without losing or even drawing a single game. But the **Spain** side who cruised their way through to the 2010 tournament in South Africa were the first to do so while playing as many as 10 matches. Qualifying for the same finals from a smaller group, Holland won eight games out of eight. West Germany also went through eight matches without dropping a point in reaching the 1982 FIFA World Cup in Spain, and Brazil won six out of six in qualifying for the 1970 competition – at which Mario Zagallo's men won another six out of six on their way to lifting the trophy.

MOVING THE FINALS AROUND

After the 1954 and 1958 finals in Europe, FIFA decided that they would be staged alternately in South America and Europe. This lasted until the award of the 1994 tournament to the United States. Things have changed since then. Japan and South Korea were the first Asian hosts in 2002 and in 2010 South Africa were the first hosts from Africa.

THE GROWTH OF THE QUALIFYING COMPETITION

This charts the number of countries entering qualifiers for the FIFA World Cup finals. Some withdrew before playing.

World Cup	Teams entering
Uruguay 1930	-
Italy 1934	32
France 1938	37
Brazil 1950	34
Switzerland 1954	45
Sweden 1958	55
Chile 1962	56
England 1966	74
Mexico 1970	75
West Germany 1974	99
Argentina 1978	107
Spain 1982	109
Mexico 1986	121
Italy 1990	116
USA 1994	147
France 1998	174
Japan/South Korea 2002	199
Germany 2006	198
South Africa 2010	204

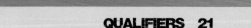

HURTADO THE LEADER

Ecuador defender **Ivan Hurtado** has made the most appearances in FIFA World Cup qualifiers. He has played 56 games, including 16 in the 2006 preliminaries. He was Ecuador's youngest-ever international when he made his debut at 17 years 285 days.

THE FASTEST SUBSTITUTION

The quickest substitution in the history of the qualifiers came on 30 December 1980, when North Korea's Chon Byong Ju was substituted in the first minute of his country's home game against Japan.

KOSTADINOV STUNS FRANCE

On 17 November 1993, in the last game of the Group Six schedule, Bulgaria's Emil Kostadinov scored one of the most dramatic goals in qualifying history to deny France a place in the 1994 finals. France seemed to be cruising with the score at 1-1 in stoppage time, but Kostadinov earned Bulgaria a shock victory after David Ginola had lost the ball. The Bulgarians reached the semi-finals of the tournament in the United States, losing 2-1 to Italy.

PALMER BEATS THE WHISTLE

Carl Erik Palmer's second goal in Sweden's 3-1 win over the Republic of Ireland in November 1949 was one of the most bizarre in qualifying history. The Irish defenders stopped, having heard a whistle, while Palmer ran on and put the ball in the net. The goal stood, because the whistle had come from someone in the crowd, not the referee. The 19-year-old forward went on to complete a hat-trick.

BWALYA LEAVES IT LATE

Zambia's **Kalusha Bwalya** is the oldest player to have scored a match-winning goal in a FIFA World Cup qualifying match. The 41-year-old netted the only goal against Liberia on 4 September 2004 after coming on as a substitute. He had also scored in his first qualifier, 20 years previously, in Zambia's 3-0 win over Uganda.

AUSTRALIA'S INCREDIBLE GOAL SPREE

Australia set a FIFA World Cup qualifying record in 2001, one that is unlikely to be beaten, as the Socceroos scored 53 goals in the space of two days. The details:

9 April 2001, Sydney: Australia 22, Tonga 0
Australia scorers: Scott Chipperfield 3, 83 mins; Damian Mori 13, 23, 40; John Aloisi 14, 24, 37, 45, 52, 63; **Kevin Muscat** (No. 2, right) 18, 30, 54, 58, 82; Tony Popovic 67; Tony Vidmar 74; David Zdrilic 78, 90; Archie Thompson 80; Con Boutsiania 87

11 April 2001, Sydney: Australia 31, American Samoa 0
Australia scorers: Boutsiania 10, 50, 84 mins; Thompson 12, 23, 27, 29, 32, 37, 42, 45, 56, 60, 65, 68, 88; Zdrilic 13, 21, 25, 33, 58, 66, 78, 89; Vidmar 14, 80; Popovic 17, 19; Simon Colosimo 51, 81; Fausto De Amicis 55

THOMPSON SETS UNLIKELY MARK

Archie Thompson eased past Iran striker Karim Bagheri's record for the number of goals in a single qualifying match (seven) as Australia thrashed American Samoa 31-0 on 11 April 2001. He netted 13 goals. David Zdrilic also beat Bagheri's total with eight goals. Australia had previously smashed Iran's scoring record two days earlier with a 22-0 victory over Tonga.

MUNICH DISASTER HITS ENGLAND

England's 1958 FIFA World Cup hopes were wrecked by the Munich air disaster on 6 February 1958, which devastated champions Manchester United. Three United players – left-back Roger Byrne, left-half Duncan Edwards and centre-forward Tommy Taylor – had been outstanding in England's unbeaten qualification campaign, with each playing in all four matches. Nineteen-year-old Edwards netted twice and Taylor scored eight goals. Byrne and Taylor died in the crash; Edwards died 15 days later.

YOUNGEST AND OLDEST

The youngest player to appear in the FIFA World Cup qualifiers is Souleymane Mamam of Togo, who was 13 years 310 days when he played against Zambia on 6 May 2001. The oldest was MacDonald Taylor, who was 46 years, 180 days when he played for the Virgin Islands against St Kitts Nevis on 18 February 2004.

DAEI TOPS THE SCORERS

Iran's **Ali Daei** is the all-time top scorer in FIFA World Cup qualifiers. His nine goals in the 2006 qualifying campaign took his total to 30, nine ahead of the previous joint record-holder, Japan's Kazu Miura. Daei also scored seven goals in the 1994 qualifiers, four in the 1998 preliminaries and ten in 2002.

HORST THE FIRST TO GIVE WAY

The first player to be substituted during a FIFA World Cup qualifier was West Germany's **Horst Eckel,** replaced by Richard Gottinger in their 3-0 victory over the short-lived protectorate of Saarland in October 1953. Eckel would go on to play on the right side of midfield in the side that beat Hungary in the 1954 FIFA World Cup final, while Gottinger's delayed appearance against Saarland was his first and last for his country. By the time of the 1958 FIFA World Cup qualifiers, Saarland had been integrated within West Germany.

UNITED STATES LEAVE IT LATE

The latest of all qualifying play-offs took place in Rome on 24 May 1934, when the USA beat Mexico 4-2 to clinch the last slot in the FIFA World Cup finals. Three days later, the Americans were knocked out 7-1 by hosts Italy in the first round of the tournament.

ITALY FORCED TO QUALIFY

Italy are the only host country who have been required to qualify for their own tournament. The 1934 hosts beat Greece 4-0 to go through. FIFA decided that, for the 1938 finals, the holders and the hosts would qualify automatically. That decision was changed for the 2006 finals. Since then, only the hosts have been exempt from qualifying, though South Africa played in the second round of qualifying for 2010. This is because it doubled up as qualifiers for the 2010 Africa Cup of Nations.

TURKEY THROUGH ON LUCK OF THE DRAW

Turkey were the first team to qualify for the FIFA World Cup finals after the drawing of lots. Their play-off against Spain, in Rome on 17 March 1954, ended 2-2. Qualification was decided by a 14-year-old Roman boy, Luigi Franco Gemma. He was blindfolded to draw the lots – and pulled out Turkey, instead of much-fancied Spain.

THE "FOOTBALL WAR"

War broke out between El Salvador and Honduras after El Salvador beat Honduras 3-2 in a play-off on 26 June 1969 to qualify for the 1970 finals. Tension had been running high between the neighbours over a border dispute and there had been rioting at the match. On 14 July, the Salvador army invaded Honduras.

MOST SUCCESSFUL QUALIFYING ATTEMPTS

Italy	13
West Germany/Germany	12
Mexico	12
Spain	12
Argentina	12
Brazil	11
England	11
Belgium	10
Sweden	10
Yugoslavia/Serbia	10
Czechoslovakia/Czech Republic	9
Hungary	9

ENGLAND IN, SCOTLAND OUT

England, led by **Billy Wright**, took part in the FIFA World Cup finals for the first time in 1950. They won their all-British group ahead of Scotland. Both teams thus qualified, but the Scots refused to go to the finals in Brazil because they had only finished second. The Scots subsequently qualified eight times, but have never advanced beyond the first round of the finals.

THIERRY'S TRICKERY

France qualified for the 2010 FIFA World Cup finals thanks to one of the most controversial goals of recent international history. The second leg of their play-off against the Republic of Ireland in November 2009 was 14 minutes into extra-time when striker **Thierry Henry** clearly controlled the ball with his hand, before crossing to William Gallas who gave his side a decisive 2-1 aggregate lead. After Swedish referee Martin Hansson allowed the goal to stand, the Football Association of Ireland first called for the game to be replayed, then asked to be allowed into the finals as a 33rd country – but both requests proved in vain.

ITALY HEAD THE QUALIFYING LIST

Italy have the best qualifying record of any nation. They have qualified 13 times – in 1934, 1954, 1962, 1966, 1970, 1974, 1978, 1982, 1994, 1998, 2002, 2006 and 2010. They were exempt as holders from qualifying in 1938, 1950 and 1986. They were hosts in 1990. They have only once been eliminated in the qualifiers, when they were knocked out by Northern Ireland in 1958.

GOING UNDERCOVER

The Kingdome in Seattle, United States, hosted the first FIFA World Cup qualifier to be played indoors, when the US beat Canada 2-0 in October 1976 – just a few months after the same venue had staged its first rock concert, by Paul McCartney's post-Beatles band Wings, and a religious rally featuring evangelist Billy Graham and country singer Johnny Cash. Canada gained revenge by beating the US 3-0 in a play-off, hosted in Haiti, to reach the next stage of the CONCACAF qualifying round. But only Mexico would go on to represent the continent at the 1978 FIFA World Cup in Argentina.

WALES IN THROUGH THE BACK DOOR

All four British teams have reached the FIFA World Cup finals only once, in 1958. England, Scotland and Northern Ireland all topped their groups, but **Wales** qualified by a roundabout route. They had been eliminated – then were offered a second chance. Israel had emerged unchallenged, for political reasons, from the Asian qualifying section. However, FIFA ruled that the Israelis could not qualify without playing a match and that they must play off against one of the second-placed European teams. Wales were drawn to meet them and qualified by winning both games 2-0.

ARGENTINA'S LONG BOYCOTT

Argentina boycotted the FIFA World Cup for nearly 20 years. They were Copa America holders in 1938, but refused to travel to France because they were upset at being passed over to host the finals. They were also unhappy at being paired with Brazil in a qualifier. They did not take part in the 1950 or 1954 competitions either, after Brazil were chosen to host the 1950 finals. Argentina did not return to FIFA World Cup competition until the qualifiers for the 1958 finals.

FIFA WORLD CUP™ TEAM RECORDS

OUT BUT UNBEATEN

Brazil were eliminated on goal difference in the 1978 semi-finals despite a seven-game unbeaten run. Since then, the expansion of the tournament and the arrival of penalty shoot-outs have meant that several more teams have been eliminated without losing a game in 90 and/or 120 minutes. Italy (1990) and France (2006) were knocked out, despite going seven games unbeaten. England (1990) and Holland (1998) went home after six-match unbeaten runs. England (twice), Brazil, Italy, Spain and Argentina have also been eliminated after going five games unbeaten.

BRAZIL'S WINNING STREAK

Brazil hold the record for the most consecutive wins at the World Cup finals. Their **2-1 win over Turkey** on 3 June 2002 started an 11-match winning run that lasted until their 1-0 quarter-final defeat by France on 1 July 2006.

SINGING THE BLUES

Spain's 2010 FIFA World Cup triumph – for whom **Xavi** was a star even in an unfamiliar all-blue kit – made them the first team to win the tournament while playing the final in their second kit since England in 1966.

BRAZIL COLOUR UP

Brazil's yellow shirts are famous throughout the world. But the national team wore **white shirts** for each of the first four World Cup tournaments. Brazil's 2-1 defeat by Uruguay, which cost them the 1950 World Cup, came as such a shock to the population that the national association decided to change the team's shirt colours, to try and wipe out the bitter memory.

SHARING THE GOALS

France in 1982 and winners Italy, in 2006, supplied the most individual goalscorers during a FIFA World Cup finals tournament – ten. Gerard Soler, Bernard Genghini, Michel Platini, Didier Six, Maxime Bossis, Alain Giresse, Dominque Rocheteau, Marius Tresor, Rene Girard and Alain Couriol netted for France. Alessandro Del Piero, Alberto Gilardino, Fabio Grosso, Vincenzo Iaquinta, Luca Toni, Pippo Inzaghi, Marco Materazzi, Andrea Pirlo, Francesco Totti and Gianluca Zambrotta all scored for Italy, who went on to win the tournament.

ITALY KEEP IT TIGHT

Italy set the record for the longest run without conceding a goal at the FIFA World Cup finals. They went five games without conceding at the 1990 finals, starting with their 1-0 group win over Austria. Goalkeeper Walter Zenga was not beaten until Claudio Caniggia scored Argentina's equalizer in the semi-final. And a watertight defence did not bring Italy the glory it craved: Argentina reached the final by winning the penalty shoot-out 4-3.

TODAY EUROPE, TOMORROW THE WORLD

Spain's 2010 trophy-lifting coach **Vicente del Bosque** became only the second manager to have won both the FIFA World Cup and the UEFA Champions League or its previous incarnation, the European Champions' Cup. Marcello Lippi won the UEFA prize with Juventus in 1996, 10 years before his Italy team became world champions. Del Bosque won the UEFA Champions League twice with Real Madrid, in 2000 and 2002, though he was sacked in summer 2003 for "only" winning the Spanish league title the previous season.

BRAZIL PROFIT FROM RIMET'S VISION

Jules Rimet, president of FIFA from 1921 to 1954, was the driving force behind the first World Cup, in 1930. The tournament in Uruguay was not the high-profile event it is now, with only 13 nations taking part. The long sea journey kept most European teams away. Only four – Belgium, France, Romania and Yugoslavia – made the trip. Regardless, Rimet's dream had been realized and the FIFA World Cup grew and grew in popularity. Brazil have been the most successful team in the competition's history, winning the trophy five times. They have won more games in the FIFA World Cup finals (67) than any other country, though Germany have now played more games – 99 to Brazil's 97. Italy have won the FIFA World Cup four times and West Germany three. The original finalists, Uruguay and Argentina, have both lifted the trophy twice. England, in 1966, and France, in 1998, have won once, both as hosts, before Spain lifted their first FIFA World Cup in South Africa in 2010.

WHY THE BRITISH TEAMS STAYED OUT

England and Scotland are considered the homelands of football, but neither country entered the FIFA World Cup until the qualifiers for the 1950 finals. The four British associations – England, Scotland, Wales and Northern Ireland – quit FIFA in the 1920s over a row over broken-time (employment compensation) payments to amateurs. The British associations did not rejoin FIFA until 1946.

MOST APPEARANCES IN THE FIFA WORLD CUP™ FINAL

1	Brazil	7
=	Germany/West Germany	7
3	Italy	6
4	Argentina	4
5	Holland	3
6	Czechoslovakia	2
=	France	2
=	Hungary	2
=	Uruguay	2
10	England	1
=	Spain	1
=	Sweden	1

ONE–TIME WONDERS

Indonesia, then known as the **Dutch East Indies**, made one appearance in the finals, in the days when the tournament was a strictly knockout affair. On 5 June 1938, they lost 6-0 to Hungary in the first round, and have never qualified for the tournament since.

MOST APPEARANCES IN FIFA WORLD CUP™ FINALS TOURNAMENTS

1	Brazil	19
2	Germany/West Germany	17
=	Italy	17
4	Argentina	15
5	Mexico	13

FIFA WORLD CUP™ STOPS THE WORLD

The FIFA World Cup finals are the biggest sporting event in history. Television was in its infancy when the first finals were held in 1930. The tournament has since become the most popular TV sporting event of all. The 2006 finals were watched by a worldwide audience of 26.3 billion, 0.1 billion fewer than the 2002 finals. In addition to the estimated 700 million fans who watched the 2010 FIFA World Cup final at Soccer City, Johannesburg, between Spain and Holland on televisions around the world, hundreds of thousands of others went to public squares and Fan Fests to watch the match on giant screens.

GOLDEN NARROWS

Before the 2010 tournament, no country had won five consecutive FIFA World Cup matches by a single-goal margin – but **Arjen Robben** and Holland became the first, thanks to their 3-2 semi-final victory over Uruguay. Before then, the record rested with Italy, who managed four single-goal wins in a row across the 1934 and 1938 FIFA World Cups. Spain's 1-0 win over Holland in the 2010 FIFA World Cup was also their fifth consecutive single-goal victory and fourth in the knockout stages.

EARLIEST RED CARD

The quickest sending off in the FIFA World Cup finals came in 1986 when Uruguay's Jose Batista was sent off after 56 seconds for a lunge at Scotland's Gordon Strachan. The latest expulsion was of Argentina's Leandro Cufre, who was dismissed after the final whistle of extra-time in the 2002 quarter-final against Germany.

EVER RED

England's victory in 1966 was not just the only time they have won the FIFA World Cup – it also now remains the only time the prize has been clinched by a side wearing red shirts in the final. Spain might have emulated England's fashion sense in 2010 but had to wear blue to avoid clashing with Holland's bright orange – they did, however, change back into their usual red to receive the trophy from FIFA president **Joseph S. Blatter**.

THE FEWEST GOALS CONCEDED

FIFA World Cup winners France (1998), Italy (2006) and Spain (2010) hold the record for the fewest goals conceded on their way to victory. All three conceded just two. Spain also now hold the record for fewest goals scored by FIFA World Cup winners. They netted just eight in 2010, below the 11 scored by Italy in 1938, England in 1966 or Brazil in 1994.

SPONSORS MAKE THE FINALS PAY

The 2010 FIFA World Cup was the most lucrative ever, with world football's governing body FIFA pocketing $3.2 million in profits from the event in South Africa. A record 700m viewers tuned in to the final between Spain and Holland – another all-time high.

FEWEST GOALS CONCEDED IN ONE TOURNAMENT:
Switzerland: 0, 2006

MOST GOALS SCORED IN ONE TOURNAMENT
Hungary: 27, 1954

MOST WINS IN ONE TOURNAMENT
Brazil: 7, 2002

MOST GOALS SCORED IN ONE TOURNAMENT
Just Fontaine (France): 13, 1958

MOST CONSECUTIVE MATCHES SCORING A GOAL AT FIFA WORLD CUP™ FINALS

18	Brazil	1930–58
18	Germany	1934–58, 1986–98
17	Hungary	1934–62
16	Uruguay	1930–62
15	Brazil	1978–90
15	France	1978–86

PERFORMANCES BY HOST NATION AT FIFA WORLD CUP™ FINALS

1930	Uruguay	Champions
1934	Italy	Champions
1938	France	Quarter-finals
1950	Brazil	Runners-up
1954	Switzerland	Third place
1958	Sweden	Runners-up
1962	Chile	Third place
1966	England	Champions
1970	Mexico	Quarter-finals
1974	West Germany	Champions
1978	Argentina	Champions
1982	Spain	Second round
1986	Mexico	Quarter-finals
1990	Italy	Third place
1994	United States	Second round
1998	France	Champions
2002	South Korea	Fourth place
	Japan	Second round
2006	Germany	Third place
2010	South Africa	First round

HOLDERS CRASH OUT

France produced the worst performance by a defending FIFA World Cup winner in Japan and South Korea in 2002: they lost their opening game 1-0 to Senegal, drew 0-0 against Uruguay and were eliminated after losing 1-0 to Denmark. They were the first defending champions to be knocked out without scoring a goal. In 2010 Italy emulated France by exiting at the first-round stage, and without winning a match – nor indeed ever taking the lead. At least Italy did achieve two draws – and scored four goals. They opened with a 1-1 draw against Paraguay, needed a penalty to force another 1-1 draw against minnows New Zealand, and they were on their way home after losing 3-2 to Slovakia.

BRAZIL LEAD THE WAY

Brazil scored the most victories in finals tournaments when they won all their seven games in 2002. They began with a 2-1 group win over Turkey and ended with a 2-0 final triumph over Germany. They scored 18 goals in their unbeaten run and conceded on only four occasions.

GERMANY'S GOAL BONANZA

West Germany conceded 14 goals in the 1954 finals, the most ever conceded by the FIFA World Cup winners. But they scored 25 – second most in FIFA World Cup history. Only their victims in the final – Hungary – scored more than the Germans: they netted 27.

FONTAINE AND JAIRZINHO HIT HOT STREAK

Brazil's **Jairzinho** and **Just Fontaine** of France are the only players to score in every match round of a FIFA World Cup finals. Fontaine netted 13 goals in six appearances in 1958 – still a FIFA World Cup record – while Jairzinho scored seven in six matches as Brazil won the trophy in 1970.

FIFA WORLD CUP™ GOALSCORING

KEEP ON SCORING

Brazil and Germany/West Germany hold the record for scoring in consecutive games in FIFA World Cup finals matches, with 18. Brazil's run lasted from their 2-1 defeat by Yugoslavia in 1930 until a 0-0 draw with England in the 1958 group stages. The Germans have achieved the feat twice. Their opening 5-2 win over Belgium in 1934 started a sequence that lasted until a 0-0 draw with Italy in the opening group game in 1962. The Germans' second run started with a 1-1 group-stage draw against Uruguay in 1986 and ended with a 3-0 defeat by Croatia in the 1998 quarter-finals.

HIGHEST SCORES

The highest-scoring game in the FIFA World Cup finals was the quarter-final between Austria and Switzerland on 26 June 1954. Austria staged a remarkable comeback to win 7-5, with centre-forward **Theodor Wagner** scoring a hat-trick, after trailing 3-0 in the 19th minute. Three other games have produced 11 goals – Brazil's 6-5 win over Poland in the 1938 first round, Hungary's 8-3 win over West Germany in their 1954 group game and the Hungarians' 10-1 rout of El Salvador at the group stage in 1982.

LOW–SCORING SPAIN

Spain won the 2010 FIFA World Cup despite scoring just eight goals in seven games on their way to the title – fewer than any world champions in history, including 11-goal Italy in 1934, England in 1966 and Brazil in 1994. Vicente del Bosque's Spain were also the first team to win 1-0 in all four of their knockout matches. **David Villa** scored the decisive goal in two of those matches.

HARD WORK

Scoring goals in the FIFA World Cup finals has become harder than ever over the years. The great days of high-scoring matches came in the finals of the 1950s, when Brazil, Hungary, West Germany and France all netted more than 20 goals in one tournament. Austria's 7-5 win over Switzerland in 1954 remains a FIFA World Cup match aggregate record, and the average of 5.38 goals scored per match in that year is also a tournament record. Since then, defences have become ever more organized and harder to break down. Changes in formation have not helped attackers either, with many coaches at the 2010 FIFA World Cup finals in South Africa using only one striker. The 2006 winners, Italy, demonstrated the trend by scoring only 12 goals in seven matches – while conceding just two – but they did score four more than 2010 winners Spain.

ZERO TOLERANCE

Paraguay's 0-0 draw and subsequent **penalty shoot-out win** over Japan in the second round at the 2010 FIFA World Cup made it seven goalless draws at the one tournament – equalling the stalemate record set in both 1982 and 2006. Andres Iniesta's late winner for Spain against Holland, in the 2010 final, meant the 1994 clash between Brazil and Italy remains the only FIFA World Cup final to remain goalless.

THE FASTEST GOAL

Turkey's **Hakan Sukur** holds the record for the quickest goal scored in the FIFA World Cup finals. He netted after 11 seconds against South Korea in the 2002 third-place play-off. Turkey went on to win 3-2. The previous record was held by Vaclav Masek of Czechoslovakia, who struck after 15 seconds against Mexico in 1962.

BIGGEST FIFA WORLD CUP™ FINALS WINS

Hungary 10, El Salvador 1 (15 June 1982)
Hungary 9, South Korea 0 (17 June 1954)
Yugoslavia 9, Zaire 0 (18 June 1974)
Sweden 8, Cuba 0 (12 June 1938)
Uruguay 8, Bolivia 0 (2 July 1950)
Germany 8, Saudi Arabia 0 (1 June 2002)

MOST GOALS IN ONE FIFA WORLD CUP™

Goals	Country	Year
27	Hungary	1954
25	West Germany	1954
23	France	1958
22	Brazil	1950
19	Brazil	1970

MOST GOALS IN FIFA WORLD CUP™ FINALS (MINIMUM 100)

1	Brazil	210
2	Germany/W Germany	206
3	Italy	126
4	Argentina	123

MOST AND LEAST

The most goals scored in a single FIFA World Cup finals tournament is 171, in France in 1998, after FIFA extended the competition to 32 teams and 64 matches for the first time. The highest number of goals per match was recorded in the 1954 finals, with 140 goals in just 26 games at an average of 5.38 goals per game. The lowest average per game came in Italy in 1990, when 115 goals were scored in 52 matches, an average of 2.21 goals per game. The 2010 FIFA World Cup saw 145 goals – at an average of 2.26 per game.

YOUNGEST AND OLDEST

Pele became the youngest-ever scorer in the FIFA World Cup finals – at 17 years and 239 days – when he scored Brazil's winner against Wales in the 1958 quarter-finals. Cameroon's **Roger Milla** – 42 years, 39 days – became the oldest scorer when he scored Cameroon's only goal in their 6-1 defeat by Russia in 1994.

COMING BACK FOR MORE

Seven footballers have scored goals at FIFA World Cup tournaments 12 years apart, the latest being Mexico's **Cuauhtemoc Blanco.** His successful penalty against France, in Polokwane in 2010, came a dozen years after his first FIFA World Cup goal, against Belgium, in 1998. Others to have scored across a similar time-span are Brazil's Pele (1958–1970), West Germany's Uwe Seeler (1958–1970), Argentina's Diego Maradona (1982–1994), Denmark's Michael Laudrup (1986–1998), Sweden's Henrik Larsson (1994–2006) and Saudi Arabia's Sami Al-Jaber (1994–2006).

GOLDEN, SILVER AND BRONZE

The top goalscorer at the FIFA World Cup traditionally receives the adidas Golden Boot. For the 2006 finals, FIFA added awards for the second and third highest scorers – the adidas Silver Boot and adidas Bronze Boot. In 2006 Argentina's Hernan Crespo took the adidas Silver Boot, behind Germany's Miroslav Klose. Brazil's 2002 Golden Boot winner Ronaldo took the adidas Bronze Boot.

EUSEBIO THE STRIKE FORCE

Portugal's **Eusebio** was the striking star of the 1966 FIFA World Cup finals. Ironically, he would not be eligible to play for Portugal now. He was born in Mozambique, then a Portuguese colony, but now an independent country. He finished top scorer with nine goals, including two as Portugal eliminated champions Brazil and four as they beat North Korea 5-3 in the quarter-finals after trailing 3-0.

HEAD FOR FIGURES

Arjen Robben's emphatic header against Uruguay, to put Holland 3-1 up in their 3-2 semi-final win at the 2010 FIFA World Cup, was the 2,200th goal ever scored in the competition. **Andres Iniesta**'s winning goal for Spain in that summer's final took the overall FIFA World Cup tally to 2,208.

ROSSI THE ITALY HERO

Paolo Rossi turned from villain to hero as Italy won the 1982 FIFA World Cup. Coach Enzo Bearzot had picked Rossi even though he had only just completed a two-year suspension after a match-fixing scandal. Rossi was criticized for a lack of fitness in the early matches, but he scored a hat-trick against Brazil, two goals as Italy beat Poland in the semi-final, and the opener in their FIFA World Cup final victory over West Germany.

FIFA WORLD CUP™ FINALS TOP SCORERS (1930–78)

Maximum 16 teams in finals

Year	Venue	Top Scorer	Country	Goals
1930	Uruguay	Guillermo Stabile	Argentina	8
1934	Italy	Oldrich Nejedly	Czechoslovakia	5
1938	France	Leonidas	Brazil	7
1950	Brazil	Ademir	Brazil	9
1954	Switzerland	Sandor Kocsis	Hungary	11
1958	Sweden	Just Fontaine	France	13
1962	Chile	Garrincha	Brazil	4
		Vava	Brazil	
		Leonel Sanchez	Chile	
		Florian Albert	Hungary	
		Valentin Ivanov	Soviet Union	
		Drazen Jerkovic	Yugoslavia	
1966	England	Eusebio	Portugal	9
1970	Mexico	Gerd Muller	West Germany	10
1974	West Germany	Grzegorz Lato	Poland	7
1978	Argentina	Mario Kempes	Argentina	6

KEMPES MAKES HIS MARK

Mario Kempes was Argentina's only foreign-based player in the hosts' squad at the 1978 finals. Twice top scorer in the Spanish league, Valencia's Kempes was crucial to Argentina's success. Coach Cesar Luis Menotti told him to shave off his moustache after he failed to score in the group games. Kempes then netted two against Peru, two more against Poland, and two decisive goals in the final against Holland.

NO GUARANTEES FOR TOP SCORERS

Topping the FIFA World Cup finals scoring chart is a great honour for all strikers, but few have gained the ultimate prize and been leading scorer. Argentina's Guillermo Stabile started the luckless trend in 1930, topping the scoring charts but finishing up on the losing side in the final. The list of top scorers who have played in the winning side is small: Garrincha and Vava (joint top scorers in 1962), Mario Kempes (top scorer in 1978), Paolo Rossi (1982) and Ronaldo (2002). Gerd Muller, top scorer in 1970, gained his reward as West Germany's trophy winner four years later. Other top scorers, such as Sandor Kocsis, 1954, Just Fontaine, 1958, and Gary Lineker, 1986, have been disappointed in the final stages. Kocsis was the only one to reach the final – and Hungary were defeated. Four players finished tied on five goals at the 2010 FIFA World Cup and one – David Villa – collected a winner's medal, but the Golden Boot went to Germany's Thomas Muller.

LINEKER LEADS ENGLAND'S LIST

Gary Lineker is England's leading FIFA World Cup scorer, and second only to FIFA World Cup winner Bobby Charlton in England's list of all-time marksmen. He netted 48 goals in 80 appearances. The high point of his FIFA World Cup career came in the 1990 semi-final, when he struck England's equalizer against West Germany. He retired from international football after the 1992 European Championships finals.

HURST MAKES HISTORY

England's **Geoff Hurst** became the first and to date only player to score a hat-trick in a FIFA World Cup final when he netted three in the hosts' 4-2 victory over West Germany in 1966. Hurst headed England level after the Germans took an early lead, then scored the decisive third goal with a shot that bounced down off the crossbar and just over the line, according to the Soviet linesman. Hurst hit his third in the last minute. The British TV commentator Kenneth Wolstenholme described Hurst's strike famously with the words: "Some people are on the pitch ... They think it's all over ... It is now!"

STABILE MAKES AN IMPACT

Guillermo Stabile, top scorer in the 1930 FIFA World Cup finals, had never played for Argentina before the tournament. He made his debut – as a 25-year-old – against Mexico because first-choice Roberto Cherro had suffered a panic attack. He netted a hat-trick then scored twice against both Chile and the United States as Argentina reached the final. He struck one of his side's goals in the 4-2 defeat by Uruguay in the final.

⚽ TWO OUT OF 10

Only two players wearing the iconic No. 10 shirt have won the Golden Boot at FIFA World Cup finals: Argentina's Mario Kempes in 1978 and England's Gary Lineker eight years later. Dutch No. 10 Wesley Sneijder was in the running for the prize in 2010, but finished second behind Germany's No. 13 Thomas Muller.

⚽ THE BRADLEY BUNCH

Michael Bradley's late equalizer for the United States, in their Group C 2-2 draw with Slovenia in June 2010, made him the first person to score a FIFA World Cup goal for a team coached by his own father – in this case, Bob Bradley.

⚽ FIFA WORLD CUP™ FINALS ALL-TIME TOP-TEN SCORERS

	Name (Country)	Tournaments	Total Goals
1	Ronaldo (Brazil)	1998, 2002, 2006	15
2	Gerd Muller (W Germany)	1970, 1974	14
=	**Miroslav Klose** (Germany)	2002, 2006, 2010	14
3	Just Fontaine (France)	1958	13
4	Pele (Brazil)	1958, 1962, 1966, 1970	12
5	Sandor Kocsis (Hungary)	1954	11
=	Jurgen Klinsmann (W Germany/Germany)	1990, 1994, 1998	11
7	Gabriel Batistuta (Argentina)	1994, 1998, 2002	10
	Teofilo Cubillas (Peru)	1970, 1978	10
	Gregorz Lato (Poland)	1974, 1978, 1982	10
	Gary Lineker (England)	1986, 1990	10
	Helmut Rahn (W Germany)	1954, 1958	10

⚽ THE GREAT GONZALO

Argentina striker **Gonzalo Higuain** ended an eight-year wait for a FIFA World Cup hat-trick when he scored three in his team's 4-1 victory over South Korea in the first round of the 2010 tournament. The 2006 FIFA World Cup was the only one without a single hat-trick, making Higuain's treble the first for eight years and seven days – since Pauleta scored three in Portugal's 4-0 trouncing of Poland at the 2002 tournament.

PELE SO UNLUCKY

Pele would surely have been the all-time FIFA World Cup top scorer but for injuries. He was sidelined early in the 1962 finals, and again four years later. He scored six goals in Brazil's 1958 triumph, including two in the 5-2 final victory over Sweden. He also netted Brazil's 100th FIFA World Cup goal as they beat Italy 4-1 in the 1970 final.

MULLER'S SCORING HABIT

West Germany's **Gerd Muller** had the knack of scoring in important games. He struck the winner against England in the 1970 quarter-final and his two goals in extra-time against Italy almost carried his side to the final. Four years later, Muller's goal against Poland ensured that West Germany reached the final on home soil. Then he scored the winning goal against Holland in the FIFA World Cup final. He also had a goal disallowed for offside – wrongly, as TV replays proved.

RONALDO SO CONSISTENT

Ronaldo was a consistent scorer in the three FIFA World Cup finals tournaments he played in. He netted four times in 1998, when they were runners-up to France, eight as Brazil won the 2002 tournament – including both goals in the final – and three more in 2006. He became the all-time top scorer when netting Brazil's opener in a 3-0 win over Ghana in the last-16 round at Dortmund on 27 June 2006. As a teenager, Ronaldo had been a member of Brazil's FIFA World Cup winning squad in the United States in 1994, but did not play.

KLINSMANN'S CONTRIBUTION

Jurgen Klinsmann has been an influential force at the FIFA World Cup both as a player and a coach. He scored three goals when West Germany won the FIFA World Cup in 1990, five more – for a unified Germany – in the 1994 finals, and three in 1998. He then coached Germany to the semi-finals in 2006.

WHO SCORED THE FIRST HAT-TRICK?

For many years, Argentina's Guillermo Stabile was considered the first hat-trick scorer in the FIFA World Cup finals. He netted three in Argentina's 6-3 win over Mexico on 19 July 1930, but has since been superseded by Bert Patenaude of the United States. FIFA changed its records in November 2006, to acknowledge that Patenaude's treble two days earlier, in the Americans' 3-0 win over Paraguay, had been the tournament's first hat-trick.

FIFA WORLD CUP™ APPEARANCES

Two players, Mexico's Antonio Carbajal and Germany's Lothar Matthaus, have appeared in a record five FIFA World Cup™ final tournaments, but for many players, appearing just once in football's ultimate event is cause enough for dreams. The following pages chart individual appearance records at football's premier competition, from the longest to the shortest, to the greatest time elapsed between FIFA World Cup™ appearances.

BRANDTS SCORED FOR BOTH SIDES

Holland defender Ernie Brandts is the only player to have scored for both sides in a FIFA World Cup finals match. Brandts's 18th-minute own goal gave Italy the lead in their decisive second group-stage game in 1978, but he then started Holland's revival with a 50th-minute equalizer before Arie Haan scored the winner to take the Dutch to the final.

YOUNGEST AND OLDEST

Northern Ireland forward **Norman Whiteside** became the then youngest player to appear in the FIFA World Cup finals when he started against Yugoslavia in 1982, aged just 17 years and 41 days. The oldest player to feature in the tournament was Cameroon forward Roger Milla, who faced Russia in 1994 aged 42 years and 39 days.

MOST APPEARANCES IN FIFA WORLD CUP™ FINALS

25 Lothar Matthaus (West Germany/ Germany)
23 Paolo Maldini (Italy)
21 Diego Maradona (Argentina)
   Uwe Seeler (West Germany)
   Wladyslaw Zmuda (Poland)

DOUBLE WINNERS

Players who have played on the winning side in two FIFA World Cup finals:

Giovanni Ferrari (Italy), 1934, 1938
Giuseppe Meazza (Italy), 1934, 1938
Pele (Brazil), 1958, 1970
Didi (Brazil), 1958, 1962
Djalma Santos (Brazil), 1958, 1962
Garrincha (Brazil), 1958, 1962
Gilmar (Brazil), 1958, 1962
Nilton Santos (Brazil), 1958, 1962
Vava (Brazil), 1958, 1962
Zagallo (Brazil), 1958, 1962
Zito (Brazil), 1958, 1962
Cafu (Brazil), 1994, 2002

THE "DOUBLE" CHAMPIONS

Franz Beckenbauer and Mario Zagallo are a unique duo. They have both won the FIFA World Cup as a player and a coach. Beckenbauer also had the distinction of captaining West Germany to victory on home soil in 1974. As coach, he steered them to the final in Mexico in 1986 and to victory over Argentina in Italy four years later. He was nicknamed "Der Kaiser" (The Emperor) both for his style and his achievements. Zagallo gained two winners' medals as a player. He was the left-winger in Brazil's triumphant march to the 1958 championship, before playing a deeper role in their 1962 victory. He took over from the controversial Joao Saldanha as Brazil coach three months before the 1970 finals and guided the side to victory in all six of its games, scoring 19 goals and routing Italy 4-1 in the final. Zagallo later filled the role of the team's technical director when Brazil won the FIFA World Cup for a fourth time in 1994.

MOST FIFA WORLD CUP™ FINALS TOURNAMENTS

These players all played in at least four FIFA World Cup finals tournaments.

5 **Antonio Carbajal** (Mexico) 1950, 1954, 1958, 1962, 1966
Lothar Matthaus (West Germany/Germany) 1982, 1986, 1990, 1994, 1998

4 **Djalma Santos** (Brazil) 1954, 1958, 1962, 1966
Pele (Brazil) 1958, 1962, 1966, 1970
Uwe Seeler (West Germany) 1958, 1962, 1966, 1970
Karl-Heinz Schnellinger (West Germany) 1958, 1962, 1966, 1970
Gianni Rivera (Italy) 1962, 1966, 1970, 1974
Pedro Rocha (Uruguay) 1962, 1966, 1970, 1974
Wladyslaw Zmuda (Poland) 1974, 1978, 1982, 1986
Giuseppe Bergomi (Italy) 1982, 1986, 1990, 1998
Diego Maradona (Argentina) 1982, 1986, 1990, 1994
Enzo Scifo (Belgium) 1986, 1990, 1994, 1998
Franky van der Elst (Belgium) 1986, 1990, 1994, 1998
Andoni Zubizarreta (Spain) 1986, 1990, 1994, 1998
Paolo Maldini (Italy) 1990, 1994, 1998, 2002
Hong Myung-Bo (South Korea) 1990, 1994, 1998, 2002
Cafu (Brazil) 1994, 1998, 2002, 2006
Sami Al-Jaber (Saudi Arabia) 1994, 1998, 2002, 2006
Denis Caniza (Paraguay) 1998, 2002, 2006, 2010
Fabio Cannavaro (Italy) 1998, 2002, 2006, 2010
Thierry Henry (France) 1998, 2002, 2006, 2010
Rigobert Song (Cameroon) 1994, 1998, 2002, 2010

MONTI AND THE "ORIUNDI"

Luisito Monti is the only man to have played in two FIFA World Cup final matches for different countries. He was on the losing side for Argentina in 1930, then gained a winner's medal for Italy in 1934. Monti was one of the "oriundi" – Argentines of Italian descent. The Italian government awarded him dual citizenship when he moved to Italy with Juventus, so he could play for the national team.

DOUBLE DUTCH, DOUBLE WHAMMY

Arjen Robben and Mark van Bommel suffered an unusual double whammy in the 2009–10 season: they ended on the losing side in both the UEFA Champions League final, for Bayern Munich against Internazionale, and the FIFA World Cup final, for Holland against Spain. Others who have endured similar fates are Oliver Neuville, Bernd Schneider and Carsten Ramelow (for Bayer Leverkusen against Real Madrid, and Germany against Brazil, in 2002) and Thierry Henry (for Arsenal against Barcelona, and France against Italy, in 2006).

IT'S THE SAME OLD SONG

Cameroon's veteran defender **Rigobert Song** played just 17 minutes of the 2010 FIFA World Cup in South Africa, but it did make him the first African to play at four editions of the tournament – nine matches, stretching across 16 years and nine days. He featured in 1994, 1998, 2002 and 2010 – missing the 2006 event because Cameroon failed to qualify. Only three players have enjoyed longer FIFA World Cup careers: Mexicans Antonio Carbajal (spanning 16 years and 25 days) and Hugo Sanchez (16 years, 17 days) and Germany's Lothar Matthaus (16 years, 14 days). Other players for whom the 2010 tournament was their fourth FIFA World Cup were Italy's Fabio Cannavaro (taking his total appearances to 18), France's Thierry Henry (14) and Paraguay's Denis Caniza (10).

MOST FIFA WORLD CUP™ FINALS MATCHES (BY POSITION)

Goalkeeper: Claudio Taffarel (Brazil, 18 matches)
Defence: Cafu (Brazil, 20); Wladyslaw Zmuda (Poland, 21); Fabio Cannavaro (Italy, 18); Paolo Maldini (Italy, 23)
Midfielders: Grzegorz Lato (Poland, 20); Lothar Matthaus (West Germany/Germany, 25); Wolfgang Overath (West Germany, 19); Enzo Scifo (Belgium, 17)
Forwards: Diego Maradona (Argentina, 21); Uwe Seeler (West Germany, 21)

PROSINECKI'S SCORING RECORD

Robert Prosinecki is the only player to have scored for different countries in FIFA World Cup finals tournaments. He netted for Yugoslavia in their 4-1 win over the United Arab Emirates in the 1990 tournament. Eight years later, following the break-up of the old Yugoslavia, he scored for Croatia in their 3-0 group-game win over Jamaica, and then netted the first goal in his side's 2-1 third-place play-off victory over Holland.

QUICKEST SUBSTITUTIONS

The three fastest substitutions in the history of the FIFA World Cup finals have all come in the fourth minute. In each case the player substituted was so seriously injured that he took no further part in the tournament: Steve Hodge came on for Bryan Robson in England's 0-0 draw with Morocco in 1986; Giuseppe Bergomi replaced Alessandro Nesta in Italy's 2-1 win over Austria in 1998; and Peter Crouch subbed for Michael Owen in England's 2-2 draw with Sweden in 2006.

UNHAPPY ENDINGS

For the second FIFA World Cup final in a row, the climactic match of the 2010 tournament featured a footballer not only playing his last international, but the final game of his career. Like Zinedine Zidane in 2006, **Giovanni van Bronckhorst** didn't complete the game four years later – though, unlike the Frenchman, he wasn't sent off but substituted, in the 105th minute. Dutch captain van Bronckhorst had scored a spectacular goal in the 2010 semi-final victory against Uruguay, but finished on the losing side in the final against Spain.

EASY FOR YOU TO SAY?

The longest single family names to have featured on the field at FIFA World Cups belong to Turkey forward Lefter Kucukandonyadis, chosen for the 1954 tournament in Switzerland, and Dutch striker Jan Vennegoor of Hesselink, who appeared as a substitute in Germany in 2006.

CAMEOS FOR CMIKIEWICZ

Polish midfielder Leslaw Cmikiewicz holds the record for most substitute appearances at one FIFA World Cup, being brought on in six different games at the 1974 tournament in West Germany as his team finished third.

BALLACK'S BITTER–SWEET SEMI–FINAL

Germany star Michael Ballack will never forget the 2002 FIFA World Cup semi-final against co-hosts South Korea in Seoul. The midfielder was yellow-carded by referee Urs Meier in the 71st minute for bringing down Lee Cun-Soo. Four minutes later, Ballack drove home a rebound to win the game for Germany, even though the yellow card he had received moments before meant he was suspended for the final.

LEADING CAPTAINS

Three players have each captained their teams in two FIFA World Cup finals – Diego Maradona of Argentina, Dunga of Brazil and West Germany's Karl-Heinz Rummenigge. Maradona lifted the trophy in 1986, but was a loser four years later. Dunga was the winning skipper in 1994, but was on the losing side in 1998. Rummenigge was a loser on both occasions, in 1982 and 1986. Maradona has made the most appearances as captain at the FIFA World Cup finals, leading out Argentina 16 times between 1986 and 1994.

FASTEST RED CARDS IN THE FIFA WORLD CUP™ FINALS

1 min	Jose Batista (Uruguay) v Scotland, 1986
3 min	Marco Etcheverry (Bolivia) v Germany, 1994
	Ion Vladoiu (Romania) v Switzerland, 1994
	Morten Wieghorst (Denmark) v South Africa, 1998
6 min	Lauren (Cameroon) v Chile, 1998
8 min	Giorgio Ferrini (Italy) v Chile, 1962
	Miklos Molnar (Denmark) v South Africa, 1998

FASTEST YELLOW CARDS IN THE FIFA WORLD CUP™ FINALS

1 min	Sergei Gorlukovich (Russia) v Sweden, 1994
	Giampiero Marini (Italy) v Poland, 1982
2 min	Jesus Arellano (Mexico) v Italy, 2002
	Henri Camara (Senegal) v Uruguay, 2002
	Michael Emenalo (Nigeria) v Italy, 1994

SIMUNIC'S THREE–CARD MATCH

Croatia's Josip Simunic holds the record for collecting the most yellow cards in one match at the FIFA World Cup finals – three against Australia in 2006. He received three yellows before he was finally sent off after a blunder by English referee Graham Poll. When Poll showed Simunic his second yellow, he clearly forgot he had already booked him.

THE LONGEST SUSPENSIONS

The longest ban imposed in FIFA World Cup finals history was the 15-month suspension of Argentina's Diego Maradona. He had tested positive for the banned drug ephedrine after Argentina's 2-1 group-game win over Nigeria in 1994. The longest suspension for on-field misconduct was the eight-match ban handed to Italy's Mauro Tassotti, also in 1994, after his elbow smashed Spain midfielder Luis Enrique's nose – out of the sight of the referee and linesmen – in the quarter-finals.

DENILSON STEPS UP FROM THE BENCH

Brazil winger **Denilson** has made the most substitute appearances at the FIFA World Cup finals – 11. He was involved in 12 of Brazil's games at the 1998 and 2002 finals, but started only one, against Norway in 1998. He was a half-time substitute for Leonardo in the 1998 final and came on for Ronaldo in stoppage time of the 2002 final (his last appearance in the finals), when Brazil beat Germany 2-0.

YOUNGEST PLAYERS IN FIFA WORLD CUP™ FINAL

Pelé (Brazil) – 17 years, 249 days, in 1958
Giuseppe Bergomi (Italy) – 18 years, 201 days, in 1982
Rubén Morán (Uruguay) – 19 years, 344 days, in 1950

OLDEST PLAYERS IN FIFA WORLD CUP™ FINAL

Dino Zoff (Italy) – 40 years, 133 days, in 1982
Gunnar Gren (Sweden) – 37 years, 241 days, in 1958
Jan Jongbloed (Holland) – 37 years, 212 days, in 1978
Nílton Santos (Brazil) – 37 years, 32 days, in 1962

PUZACH THE FIRST SUB

The first substitute in FIFA World Cup finals history was Anatoli Puzach of the Soviet Union. He replaced Viktor Serebrianikov at half-time of the Soviets' 0-0 draw with hosts Mexico on 31 May 1970. The 1970 tournament was the first in which substitutes were allowed, with two permitted for each team. FIFA increased this to three per team for the 1998 finals.

FOUR AND OUT

The most players sent off in one FIFA World Cup finals game is four. Costinha and Deco of Portugal and Khalid Boulahrouz and Gio van Bronckhorst of Holland were sent off by Russian referee Valentin Ivanov in their second-round match in Germany in 2006.

CANIGGIA – SENT OFF, WHILE ON THE BENCH…

Claudio Caniggia of Argentina became the first player to be sent off from the substitutes' bench, during the match against Sweden in 2002. Caniggia was dismissed in first-half stoppage time for dissent towards UAE referee Ali Bujsaim. Caniggia carried on protesting after the referee warned him to keep quiet, so Bujsaim showed him a red card.

MALDINI'S MINUTES RECORD

Lothar Matthaus of West Germany/Germany has started the most FIFA World Cup finals matches – 25. But Italy defender **Paolo Maldini** has stayed on the field for longer, despite starting two games fewer. Maldini played for 2,220 minutes, Matthaus for 2,052. According to the stopwatch, the top four are completed by Uwe Seeler of West Germany, who played for 1,980 minutes, and Argentina's Diego Maradona, who played for 1,938.

SHOOT–OUT SAVIOURS

West Germany's Harald "Toni" Schumacher and Sergio Goycochea of Argentina hold the record for the most penalty shoot-out saves in the finals – four each. Schumacher's saves came over two tournaments – in 1982 and 1986, including the decisive stop in the 1982 semi-final against France. Goycochea made his crucial saves in 1990, first in Argentina's quarter-final win over Yugoslavia and then against Italy to take his team to the final. His four shoot-out saves in one tournament is also a record. The record for the most shoot-out saves in one game is held by Portugal goalkeeper Ricardo. He saved three times to knock out England in the quarter-finals of the 2006 FIFA World Cup.

UNBEATEN GOALKEEPERS IN THE FIFA WORLD CUP™ FINALS*

Walter Zenga (Italy)	517 minutes without conceding a goal, 1990
Peter Shilton (England)	502 minutes, 1986–90
Sepp Maier (W Germany)	475 minutes, 1974–78
Gianluigi Buffon (Italy)	460 minutes, 2006
Emerson Leao (Brazil)	458 minutes, 1978
Gordon Banks (England)	442 minutes, 1966

* Pascal Zuberbuhler did not concede a goal in all 390 minutes played by Switzerland in the 2006 FIFA World Cup. Iker Casillas of Spain completed 433 minutes without conceding a goal in 2010.

FIFA WORLD CUP™ GOALKEEPING

IKER'S REPEAT PERFORMANCE

Spain's **Iker Casillas** became only the third goalkeeper to save two FIFA World Cup penalties – aside from shoot-outs – and the first to spread them across different tournaments. First he pushed away Ian Harte's spot-kick in a second-round tie against the Republic of Ireland in 2002. Even more impressive was how he caught Paraguayan forward Oscar Cardozo's effort in their 2010 quarter-final. Spain went on to win both matches. The two goalkeepers who had enjoyed such double success before were Poland's Jan Tomaszewski in 1974 and the United States' Brad Friedel in 2002.

NOT THINKING OUTSIDE THE BOX

Italy's Gianluca Pagliuca was the first goalkeeper to be sent off at a FIFA World Cup match when he was dismissed for handball outside his penalty area after 21 minutes against Norway at Giants Stadium, New York, in 1994. Despite sacrificing playmaker Roberto Baggio for goalkeeper Luca Marchegiani, Italy still won 1-0.

ITALY'S ELDER STATESMAN

Dino Zoff became both the oldest player and oldest captain to win the FIFA World Cup when his Italian side lifted the trophy in Spain in 1982. He was 40 years and 133 days old at the time. Alongside him in the team was defender Giuseppe Bergomi, aged 18 years and 201 days, a difference of 21 years and 297 days.

END-TO-END STUFF

When German striker Miroslav Klose raced on to a long ball from team-mate **Manuel Neuer** to give his side the lead against England in their 2010 second-round tie, it made Neuer the first goalkeeper to directly set up a FIFA World Cup goal for 44 years. The last before then had been the Soviet Union's Anzor Kavazashvili, who provided the assist for Valery Porkuyan's late winner against Chile in the 1966 first round.

NOT SO SWEET 16

No goalkeeper had conceded more goals in one FIFA World Cup than the 16 put past South Korea's Hong Duk-Yung in Switzerland in 1954. They all came in just two games, a 9-0 trouncing by eventual finalists Hungary and a 7-0 defeat to Turkey.

FIVE-STAR CARBAJAL

Antonio Carbajal, of Mexico, is one of only two men to have appeared at five FIFA World Cup finals – the other was Germany's versatile Lothar Matthaus. Carbajal, who played in 1950, 1954, 1958, 1962 and 1966, conceded a record 25 goals in his 11 FIFA World Cup finals appearances – the same number let in by Saudi Arabia's Mohamed Al-Deayea across ten games in 1994, 1998 and 2002. Al-Deayea was a member of the Saudi squad for the 2006 tournament but did not play.

NUMBER-ONE NUMBER ONES

The Lev Yashin Award was introduced in 1994 for the man voted best goalkeeper of the FIFA World Cup – though a goalkeeper has been picked for an all-star team at the end of every tournament dating back to 1930. The all-star team was expanded from 11 to 23 players in 1998, allowing room for more than one goalkeeper, but returned to 11 players in 2010. Players who were picked for the all-star teams but missed out on the Lev Yashin Award were Paraguay's Jose Luis Chilavert in 1998, Turkey's Rustu Recber in 2002, and Germany's Jens Lehmann and Portugal's Ricardo in 2006. The first Lev Yashin Award was presented to Belgium's Michel Preud'homme, even though he only played four games, conceding four goals, at the 1994 competition – his side were edged out 3-2 by Germany in the second round. Legendary Soviet goalkeeper Lev Yashin, after whom the trophy is named, played in the 1958, 1962 and 1966 FIFA World Cups and was a member of his country's 1970 squad as third-choice keeper and assistant coach – although he was never chosen for a FIFA World Cup team of the tournament. Yashin conceded the only FIFA World Cup finals goal scored directly from a corner-kick, taken by Colombia's Marcos Coll during a 4-4 draw in 1962.

OLIVER'S ARMS

Germany's **Oliver Kahn** is the only goalkeeper to have been voted FIFA's Player of the Tournament, winning the award at the 2002 FIFA World Cup – despite taking a share of the blame for Brazil's winning goals in the final.

RIGHT WAY FOR RICARDO

Spain's Ricardo Zamora became the first man to save a penalty in a FIFA World Cup finals match, stopping Valdemar de Brito's spot-kick for Brazil in 1934. Spain went on to win 3-1.

BROTHERS IN ARMS

Brothers Viktor and Viacheslav Chanov were two of the three goalkeepers in the Soviet Union's 1982 FIFA World Cup squad, but first-choice Rinat Dasayev was preferred to them both throughout. Viktor, eight years younger than Vyacheslav, did make one appearance at the 1986 FIFA World Cup four years later and ended his career with 21 caps. Vyacheslav had to wait until 1984 for his first and only international appearance.

UNLUCKY BREAK

Goalkeeper Frantisek Planicka broke his arm during Czechoslovakia's 1938 second-round clash against Brazil, but played on, even though the game went to extra-time before ending in a 1-1 draw. Not surprisingly, given the extent of his injury, Planicka missed the replay two days later, which the Czechs lost 2-1, and the goalkeeper of the 1938 FIFA World Cup never added to his tally of 73 caps.

PLAYERS VOTED BEST GOALKEEPER OF THE TOURNAMENT

1930	Enrique Ballestrero (Uruguay)	1978	Ubaldo Fillol (Argentina)
1934	Ricardo Zamora (Spain)	1982	Dino Zoff (Italy)
1938	Frantisek Planicka (Czechoslovakia)	1986	Harald Schumacher (West Germany)
1950	Roque Maspoli (Uruguay)	1990	Sergio Goycoechea (Argentina)
1954	Gyula Grosics (Hungary)	1994	Michel Preud'homme (Belgium)
1958	Harry Gregg (Northern Ireland)	1998	Fabien Barthez (France)
1962	Viliam Schrojf (Czechoslovakia)	2002	Oliver Kahn (Germany)
1966	Gordon Banks (England)	2006	Gianluigi Buffon (Italy)
1970	Ladislao Mazurkiewicz (Uruguay)	2010	Iker Casillas (Spain)
1974	Jan Tomaszewski (Poland)		

BATTERING RAMON

Argentina's 6-0 win over Peru at the 1978 FIFA World Cup aroused suspicion because the hosts needed to win by four goals to reach the final at the expense of arch-rivals Brazil – and Peruvian goalkeeper Ramon Quiroga had been born in Argentina. He insisted, though, that his saves prevented the defeat from being even more embarrassingly emphatic. Earlier in the same tournament, Quiroga had been booked for a foul on Grzegorz Lato after running into the Polish half of the field.

KHUNE LOSES HIS COOL

Host nation South Africa's **Itumeleng Khune** became only the second goalkeeper to be sent off at a FIFA World Cup when he was red-carded during their 3-0 defeat to Uruguay in the 2010 first round. He was penalized for a professional foul on Luis Suarez, also conceding a penalty at the same time. Khune, 22, had been one of the team's best performers in the opening game of the tournament, a 1-1 draw with Mexico.

MORE AND MORA

Luis Ricardo Guevara Mora holds the unenviable record for most goals conceded in just one FIFA World Cup finals match. The 20-year-old had to pick the ball out of the net ten times in El Salvador's thrashing by Hungary in 1982 – and his team-mates managed only one goal of their own in reply. In this game he also set the record for being the youngest goalkeeper to participate in the FIFA World Cup finals.

TONY AWARD

United States goalkeeper **Tony Meola** left the national team after the 1994 FIFA World Cup because he wanted to switch sports and take up American football instead. He failed to make it in gridiron and returned to soccer, but did not play for his country again until 1999. He retired for a second time after reaching a century of international appearances and still holds the record for being the youngest FIFA World Cup captain, having worn the armband for the US's 5-1 defeat to Czechoslovakia in 1990, aged 21 years 316 days.

THREE'S COMPANY

Both Czechoslovakia and Belgium used all three of their goalkeepers at the 1982 FIFA World Cup in Spain – Zdenek Hruska, Stanislav Seman and Karel Stromsik for the Czechs, and Jean-Marie Pfaff, Theo Custers and Jacques Munaron for the Belgians.

PUTTING THE LOVE IN GLOVE

For the third time since it was first handed out five FIFA World Cups ago, the 2010 Golden Glove prize went to the man between the sticks for the newly crowned world champions. Spain captain **Iker Casillas** received the award as best goalkeeper in South Africa, adding it to a winner's medal just as Italy's Gianluigi Buffon had in 2006 and France's Fabien Barthez had in 1998. Casillas's exploits included saving a penalty by catching the ball, in the quarter-final win over Paraguay. He celebrated winning the final by giving a passionate on-air kiss to his TV presenter girlfriend **Sara Carbonero**. Perhaps they were kissing and making up – she had appeared to criticize Casillas when interviewing him in the immediate aftermath of Spain's first game of the competition, a surprise 1-0 defeat to Switzerland.

TOP GOALS

1930	70	(3.89 per match)
1934	70	(4.12 per match)
1938	84	(4.67 per match)
1950	88	(4 per match)
1954	140	(5.38 per match)
1958	126	(3.6 per match)
1962	89	(2.78 per match)
1966	89	(2.78 per match)
1970	95	(2.97 per match)
1974	97	(2.55 per match)
1978	102	(2.68 per match)
1982	146	(2.81 per match)
1986	132	(2.54 per match)
1990	115	(2.21 per match)
1994	141	(2.71 per match)
1998	171	(2.67 per match)
2002	161	(2.52 per match)
2006	147	(2.3 per match)
2010	145	(2.27 per match)
Total 2,063		(2.91 per match)

TRADING PLACES

The first goalkeeper to be substituted at a FIFA World Cup was Romania's Stere Adamache, who was replaced by Rica Raducanu 27 minutes into a 3-2 defeat to Brazil in 1970. Romania were 2-0 down at the time.

INCONSOLABLE JULIO CESAR

Despite being widely acclaimed as one of the best goalkeepers in the world – and going into the 2010 FIFA World Cup having just won the UEFA Champions League with Italy's Internazionale – Brazil's **Julio Cesar** had a quarter-final to forget in Port Elizabeth. He misjudged the free-kick by Wesley Sneijder which provided Holland with a crucial equalizer – though Cesar's team-mate Felipe Melo appeared to deflect the ball into his own net. The Dutch won the game 2-1 and the distraught Cesar was later filmed sobbing in his mother's arms after landing back home in Brazil.

PLAYING THROUGH THE PAIN BARRIER

The first FIFA World Cup clean sheet was kept by Jimmy Douglas of the United States in a 3-0 win over Belgium in 1930. He followed that up with another, as Paraguay were beaten by the same scoreline – but Argentina proved too good, winning 6-1 in the semi-final. Douglas injured his knee after only four minutes, but had to play on as this occurred in the days before substitutes were allowed.

THE PETER PRINCIPLE

Peter Shilton became the oldest FIFA World Cup captain when he led England for their 1990 third-place play-off against hosts Italy. He was 40 years and 292 days old as he made his 125th and final appearance for his country – though his day was spoiled by a 2-1 defeat, including a goalkeeping error that gifted Roberto Baggio Italy's opener. Shilton, born in Leicester on 18 September 1949, also played for England at the 1982 and 1986 tournaments. He became captain in Mexico in 1986 after Bryan Robson was ruled out of the tournament by injury and Ray Wilkins by suspension, and featured in one of the FIFA World Cup's all-time memorable moments, when he was out-jumped by Argentina's Diego Maradona for the infamous "Hand of God" goal. Shilton jointly holds the record for most FIFA World Cup clean sheets, with ten – along with France's Fabien Barthez, who played at the 1998, 2002 and 2006 tournaments. Both men made 17 FIFA World Cup finals appearances apiece.

FIFA WORLD CUP™ MANAGERS

ELDEST STATESMAN OTTO

Otto Rehhagel was not only the oldest coach at the 2010 FIFA World Cup, but the oldest in the competition's history. The German was 71 years 317 days old when his Greece team played their third and final game of the tournament, a 2-0 defeat to Argentina.

OUTSIDE INFLUENCES

Every single FIFA World Cup has featured at least one team led by a foreign coach. The most were at the 2006 tournament, with 15 of the 32 competing countries spearheaded by chiefs from overseas. These included Luiz Felipe Scolari, the Brazilian coach of fourth-placed Portugal. Twelve different countries taking part in the 2010 FIFA World Cup were led by foreign managers: Chile's Marcelo Bielsa (Argentine), England's Fabio Capello (Italian), Ivory Coast's Sven-Goran Eriksson (Swedish), Switzerland's Ottmar Hitzfeld (German), Nigeria's Lars Lagerback (Swedish), Cameroon's Paul Le Guen (French), Paraguay's Gerardo Martino (Argentine), South Africa's Carlos Alberto Parreira (Brazilian), Ghana's Milovan Rajevac (Serbian), Greece's Otto Rehhagel (German), Honduras' Reinaldo Rueda (Colombian) and Australia's Pim Verbeek (Dutch). Brazilian managers lead the way since 1930, having led 14 different non-Brazilian squads at FIFA World Cups, followed by French coaches (11), English (10) and Yugoslavian/Serbian (nine).

CRASHING BORA

Only one tournament behind record-holder Carlos Alberto Parreira, **Bora Milutinovic** has coached at five different FIFA World Cups – with a different country each time, two of them being the hosts. As well as Mexico in 1986 and the United States in 1994, he led Costa Rica in 1990, Nigeria in 1998 and China in 2002. He reached the knockout stages with every country except China – who failed to score a single goal.

DREAM ELEVEN

Luiz Felipe Scolari managed a record 11 FIFA World Cup finals wins in a row, across the 2002 tournament, when he was in charge of Brazil, and 2006, when coach of Portugal. That winning run extends to 12 games if one counts Portugal's victory over England in the 2006 quarter-final, though that was on penalties after a goalless draw.

SOCCER SIX

Only one man has gone to six FIFA World Cups as coach: Brazilian **Carlos Alberto Parreira**, whose greatest moment came when he guided Brazil to the trophy for the fourth time in 1994. His second stint as Brazil coach was less successful – they fell in the quarter-finals in 2006. Parreira also led Kuwait (1982), the United Arab Emirates (1990), Saudi Arabia (1998) and hosts South Africa (2010) at the finals. He had stepped down as South Africa coach in April 2008, for family reasons, but returned late the following year. Parreira was once sacked midway through a FIFA World Cup. In 1998 he led Saudi Arabia for the first two of their three games – losing 1-0 to Denmark and 4-0 to France – before receiving his marching orders.

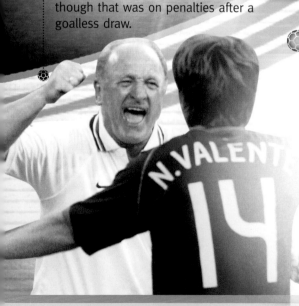

PUFF DADDIES

The coaches of the two sides appearing at the 1978 FIFA World Cup final were such prolific smokers that an oversized ashtray was produced for Argentina's Cesar Luis Menotti and Holland's Ernst Happel so they could share it on the touchline.

DIVIDED LOYALTIES

No coach has won the FIFA World Cup in charge of a foreign country, but several have found themselves taking on their homelands in the FIFA World Cup. These include Brazilian 1958 FIFA World Cup-winning midfielder Didi, whose Peru side lost 4-2 to his home country in 1970. Sven-Goran Eriksson was England coach for their 1-1 draw against his native Sweden in 2002, the same year Frenchman Bruno Metsu led Senegal to a 1-0 opening-match win over France. Former Yugoslavia goalkeeper Blagoje Vidinic endured the most bittersweet moment – he coached Zaire to their first and only FIFA World Cup in 1974, and then had to watch his adopted players lose 9-0 to Yugoslavia.

YOUNG JUAN

Juan Jose Tramutola remains the youngest-ever FIFA World Cup coach, leading Argentina in the 1930 tournament at the age of 27 years and 267 days. Italian Cesare Maldini became the oldest in 2002, taking charge of Paraguay when aged 70 years and 131 days.

FIFA WORLD CUP™– WINNING COACHES

1930	Alberto Suppici
1934	Vittorio Pozzo
1938	Vittorio Pozzo
1950	Juan Lopez
1954	Sepp Herberger
1958	Vicente Feola
1962	Aymore Moreira
1966	Alf Ramsey
1970	Mario Zagallo
1974	Helmut Schon
1978	Cesar Luis Menotti
1982	Enzo Bearzot
1986	Carlos Bilardo
1990	Franz Beckenbauer
1994	Carlos Alberto Parreira
1998	Aime Jacquet
2002	Luiz Felipe Scolari
2006	Marcello Lippi
2010	Vicente del Bosque

SCHON SHINES

West Germany's **Helmut Schon** was coach for more FIFA World Cup matches than any other man – 25, across the 1966, 1970, 1974 and 1978 tournaments. He has also won the most games as a coach, 16 in all – including the 1974 final against Holland. The 1974 tournament was third time lucky for Schon. He he had taken West Germany to second place in 1966 and to third in 1970. Before taking charge of the national side, Schon had worked as an assistant to Sepp Herberger, coach of West Germany's 1954 FIFA World Cup-winning team – Schon was coach of the then-independent Saarland regional side at the time. Dog-lover Schon, born in Dresden on 15 September 1915, scored 17 goals in 16 internationals for Germany between 1937 and 1941. He succeeded Herberger in 1964 and spent 14 years in charge of his country. He was the only coach to win both the FIFA World Cup (1974) and the European Championship (1972).

FIFA WORLD CUP™ REFEREEING

YEARS OF EXPERIENCE

Spain's Juan Gardeazabal Garay remains the youngest man to referee at a FIFA World Cup, being just 24 years 193 days old when he took charge at the 1958 tournament in Sweden. He also officiated in 1962 and 1966. Englishman George Reader is not only the oldest man to have refereed a FIFA World Cup final – 56 years 236 days old when he ran the effective climax between Brazil and Uruguay in 1950 – but also the oldest referee at any FIFA World Cup. He died on 13 July 1978, exactly 48 years to the day since the very first FIFA World Cup fixture.

BAKU OF THE NET

The official who signalled that Geoff Hurst's controversial extra-time goal for England in the 1966 FIFA World Cup final had crossed the line is often wrongly described as a Russian linesman. In fact, Tofik Bakhramov was from Azerbaijan, so he was officially a Soviet Union linesman. The Azeri national football stadium, in the capital Baku, is now named after him.

DOUBLE DUTY

Only two men have refereed a FIFA World Cup final and a European Championship final. Italian Sergio Gonella officiated at the 1978 World Cup final between Argentina and Holland, two years after overseeing the European Championship final between West Germany and Czechoslovakia. Swiss official Gottfried Dienst took control of the 1966 FIFA World Cup final, between England and West Germany, and the drawn 1968 European Championship final between Italy and Yugoslavia – Spain's Jose Maria Ortiz de Mendibil was awarded the replay.

MOTHER'S PRIDE

Guatemala's **Carlos Batres** refereed the 2010 FIFA World Cup first-round match between Algeria and Slovenia despite the death of his terminally ill mother just four days earlier. Amanda Rosa Gonzalez had told her son beforehand to stay in South Africa should she die while he was away. He went on to referee two more games in South Africa: the Group F draw between Italy and New Zealand and Spain's quarter-final win over Paraguay.

FRENCH CONNECTION

Frenchman **Georges Capdeville**, in charge for Italy's win over Hungary in 1938, is the only man to referee the final in a FIFA World Cup hosted by his own country.

FIFA WORLD CUP™ FINAL REFEREES

1930	Jean Langenus (Belgium)
1934	Ivan Eklind (Sweden)
1938	Georges Capdeville (France)
1950	George Reader (England)
1954	William Ling (England)
1958	Maurice Guigue (France)
1962	Nikolay Latyshev (USSR)
1966	Gottfried Dienst (Switzerland)
1970	Rudi Glockner (West Germany)
1974	Jack Taylor (England)
1978	Sergio Gonella (Italy)
1982	Arnaldo Cezar Coelho (Brazil)
1986	Romualdo Arppi Filho (Brazil)
1990	Edgardo Codesal (Mexico)
1994	Sandor Puhl (Hungary)
1998	Said Belqola (Morocco)
2002	Pierluigi Collina (Italy)
2006	Horacio Elizondo (Argentina)
2010	Howard Webb (England)

COUPE DU MONDE 1938

WORLDWIDE WEBB

Former Yorkshire policeman **Howard Webb** became the fourth Englishman to referee a FIFA World Cup final when he was chosen for the 2010 showdown between Spain and Holland. He had earlier controlled two group games and a second-round tie between Spain and Chile. The honour came less than two months after he refereed the UEFA Champions League final between Inter Milan and Bayern Munich, making him the first man in charge of both World Cup and European Cup final matches in the same summer. Webb also became the first FIFA World Cup debutant ref to be given the final. At just three days short of his 39th birthday, Webb was also the youngest FIFA World Cup final referee since Frenchman Georges Capdeville, who took charge of the 1938 final aged 38 years and 232 days. Even younger was Swedish 28-year-old Ivan Eklind, in 1934.

IDENTITY PARADE

Hungarian referee Istvan Zsolt threatened to call off England's opening game of the 1966 FIFA World Cup, against Uruguay, when he demanded to see the players' identity cards – and found that seven English players had left their passports at the team hotel. A police motorcyclist was sent to collect them and bring them back to Wembley Stadium so the match could go ahead.

NETTO'S NET

Soviet captain Igor Netto persuaded Italian referee Cesare Jonni to disallow a goal for his own team at the 1962 FIFA World Cup, pointing out that Igor Chislenko had shot wide – the ball entered the Uruguayan goal through a hole in the net. His side still won the first-round match, 2-1.

TIME, GENTLEMEN

Welsh referee Clive Thomas disallowed what would have potentially been a winning goal by Brazil against Sweden in the 1978 FIFA World Cup. Thomas said he had blown the final whistle seconds before Zico headed in from a corner, and the game ended in a 1-1 draw. In contrast, Israeli referee Abraham Klein tried to blow the final whistle several times when England played Brazil at the 1970 FIFA World Cup in Guadalajara, but none of the players appeared to hear him.

PROLIFIC OFFICIALS

No referees have run more FIFA World Cup matches than Joel Quiniou and Benito Archundia. Frenchman Quiniou took charge of eight games across the 1986, 1990 and 1994 tournaments. In the last of these, he became the first man to referee four matches in one FIFA World Cup – including Italy's semi-final victory over Bulgaria. Since then, others have officiated in even more matches in a single FIFA World Cup: Mexico's Archundia and Argentina's **Horacio Elizondo** each controlled five games in 2006, as did Uzbekistan's Ravshan Irmatov in 2010. Elizondo was referee for both the first and final matches in 2006, emulating the feat of English referee George Reader in 1950. Elizondo's memorable moments included a red card for Zinedine Zidane following the French star's headbutt on Marco Materazzi in the 2006 final, a red card for England's Wayne Rooney for stamping on Portugal's Ricardo Carvalho in their quarter-final that summer, and a yellow card for Ghana's Asamoah Gyan, for taking a penalty against the Czech Republic too quickly. Gyan then missed his second attempt. After five games in 2006, Archundia was given responsibility for three matches in 2010 – including the third-place play-off between Germany and Uruguay.

FIFA WORLD CUP™ DISCIPLINE

ADVANCE BOOKING

Two players have been booked within a minute of kick-off – Italy's **Giampiero Marini**, against Poland, in 1982, and Russia's Sergei Gorlukovich against Sweden 12 years later. But Uruguayan Jose Batista went one worse in a 1986 first-round match against Scotland, receiving a red card after just 56 seconds for a gruesome foul on Gordon Strachan. His team-mates held on for a goalless draw.

NOT LEADING BY EXAMPLE

The first man to be sent off at a FIFA World Cup was Peru's Placido Galindo, at the first tournament in 1930 during a 3-1 defeat to Romania. Chilean referee Alberto Warnken dismissed the Peruvian captain for fighting.

REPEAT OFFENDERS

France's **Zinedine Zidane** and Brazil's **Cafu** are both FIFA World Cup winners – and both notched up a record six FIFA World Cup cards, though Cafu escaped any reds, while Zidane was sent off twice. Most famously, Zidane was dismissed for headbutting Italy's Marco Materazzi in extra-time of the 2006 final in Berlin – the final match of the Frenchman's career. He had also been sent off during a first-round match against Saudi Arabia in 1998, but returned from suspension in time to help France win the trophy with a sensational two-goal performance in the final. The only other man to have been sent off twice at two different FIFA World Cups is Cameroon's Rigobert Song. When dismissed against Brazil in 1994, he became the FIFA World Cup's youngest red card offender – aged just 17 years and 358 days. He saw red for the second time against Chile in 1998.

LATE BREAKERS

Argentina goalkeeper Carlos Roa was booked after the final whistle, for time-wasting during his team's second-round penalty shoot-out against England in 1998. Brazilian defender Edinho was shown a yellow card during the quarter-final shoot-out against France in 1986. French midfielder Jacques Simon was booked after his team's 2-1 defeat to Uruguay at the 1966 FIFA World Cup had ended, for spitting at Czech referee Karol Galba. But Argentina's unused substitute Leandro Cufre outdid them all, receiving a red card for his part in a brawl minutes after his team lost on penalties to Germany in their 2006 FIFA World Cup quarter-final clash.

CARDS CLOSE TO CHEST

Only one group in FIFA World Cup finals history has featured no bookings at all – Group 4 in 1970, featuring West Germany, Peru, Bulgaria and Morocco. In contrast, the 2006 FIFA World Cup in Germany was the worst for both red and yellow cards, with 28 dismissals and 345 bookings in 64 matches.

GOOD SON, BAD SON

Cameroon's Andre Kana-Biyik served two suspensions during the 1990 FIFA World Cup. The first came after he was sent off in the opening match against Argentina – six minutes before his brother Francois Omam-Biyik scored the only goal. His second ban came after yellow cards in the final group game against Russia and in the second-round defeat of Colombia.

FIFA WORLD CUP™ RED CARDS, BY TOURNAMENT

1930	1
1934	1
1938	4
1950	0
1954	3
1958	3
1962	6
1966	5
1970	0
1974	5
1978	3
1982	5
1986	8
1990	16
1994	15
1998	22
2002	17
2006	28
2010	17

FINAL COUNT

Before 14 yellow cards were shown in the 2010 FIFA World Cup final, the previous 18 finals had featured 40 bookings between them – an average of 2.2 per game. The 15 cards flourished by 2010 final referee **Howard Webb** – 14 yellows and one red – were nine more than those shown by previous record-holder Romualdo Arppi Filho, who "awarded" Argentina four and West Germany two yellows in the 1986 final.

LUCKY ESCAPE

Brazil's FIFA World Cup history and legend could have been very different had the present system of automatic suspension for a sending-off been in place in 1962. In the absence of the injured Pele, outside-right Garrincha had emerged as the defending champions' attacking inspiration. He was sent off in the closing minutes of the semi-final win over Chile ... but it was recorded only as a booking and he went on to play in the final against Czechoslovakia, which Brazil won 3-1.

BREAKING COVER

Zaire defender Mwepu Llunga was booked for running out of the wall and kicking the ball away as Brazil prepared to take a free-kick, at the 1974 FIFA World Cup. Romanian referee Nicolae Rainea ignored Llunga's pleas of innocence.

YELLOW MELO'S RED MIST

Felipe Melo's red card for stamping on Arjen Robben, in Brazil's 2010 FIFA World Cup quarter-final defeat to Holland, means Brazil have now had more players sent off in FIFA World Cup history than any other team – one more than Argentina. Melo was Brazil's 11th dismissal, after Kaka had become the 10th in a first-round victory over the Ivory Coast. Melo could also have gone down as the first player ever to score an own goal and be sent off in the same FIFA World Cup match, but the first Dutch goal was later officially awarded to their own playmaker Wesley Sneijder.

SOLE CHANCE OF GLORY

India withdrew from the 1950 FIFA World Cup because some of their players wanted to play barefoot but FIFA insisted all players must wear football boots. India have not qualified for the tournament since.

ELBOWED OUT

Italian defender Mauro Tassotti was given an unprecedented eight-game ban for smashing Spain's Luis Enrique in the face with his elbow in 1994 – an offence missed by match referee Sandor Puhl. Spain lost 2-1 and were further enraged when the Hungarian official was then selected to referee the final.

ABSENT FRIENDS

Only 8,521 spectators turned up at Solna's Rasunda Stadium in Stockholm to see Wales play Hungary in a first-round play-off match during the 1958 FIFA World Cup. More than 40,000 had attended the first game between the two sides but how could the replay in tribute to executed Hungarian uprising leader Imre Nagy.

RIO BRAVO

The 162,764 people who watched Brazil play Colombia in Rio's Maracana in March 1977 provided the biggest crowd for a FIFA World Cup qualifying match. Sadly the game failed to live up to the occasion: it ended in a disappointing 0-0 draw.

SOUTH AFRICAN SUCCESS

The 2010 FIFA World Cup in South Africa was watched by a total of 3,178,856 spectators, across the 64 matches in 10 different stadiums – the third-highest aggregate attendance in the tournament's history, behind the United States in 1994 and Germany in 2006. The average attendance was 49,670 and though some concerns were raised about patches of empty seats at several games, organizers said they were happy that 92.9 per cent of places were filled.

GENDER EQUALITY

Only two stadiums have hosted the finals of the FIFA World Cup for both men and women. The Rose Bowl, in Pasadena, California, was the venue for the men's final in 1994 – when Brazil beat Italy – and the women's showdown between the victorious US and China five years later, which was watched by 90,185 people. But Sweden's Rasunda Stadium, near Stockholm, just about got there first – though it endured a long wait between the men's final in 1958 and the women's in 1995. Both sets of American spectators got their money's worth, watching games that went into extra-time and which were settled on penalties.

CITY SLICKER

The capacity of South Africa's 2010 FIFA World Cup showpiece venue, **Soccer City** in Johannesburg, was increased from 78,000 to 84,490. The design of the newly revamped stadium was based on traditional African pottery and nicknamed the Calabash. Soccer City hosted both the opening game and the final – as well as four more first-round fixtures, a second-round clash and a quarter-final.

FIFA WORLD CUP™ FINAL ATTENDANCES

Year	Attendance	Stadium	City
1930	93,000	Estadio Centenario	Montevideo
1934	45,000	Stadio Nazionale del PNF	Rome
1938	60,000	Stade Olympique de Colombes	Paris
1950	174,000	Estadio do Maracana	Rio de Janeiro
1954	60,000	Wankdorfstadion	Berne
1958	51,800	Rasunda Fotbollstadion	Solna
1962	68,679	Estadio Nacional	Santiago
1966	98,000	Wembley Stadium	London
1970	107,412	Estadio Azteca	Mexico City
1974	75,200	Olympiastadion	Munich
1978	71,483	Estadio Monumental	Buenos Aires
1982	90,000	Estadio Santiago Bernabeu	Madrid
1986	114,600	Estadio Azteca	Mexico City
1990	73,603	Stadio Olimpico	Rome
1994	94,194	Rose Bowl	Pasadena
1998	80,000	Stade de France	Paris
2002	69,029	International Stadium	Yokohama
2006	69,000	Olympiastadion	Berlin
2010	84,490	Soccer City	Johannesburg

TOURNAMENT ATTENDANCES

Year	Total	Average
1930	434,500	24,139
1934	358,000	21,059
1938	376,000	20,889
1950	1,043,500	47,432
1954	889,500	34,212
1958	919,580	26,274
1962	899,074	28,096
1966	1,635,000	51,094
1970	1,603,975	50,124
1974	1,768,152	46,530
1978	1,546,151	40,688
1982	2,109,723	40,572
1986	2,393,331	46,026
1990	2,516,348	48,391
1994	3,587,538	68,991
1998	2,785,100	43,517
2002	2,705,197	42,269
2006	3,359,439	52,491
2010	3,178,856	49,670
TOTAL	34,108,964	44,182

MORBID MARACANA

The largest attendance for a FIFA World Cup match was at Rio de Janeiro's Maracana for the last clash of the 1950 tournament – though no one is quite sure how many were there. The final tally was officially given as 174,000, though some estimates suggest as many as 210,000 witnessed the host country's traumatic defeat. Tensions were so high at the final whistle, winning Uruguay captain Obdulio Varela was not awarded the trophy in a traditional manner, but had it surreptitiously nudged into his hands. FIFA president Jules Rimet described the crowd's overwhelming silence as "morbid, almost too difficult to bear". Uruguay's triumphant players barricaded themselves inside their dressing room for several hours before they judged it safe enough to emerge. Those spectators, however many there were, were the last to see Brazil play in an all-white kit – the unlucky colours were scrapped and, after a competition was held to find a new national strip, were replaced by the now-familiar yellow and blue.

FAN FESTS FIND FAVOUR

After city centre **"Fan Fests"**, including giant TV screens and food stalls, proved popular at the 2006 FIFA World Cup in Germany, they were staged again in 2010 – not only across South African cities (such as **Durban**, below), but also elsewhere in the world including Rio in Brazil, Rome in Italy, Paris in France and Sydney in Australia. A total of 6,151,823 people visited the Fan Fests for the tournament's 64 games, including 2,634,018 across South Africa and 3,517,805 abroad. German capital Berlin attracted the biggest crowd, with 350,000 flocking to the Fan Fest there to watch Germany's semi-final defeat to Spain.

RIO'S MARIO

Most people know Brazil's largest stadium as the Maracana, named after the Rio neighbourhood and a small nearby river. But, since the mid-1960s, the official title has actually been "Estadio Jornalista Mario Filho", after a Brazilian journalist who had helped in the campaign for the stadium to be built.

OLYMPIC NAMES

The stadium hosting the opening match of the 1930 FIFA World Cup had stands named after great Uruguayan footballing triumphs: Colombes, in honour of the 1924 Paris Olympics venue; Amsterdam, after the site where that title was retained four years later; and Montevideo, even though it would be another fortnight before the home team clinched the first FIFA World Cup in their own capital city.

BERLIN CALL

Despite later becoming the capital of a united Germany, then-divided Berlin only hosted three group games at the 1974 FIFA World Cup in West Germany – the host country's surprise loss to East Germany took place in Hamburg. An unexploded World War Two bomb was discovered beneath the seats at Berlin's Olympiastadion in 2002, by workers preparing the ground for the 2006 tournament. Germany, along with Brazil, had applied to host the tournament in 1942, before it was cancelled due to the outbreak of World War Two.

MEXICAN SAVE

Mexico was not the original choice to host the 1986 FIFA World Cup, but stepped in when Colombia withdrew in 1982 due to financial problems. Mexico held on to the staging rights despite suffering from an earthquake in September 1985 that left approximately 10,000 people dead, but which left the stadiums unscathed. FIFA kept faith in the country, and the **Azteca Stadium** went on to become the first venue to host two FIFA World Cup final matches – and Mexico the first country to stage two FIFA World Cups. The Azteca – formally named the "Estadio Guillermo Canedo", after a Mexican football official – was built in 1960 using 100,000 tonnes of concrete, four times as much as was needed for the old Wembley.

TWIN PEAKS

Five stadiums have the distinction of staging both the final of a FIFA World Cup and the Summer Olympics athletics: Berlin's Olympiastadion (1936 Olympics, 2006 FIFA World Cup); London's Wembley (1948 Olympics, 1966 FIFA World Cup); Rome's Stadio Olimpico (1960 Olympics, 1990 FIFA World Cup); Mexico City's Azteca (1968 Olympics, 1970 and 1986 FIFA World Cups); and Munich's Olympiastadion (1972 Olympics, 1974 FIFA World Cup). The Rose Bowl in Pasadena, California, hosted both the final of the 1994 FIFA World Cup and the 1984 Olympics football tournament, but not the main Olympics track-and-field events.

THE REAL THING?

Official rules mean stadiums used at FIFA World Cups must shed any sponsors' names for the duration of the tournament. The only South African stadium affected by this in 2010 was Johannesburg's Ellis Park venue, otherwise known locally under separate sponsors' names when staging other football and rugby fixtures. Three 2010 venues were named after former African National Congress figures: the Nelson Mandela Bay stadium in Port Elizabeth, the Peter Mokaba stadium in Polokwane and the Moses Mabhida stadium in Durban.

ARCHITECTS' PREROGATIVE

Distinctive and creative elements were added to the stadiums built especially for the 2010 FIFA World Cup in South Africa, including the giraffe-shaped towers at **Nelspruit's Mbombela stadium,** the 350-metre-long arch and rope-swing soaring above **Durban's main arena,** and the white "petals" shrouding the Nelson Mandela Bay stadium in Port Elizabeth.

HOSTS WITH THE MOST

No other single-hosted FIFA World Cup has used as many venues as the 14 spread across Spain in 1982. The 2002 tournament was played at 20 different venues, but ten of these were in Japan and ten in co-host country South Korea.

RULES OF SELECTION

FIFA World Cup hosting rights alternated between Europe and the Americas until the 2002 tournament, which went to Asia for the first time as Japan and South Korea co-hosted the event. The first FIFA World Cup held in Africa was hosted by South Africa in 2010, before the tournament goes to Brazil four years later – the first return to South America in 36 years. FIFA's latest rules mean no continent can apply to host more than one FIFA World Cup every eight years – and host nations for 2018 and 2022 will be named on the same day in December 2010. South Africa had only missed out on hosting the 2006 FIFA World Cup by just one solitary vote, to Germany.

UNSUCCESSFUL HOSTING BIDS

1930	Hungary, Italy, Holland, Spain, Sweden
1934	Sweden
1938	Argentina, Germany
1950	None
1954	None
1958	None
1962	Argentina, West Germany
1966	Spain, West Germany
1970	Argentina
1974	Spain
1978	Mexico
1982	West Germany
1986	Colombia*, Canada, USA
1990	England, Greece, USSR
1994	Brazil, Morocco
1998	Morocco, Switzerland
2002	Mexico
2006	Brazil, England, Morocco, South Africa
2010	Egypt, Libya/Tunisia, Morocco
2014	None

* Colombia won hosting rights for 1986 but later withdrew.

BREAKING THE CODE

Not all the stadiums at the 2010 FIFA World Cup were entirely new constructions – several were old-fashioned mainly rugby venues given enough of a facelift to cope with the new football-led demand. These included Johannesburg's Ellis Park and Pretoria's **Loftus Versfeld.** The Pretoria arena is the usual home ground of popular rugby team the Blue Bulls, though they did play a pre-FIFA World Cup game at Johannesburg's showpiece Soccer City stadium. Soccer City also staged an August 2010 rugby international between the Springboks of South Africa and the All-Blacks of New Zealand.

FIFA WORLD CUP™ PENALTIES

FIFA WORLD CUP™ PENALTY SHOOT-OUTS

Year	Round	120-minute Score	Winner
1982	Semi-final	West Germany 3 France 3	West Germany
1986	Quarter-final	West Germany 0 Mexico 0	West Germany
1986	Quarter-final	France 1 Brazil 1	France
1986	Quarter-final	Belgium 1 Spain 1	Belgium
1990	Second round	Republic of Ireland 0 Romania 0	Republic of Ireland
1990	Quarter-final	Argentina 0 Yugoslavia 0	Argentina
1990	Semi-final	Argentina 1 Italy 1	Argentina
1990	Semi-final	West Germany 1 England 1	West Germany
1994	Second round	Bulgaria 1 Mexico 1	Bulgaria
1994	Quarter-final	Sweden 2 Romania 2	Sweden
1994	Final	Brazil 0 Italy 0	Brazil
1998	Second round	Argentina 2 England 2	Argentina
1998	Quarter-final	France 0 Italy 0	France
1998	Semi-final	Brazil 1 Netherlands 1	Brazil
2002	Second round	Spain 1 Republic of Ireland 1	Spain
2002	Quarter-final	South Korea 0 Spain 0	South Korea
2006	Second round	Ukraine 0 Switzerland 0	Ukraine
2006	Quarter-final	Germany 1 Argentina 1	Germany
2006	Quarter-final	Portugal 0 England 0	Portugal
2006	Final	Italy 1 France 1	Italy
2010	Second round	Paraguay 0 Japan 0	Paraguay
2010	Quarter-final	Uruguay 1 Ghana 1	Uruguay

FIRST IS BEST

Paraguay's defeat of Japan and **Diego Forlan** and Uruguay's win against Ghana in 2010 mean seven straight FIFA World Cup penalty shoot-outs have been won by the team taking the first kick. The last side to go second and win was Spain, against the Republic of Ireland in 2002.

THREE IN ONE

Argentina's stand-in goalkeeper Sergio Goycochea set a tournament record by saving four shoot-out penalties in 1990 – though West Germany's Harald Schumacher managed as many, across the 1982 and 1986 tournaments. Portugal's **Ricardo** achieved an unprecedented feat by stopping three spot-kicks in just the one shoot-out, becoming an instant hero in his side's quarter-final win over England in 2006.

NOT SO SUPREME

The 1994 tournament in the US was simply fated to end with a missed penalty. The opening ceremony featured soul-pop singer Diana Ross taking a spot-kick in Chicago's Soldier Field stadium – only for the former Supremes frontwoman (then aged 50) to toe-poke the ball wide. The goal collapsed in half, as choreographed, nevertheless.

BAGGIO OF DISHONOUR

Pity poor Roberto Baggio: the Italian maestro has taken part in three FIFA World Cup penalty shoot-outs, more than anyone else – and lost each and every one. Most grievously, it was his shot over the bar that gifted Brazil the trophy at the end of the 1994 final. But he also ended up on the losing side against Argentina in a 1990 semi-final and France in a quarter-final eight years later. At least on those two occasions, his own attempts did hit the back of the net.

FRENCH KICKS

The first penalty shoot-out at a FIFA World Cup finals came in the 1982 semi-final in Seville between West Germany and France, when French takers Didier Six and **Maxime Bossis** were the unfortunate players to miss. The same two countries met in the semi-finals four years later – and West Germany again won, though this time in normal time, 2-0. But the record for most shoot-outs is shared by the 1990 and 2006 tournaments, with four apiece. Both semi-finals in 1990 went to penalties, while the 2006 final was the second to be settled that way – Italy beating France 5-3 thanks to David Trezeguet's shot hitting the crossbar.

CLOSE SAVES

Just two minutes and three seconds separated the two penalties awarded by Guatemalan referee Carlos Batres in the second-round clash between Paraguay and Spain in 2010 – a FIFA World Cup record. Not only were the spot-kicks given at either end of the pitch in Johannesburg's Ellis Park stadium, but both were saved. First, Spanish goalkeeper Iker Casillas caught Oscar Cardozo's attempt, after the Paraguay striker was fouled by Gerard Pique. Then, after striker David Villa was brought down by Antolin Alcaraz, **Justo Villar** palmed away Xabi Alonso's penalty. Alonso actually scored with his attempt, but Batres ordered a retake due to Spanish encroachment in the area. Spain had scored all 14 of their FIFA World Cup penalties going into the 2010 tournament – excluding shoot-outs – but Alonso's miss came just 12 days after David Villa fired a spot-kick wide against Honduras.

THREE LIONS TAMED

Italy and England have lost more FIFA World Cup penalty shoot-outs than any other nation – three each. At least Italy finally managed to win one, in the 2006 final, but England have yet to triumph from 12 yards – losing to West Germany in their 1990 semi-final, Argentina in the second round in 1998 and Portugal in the quarter-finals eight years later. The penalty-missing culprits have been Stuart Pearce and Chris Waddle (1990), Paul Ince and David Batty (1998), and Frank Lampard, Steven Gerrard and Jamie Carragher (2006).

THE PLAYERS WHO MISSED IN SHOOT-OUTS

Argentina: Diego Maradona (1990), Pedro Troglio (1990), Hernan Crespo (1998), Roberto Ayala (2006), Esteban Cambiasso (2006)
Brazil: Socrates (1986), Julio Cesar (1986), Marcio Santos (1994)
Bulgaria: Krassimir Balakov (1994)
England: Stuart Pearce (1990), Chris Waddle (1990), Paul Ince (1998), David Batty (1998), Frank Lampard (2006), Steven Gerrard (2006), Jamie Carragher (2006)
France: Didier Six (1982), Maxime Bossis (1982), Michel Platini (1986), Bixente Lizarazu (1998), David Trezeguet (2006)
Germany/West Germany: Uli Stielike (1982)
Ghana: John Mensah (2010), Dominic Adiyiah (2010)
Italy: Roberto Donadoni (1990), Aldo Serena (1990), Franco Baresi (1994), Daniele Massaro (1994), Roberto Baggio (1994), Demetrio Albertini (1998), Luigi Di Biagio (1998)
Japan: Yuichi Komano (2010)
Mexico: Fernando Quirarte (1986), Raul Servin (1986), Alberto Garcia Aspe (1994), Marcelino Bernal (1994), Jorge Rodriguez (1994)
Holland: Phillip Cocu (1998), Ronald de Boer (1998)
Portugal: Hugo Viana (2006), Petit (2006)
Republic of Ireland: Matt Holland (2002), David Connolly (2002), Kevin Kilbane (2002)
Romania: Daniel Timofte (1990), Dan Petrescu (1994), Miodrag Belodedici (1994)
Spain: Eloy (1986), Juanfran (2002), Juan Carlos Valeron (2002), Joaquin (2002)
Sweden: Hakan Mild (1994)
Switzerland: Marco Streller (2006), Tranquillo Barnetta (2006), Ricardo Cabanas (2006)
Ukraine: Andriy Shevchenko (2006)
Uruguay: Maximiliano Pereira (2010)
Yugoslavia: Dragan Stojkovic (1990), Dragoljub Brnovic (1990), Faruk Hadzibegic (1990)

PENALTY SHOOT-OUTS BY COUNTRY

4	Germany/West Germany (4 wins)	1	Belgium (1 win)
4	Argentina (3 wins, 1 defeat)	1	Bulgaria (1 win)
4	France (2 wins, 2 defeats)	1	Paraguay (1 win)
4	Italy (1 win, 3 defeats)	1	Portugal (1 win)
3	Brazil (2 wins, 1 defeat)	1	South Korea (1 win)
3	Spain (1 win, 2 defeats)	1	Sweden (1 win)
3	England (3 defeats)	1	Ukraine (1 win)
2	Republic of Ireland (1 win, 1 defeat)	1	Uruguay (1 win)
2	Mexico (2 defeats)	1	Yugoslavia (1 win)
2	Romania (2 defeats)	1	Ghana (1 defeat)
		1	Holland (1 defeat)
		1	Japan (1 defeat)
		1	Switzerland (1 defeat)

GERMAN EFFICIENCY

Germany, or West Germany, have won all four of their FIFA World Cup penalty shoot-outs, more than any other team. Their run began with a semi-final victory over France in 1982, when goalkeeper Harald Schumacher was the matchwinner, despite being lucky to stay on the pitch for a vicious extra-time foul on France's Patrick Battiston. West Germany also reached the 1990 final thanks to their shoot-out expertise, this time proving superior to England – as they similarly did in the 1996 European Championships semi-final. Germany were better at spot-kicks than Argentina in their 2006 quarter-final, when goalkeeper **Jens Lehmann** consulted a note predicting the direction the Argentine players were likely to shoot towards. The vital information was scribbled on a scrap of hotel notepaper by Germany's chief scout Urs Siegenthaler. The only German national team to lose a major tournament penalty shoot-out were the West Germans, who contested the 1976 European Championships final against Czechoslovakia – their first shoot-out experience, and clearly an effective lesson, as they have not lost a shoot-out since.

PART 2: THE COUNTRIES

ALL the world's sports data provides the most glowing testament to the ever-increasing popularity of association football. The game – whether locally known as *futbol* or *calcio* or *futebol* or soccer or any of a linguistic flood of other labels – knows no boundaries of race or politics or religion. The structure is simple, a contributory factor to the game's international success. At the head of the world football pyramid is FIFA, the world federation. Supporting FIFA's work are the six regional geographical confederations representing Africa, Asia, Europe, Oceania, South America, plus the Caribbean, Central and North America. Supporting the regions in turn are the national associations of 208 countries – and thus FIFA can boast more member countries than even the United Nations and the Olympic movement. The countries are pivotal. They field the national teams who have built sporting history through their many and varied achievements in world-focused competitions such as the FIFA World Cup. But they also oversee the growth of football in their country – from professional leagues to the game at grassroots level.

Representative teams from England and Scotland played out the first formal internationals in the late 19th century, thus laying the foundation for the four British home nations' unique independent status within a world football family otherwise comprised of nation states. The original British Home Championships was the first competition for national teams, but its demise, as a result of a congested fixture list, has left the Copa America in South America as the oldest survivor, apart from the Olympic Games.

And it was out of the interest in the Olympic Games in the 1920s that was born the FIFA World Cup in 1930 – and subsequently the regional championships whose winners now compete every four years at the FIFA Confederations Cup. The next such event will be staged in Brazil in 2013, one year ahead of the country's staging of the FIFA World Cup finals, the ultimate celebration of world's favourite sport.

> **Representatives of all 32 nations competing at the 2010 FIFA World Cup made for a colourful spectacle at the opening ceremony in the magnificent surroundings of the Soccer City stadium in Johannesburg, South Africa.**

EUROPE

Europe was the cradle of modern association football. The laws were compiled in England in the middle of the nineteenth century but within only a few years they were being carried across the continent by students, engineers, sailors, soldiers and businessmen – igniting the passion evident from fans on any given day in any given country (as thousands of Spaniards will happily testify).

ENGLAND

England is where football began, the country where the game was first developed, which saw the creation of the game's first Football Association and the first organized league, and which now plays host to the richest domestic league in the world. But, while England have not had it all their own way on the international scene. Far from it. One solitary FIFA World Cup™ win apart, as hosts in 1966, the Three Lions have found it hard to shake off the "underachievers" tag when it comes to major tournaments.

IF THE CAP FITS

England's players in the historic first game against Scotland all wore **cricket-style caps** while the Scots wore hoods. England's "fashion statement" prompted the use of the term "cap" to refer to any international appearance. The tradition of awarding a cap to British international footballers still survives today.

NAUGHTY BOYS

Alan Mullery was the first of 12 England players sent off in senior internationals. Mullery was dismissed in the semi-final of the UEFA European Championship against Yugoslavia in Florence on 5 June 1968. David Beckham is the only one of the 12 to have been sent off twice for England.

IN THE BEGINNING

The day it all began ... 30 November 1872, when England played their first official international match, against Scotland, at Hamilton Crescent, Partick. The result was a 0-0 draw in front of a then massive crowd of 4,000, who each paid an admission fee of one shilling (5p). In fact, teams representing England and Scotland had played five times before, but most of the Scottish players had been based in England and the matches are considered unofficial. England's team for the first official game was selected by Charles Alcock, the secretary of the Football Association. His one regret was that, because of injury, he could not pick himself to play. In contrast, the first rugby union international between England and Scotland had been played in 1871, but England's first Test cricket match was not played until March 1877, against Australia in Melbourne.

RUNAWAY SUCCESS

England have hit double figures five times: beating Ireland 13-0 and 13-2 in 1882 and 1899, thrashing Austria 11-1 in 1908, crushing Portugal 10-0 in Lisbon in 1947 and then the United States 10-0 in 1964 in New York. The ten goals were scored by Roger Hunt (four), Fred Pickering (three), Terry Paine (two) and **Bobby Charlton**.

FIRST DEFEAT

Hungary's 6-3 win at Wembley in 1953 was the first time England had lost at home to continental opposition. Their first home defeat by non-British opposition came against the Republic of Ireland, who beat them 2-0 at Goodison Park, Liverpool, in 1949.

TELLING THE TIME

In 1961 England demolished Scotland 9-3 at Wembley. The unfortunate Scottish goalkeeper was Frank Haffey. England also had a goal disallowed. That prompted an England fan, asked the time by a sad Scottish supporter, to answer: "Almost ten past Haffey..."

ENGLAND'S BIGGEST WINS

1882	Ireland 0 England 13
1899	England 13 Ireland 2
1908	Austria 1 England 11
1964	United States 0 England 10
1947	Portugal 0 England 10
1982	England 9 Luxembourg 0
1960	Luxembourg 0 England 9
1895	England 9 Ireland 0
1927	Belgium 1 England 9
1896	Wales 1 England 9
1890	Ireland 1 England 9

ENGLAND'S BIGGEST DEFEATS

1954	Hungary 7 England 1
1878	Scotland 7 England 2
1881	England 1 Scotland 6
1958	Yugoslavia 5 England 0
1964	Brazil 5 England 1
1928	England 1 Scotland 5
1882	Scotland 5 England 1
1953	England 3 Hungary 6
1963	France 5 England 2
1931	France 5 England 2

SENIOR MOMENT

Goalkeeper **David James** became the oldest player to make his FIFA World Cup debut, aged 39 years and 321 days when he first appeared for England at the 2010 competition in South Africa. He kept a clean sheet in a goalless Group C draw against Algeria after coming into the side to replace Robert Green, who had made an embarrassing error in England's opening game against the USA.

FAITH IN EXPERIENCE

England's 2010 FIFA World Cup squad was the oldest they have ever taken to the tournament, with an average age of 28.7. The record was previously held by the country's 1954 squad, with an average age of 28.4. Both selections featured a 39-year-old – goalkeeper David James in 2010, winger Stanley Matthews in 1954. The 2010 selection also went into the tournament with a total tally of 900 international appearances between them, an average of 39.1 apiece – beating the earlier record of England's 1990 squad with its average of 32.2 caps per player.

THE CLASSIC

Because of England's status as being the home of modern football and Brazil's record five FIFA World Cup wins, **England v Brazil** is considered one of the game's classic rivalries. England have won only three times in 23 games – and never in major competition.

BLANKS OF ENGLAND

A goalless draw against Algeria, in Cape Town in June 2010, made England the first country to finish 10 different FIFA World Cup matches 0-0. Their first was against Brazil in 1958, while the tally also includes both second-round group games in 1982 against eventual runners-up West Germany and hosts Spain.

BEST GERMANY

England suffered their heaviest-ever FIFA World Cup finals defeat when losing 4-1 to Germany in Bloemfontein, South Africa, in the second round of the 2010 tournament. Before then, their largest loss had been 4-2 against Uruguay, in a 1954 quarter-final. Germany managed more goals in one match than England scored in the entire 2010 tournament – defender Matthew Upson scored England's consolation goal in Bloemfontein, after only **Steven Gerrard** and Jermain Defoe had scored in three first-round matches. Back in September 2001, England enjoyed a 5-1 away win over Germany, in a FIFA World Cup qualifier in Munich, thanks to Michael Owen's hat-trick and goals by Steven Gerrard and Emile Heskey. Germany still progressed further at the following year's FIFA World Cup in South Korea and Japan, though, losing to Brazil in the same final after England were knocked out by the same opponents in the quarter-finals.

GRAND OLD MAN

Stanley Matthews became England's oldest-ever player when he lined up at outside-right against Denmark on 15 May 1957 at the age of 42 years 104 days. That was 22 years and 229 days after his first appearance. Matthews was also England's oldest marksman. He was 41 years eight months old when he scored against Northern Ireland on 10 October 1956.

BECKHAM'S RECORD

David Beckham played for England for the 109th time when he appeared as a second-half substitute in the 4-0 win over Slovakia in a friendly international on 28 March 2009. That overtook the record number of England games for an outfield player, which had been set by Bobby Moore, England's 1966 FIFA World Cup-winning captain. Beckham, born on 2 May 1975, in Leytonstone, London, made his first appearance for his country on 1 September 1996, in a FIFA World Cup qualifying match against Moldova. He was appointed full-time England captain in 2001 by the then new manager Sven-Goran Eriksson – stepping down after England's quarter-final defeat by Portugal in the 2006 FIFA World Cup.

THE LONG AND THE SHORT OF IT

At 6ft 7in, centre-forward **Peter Crouch** is the tallest player ever to stretch above opposing defences for England – while **Fanny Walden**, the Tottenham winger who won two caps in 1914 and 1922, was the shortest at 5ft 2in. Sheffield United goalkeeper Billy "Fatty" Foulke was the heaviest England player at 18st when he played against Wales on 29 March 1897.

TEENAGE PROMISE

Theo Walcott became England's youngest full international when he played against Hungary at Old Trafford on 30 May 2006 at the age of 17 years 75 days. On 10 September 2008, he became England's youngest scorer of a hat-trick in a 4-1 win away to Croatia in Zagreb, aged 19 years 178 days. The previous youngest international was Wayne Rooney, who was 17 years 111 days old when he played against Australia in February 2003.

MEET THE NEW BOSS

Striker Andy Cole had a different England manager for each of his first four international appearances: Terry Venables for his debut against Uruguay in 1995, Glenn Hoddle against Italy in 1997, caretaker boss Howard Wilkinson against France and permanent replacement Kevin Keegan against Poland, both in 1999. Cole would win only 11 more caps, under both Keegan and Sven-Goran Eriksson.

LAMPARD'S HARD LUCK

Frank Lampard has had more shots on goal without scoring than any other player at FIFA World Cups since tallies began in 1966. England's 4-1 second-round defeat to Germany in 2010 took his catalogue of unsuccessful efforts to 37, though this does include one that crossed the line but was not given by the referee or his assistant.

ALEXANDER THE LATE

The oldest player to make his debut for England remains Alexander Morten, who was 41 years and 114 days old when facing Scotland on 8 March 1873 in England's first home game, at The Oval in Kennington, London. He was also captain that day, and is still the country's oldest-ever skipper.

TOP SCORERS

#	Player	Goals
1	Bobby Charlton	49
2	Gary Lineker	48
3	Jimmy Greaves	44
4	Michael Owen	40
5	Tom Finney	30
=	Nat Lofthouse	30
=	Alan Shearer	30
8	Viv Woodward	29
9	Steve Bloomer	28
10	David Platt	27

CLOSE BUT NO CIGAR

Jimmy Greaves is one of the greatest goalscorers ever to play for England, with a phenomenal record of 44 goals in just 57 appearances – including six hat-tricks. But Greaves missed out on a career highlight when he was injured in the final group game of the 1966 FIFA World Cup. His replacement, Geoff Hurst, scored the only goal in the second round, kept his place and went on to make history with his hat-trick in the final. Greaves and the other unused reserves of World Cup-winning sides were finally awarded medals by FIFA in 2007.

DEFOE SPECIAL

Jermain Defoe's goal against Slovenia in the first round of the 2010 FIFA World Cup not only clinched England's place in the knockout stages. It was also the 184th goal scored for England by a Tottenham Hotspur player – more than from any other club.

CAPTAIN SOLO

Claude Ashton, the Corinthians centre-forward, set a record when he captained England on his only international appearance. This was a 0-0 draw against Northern Ireland in Belfast on 24 October 1925.

CAPTAINS COURAGEOUS

The international careers of Billy Wright and **Bobby Moore**, who both captained England a record 90 times, very nearly overlapped. Wright, from Wolves, played for England between 1946 and 1959 and Moore, from West Ham, between 1962 and 1973, including England's FIFA World Cup win in 1966.

TOP CAPS

#	Player	Caps
1	Peter Shilton	125
2	David Beckham	115
3	Bobby Moore	108
4	Bobby Charlton	106
5	Billy Wright	105
6	Bryan Robson	90
7	Michael Owen	89
8	Kenny Sansom	86
9	Gary Neville	85
10	Steven Gerrard	84
=	Ray Wilkins	84

WRONG WAY!

Though the goal is sometimes credited to Scottish striker John Smith, it is believed that Edgar Field was the first England player to score an "own goal", which was his fate as Scotland crushed England 6-1 at The Oval on 12 March 1881. By the time Field put the ball in his own net, Scotland were already 4-1 up. The full-back, who was an FA Cup winner and loser with Clapham Rovers, is in good company. Manchester United's Gary Neville has scored two own goals "against" England.

COMING OVER HERE

Argentina were the first non-UK side to play at Wembley – England won 2-1 on 9 May 1951 – while Ferenc Puskas and the "Magical Magyars" of Hungary were the first "foreign", or "continental", side to beat England at Wembley, with their famous 6-3 victory in 1953. This humiliation marked Alf Ramsey's last game as an England player. England first tasted defeat to a "foreign" side when they lost 4-3 to Spain in Madrid on 15 May 1929. Two years later England gained their revenge with a 7-1 win at Highbury.

THE REAL HOME OF FOOTBALL

Contrary to popular belief, myth and most football record books, the original home of the England football team is The Oval. It was The Oval in Kennington, London – more famous for cricket (and the venue for the first Test match in England in 1880) – which hosted the first "unofficial" international games (five in all) between representative teams from England and Scotland between 1870 and 1872. The Oval went on to host England's first "official" home international (their second game), which turned out to be England's first international victory (4-2 over Scotland), as well as wins against Wales and Ireland in the fledgling British Home Championship.

WHO'S THE GREATEST?

Fabio Capello is the most statistically successful England manager, with a win ratio of 68 per cent, followed by **Sir Alf Ramsey (below)** and **Glenn Hoddle** tied on 61 per cent. Sir Alf's 1966 FIFA World Cup victory, however, puts him head and shoulders above all the rest. Technically, caretaker manager Peter Taylor has the worst record – a 100 per cent record of defeat. But then, he was in charge for only one game – a 1-0 defeat to Italy in Turin, a game that saw David Beckham making his first appearance as England captain. Don Revie, in the 1970s, and Steve McClaren, in the 2000s, are the only full-time managers to have failed to qualify for any international tournament. Terry Venables was spared the need to qualify for his only tournament, Euro 1996, since England were hosts. McClaren's 16-month tenure (during which Venables served as his assistant) is also the shortest full-time reign as national team manager.

UNFINISHED BUSINESS

England's friendly, away to Argentina in Buenos Aires, on 17 May 1953, was abandoned with the score at 0-0 due to torrential rain. The two FAs decided to record the "official" result as 0-0. However, when England's 1995 match against the Republic of Ireland in Dublin was abandoned after 27 minutes due to crowd trouble, the 0-1 scoreline at the time was not recognized. England's players kept the caps they were awarded for the match.

SHARED RESPONSIBILITY

Substitutions meant the captain's armband passed between four different players during England's 2-1 friendly win over Serbia and Montenegro on 3 June 2003. Regular captain David Beckham was missing so Michael Owen led the team out, but was substituted at half-time. England's second-half skippers were Owen's then-Liverpool team-mates Emile Heskey and Jamie Carragher and Manchester United's Philip Neville.

ROLL UP, ROLL UP

The highest attendance for an England game came at Hampden Park on 17 April 1937, when 149,547 spectators crushed in to see Scotland's 3-1 victory in the British Home Championships. Only 2,378 turned up in Bologna, Italy, to see San Marino stun England after nine seconds in Graham Taylor's side's 7-1 victory that was not enough to secure qualification to the 1994 FIFA World Cup.

FIRST AND FOREMOST

England's first official international was a 0-0 draw against Scotland in Glasgow on 30 November 1872, though England and Scotland had already played a number of unofficial representative matches against each other prior to that. Given that England's only opponents for four decades were the home nations – and only Scotland for the first seven years, it is not surprising that England's first draw, win and defeat were all against their northern neighbours. After the goalless first game, the second fixture – played at The Oval on 8 March 1873 – proved a more exciting affair: England won 4-2 in a six-goal thriller. In their third game, back in Glasgow almost exactly a year later, Scotland evened things up with a 2-1 win. These fixtures completed the trio of first wins, defeats and draws for the oldest participants in international football.

THE ITALIAN JOB

Italian **Fabio Capello** became England's second foreign coach when he took over from Steve McClaren in January 2008 and led the country to the 2010 FIFA World Cup in South Africa. Capello already had happy memories of national stadium Wembley from his playing days – he scored the only goal for Italy on 14 November 1973, giving them their first-ever away win against England.

YOUR COUNTRY NEEDS YOU

The first England teams were selected from open trials of Englishmen who responded to the FA's adverts for players. It was only when these proved too popular and unwieldy that, in 1887, the FA decided that it would be better to manage the process through an International Selection Committee, which continued to pick the team until Sir Alf Ramsey's appointment in 1962.

MANAGERIAL ROLL OF HONOUR

Name		P	W	D	L	F	A
Walter Winterbottom	(1946–62)	138	77	33	28	380	195
Sir Alf Ramsey	(1962–74)	113	69	27	17	224	98
Joe Mercer	(1974)	7	3	3	1	9	7
Don Revie	(1974–77)	29	14	7	8	49	25
Ron Greenwood	(1977–82)	55	33	12	10	93	40
Bobby Robson	(1982–90)	95	47	30	18	154	60
Graham Taylor	(1990–93)	38	18	13	7	62	32
Terry Venables	(1994–96)	24	11	11	2	35	14
Glenn Hoddle	(1996–98)	28	17	6	5	42	13
Howard Wilkinson	(1999–2000)	2	0	1	1	0	2
Kevin Keegan	(1999–2000)	18	7	7	4	26	15
Peter Taylor	(November 2000)	1	0	0	1	0	1
Sven-Goran Eriksson	(2001–06)	67	40	17	10	127	60
Steve McClaren	(2006–07)	18	9	4	5	32	12
Fabio Capello	(2008–)	28	19	4	5	64	25

NOT QUITE HOME…

Wembley Stadium has not always been England's home. Opened in 1923, the first England international to be staged there – when it was still called the "Empire Stadium" – was a 1-1 draw with Scotland on 12 April 1924.

WONDERFUL WALTER

Walter Winterbottom was the England national team's first full-time manager – and remains both the longest-serving (with 138 games in charge) and the youngest-ever England manager, aged just 33 when he took the job in 1946 (initially as a coach and then, from 1947, as manager). The former teacher and Manchester United player led England to four FIFA World Cups.

FRANCE

France – nicknamed "Les Bleus" – are one of the most successful teams in the history of international football. They are one of only three countries to be World and European champions at the same time. They won the FIFA World Cup™ in 1998 as tournament hosts, routing Brazil 3-0 in the final. Two years later they staged a sensational, last-gasp recovery to overhaul Italy in the Euro 2000 final. The French equalized in the fifth minute of stoppage time, then went on to win 2-1 on a golden goal. France had previously won the UEFA European Championship in 1984, beating Spain 2-0 in the final in Paris. They reached the 2006 FIFA World Cup™ final too, but lost to Italy in a penalty shoot-out. France also won the 2001 and 2003 FIFA Confederations Cup and took the Olympic football gold medal in 1984.

KOPA – FRANCE'S FIRST SUPERSTAR

Raymond Kopa (born on 13 October 1931) was France's first international superstar. Born into a family of Polish immigrants (the family name was Kopaszewski), he was instrumental in Reims's championship successes of the mid-1950s. He later joined Real Madrid and became the first French player to win a European Cup winner's medal. He was the playmaker of the France team that finished third in the 1958 FIFA World Cup finals. His performances for his country that year earned him the European Footballer of the Year award.

MICHEL PLATINI (league and national career)

Duration	Team	Appearances	Goals
1972–79	Nancy	181	98
1979–82	Saint-Etienne	104	58
1982–87	Juventus	147	68
1976–87	France	72	41

PLATINI'S GLITTERING CAREER

Michel Platini (born in Joeuf on 21 June 1955) has enjoyed a glittering career, rising from a youngster at Nancy to become one of France's greatest-ever players, a hero in Italy, and now the president of UEFA. He was also joint organizing president (along with Fernand Sastre) of the 1998 FIFA World Cup finals in France. Platini was the grandson of an Italian immigrant who ran a café in Joeuf, Lorraine. He began with the local club, Nancy, before starring for Saint-Etienne, Juventus and France. He was instrumental in France's progress to the 1982 FIFA World Cup semi-finals and was the undisputed star of the UEFA European Championship two years later, when France won the tournament on home soil.

PARTYING IN PARIS

France's 1998 FIFA World Cup victory led to the greatest scenes of celebration in Paris since the French capital was liberated from German occupation in 1944. According to police estimates, around two million people burst on to the streets; with nearly a million dancing along the Champs-Elysées in the centre of Paris. The supporters' favourite chant was for Zinedine Zidane: "Zidane – president!"

UP FOUR THE CUP

Reaching the 2010 FIFA World Cup might have been a struggle – and a controversial one at that – but it did mean France had qualified for four FIFA World Cups in a row for the first time ever. Include the 2008 UEFA European Championship and that made Raymond Domenech the first France coach to lead his country at three consecutive major finals tournaments.

FRANCE AND FIFA

France were one of FIFA's founding members in 1904. Frenchman Robert Guerin became the first president of the governing body. Another Frenchman, Jules Rimet, was president from 1921 to 1954. He was the driving force behind the creation of the FIFA World Cup and the first version of football's most coveted trophy was named in his honour.

CROSSING THE BARRIERS

France's teams have usually included a high proportion of players from immigrant backgrounds or ethnic minorities. Three of France's greatest players – Raymond Kopa, Michel Platini and Zinedine Zidane – were the sons or grandsons of immigrants. In 2006, 17 of France's 23-man FIFA World Cup squad had links to the country's former colonies.

IT'S A SHAME ABOUT RAY

France's failure to win a match at the 2010 FIFA World Cup meant coach **Raymond Domenech** equalled but failed to exceed Michel Hidalgo's record of 41 victories in charge of the national side. Domenech did at least end his six-year reign having surpassed Euro 84-winning Hidalgo's tally of matches in the job. Domenech's final game, against South Africa, was his 79th as coach, four more than Hidalgo achieved. Domenech, a tough-tackling defender who was picked for France by Hidalgo, proved an eccentric as national coach. He admitted partly judging players by their star signs and responded to being knocked out of the 2008 UEFA European Championship by proposing to his girlfriend on live television.

KISSING COLLEAGUES

Marseille colleagues centre-back **Laurent Blanc** and goalkeeper **Fabien Barthez** had a special ritual during France's run to the 1998 FIFA World Cup crown. Before the game, Blanc would always kiss Barthez's shaven head, even when the veteran defender was suspended for the final.

WRONG KIND OF STRIKERS

During France's disastrous 2010 FIFA World Cup campaign, the players went on strike, refusing to train two days before their final Group A match, in protest at striker Nicolas Anelka being sent home early for insulting coach Raymond Domenech. France finished bottom of the group after a goalless draw with Uruguay and defeats to Mexico and hosts South Africa. The country's president Nicolas Sarkozy ordered an investigation into all that had gone wrong, while former French international defender Lilian Thuram called for captain **Patrice Evra** to be banned from playing for the team ever again. New coach Laurent Blanc later announced that none of the 23 in the FIFA World Cup 2010 squad would be considered for France's first match after the finals, a friendly in Norway.

TOP CAPS

1	Lilian Thuram	142
2	Thierry Henry	123
3	Marcel Desailly	116
4	Zinedine Zidane	108
5	Patrick Vieira	107
6	Didier Deschamps	103
7	Laurent Blanc	97
=	Bixente Lizarazu	97
9	Sylvain Wiltord	92
10	Fabien Barthez	87

HENRY BENCHED

France's record scorer Thierry Henry missed out on an appearance in the 1998 FIFA World Cup final because of Marcel Desailly's red card. Henry was France's leading scorer in the competition with three goals in the group games. Coach Aime Jacquet planned to use him as a substitute in the final, but Desailly's sending-off forced a re-think. Jacquet decided to reinforce the midfield – Arsenal team-mate Patrick Vieira going on instead – so Henry spent the full 90 minutes of the final on the bench.

TOP SCORERS

1	Thierry Henry	51
2	Michel Platini	41
3	David Trezeguet	34
4	Zinedine Zidane	31
5	Just Fontaine	30
=	Jean-Pierre Papin	30
7	Youri Djorkaeff	28
8	Sylvain Wiltord	26
9	Jean Vincent	22
10	Jean Nicolas	21

HAND OF GAUL

France qualified controversially for the 2010 FIFA World Cup finals. All-time leading scorer Thierry Henry was cast as the villain of their play-off against the Republic of Ireland in November 2009, when he clearly controlled the ball with his hand before setting up William Gallas's extra-time winner. Henry later apologized for what was dubbed "The Hand of Gaul" or "Le Main de Dieu". FIFA turned down the Irish FA's pleas for a replay or an unprecedented 33rd place in the following year's finals.

DESCHAMPS THE LEADER

Didier Deschamps was the most successful captain in France's history, leading them to victory in the 1998 FIFA World Cup and at Euro 2000. He won 103 caps and skippered the team a record 55 times between 1996 and his international retirement in July 2000. He first wore the captain's armband in a 1-0 win over Germany on 1 June 1996 and led the team that lost on penalties to the Czech Republic in the Euro 96 semi-finals.

ZIDANE AND SAINT–DENIS

The Stade de France, at Saint-Denis in Paris, was the scene of **Zinedine Zidane**'s greatest triumph, in the 1998 FIFA World Cup final. There was another family connection. Zidane's father Smail had settled in Saint-Denis after emigrating to France from Algeria. He later moved to Marseille, where Zinedine was born.

BITTERSWEET FOR TREZEGUET

Striker **David Trezeguet** has bittersweet memories of France's clashes with Italy in major finals. He scored the "golden goal" that beat the Italians in extra-time in the Euro 2000 final, but six years later, he was the man who missed as France lost the FIFA World Cup final on penalties. Trezeguet's shot bounced off the bar and failed to cross the line.

PRESIDENTIAL PARDON

Imperious centre-back Laurent Blanc was known as "Le President" during his playing days – now he is the national coach, succeeding Raymond Domenech after the 2010 FIFA World Cup. Blanc was unlucky to miss the 1998 FIFA World Cup final after being sent off in the semi-final for pushing Slaven Bilic in the face, though replays showed the Croatian defender to have over-reacted. Blanc did enjoy some redemption by being part of the French team that won the UEFA European Championship two years later. He took the French manager's job 12 months after leading Bordeaux to the 2008–09 domestic championship, ending Olympique Lyonnais's run of seven league titles in a row.

FRENCH EXODUS

France's 23-man squad for the 2010 FIFA World Cup was reduced to 22, just three days after their opening game, when third-choice goalkeeper Cedric Carrasso suffered a thigh injury. Uncapped Monaco goalkeeper Stephane Ruffier cut short a holiday and flew to South Africa, but was barred from replacing Carrasso because the tournament had already started. The French squad was then reduced to 21 before what would be their last match, against South Africa, when disgruntled striker Nicolas Anelka was expelled for disciplinary reasons.

THE FULL SET

Four France stars have a full set of top international medals – FIFA World Cup, UEFA European Championship and European Cup winners. Marcel Desailly, Bixente Lizarazu, Didier Deschamps and Zinedine Zidane all played in France's winning teams of 1998 and 2000. In addition, Desailly won the European Cup with Marseille in 1993 and Milan the following year. Deschamps won with Marseille in 1993 and Juventus in 1996; Lizarazu with Bayern Munich in 2001; and Zidane with Real Madrid in 2002.

LILIAN IN THE PINK

Defender **Lilian Thuram** made his 142nd and final appearance for France in their defeat by Italy at Euro 2008. His international career had spanned nearly 14 years, since his debut against the Czech Republic on 17 August 1994. Thuram was born in Pointe a Pitre, Guadeloupe on 1 January 1972. He played club football for Monaco, Parma, Juventus and Barcelona before retiring in the summer of 2008 because of a heart problem. He was one of the stars of France's 1998 FIFA World Cup-winning side and scored both goals in the semi-final victory over Croatia – the only international goals of his career. He gained another winner's medal at Euro 2000. He first retired from international football after France's elimination at Euro 2004, but was persuaded by coach Raymond Domenech to return for the 2006 FIFA World Cup campaign and made his second appearance in a FIFA World Cup final. He broke Marcel Desailly's record of 116 caps in the group game against Togo.

ALBERT THE FIRST

Albert Batteux (1919–2003) was France's first national manager. Before his appointment in 1955, a selection committee had picked the team. Batteux was also the most successful coach in the history of French football. He combined managing France with his club job at Reims. His biggest achievement was guiding the national team to third place in the 1958 FIFA World Cup finals. The team's two big stars, Raymond Kopa and Just Fontaine, had both played under his charge at Reims.

HIDALGO REIGNS LONGEST

The longest-serving France manager was Michel Hidalgo, another who played under Albert Batteux at Reims. He was appointed on 27 March 1976 and stayed for more than eight years. Hidalgo was also the first France coach to win a major trophy – the UEFA European Championship in 1984. He retired straight after France's victory on 27 June. He had also steered France to the FIFA World Cup semi-finals in 1982, when they lost to West Germany in highly controversial circumstances.

JACQUET'S TRIUMPH

Aime Jacquet, who guided France to FIFA World Cup victory in 1998, was one of their most controversial national coaches. He had been attacked for alleged defensive tactics despite France's run to the semi-finals of Euro 96 and a record of only three defeats in four years. A month before the 1998 finals, the sports daily *L'Equipe* claimed he was not capable of building a successful team!

NO TIME FOR FONTAINE

Former striker **Just Fontaine** spent the shortest-ever spell in charge of the France team. He took over on 22 March 1967 and left on 3 June after two defeats in friendlies.

OVAL BALL

The father of France's most capped goalkeeper Fabien Barthez was also a French international. Alain Barthez was a fine rugby union player who won one cap for France.

FRANCE MANAGERS

Albert Batteux	1955–62
Henri Guerin	1962–66
Jose Arribas/Jean Snella	1966
Just Fontaine	1967
Louis Dugauguez	1967–68
Georges Boulogne	1969–73
Stefan Kovacs	1973–75
Michel Hidalgo	1976–84
Henri Michel	1984–88
Michel Platini	1988–92
Gerard Houllier	1992–93
Aime Jacquet	1993–98
Roger Lemerre	1998–2002
Jacques Santini	2002–04
Raymond Domenech	2004–10
Laurent Blanc	2010–

JACQUES HAMMERED

Jacques Santini is statistically France's most successful manager, despite being in charge when they failed to retain their UEFA European Championship crown in 2004. He won 22 of his 28 games in charge, between 2002 and 2004, a success rate of 79 per cent – ahead of closest challengers Aime Jacquet and Roger Lemerre, both on 64 per cent. Former Lyon coach Santini lost just two games for France – though the last of these was their Euro 2004 quarter-final against eventual champions Greece. He had already upset supporters back home by announcing a post-tournament move to English club Tottenham Hotspur.

HEROES TO VILLAINS

The failure of both France and Italy to get through the first round of the 2010 FIFA World Cup marked the first time this has happened to both finalists from the previous tournament. France coach Raymond Domenech and Italy's Marcello Lippi were in charge both times, reaching the showdown in Berlin, Germany, in 2006 but each finished bottom of their group in South Africa four years later.

WINNING WITH YOUTH

In the early 1990s, France became the first European country to institute a national youth development programme. The best young players were picked to attend the national youth academy at Clairefontaine. Then they went on to the top clubs' academies throughout the nation. The scheme has produced a rich harvest of stars. FIFA World Cup winners Didier Deschamps, Marcel Desailly and Christian Karembeu started at Nantes. Lilian Thuram, Thierry Henry, Manu Petit and David Trezeguet began with Monaco and **Zinedine Zidane** and Patrick Vieira were graduates from Cannes.

ROUX SETS THE PACE

Former Auxerre coach Guy Roux holds the record for the most Ligue 1 games in charge. Roux (born on 18 October 1938) guided his team through 890 matches during a 44-year spell. He took over as player/coach in 1961 and only retired as coach in 2005. He led Auxerre from languishing in the old third division to becoming French champions in 1996. They also won the French Cup four times, in 1994, 1996, 2003 and 2005. Roux knew that an unfashionable provincial club like Auxerre could not compete financially with the big clubs, so he developed a youth policy that produced a succession of stars, such as Eric Cantona and Basile Boli. Roux's success was one of the catalysts for the now highly successful French Federation's national youth development programme.

EARNING THEIR STRIPES

France are the only country to play at a FIFA World Cup wearing another team's kit. In the 1978 tournament in Argentina, for a first-round match at Mar del Plata, *Les Bleus* were forced to wear the green and white stripes of a local club side, Atletico Kimberley, when they met Hungary. France brought their second, white, kit instead of their normal blue, while Hungary turned up in their second strip, white, too. The quick-change did not seem to affect France, who won the match 3-1.

GERMANY

Politics may have divided the country in two for over 40 years, but few countries can match Germany's record in international football. Three-time winners of the FIFA World Cup™ (1954, 1974 and 1990) and three-time UEFA European Championship winners (1972, 1980 and 1996), in 1974 they became the first country in history to hold the World and European titles at the same time – and have remained a fearsome opponent in top-level football matches ever since.

SHOOT–OUT SURE–SHOTS

German teams have always put in hours of preparation for penalty shoot-outs. Their last two major successes – the 1990 FIFA World Cup and Euro 96 successes – both came after shoot-out victories in the semi-finals. England were the Germans' victims on both occasions.

BOTH SIDES NOW

Eight players appeared for both the old East Germany and then Germany after reunification in October 1990.

Player	East Germany	Germany
Ulf Kirsten	49	51
Matthias Sammer	23	51
Andreas Thom	51	10
Thomas Doll	29	18
Dariusz Wosz	7	17
Olaf Marschall	4	13
Heiko Scholz	7	1
Dirk Schuster	4	3

THE 1954 "MIRACLE OF BERN"

West Germany's FIFA World Cup victory in 1954 was considered crucial to the country's unity and future economic success. Winning coach Sepp Herberger's biographer wrote: "That was the real founding day of the West German state." The victory was portrayed again by the movie-maker Sonke Wortmann more than 50 years later in a film called Das Wunder von Bern ("The Miracle of Bern").

FOR CLUB AND COUNTRY

Italy's first-round departure from the 2010 FIFA World Cup, after Internazionale were crowned European club champions, means West Germany remains the only country to have won the FIFA World Cup in the same year that one of its clubs has clinched the European Cup or UEFA Champions League. Captain Franz Beckenbauer lifted both trophies in 1974, one for West Germany and the other for **Bayern Munich**.

AUSTRIAN CONNECTION

Germany's squad for the 1938 FIFA World Cup finals in France contained several Austrian players. After Germany had swallowed up Austria in 1938, Adolf Hitler and his Nazi regime insisted that, for political reasons, the Germany squad should include several Austrians. However, it caused friction in the camp, coach Sepp Herberger could not unite the contrasting styles and they were knocked out in the first round by Switzerland, 4-2 in a replay.

EAST GERMANY –
TOP APPEARANCES AND GOALS

Appearances

1	Joachim Streich	98
2	**Hans-Jurgen Dorner**	96
3	Jurgen Croy	86
4	Konrad Weise	78
5	Eberhard Vogel	69

Goals

1	Joachim Streich	53
2	Eberhard Vogel	24
3	Hans-Jurgen Kreische	22
4	Rainer Ernst	20
5	Henning Frenzel	19

PARTY LIKE IT'S MATCHDAY 99

Germany (and West Germany) have now played more FIFA World Cup finals matches than any other country. Their 2010 semi-final defeat to Spain was their 98th in the competition, one ahead of losing quarter-finalists Brazil. **Germany's third-place play-off win** took their overall tally to 99 matches – comprising 60 wins, 19 draws and 20 losses, with 203 goals scored and 115 conceded.

GERMANY JOIN THE 200 CLUB

Thomas Muller's third-minute goal for Germany against Argentina in their 2010 FIFA World Cup quarter-final, setting his side on the way to a 4-0 victory, also made Germany the second country to complete a double century of World Cup goals. Joachim Low's side ended the 2010 competition on 203 overall, just seven behind Brazil. Germany's first finals goal was scored by Stanislaus Kobierski in a 5-2 victory over Belgium in 1934. Germany's 2010 team became the first since Brazil in 1970 to enjoy three separate four-goal sprees at one FIFA World Cup, by trouncing Australia 4-0, England 4-1 and Argentina 4-0.

DIAMOND STUDS

The Germans have always been in the forefront of technical innovation – as they showed in the 1954 FIFA World Cup final. The pitch in Bern was wet and rain was falling. West Germany were one of the first teams to wear removable studs, so were able to change them at half-time. Their Hungarian opponents wore traditional fixed-studded boots – and Hungary's goalkeeper, Gyula Grosics, slipped on the wet turf as Helmut Rahn scored West Germany's winning goal.

HISTORY MAN

East and West Germany met only once at senior national team level. That was on 22 June 1974, in the FIFA World Cup finals for which the West played hosts. Drawn in the same group, East Germany produced a shock 1-0 win in Hamburg. Both teams progressed to the second round.

GOLDEN WONDER

Germany became the first team to win a major title thanks to the now-discarded golden goal system when they beat the Czech Republic in the Euro 96 final at Wembley. **Oliver Bierhoff's** equalizer forced extra-time after Patrik Berger scored a penalty for the Czechs. Bierhoff grabbed Germany's winner five minutes into extra-time to end the game and the championship.

DOUBLING UP

West Germany were the first side to hold the UEFA European Championship and the FIFA World Cup at the same time. They beat the Soviet Union 3-0 in the 1972 European final, then surprised Holland 2-1 in the FIFA World Cup final two years later.

MULLER TIME

Twenty-year-old **Thomas Muller** was one of the undoubted stars of the 2010 FIFA World Cup, despite only having made his international debut in March that year, in a 1-0 defeat to Argentina. At a post-match press conference, he was mistaken for a ballboy by Argentina coach Diego Maradona, but had his revenge with the opening goal in Germany's convincing 4-0 win over the same opposition in the 2010 quarter-finals. Muller made both his Bayern Munich club debut and his first appearance for the German under-21s at the start of the 2009–10 season, but his impressive form in midfield and attack convinced Germany coach Joachim Low to fast-track him to full international status. Muller had played just twice for his country by the time the tournament started, but scored five goals in six games in South Africa. He missed the semi-final defeat to Spain as he was serving a suspension after receiving a yellow card – his second of the tournament – for handball in the Argentina match. Like his (unrelated) namesake Gerd at the 1970 and 1974 FIFA World Cups, Muller's exploits in South Africa came while wearing the number 13 shirt.

"DER BOMBER"

Gerd Muller was the most prolific scorer of the modern era. Neither tall nor graceful, he was quick, strong and had a predator's eye for the net. He also had the temperament to score decisive goals in big games, including the winner in the 1974 FIFA World Cup final, the winner in the semi-final against Poland and two goals in West Germany's 1972 UEFA European Championship final victory over the USSR. He netted 68 goals in 62 appearances for West Germany and remains the leading scorer in the Bundesliga and all-time record scorer for his club, Bayern Munich.

EURO GLORIES

Five German players have been voted European Player of the Year. Gerd Muller was the first West German winner in 1970. He was followed by Franz Beckenbauer in 1972 and 1976, Karl-Heinz Rummenigge in 1980 and 1981 and Lothar Matthaus in 1990. Matthias Sammer, who began his career in East Germany, was the first winner from the reunified Germany, picking up the award in 1996.

VOGTS THE "GUARD DOG"

Berti Vogts was known as "the guard dog" because of his tigerish marking jobs on some of the world's top players. The high point of Vogts's playing career came in West Germany's FIFA World Cup victory over Holland, when – apart from failing to stop his run for the first-minute penalty – he marked Johan Cruyff out of the match. Vogts later went on to coach the reunified Germany to victory at Euro 96.

DER KAISER

Franz Beckenbauer is widely regarded as the greatest player in German football history. He has also made a huge mark as a FIFA World Cup-winning coach, administrator and organizer. Beckenbauer (born on 11 September 1945) was a 20-year-old attacking wing-half when West Germany reached the 1966 FIFA World Cup final. He later defined the role of attacking sweeper, first in the 1970 FIFA World Cup finals, and then as West Germany won the 1972 UEFA European Championship and the 1974 FIFA World Cup. When West Germany needed a coach in the mid-1980s, they turned to Beckenbauer, despite his lack of experience. He delivered a FIFA World Cup final appearance in 1986, a Euro 88 semi-final and 1990 FIFA World Cup triumph in his final game in charge. He later became president of Bayern Munich, the club he captained to three consecutive European Cup victories between 1974 and 1976. He also led Germany's successful bid for the 2006 FIFA World Cup finals and headed the organizing committee. No wonder he is known as "Der Kaiser" ("the Emperor") for his enormous influence on German football.

MAGICAL MATTHAUS

Lothar Matthaus is Germany's most-capped player. He appeared in five FIFA World Cup finals – 1982, 1986, 1990, 1994 and 1998 – a record for an outfield player. Versatile Matthaus could operate as a defensive midfielder, an attacking midfielder, or as a sweeper. He was a FIFA World Cup winner in 1990, a finalist in 1982 and 1986 and a UEFA European Championship winner in 1980. His record 150 appearances – spread over a 20-year international career – were split 87 for West Germany and 63 for Germany. He also scored 23 goals and was voted top player at the 1990 FIFA World Cup.

TOP CAPS
(West Germany & Germany)

1	Lothar Matthaus	150
2	Jurgen Klinsmann	108
3	Jurgen Kohler	105
4	Franz Beckenbauer	103
5	Thomas Hassler	101
=	Miroslav Klose	101
7	Michael Ballack	98
8	Berti Vogts	96
9	Sepp Maier	95
=	Karl-Heinz Rummenigge	95

TOP SCORERS

1	Gerd Muller	68
2	Miroslav Klose	52
3	Jurgen Klinsmann	47
=	Rudi Voller	47
5	Karl-Heinz Rummenigge	45
6	Uwe Seeler	43
7	Michael Ballack	42
8	Lukas Podolski	40
9	Oliver Bierhoff	37
10	Fritz Walter	33

KLOSE ENCOUNTERS

Miroslav Klose drew level with Gerd Muller as the country's most prolific FIFA World Cup scorer when he took his tournament tally to 14 in South Africa in 2010. He had opened his overall account with a hat-trick against Saudi Arabia in 2002, scoring five goals that summer, before winning the Golden Boot with five strikes in his homeland four years later. His four goals at the 2010 FIFA World Cup included the opener against England in the second round and two in the quarter-final against Argentina. Polish-born Klose managed more goals for Germany at the 2010 FIFA World Cup than his meagre three during a disappointing 2009–10 domestic season for Bayern Munich. Klose also holds a rather more unenviable FIFA World Cup record, having been substituted an unlucky 13 times – more than any other player.

SUPER SEELER

All-action centre-forward Uwe Seeler was the top West German player of the late 1950s and '60s. He scored 43 goals in 72 appearances and played, and scored, in four FIFA World Cup finals tournaments (1958, 1962, 1966 and 1970). He also skippered the Germans to the 1966 FIFA World Cup final and the semi-final in 1970. He scored more than 400 league goals in a 19-year career with his home club, Hamburg.

GOLDEN GLOVES

Sepp Maier was at the heart of West Germany's triumphs of the early 1970s, including the 1972 UEFA European Championship and the 1974 FIFA World Cup. He remains West Germany's most-capped goalkeeper, winning 95 caps in an international career lasting from 1965 to 1979. He played his whole club career for Bayern Munich and helped them win the European Cup three times. A car crash in 1979, in which he received life-threatening injuries, ended his playing days, but he went on to become a goalkeeping coach for both Germany and his old club.

KEEPING A LOW PROFILE

Until **Joachim Low**, Germany had followed a recent trend of being led into FIFA World Cup finals by former playing legends who had already starred in the competition on the field rather than on the touchline: 1974 FIFA World Cup winners Franz Beckenbauer (coach in 1986 and 1990) and Berti Vogts (1994 and 1998), and 1990 FIFA World Cup winners Rudi Voller (coach in 2002) and Jurgen Klinsmann (2006). Low, Klinsmann's assistant in 2006, then became the first man to coach Germany at a FIFA World Cup without having been to any finals as a player since Jupp Derwall in 1982. Derwall had at least won two international caps during his player career, both in 1954 – but missed out on a call-up for that year's FIFA World Cup, which West Germany won.

GERMANY'S BRONZE AGES

The 2010 FIFA World Cup third-place play-off between Germany and Uruguay was a rematch of the same tie at the 1970 tournament, when West Germany won 1-0. The German side again took third place 40 years later, thanks to a dramatic 3-2 victory in Port Elizabeth's Nelson Mandela Bay stadium. The result, secured by Sami Khedira's late goal, meant Germany had a record four third-place finishes at FIFA World Cups, having also come third in 1934 and 2006.

OTTO THE FIRST

Germany's first international manager was Otto Nerz, a qualified doctor who played for Mannheim and Tennis Borussia Berlin as an amateur. A strict disciplinarian and an admirer of English football, he led Germany to third place in the 1934 FIFA World Cup finals. They lost 3-1 to Czechoslovakia in the semi-finals, but beat Austria 3-2 in the third-place play-off. The Nazi government sacked Nerz in 1936 after Germany's shock defeat by Norway in the football tournament at the Nazi showcase Berlin Olympics.

GERMANY'S MANAGERS

Otto Nerz	1928–36
Sepp Herberger	1936–64
Helmut Schoen	1964–78
Jupp Derwall	1978–84
Franz Beckenbauer	1984–90
Berti Vogts	1990–98
Erich Ribbeck	1998–2000
Rudi Voller	2000–04
Jurgen Klinsmann	2004–06
Joachim Low	2006–

BONUS BATTLE

Helmut Schon's 1974 FIFA World Cup winners came close to walking out before the finals started. Schon was prepared to send his squad home in a row over bonuses. A last-minute deal was brokered between Franz Beckenbauer and federation vice-president Hermann Neuberger. The vote among the squad went 11-11, but Beckenbauer persuaded the players to accept the DFB's offer. It was a great decision: they beat Holland 2-1 in the final.

GOAL RUSH

Germany's biggest win was 16-0 against Russia in the 1912 Olympic Games in Stockholm. Gottfried Fuchs of Karlsruhe scored ten of the goals, which remains a national team record to this day.

CHANGE OF DIRECTION

Germany has a tradition for continuity in team management. Helmut Schon took over in 1964 after being Sepp Herberger's assistant; Jupp Derwall, who took over from Schon, had been his No. 2. But that policy changed after West Germany's exit from the 1984 UEFA European Championship. Instead of replacing Derwall with his assistant, Erich Ribbeck, the DFB preferred the star quality of Franz Beckenbauer instead. Later managerial "outsiders" included Rudi Voller and Jurgen Klinsmann.

SCHON IN SAARLAND

Helmut Schon is remembered as one of Germany's most successful managers. He started his international coaching career with Saarland, now part of Germany, but which had been made a separate state (with a population of 970,000) after the country's post-war division. Saarland's greatest moment came in the 1954 FIFA World Cup qualifiers, when they beat Norway 3-2 in Oslo to top their qualifying group. They were eventually eliminated by Sepp Herberger's West Germany.

QUICK START

Defender **Arne Friedrich** had made only two Bundesliga appearances when he was selected for his Germany senior debut in a 2-2 draw against Bulgaria in 2002. After switching from full-back to centre-back, he finally scored his first international goal in his 77th appearance for Germany – against Argentina, in a 2010 FIFA World Cup quarter-final. When not playing football, Friedrich is a keen cook and has even published his own book of recipes.

BAYERN BRILLIANCE

Bayern Munich are Germany's record champions. They have won the title on 22 occasions – 21 since the creation of the unified national league (the Bundesliga) in 1963. Until then the championship had been decided by end-of-season play-offs between the top teams of the country's regional leagues. Bayern's only championship under the old system came in 1932 when they beat Eintracht Frankfurt 2-0 in the final.

SEPP'S SURPRISE

Sepp Herberger (1897–1977) was one of the most influential figures in Germany's football history. He was their longest-serving coach (28 years at the helm) and his legendary status was assured after West Germany surprised odds-on favourites Hungary to win the 1954 FIFA World Cup final – a result credited with dragging the country out of a post-war slump. Herberger took charge in 1936 and led the team into the 1938 FIFA World Cup finals. During the war years he used his influence to try to keep his best players away from the heavy fighting. When organized football resumed in 1949, the federation decided to advertise for a national coach, but Herberger persuaded DFB chief Peco Bauwens to give him back his old job. He had a clause in his contract guaranteeing him a totally free hand in organization and selection policy. Among Herberger's favourite sayings was: "The ball is round and the match lasts 90 minutes. Everything else is just theory."

NETHERLANDS

The walled banks of orange-shirted Holland fans may have become a regular feature at the world's major football tournaments, but that has not always been the case. It wasn't until the 1970s, with Johan Cruyff and his team's spectacular brand of Total Football, that the country possessed a side worthy of the modern legend. They won the UEFA European Championship in 1988 and have regularly challenged for the game's major honours.

HOLLAND MANAGERS (SINCE 1980)

Jan Zwartkruis	1978–81
Rob Baan	1981
Kees Rijvers	1981–84
Rinus Michels	1984–85
Leo Beenhakker	1985–86
Rinus Michels	1986–88
Thijs Libregts	1988–90
Nol de Ruiter	1990
Leo Beenhakker	1990
Rinus Michels	1990–92
Dick Advocaat	1992–95
Guus Hiddink	1995–98
Frank Rijkaard	1998–2000
Louis van Gaal	2000–02
Dick Advocaat	2002–04
Marco van Basten	2004–08
Bert van Marwijk	2008–

MICHELS THE MASTER

Rinus Michels (1928–2005) was named FIFA's Coach of the Century in 1999 for his achievements with Holland and Ajax. The former Ajax and Holland striker took over the manager's job at his old club in 1965 and began creating the side that would go on to dominate European football in the early 1970s. Michels built the team around Johan Cruyff – as he later did with the national side – and introduced the concept known as "Total Football". He moved to Barcelona after Ajax's 1971 European Cup victory, but he was called back to mastermind Holland's 1974 FIFA World Cup bid. Nicknamed "The General", he was known as a disciplinarian who could impose order on the many different factions within the Dutch dressing room. Michels used that skill to great effect after taking over the national team again for their 1988 UEFA European Championship campaign. In the finals, Holland beat England and the Republic of Ireland to reach the last four. Then they knocked out hosts West Germany, before beating the Soviet Union 2-0 in the final. Michels had taken charge for a third spell as manager when Holland reached the semi-finals of Euro 92. He retired straight after the tournament.

CRUYFF THE MAGICIAN

Johan Cruyff's footballing achievements have made him the most famous living Dutchman. Cruyff (born in Amsterdam on 25 April 1947) was the catalyst for the rise of both Ajax and the national team. As one Dutch paper wrote before the 1974 FIFA World Cup final: "Cruyff woke up Holland and took us to a world-class level." His great opponent, Franz Beckenbauer, said: "He is the best player to have come from Europe." Cruyff joined Ajax as a ten-year-old and made his league debut at 17. He led them to eight championships and the European Cup three years in a row. He and coach Rinus Michels also developed the style of playing known as "Total Football", which became a trademark for club and country. Cruyff made his international debut, against Hungary, on 7 September 1966. He scored 33 goals in 48 appearances and captained his country 33 times. He was named Player of the Tournament in the 1974 FIFA World Cup finals and was voted European Player of the Year three times.

HOLLAND'S HOT STREAK

Going into the 2010 FIFA World Cup final, Holland had won all 14 games of their campaign – eight in qualifying and six in South Africa. This run of 14 consecutive competitive victories, dating back to September 2008, equalled a record set by France from September 2002 to June 2004. The Dutch route to the final was also the ninth time a team got there with a 100 per cent record in games up to and including the semi-final. Under captain **Giovanni van Bronckhorst** and with **Wesley Sneijder** in top form, Holland matched Brazil's 2002 FIFA World Cup achievement of six victories in a row. Their run to the final also extended their unbeaten run to a Dutch record of 25 games. Holland's last defeat before the final was to Australia, 2-1 in a September 2008 friendly.

HERO HAPPEL

Ernst Happel is second only to Rinus Michels for his coaching achievements with Dutch teams. The former Austria defender made history by steering Feyenoord to the European Cup in 1970 – the first Dutch side to win the trophy. He was drafted in to coach Holland at the 1978 FIFA World Cup finals after guiding Belgian side Brugge to the European Cup final. In Johan Cruyff's absence, Happel drew the best from Ruud Krol, Johan Neeskens and Arie Haan as Holland reached the final before losing in extra-time to Argentina in Buenos Aires.

AMSTERDAM ARENA

Construction work on Holland's major venue, the Amsterdam ArenA, started in 1993. The project cost £100m and the stadium was opened on 14 August 1996. It has been Ajax's home ground ever since and was also one of the leading venues when Holland co-hosted Euro 2000. The unusual spelling was adopted after a complaint by a nightclub of the same name.

PATIENT VAN BASTEN

The Holland manager's job is one of the most precarious in world football. The longest-serving manager in the modern era is Marco van Basten. He was appointed on 29 July 2004 and resigned in June 2008 after Holland's quarter-final elimination from Euro 2008.

VAN BASTEN'S TOURNAMENT

Marco van Basten was the hero of Holland's 1988 UEFA European Championship success. He netted a hat-trick to see off England in the group games, scored a semi-final winner against West Germany, and then cracked a spectacular flying volley to clinch a 2-0 victory over the Soviet Union in the final. The Holland forward also starred in Italy's Serie A with AC Milan, and was twice the league's top scorer before persistent ankle trouble ended his career prematurely.

WAITING IS THE HARDEST PART

Holland had to wait 32 years between reaching the FIFA World Cup final in 1978 and going so far again, in 2010 – equalling the time-span between finals Italy endured from 1938 to 1970. Only Argentina have had to wait longer, from their first final in 1930 to their next in 1978.

LUCKY RINUS

In 1974, Rinus Michels succeeded Frantisek Fadrhonc, the Czech who had steered Holland through the FIFA World Cup qualifiers, as Holland manager with Fadrhonc becoming his assistant. Holland were fortunate to qualify on goal difference. Belgium's Jan Verheyen had a "winner" disallowed for offside in the final qualifier in Amsterdam. TV replays showed the Russian referee had made a mistake. Had the goal stood, Belgium would have gone through at Holland's expense.

THE MISSING LINK

Johan Cruyff remains one of the most influential figures in Dutch football. His negotiations with the Dutch Federation to become national coach before the 1994 FIFA World Cup finals broke down and he twice refused offers by Van Basten to step down and become his assistant.

HOLLAND'S TABLOID WOES

Holland were drawn into a tabloid "scandal" the day before the 1974 FIFA World Cup final against West Germany. The German newspaper *Bild* claimed that four Dutch players and four German girls had taken part in a "naked party" at the team hotel before the semi-final win over Brazil that clinched Holland's final place. Coach Rinus Michels simply accused the German media of trying to stir up trouble.

FLYING FEAR DENIED BERGKAMP MORE CAPS

Dennis Bergkamp would have won many more than 79 caps, but for his fear of flying. Bergkamp refused to board aircraft after the Holland squad were involved in a bomb hoax incident during the 1994 FIFA World Cup in the United States. He missed away games for Holland and his clubs unless he could reach them by road, rail or boat.

DIFFERENT SIDES OF SNEIJDER

Wesley Sneijder was hoping to achieve an unprecedented quintuple when his Holland team took on Spain in the 2010 FIFA World Cup final. No footballer had ever before won the FIFA World Cup in the same season as a domestic league and cup double and the UEFA Champions League or European Cup – let alone adding the FIFA World Cup Golden Boot. Sneijder won the 2009–10 treble with his club side, Internazionale, before only just missing out on the FIFA World Cup and the Golden Boot. Despite his FIFA World Cup final heartbreak, Sneijder did enjoy some romantic solace six days after defeat to Spain, when he married Dutch actress and TV presenter Yolanthe Cabau van Kasbergen.

TOP CAPS

1	Edwin Van der Sar	130
2	Frank De Boer	112
3	Gio Van Bronckhorst	106
4	Philip Cocu	101
5	Clarence Seedorf	87
6	Marc Overmars	86
7	Aaron Winter	84
8	Ruud Krol	83
=	Rafael van der Vaart	83
10	Dennis Bergkamp	79
=	Patrick Kluivert	79

NEESKENS'S EARLY GOAL

Holland took a first-minute lead in the 1974 World Cup without a West German player having touched the ball. The Dutch built a move of 14 passes from the kick-off and Johan Cruyff was tripped in the box by Uli Hoeness. Johan Neeskens converted the first penalty in a World Cup final history . . . but they still went on to lose.

HOLLAND'S DOUBLE LOSERS

Nine Holland players were on the losing side in both the 1974 (2-1 to West Germany) and 1978 (3-1 to Argentina) FIFA World Cup finals. Jan Jongbloed, Ruud Krol, Wim Jansen, Arie Haan, Johan Neeskens, Johnny Rep and Rob Rensenbrink started both games. Wim Suurbier started in 1974 and was a substitute in 1978. Rene Van der Kerkhof was a sub in 1974 and started in 1978.

KEEPING IN WITH THE IN–LAWS

Midfield enforcer **Mark van Bommel** was left out of coach Marco van Basten's Holland squad for the 2008 UEFA European Championship, but was ever-present at the 2010 FIFA World Cup. Van Basten's replacement Bert van Marwijk is his father-in-law: van Bommel being married to van Marwijk's daughter Andra.

THE WINNING CAPTAIN

With his distinctive dreadlocks, Ruud Gullit cut a swathe through world football through the 1980s and '90s. Twice a European Cup winner with AC Milan and a former European Footballer of the Year, he will always be remembered fondly by the Dutch fans as being the first man in a Holland shirt to lift a major trophy – the 1988 UEFA European Championship.

HOLLAND'S EURO STARS

Three Dutch players have won the European Footballer of the Year award: Johan Cruyff, Ruud Gullit and Marco Van Basten. Cruyff picked up the award in 1971, 1973 and 1974; Gullit was honoured in 1987, and Van Basten was chosen in 1988, 1989 and 1992.

"HOLLAND ON TOUR"

The great Milan side of the late 1980s were often known as "Holland on tour" because of their Dutch stars – Ruud Gullit, Marco van Basten and Frank Rijkaard. All three players were key figures in Holland's 1988 UEFA European Championship victory, and they were equally important in Milan's 1989 and 1990 European Cup wins. Gullit and van Basten both scored twice in the 1989 victory over Steaua Bucharest. Rijkaard scored the only goal against Benfica a year later.

DE BOER BOYS SET RECORD

Twins Frank and Ronald De Boer hold the record for the most games played by brothers together for Holland. Frank won 112 caps, while Ronald won 67.

CRUYFF'S CONVERSION

Johan Cruyff used to smoke 20 cigarettes a day before undergoing heart bypass surgery in 1991 while he was coach of Barcelona. He gave up smoking after the operation and later fronted an anti-smoking campaign on behalf of the Catalan regional government.

TOP SCORERS

1	Patrick Kluivert	40
2	Dennis Bergkamp	37
3	Faas Wilkes	35
4	Johann Cruyff	33
=	Abe Lenstra	33
=	Ruud van Nistelrooy	33
7	Bep Bakhuys	28
8	Kick Smit	26
9	Marco van Basten	24
10	Leen Vente	19
=	Wesley Sneijder	19
=	Robin van Persie	19

DUTCH DESPAIR

One of Holland's most painful defeats in recent years came on 1 September 2001. Their 1-0 loss to the Republic of Ireland in Dublin ended their hopes of reaching the 2002 FIFA World Cup finals. The Dutch conceded a shock 68th-minute goal, even though they were playing against ten men after Gary Kelly was sent off. It was the result that forced the resignation of coach Louis van Gaal.

EARLY DAYS

Holland played their first international against Belgium in Brussels on 30 April 1905. Eddy de Neve scored all the goals in Holland's 4-1 win. The Dutch and their Belgian neighbours have been arch-rivals ever since.

"TOTAL FOOTBALL"

Holland's 1974 FIFA World Cup finalists played a revolutionary style of football described as "Total Football" ("totaalvoetbal"), which Rinus Michels and Johan Cruyff had pioneered at Ajax. The game was based on quick passing and fluid movement, with players frequently interchanging positions. Hence full-backs Wim Suurbier and Ruud Krol often appeared in attack and midfielder Johan Neeskens was a frequent scorer with well-timed breaks from midfield.

ALL-TIME LEADING SCORER

Born in Amsterdam on 1 July 1976, centre-forward Patrick Kluivert made his debut for Holland in 1994. In the following ten years he made 79 appearances for the national side, scoring an all-time Dutch record 40 goals.

HOLLAND – MODERN GREATS

Holland have been one of the strongest nations in world football for the past 35 years. The Dutch "Total Football" team – led by Johan Cruyff – reached the 1974 FIFA World Cup final, only to lose 2-1 to West Germany. Four years later, the Dutch lost the final against Argentina, 3-1 in extra-time in Buenos Aires. In between, they reached the UEFA European Championship semi-finals in 1976. Coach Rinus Michels steered Holland to their one major honour, in 1988, when they beat the Soviet Union 2-0 in the UEFA European Championship final. They had gained revenge over West Germany for the 1974 defeat by winning 2-1 in the semi-finals. Before reaching the 2010 FIFA World Cup final, the Dutch suffered a series of semi-final setbacks: they lost the 1998 FIFA World Cup semi-final on penalties to Brazil, and were also beaten in UEFA European Championship semi-finals in 1992, 2000 and 2004.

DUTCH CLOGS

Holland became the first team to be shown as many as nine cards during a single FIFA World Cup match, when they received eight yellows, including a lenient one for **Nigel de Jong**'s chest-high challenge on Xabi Alonso, and a red during the 2010 final against Spain. Holland were also involved in the FIFA World Cup game with the most cards: their second-round defeat to Portugal four years earlier, when 20 cards were shown in total – 16 yellows and four reds.

HOLLAND SO CLOSE

Holland came within a post's width of winning the 1978 FIFA World Cup final. Rob Rensenbrink's shot bounced off an upright in the last minute of normal time. It was 1-1 after 90 minutes and Argentina won 3-1 in extra-time, enough to shatter Dutch final dreams for the second FIFA World Cup in a row.

PENALTY PLAGUE

Missed penalties have become a nightmare for Holland, causing their downfall in several major tournaments. The jinx started in the Euro 92 semi-final when Peter Schmeichel saved Marco van Basten's kick, enabling Denmark to win the penalty shoot-out. Holland lost their Euro 96 quarter-final to France 5-4 on penalties and, two years later, went down 4-2 to Brazil in a FIFA World Cup semi-final shoot-out. Worse followed when Holland co-hosted Euro 2000. They missed two penalties in normal time in the semi-final against Italy. Then Italy keeper Francesco Toldo saved two spot-kicks to eliminate the Dutch in the shoot-out.

KEY PLAYER

Maintaining harmony has often been a tricky task for Dutch coaches at major international tournaments – but Bert Van Marwijk managed to do so at the 2010 FIFA World Cup, despite rumoured tension between several of his star starters. When not conducting his team from the touchline, Van Marwijk could occasionally be found playing the piano in the lobby of the squad's Johannesburg hotel.

VAN DER SAR TOPS THE LOT

Goalkeeper **Edwin van der Sar** (born in Voorhout, on 29 October 1970) is Holland's most-capped player, having made 130 appearances for the national side. He joined Ajax in 1990 and helped them win the European Cup five years later. He made his Holland debut on 7 June 1995, against Belarus, and was their first-choice keeper for 13 years. He quit international football after Holland's elimination at Euro 2008, but new coach Bert van Marwijk persuaded him to return briefly after injuries to his successors, Maarten Stekelenburg and Henk Timmer. Van der Sar has also won the European Cup with Manchester United, as well as spending spells with Juventus and Fulham.

GOING DUTCH FULL-TIME

Professionalism was not introduced into Dutch football until 1954. Holland's emergence as a major power came even later, after Ajax and Feyenoord decided to go full-time professional in the early 1960s. Until then, even stars such as Ajax left winger Piet Keizer – who worked in a tailor's – had part-time jobs outside the game.

BEST AND WORST

Holland's record win is 9-0, which they have achieved twice. The first time came against Finland at the Stockholm Olympics on 4 July 1912. The second time was when they thrashed Norway in a FIFA World Cup qualifier in Rotterdam on 1 November 1972. The Dutch suffered their worst defeat on 21 December 1907, when they lost 12-2 to England's amateurs at Darlington!

HOLLAND'S RISE

Holland were eliminated in the early stages of the 1934 and 1938 FIFA World Cups and they did not qualify for the World Cup finals again until 1974, after narrowly pipping Belgium in their group. The rise of Dutch football coincided with a move to full-time professionalism by the leading clubs in the early 1960s.

ITALY

Only Brazil (with five victories) can claim to have won the FIFA World Cup™ more times than Italy. The Azzurri became the first nation to retain the trophy (through back-to-back successes in 1934 and 1938), snatched a surprise win in Spain in 1982, and collected football's most coveted trophy for a fourth time in 2006 following a dramatic penalty shoot-out win over France. Add the 1968 UEFA European Championship success to the mix and few nations can boast a better record. The success story does not end there. Italian clubs have won the European Cup on 11 occasions and the country's domestic league, Serie A, is considered among the strongest in the game. Italy are a true powerhouse of world football.

TRIED AND TRUSTED

Marcello Lippi's reliance on his 2006 FIFA World Cup-winning stars for the 2010 campaign meant nine players featured in both squads, including captain Fabio Cannavaro and full-back **Gianluca Zambrotta** who both played most in qualifiers – 810 minutes, or nine out of 10 matches – and then all 270 minutes in South Africa.

SECOND TIME LUCKY

The only time a major international tournament has been settled by a replay was Italy's win over Yugoslavia in the 1968 UEFA European Championship. To the delight of their fans, hosts Italy won the second game 2-0, two days after a 1-1 draw in the same Stadio Olimpico in Rome.

RECORD RUN

In two spells as Italy coach, 2004–06 and 2008–10, Marcello Lippi achieved a run of 31 consecutive matches unbeaten – equalling the world record held by Javier Clemente of Spain and Alfio Basile with Argentina.

ROTTEN RETURN

Italy's players were pelted with tomatoes by angry fans when they returned home after crashing out of the 1966 FIFA World Cup at the group stages. After a nervy and unconvincing 2-0 opening victory over Chile, they slumped to a 1-0 defeat to the Soviet Union – and then crashed to a humiliating reverse against North Korea, by the same scoreline.

WE'LL MEET AGAIN

Italy and Argentina are the only two countries to have met each other in five successive FIFA World Cups. They drew in 1974, Italy won in 1978 and 1982, they drew again in 1986, and Argentina dramatically won on penalties in their FIFA World Cup semi-final clash in Naples in 1990.

OFF THE SPOT

Only England have lost as many FIFA World Cup penalty shoot-outs as Italy – three apiece. **Roberto Baggio**, nicknamed "The Divine Ponytail", was involved in all three of Italy's spot-kick defeats, in 1990, 1994 and 1998. Left-back Antonio Cabrini is the only man to have missed a penalty during normal time in a FIFA World Cup final – the score was 0-0 at the time but, fortunately for him, Italy still beat West Germany 3-1 in 1982.

IN SAFE KEEPING

During World War Two, the Jules Rimet Trophy, the FIFA World Cup – won by Italy in 1938 – was hidden in a shoebox under the bed of football official Ottorino Barassi. He preferred to keep it there, rather than its previous home – a bank in Rome. The trophy was handed back to FIFA, safe and untouched, only when the FIFA World Cup resumed in 1950.

SLOW STARTERS

Italy are the only country to have won the FIFA World Cup despite failing to win a first-round game. They drew all three group matches against Peru, Poland and Cameroon at the 1982 tournament in Spain. The Azzurri ("The Blues") sneaked through to the second round only by dint of having scored one more goal in the group stages than Cameroon, who had been unlucky not to have beaten the Italians in the two sides' final group-game encounter, which ended in a 1-1 draw. The Italians made the most of their luck, progressing to the final, where they beat West Germany 3-1 to win the trophy for the third time.

TOURNAMENT SPECIALISTS

FIFA WORLD CUP™: 17 appearances – winners 1934, 1938, 1982, 2006
UEFA EUROPEAN CHAMPIONSHIP: 7 appearances – winners 1968
FIRST INTERNATIONAL: Italy 6 France 2 (Milan, 15 May 1910)
BIGGEST WIN: Italy 9 USA 0 (Brentford, London, 17 August 1948 – Olympic Games)
BIGGEST DEFEAT: Hungary 7 Italy 1 (Budapest, 6 April 1924)

FLYING HIGH

Vittorio Pozzo is the only man to have won the FIFA World Cup twice as manager – both times with Italy, in 1934 and 1938 (only two players, Giuseppe Meazza and Giovanni Ferrari, were selected in both finals). Pozzo also led Italy to the 1936 Olympics title. Born in Turin on 2 March 1886, Pozzo learned to love football as a student in England, watching Manchester United. He returned home reluctantly when his family bought him a return ticket for his sister's wedding – and then refused to let him leave Italy again. Pozzo fired up his Italian team ahead of their 1938 semi-final against Brazil by revealing their opponents had already booked their plane to Paris for the final – Italy won 2-1.

TOP DRAW

No team has finished more FIFA World Cup matches level than Italy, who took their tally to 21 with 1-1 draws against both Paraguay and New Zealand in Group F, at the 2010 competition in South Africa. Their first draw had also been 1-1, against Spain in a 1934 quarter-final tie. Italy's Giuseppe Meazza scored the only goal of a replay the following day, and Italy went on to lift the trophy for the first time that year.

CHAMPS TO CHUMPS

Italy's dismal 2010 FIFA World Cup campaign was the worst in their history, despite going into the tournament as defending world champions. Their two draws, and 3-2 defeat to Slovakia, meant they ended a FIFA World Cup without a win for the first time ever. Finishing bottom of their first-round group was also unprecedented. The poor showing must have left 2006 World Cup-winning coach **Marcello Lippi** regretting his decision to resume control in 2008. Immediately after the Slovakia match, which ended the defending champions' run, Lippi insisted the players should not be faulted and he should take all blame. He had already announced his intention to resign after the finals.

ITALY'S NATIONAL COACHES

Vittorio Pozzo	1912, 1924
Augusto Rangone	1925–28
Carlo Carcano	1928–29
Vittorio Pozzo	1929–48
Ferruccio Novo	1949–50
Carlino Beretta	1952–53
Giuseppe Viani	1960
Giovanni Ferrari	1960–61
Giovanni Ferrari/Paolo Mazza	1962
Edmondo Fabbri	1962–66
Helenio Herrera/Ferruccio Valcareggi	1966–67
Ferruccio Valcareggi	1967–74
Fulvio Bernardini	1974–75
Enzo Bearzot	1975–86
Azeglio Vicini	1986–91
Arrigo Sacchi	1991–96
Cesare Maldini	1997–98
Dino Zoff	1998–2000
Giovanni Trapattoni	2000–04
Marcello Lippi	2004–06
Roberto Donadoni	2006–08
Marcello Lippi	2008–10
Cesare Prandelli	2010–

COMEBACK KID

Paolo Rossi was the unlikely hero of Italy's 1982 FIFA World Cup triumph, winning the Golden Boot with six goals – including a memorable hat-trick against Brazil in the second round, and the first of Italy's three goals in their final win over West Germany. But he only just made it to the tournament at all, having completed a two-year ban for his alleged involvement in a betting scandal only six weeks before the start of the tournament.

HELPING HANDS

Goalkeeper Angelo Peruzzi was a 14-year-old ballboy at the 1984 European Cup final between Roma and Liverpool. He made 16 appearances for Roma before playing for Juventus, Internazionale and Lazio as well as 31 times for Italy between 1995 and 2006.

JUVE GOT A FRIEND

Although their performances turned out disappointingly in the end, former Italy under-21s captain **Giorgio Chiellini** might have felt happy just to be lining up alongside legendary Juventus team-mate Fabio Cannavaro in central defence for the 2010 FIFA World Cup. Despite winning his first cap in 2004, Chiellini was left out of the 2006 FIFA World Cup squad and then was inadvertently responsible for Cannavaro missing the 2008 UEFA European Championship with an ankle injury caused by Chiellini's training-ground tackle.

INTERNATIONAL INTER

The 2010 treble-winners Internazionale provided more different countries with players for the 2010 FIFA World Cup than any other club – except for mid-table German side Wolfsburg. Both clubs were represented in eight different squads at the tournament in South Africa. Just weeks after completing a treble of the Italian league and cup and the UEFA Champions League, the Milan club's players featured for Italy, Argentina, Brazil, Cameroon, Ghana, Holland, Serbia and Slovenia.

TOP CAPS

1	Fabio Cannavaro	136
2	Paolo Maldini	126
3	Dino Zoff	112
4	Gianluigi Buffon	102
5	Gianluca Zambrotta	97
6	Giacinto Facchetti	94
7	Alessandro Del Piero	91
8	Franco Baresi	81
=	Giuseppe Bergomi	81
=	Marco Tardelli	81

TOP SCORERS

1	Luigi Riva	35
2	Giuseppe Meazza	33
3	Silvio Piola	30
4	Roberto Baggio	27
=	Alessandro Del Piero	27
6	Adolfo Baloncieri	25
=	Filippo Inzaghi	25
=	Alessandro Altobelli	25
9	Christian Vieri	23
=	Francesco Graziani	23

ZOFF THE SCALE

Goalkeeper **Dino Zoff** set an international record by going 1,142 minutes without conceding a goal between September 1972 and June 1974. Zoff was Italy's captain when they won the 1982 FIFA World Cup – emulating the feat of another Juventus goalkeeper, Gianpiero Combi, who had been the victorious skipper in 1934. Zoff coached Italy to the final of the 2000 UEFA European Championship, which they lost 2-1 to France thanks to an extra-time "golden goal" – then quit a few days later, unhappy following the criticism levelled at him by Italy's prime minister, Silvio Berlusconi.

RIGHT CALL

Italy captain **Giacinto Facchetti** called correctly when their 1968 UEFA European Championship semi-final against the Soviet Union ended in a draw after extra-time (in the days before penalties) and had to be settled by tossing a coin. The attacking left-back had luck on his side that time, then lifted the trophy after a 2-0 replay victory in the final against Yugoslavia. Facchetti, who also won the European Cup with Internazionale in 1964 and 1965, had an impressive scoring record for a defender, ending his career with 59 goals in 476 league appearances. He played on the left flank, even though he was a naturally right-footed player.

HAPPY CENTENARY

After captaining Italy to the 2006 FIFA World Cup title, **Fabio Cannavaro** was named FIFA World Player of the Year – at 33, the oldest winner of the prize, as well as the first defender. Cannavaro, born in Naples in 1973, played every minute of the 2006 tournament and the final triumph against France was the ideal way to celebrate his 100th international appearance.

ROLLING RIVA

Italy's all-time top scorer is **Luigi "Gigi" Riva**, who scored 35 goals in 42 appearances for his country. One of his most important strikes was the opening goal in the 1968 UEFA European Championship final win over Yugoslavia. Despite his prolific form after having switched from left-winger to striker, he never played for one of Italy's traditional club giants. Instead, Riva – born in Leggiuno on 7 November 1944 – spent his entire league career with unfashionable Sardinian club Cagliari, and at one point turned down a move to the mighty Juventus. His goals (21 of them) fired the club to their one and only league championship in 1970. Riva suffered his fair share of bad luck with injuries, breaking his left leg while playing for Italy in 1966, then his right leg in 1970, again when he was away on international duty.

HOME GROWN

More than 80 years separated the first and latest foreign-born players to wear the blue Azzurri shirt. Argentina-born Julio Libonatti made the first of his 17 appearances in a 3-1 defeat by Czechoslovakia in Prague on 28 October 1926. Most recently, Brazilian-born Amauri Carvalho de Oliveira debuted in a 1-0 defeat by the Ivory Coast on 10 August 2010, in a friendly at Upton Park, London.

FED UP ... THEN DOWN

After **Gianluigi Buffon** conceded just two goals throughout Italy's 2006 FIFA World Cup-winning campaign, the last thing Italy would have wanted was losing him to a back injury halfway through their first game in South Africa four years later. Substitute Federico Marchetti kept a clean sheet as Italy came back from a goal down to draw 1-1 with Paraguay. But the Cagliari goalkeeper then conceded five goals from the six shots he faced in the following two games. While other veterans such as Fabio Cannavaro and Gennaro Gattuso ended their international careers after Italy's elimination, Buffon insisted he wanted to keep on playing – and was named Cannavaro's replacement as captain by new Italy coach Cesare Prandelli.

GLOVE CONQUERS ALL

Walter Zenga went 517 minutes without conceding a goal at the 1990 FIFA World Cup – a tournament record. The only two goals conceded by Gianluigi Buffon during the 2006 FIFA World Cup were an own goal and a penalty.

TRAVELLING TRAPATTONI

Italian **Giovanni Trapattoni** has won domestic league titles as a coach in Italy, Germany, Portugal and Austria – with Juventus, Bayern Munich, Benfica and Salzburg. Only the German Udo Lattek has also coached teams in four different countries to league title success. Trapattoni is the only manager to have won all three UEFA club competitions as well as the World Club Cup, all with the great Juventus sides of the 1980s.

ITALY'S GREATEST PLAYERS

(as chosen by the Italian football association)

1 Giuseppe Meazza
2 Luigi Riva
3 Roberto Baggio
4 Paolo Maldini
5 Giacinto Facchetti
6 Sandro Mazzola
7 Giuseppe Bergomi
8 Valentino Mazzola

KEEPING IT IN THE FAMILY

Cesare and **Paolo Maldini** are the only father and son to have hoisted the European Cup as winning captains – both with AC Milan, and both for the first time in England. Cesare lifted the trophy after his team beat Benfica at Wembley, London, in 1963. Paolo repeated the feat 40 years later, when Milan defeated Juventus at Old Trafford, Manchester. Cesare was Italy coach and Paolo Italy captain at the 1998 FIFA World Cup, and they both featured at the 2002 tournament – though by now Cesare was in charge of Paraguay. The Maldini dynasty may not end there – Paolo's son, Christian, is emerging through the youth ranks at Milan. If he makes it into the first team, Christian will be the only player allowed to wear Paolo's famous No. 3 jersey. Although he is now Italy's second most-capped player, Paolo narrowly failed to win an international tournament – he played for Italy sides that finished third and runners-up in both FIFA World Cup and UEFA European Championship tournaments.

PRANDELLI'S PLEDGE

After agreeing to take over from Marcello Lippi as Italy coach after the 2010 FIFA World Cup, ex-Fiorentina boss Cesare Prandelli did travel to Africa during the tournament – but watching the football was not his only aim. He watched Italy play New Zealand on television in Zanzibar, Tanzania, where he and his daughter were opening a school in memory of Prandelli's wife Manuela, who died of cancer three years earlier.

MEDAL COLLECTORS

Giovanni Ferrari not only enjoys the status of having won both the 1934 and 1938 FIFA World Cups with Italy, he also shares the record for most Serie A titles, with eight triumphs. Five were with Juventus, two with Internazionale and one with Bologna. He shares the record of eight league championship medals with Virginio Rosetta, twice with Pro Vercelli and six times with Juventus, and Giuseppe Furino, all with Juventus.

BEEFING UP

The stadium shared by AC Milan and Internazionale is popularly known as San Siro, after the district in which it is located. Its official title, however, is Stadio **Giuseppe Meazza**, named after the star inside-forward on the pitch and dance enthusiast off it who played for both clubs as well as Italy's 1934 and 1938 FIFA World Cup-winning sides. Meazza, born in Milan on 23 August 1910, was first spotted by an Inter scout while playing keepy-uppy in the street with a ball made of rags – but was so thin he had to be fattened up with plenty of steaks. His last goal for Italy was a penalty in the 1938 World Cup semi-final against Brazil – taken while trying to pull up his shorts, whose elastic had broken.

ITALIAN LEAGUE TITLES

Juventus	27
Internazionale	18
AC Milan	17
Genoa	9
Bologna	7
Pro Vercelli	7
Torino	7
Roma	3
Fiorentina	2
Lazio	2
Napoli	2
Cagliari	1
Casale	1
Hellas Verona	1
Novese	1
Sampdoria	1
Spezia	1

GRAND OLD TEAM TO PLAY FOR

Every Italian FIFA World Cup squad has featured at least one Juventus player. The Turin team, known as the "Grand Old Lady" of Italian club football, were relegated a division in 2006 after being found guilty of match-fixing – and, as a result, were forced to endure their first season outside the top division since the club's foundation in 1897. Their 51 trophies are an Italian club record – and, in 1985, they became the first team to have won the European, UEFA and Cup-Winners' Cups.

SECONDS OUT

The world's fastest red card after kick-off was shown to Bologna's Giuseppe Lorenzo when he hit a Parma player in a Serie A match in December 1990 – he was sent off just ten seconds into the match.

CLEAN SWEEP

Italian clubs won all three UEFA trophies in the 1989–90 season, a unique treble. AC Milan took the European Cup (beating Benfica 1-0 in the final), Juventus the UEFA Cup (beating Fiorentina 3-1) and Sampdoria the Cup-Winners' Cup (beating Anderlecht 2-0 in the final).

TRAGIC TORINO

Torino were Italy's most successful club side when their first-team squad was wiped out in an air crash at Superga, above Turin, on 4 May 1949. The club has only won the Serie A title once since then, in the 1976–77 season. Among the victims was star forward Valentino Mazzola, who had gone along on the trip despite being ill. His son **Sandro Mazzola**, only six at the time of the disaster, went on to star in the Italy teams that won the 1968 UEFA European Championship and finished as FIFA World Cup runners-up two years later.

SPAIN

Spain is home to some of the strongest club sides in Europe (boasting a total of 12 European Cups between them) and has produced some of the biggest names in the sport. For years, as major tournament failures became the depressing norm (the 1964 UEFA European Championship triumph apart), *La Roja* were considered the world game's major underachievers. But that started to change in 2008, in the UEFA European Championship final, when Spain beat Germany 1-0 to give the country its first taste of international success for 44 years and a first-ever top position in the Coca-Cola/FIFA World Rankings. Fast forward to 2010, and the 1-0 defeat of Holland in the FIFA World Cup™ final cemented Spain's place as the world's No. 1 football nation.

CIVIL SPANISH

The FIFA World Cup was not the only prize Spain claimed at the 2010 tournament in South Africa. They also received the Fair Play award, having been shown just eight yellow cards – and no red cards – in their seven matches. The Spanish were also Fair Play Award winners at the 2006 FIFA World Cup, though that time they did share the honour with Brazil.

DOUBLING UP

Spain's 2010 FIFA World Cup triumph made them the first country since West Germany, in 1974, to lift the trophy as the reigning European champions. When France combined the two titles, they did it the other way around, by winning the 1998 FIFA World Cup and then the UEFA European Championship two years later.

KEEPING IT CLEAN

Spanish goalkeeper **Iker Casillas** kept clean sheets in all seven of his country's knockout-round matches across the 2008 UEFA European Championship and the 2010 FIFA World Cup. The team scored four goals in three games at Euro 2008 and four in four in South Africa.

GROUNDS FOR APPEAL

No single country has provided more venues when hosting a FIFA World Cup finals than the 17 stadiums – in 14 cities – used by Spain in 1982. The 2002 tournament was played at 20 different venues but ten were in Japan and ten in South Korea. The 1982 competition was the first FIFA World Cup to be expanded from 16 to 24 teams. The final was played in Madrid's Estadio Santiago Bernabeu.

THREE AND EASY

Only three players have scored for Spain in three separate FIFA World Cup final tournaments – Raul (in 1998, 2002 and 2006), Julio Salinas (1986, 1990 and 1994) and Fernando Hierro (1994, 1998 and 2002). The latter is also Spain's third top scorer despite spending a large part of his career as a defender.

RIGHT SAID FRED

When Spain came back from 2-0 and then 3-2 down to win 4-3 in Madrid in May 1929, they became the first non-British team to beat England. Spain's victory, in the Estadio Metropolitano, came with the help of their English coach Fred Pentland, who had moved to Spain in 1920. He had most success with Athletic Bilbao, leading them to league and cup doubles in 1930 and 1931 – and inflicting Barcelona's worst-ever defeat, a 12-1 rout in 1931.

MAJOR TOURNAMENTS

FIFA WORLD CUP™:
13 appearances – winners 2010

UEFA EUROPEAN CHAMPIONSHIP:
Eight appearances – winners 1964, 2008

FIRST INTERNATIONAL:
Spain 1 Denmark 0 (Brussels, Belgium, 28 August 1920)

BIGGEST WIN:
Spain 13 Bulgaria 0 (Madrid, 21 May 1933)

BIGGEST DEFEAT:
Italy 7 Spain 1 (Amsterdam, Holland 4 June 1928); England 7 Spain 1 (London, England, 9 December 1931)

RED ALERT

Spain refused to play in the first UEFA European Championship in 1960, in protest at having to travel to the Soviet Union, a Communist country. But they changed their minds four years later, not only hosting the tournament but also winning it – by beating the visiting Soviets 2-1 in the final. Spain were captained by Fernando Olivella and managed by Jose Villalonga, who had been the first coach to win the European Cup, with Real Madrid in 1956.

SWOON IN JUNE

The date 22 June has been an unfortunate one for Spain, especially when it comes to penalty shoot-outs. They lost on spot-kicks on this date to Belgium in the 1986 FIFA World Cup, England in the 1996 UEFA European Championship and South Korea in the 2002 World Cup. But their luck changed on 22 June 2008, when they beat Italy on penalties in the quarter-finals of the UEFA European Championship, after the game had ended in a 0-0 draw. The win also marked Spain's first victory over Italy in a competitive match since 1920.

WISE HEAD, OLD SHOULDERS

Luis Aragones became the oldest coach to win the UEFA European Championship when Spain won the 2008 tournament, a month short of his 70th birthday. Aragones, a former centre-forward and known only as "Luis" during his playing days, had lined up for Spain in the run-up to the 1964 finals, but had to watch the team win the competition from the sidelines after being left out of the squad. During his time as national coach between 2004 and 2008, the so-called "Wise Man of Hortaleza" won more matches than any other Spanish boss – 38. Aragones, born in Hortaleza, Madrid on 28 July 1938, spent most of his playing career with Atletico Madrid, where he was surprisingly appointed as club coach (at the surprisingly young age of 36) immediately after retiring in 1974.

TRI-NATIONS

Ladislav Kubala is the only man to have played for not one, not two, but three different countries – though he never played in the finals of a major international tournament. Despite being born in Budapest on 10 June 1927, he made his international debut for Czechoslovakia in 1946 – winning five more caps for the country of his parents' birth. He then appeared three times for birthplace Hungary after moving back to the country in 1948, before playing 19 games for Spain after leaving Hungary as a refugee and securing a transfer to Barcelona in 1951.

TOP CAPS

1	Andoni Zubizarreta	126
2	Iker Casillas	111
3	Raul	102
4	Xavi	94
5	Carles Puyol	90
6	Fernando Hierro	89
7	Jose Antonio Camacho	81
8	Fernando Torres	80
9	Xabi Alonso	76
10	Rafael Gordillo	75

TOP SCORERS

1	Raul	44
2	David Villa	43
3	Fernando Hierro	29
4	Fernando Morientes	27
5	Emilio Butragueno	26
6	Fernando Torres	24
7	Alfredo Di Stefano	23
=	Julio Salinas	23
9	Michel	21
10	Telmo Zarra	20

TORRES! TORRES!

Fernando Torres originally wanted to be a goalkeeper as a child, before becoming a striker. Torres, born in Madrid on 20 March 1984, was only 19 when he was made captain of his boyhood heroes Atletico Madrid. He has a knack for scoring the only goal in tournament finals – most famously in the 2008 UEFA European Championship, for Spain against Germany in Vienna. He had already achieved the feat in the Under-16 UEFA European Championships in 2001 and for the Under-19s the following year.

VICTORY MARCH

Centre-back Carlos Marchena became the first footballer to go 50 internationals in a row unbeaten, when he played in Spain's 3-2 victory over Saudi Arabia in May 2009 – one more than Brazil's 1950s and 1960s winger Garrincha. Marchena was a member of Spain's successful 2010 FIFA World Cup squad, ending the tournament on 54 consecutive internationals without defeat – and counting. His one and only loss while playing for Spain was when Greece won 1-0 at the 2004 UEFA European Championship.

BEST CAS SCENARIO

No man has captained Spain more often than **Iker Casillas**, who took his appearances with the armband to 54 while leading his country to glory in the 2010 FIFA World Cup final against Holland. The previous record of 50 was also held by a goalkeeper, Andoni Zubizarreta, who appeared for Spain at the 1986, 1990, 1994 and 1998 FIFA World Cups. Casillas broke the record in the second-round 1-0 win over Portugal, in Cape Town.

David Villa became Spain's all-time top scorer in FIFA World Cups with his first-round goal against Chile, his sixth overall across the 2006 and 2010 tournaments – then knockout-round strikes against Portugal and Paraguay took his World Cup tally to eight. Emilio Butragueño, Fernando Hierro, Fernando Morientes and Raul had each scored five FIFA World Cup goals for Spain. Villa also became the first Spaniard to miss a penalty in a FIFA World Cup match, when he missed the chance of a hat-trick against Honduras by shooting his spot-kick wide. Spain had scored their previous 14 FIFA World Cup penalties, not counting shoot-outs.

THE RAUL THING

Former Real Madrid striker **Raul Gonzalez Blanco** – known as Raul – is not only Spain's most prolific international goalscorer, with 44 goals in 102 games, he also tops the scoring charts for both the European Cup, with 66 goals, and Real Madrid – after passing Alfredo Di Stefano's tally of 309 club goals during the 2008–09 season. Raul scored seven goals for Spain in just four days in March 1999 – four in a 9-0 thrashing of Austria, followed by three as San Marino were crushed 6-0, but he was controversially left out of Spain's Euro 2008-winning squad by coach Luis Aragones, who condemned the player's lack of success in big international tournaments. Raul also missed out on FIFA World Cup glory in 2010 and, as a club free agent, joined German club Schalke 04 a few weeks after the FIFA World Cup final. Football and family are closely entwined for the man born in Madrid on 27 June 1977 – he celebrates each goal by kissing his wedding ring, a gesture reserved for his wife, Mamen Sanz.

GIFT OF THE FAB

Arsenal's **Cesc Fabregas** became Spain's youngest-ever FIFA World Cup player – and the country's youngest international for 70 years – when he came on as a substitute against Ukraine at the 2006 FIFA World Cup aged 19 years 41 days. Despite wearing the name "Fabregas" on the back of his Arsenal shirt, he is better known in Spain as simply "Cesc".

YELLOW PERIL

Julio Alberto was booked after just six minutes of Spain's game against Brazil at the 1986 FIFA World Cup – though his record for the quickest FIFA World Cup yellow card was broken eight years later, when Russia's Sergei Gorlukovich was cautioned inside the first minute against Sweden.

FIT FOR PURPOSE

Luis Suarez played through injury for Spain in the 1964 UEFA European Championship final – luckily for his team-mates, since he set up both goals in a 2-1 triumph. He was named European Footballer of the Year in 1960 – the only Spanish-born player to have taken the prize.

TREASURE CHEST

The Spanish first division goalkeeper who concedes the fewest goals per game each season is awarded the Zamora Trophy. This is named after legendary keeper **Ricardo Zamora**, who played 46 times for Spain between 1920 and 1936 – including the legendary 4-3 win over England in Madrid in 1929. Zamora was the first Spanish star to play for both Barcelona and Real Madrid. Later he was league title-winning coach of ... Atletico Madrid.

LUCKY JUAN

Only one player has failed to score in a FIFA World Cup penalty shoot-out with a spot-kick that would have won the game had it gone in: Spain's Juan Carlos Valeron, whose effort went wide against Republic of Ireland in 2002. The shoot-out score was 2-1 in Spain's favour, with just an Irish attempt to follow, when he missed – but his team went on to win anyway.

SPANISH STREAKS

Only two clubs have gone through an entire top division season unbeaten – Athletic Bilbao in 1929–30 and Real Madrid two years later. This was the first of Real Madrid's record 31 Spanish league

SPANISH LEAGUE CHAMPIONSHIPS

Real Madrid	31
Barcelona	20
Atletico Madrid	9
Athletic Bilbao	8
Valencia	6
Real Sociedad	2
Deportivo de la Coruna	1
Sevilla	1
Betis	1

TOP OF THE WORLD

Spain rose to the top of the FIFA world rankings for the first time in July 2008, after winning the UEFA European Championship co-hosted by Austria and Switzerland. They became only the sixth team to reach the No. 1 spot and the first to do so without ever having won the FIFA World Cup.

LEADING LIGHTS

Spain have become experts in holding on to a lead, winning 43 games in a row having opened the scoring – including all six of their victories at the 2010 FIFA World Cup. The last team to go a goal down to Spain but end up winning the game were Northern Ireland, securing a 3-2 success in a Euro 2008 qualifier in September 2006.

SEMI PRECIOUS

Centre-back **Carles Puyol**'s thumping header not only gave Spain victory in their 2010 FIFA World Cup semi-final – it was also the country's first win over Germany in four FIFA World Cup matches. West Germany had won 2-1 in both 1966 and 1982, before a 1-1 draw at the 1994 tournament. But Spain's 1-0 win in 2010 was a repeat of their triumph over Germany in the UEFA European Championship final two years earlier. Nineteen members of the two 2010 FIFA World Cup squads had played in that Euro 2008 showdown, 11 Spanish and eight German.

MORE THAN JUST A CLUB

Barcelona, founded in 1899 by a Swiss businessman Hans Gamper, prides itself on being "more than a club". The club's famous blue and purple resisted the march of commercialism for more than a century until 2006, when the club signed a deal with (and gave money to) the United Nations Children's Fund (UNICEF) in exchange for using the charity's logo on its shirts.

PERFECT PICHICHI

The annual award for top scorer in La Liga is called the "Pichichi" – the nickname of Rafael Moreno, a striker for Athletic Bilbao between 1911 and 1921. He scored 200 goals in 170 games for the club, and once in five matches for Spain. Pichichi, who often took the field wearing a large white cap, died suddenly in 1922, aged just 29.

MAIN STADIUMS

Name	City	Capacity
Camp Nou	Barcelona	98,772
Santiago Bernabeu	Madrid	80,354
Estadio de la Cartuja	Seville	72,000
Vicente Calderon	Madrid	57,200
Lluis Companys	Barcelona	56,000
Mestalla	Valencia	55,000
Manuel Ruiz de Lopera	Seville	52,500
Ramon Sanchez Pizjuan	Seville	45,500
San Mames	Bilbao	40,000
Manuel Martinez Valero	Elche	38,750

THE VULTURE

Born in the Spanish capital and a star for Real for over a decade, **Emilio Butragueno** was a man made in Madrid. Nicknamed The Vulture for his predatory instincts in the penalty area, he made 69 appearances for the Spanish national side, scoring 26 goals.

WHO CAN TELMO

Telmo Zarraonaindia, commonly known as "Zarra", scored a Spanish championship record of 251 goals in 277 games for Athletic Bilbao between 1940 and 1955 – and 20 goals in 20 games for Spain, between 1945 and 1951. He was nicknamed the "finest head in Europe after Churchill".

FIFA FIRST

Real Madrid were the only club formally represented at FIFA's first meeting in Paris in 1904 – though the club was then known simply as Madrid FC. Spanish clubs, such as Real Madrid and Real Betis, dropped the word "Real" – meaning "Royal" – from their names during the Second Spanish Republic, between 1931 and 1939.

BELGIUM

For eight decades Belgium remained a nation capable of challenging for honours. Then came the golden period. 1980 UEFA European Championship runners-up at the 1986 FIFA World Cup qualifiers – and even competed at major tournaments. Recent times have been tougher, and a nation hopes that failure to qualify for UEFA Euro 2004 and 2008 and the FIFA World Cup™ in 2006 and 2010 does not signal a slide back into darker times.

TOP CAPS

1	Jan Ceulemans	96
2	Eric Gerets	86
=	Franky van der Elst	86
4	Enzo Scifo	84
5	Paul van Himst	81
6	Bart Goor	78
7	Georges Grun	77
8	Timmy Simons	74
9	Lorenzo Staelens	70
=	Marc Wilmots	70

TOP SCORERS

1	Paul van Himst	30
=	Bernard Voorhoof	30
3	Marc Wilmots	28
4	Joseph Mermans	27
5	Raymond Braine	26
=	Robert De Veen	26
7	Wesley Sonck	24
8	Jan Ceulemans	23
=	Marc Degryse	23
10	Henri Coppens	21

SIXTH SENSE

By qualifying for the 2002 FIFA World Cup, Belgium became the first country to reach six successive tournaments without benefiting once from being either hosts or defending holders. But although they beat reigning champions Argentina at the 1982 finals, they would lose to the same opposition – eventual champions – in the semi-finals four years later.

CONSOLATION FOR KEEPER

The Lev Yashin Award (for the best goalkeeper at a FIFA World Cup) was introduced in 1994. The first recipient was Belgium goalkeeper **Michel Preud'homme**, despite his country only making it as far as the second round.

HOME ALONE

In 2000, when they co-hosted the tournament with Holland, Belgium became the first UEFA European Championship hosts not to make it through the first round of the finals.

MOTHER'S BOY

Not many footballers turn down a move to AC Milan, but Jan Ceulemans did just that, after seeking the advice of his mum. Belgium's most-capped player (he played 96 times for his country) spent the bulk of his career with Club Brugge, but is best remembered by fans for his contributions to three consecutive FIFA World Cup campaigns. Belgium's finest performance came in finishing fourth at the 1986 tournament in Mexico, when midfielder and captain Ceulemans scored three goals. Born in Lier on 28 February 1957, he retired from international football after the 1990 FIFA World Cup – and later, between 2005 and 2006, returned to Club Brugge as manager.

ALL CHANGE AT THE TOP

Belgium went through four different coaches in the 13 months from April 2009 to May 2010. Rene Vandereycken's three-year reign came to an end on 7 April 2009, during a disappointing World Cup qualification campaign – but successor Franky Vercauteren lasted just four months. Dutch coach Dick Advocaat took over in October 2009 but quit the following April, after five matches, to be replaced by Georges Leekens – who was himself returning to the job he filled from 1997 to 1999.

GOLDEN NOT–SO–OLDIE

Fernand Nisot held the record for being the youngest-ever international footballer for 60 years. He made his Belgium debut in 1911 aged 16 years and 19 days.

CLUB MATES

Belgium ended a 1964 match against Holland with a team entirely made up of Anderlecht players, after Liege goalkeeper Guy Delhasse was substituted by Anderlecht's Jan Trappeniers.

SPECS APPEAL

Many footballers wear contact lenses, but Belgium captain **Jef Jurion** was notable in the late 1950s and early 1960s for wearing a pair of specially made glasses during the matches he played.

LIMITED KOMPANY

Belgium won Olympic bronze in 1900 and gold 20 years later, but they just missed out on a medal at the 2008 Beijing Games, when they lost to Brazil in the bronze medal play-off. Star player **Vincent Kompany** missed the match after being summoned back to Europe by his German club Hamburg.

HE'S OUR GUY

Belgium's longest-serving, and most successful, coach was **Guy Thys**, who led them to the final of the 1980 UEFA European Championships and to the semi-finals of the FIFA World Cup six years later. He served 13 years in the job – from 1976 to 1989 – then returned to the role just eight months after stepping down, to take his country to the 1990 FIFA World Cup.

BULGARIA

The glory days of the "golden generation" apart – when Bulgaria finished fourth at the 1994 FIFA World Cup™ in the United States, sensationally beating defending champions Germany 2-1 in the quarter-finals – a consistent pattern emerges with Bulgarian football. Regular qualifiers for the game's major competitions, and the birthplace of some of the sport's biggest names (such as Hristo Stoichkov and Dimitar Berbatov), the country has too often failed to deliver on the big occasions and make its mark on world football.

TOP CAPS

1	Borislav Mikhailov	102
2	Hristo Bonev	96
3	Stilian Petrov	92
=	Krassimir Balakov	92
5	Dimitar Penev	90
6	Radostin Kishishev	88
7	Hristo Stoichkov	83
8	Nasko Sirakov	82
9	Zlatko Yankov	80
10	Ayan Sadkov	79

A NATION MOURNS

Bulgaria lost two of its most popular footballing talents in a June 1971 car crash that killed strikers Georgi Asparukhov, aged 28, and Nikola Kotkov, aged 32. Asparukhov scored 19 goals in 50 internationals, including Bulgaria's only goal of the 1966 FIFA World Cup finals in a 3-1 defeat by Hungary.

SAINT STEFAN

Bulgaria's best football performances at the Olympics were a bronze medal in Melbourne in 1956 and a silver in Mexico City 12 years later. Stefan Bozhkov was a playing member of the Melbourne team and the coach of the Mexico City side.

MOB RULES

Manchester United and Bulgaria centre-forward **Dimitar Berbatov** claims to have learned English by watching the *Godfather* movies. Berbatov joined United from Tottenham in 2008 for a club and Bulgarian record fee of £30.75m. Before joining Spurs, he had been a member of the Bayer Leverkusen side who narrowly missed out on a treble in 2002. They lost in the final of both the UEFA Champions League and the German cup and finished runners-up in the German Bundesliga.

SNEAKING THROUGH

Ivan Vutsov's Bulgaria side reached the second round of the 1986 FIFA World Cup despite achieving just two draws and a defeat in their first-round group. They and Uruguay, in the same tournament, became the first teams to make it through a first round and into the knockout stages without winning a game. Their fortune ran out, though, when they fell 2-0 to hosts Mexico.

PENEV MIGHTIER

Dimitar Penev, Bulgaria's coach as they finished fourth at the 1994 FIFA World Cup, had previously represented his country as a defender at the tournaments in 1966, 1970 and 1974. After a brief second spell in charge of the national side in 2007, he then coached leading club CSKA Sofia – but was sacked in March 2009 and replaced as manager by his own nephew, Luboslav Penev.

GO FOURTH AND MULTIPLY

The so-called "Golden Generation" of 1994 was the only Bulgarian side to win a match at a FIFA World Cup finals – finishing fourth after beating Greece, Argentina, Mexico and Germany. Bulgaria had only just qualified for the tournament, thanks to Emil Kostadinov's last-minute goal in Paris that knocked out Gerard Houllier's France.

ALL–ROUNDER ALEKSANDAR

Defender Aleksandar Shalamanov played for Bulgaria at the 1966 FIFA World Cup, six years after representing his country as an alpine skier at the Winter Olympics. He also went to the 1964 Olympics as an unused member of the volleyball squad. Shalamanov was voted Bulgaria's best sportsman in 1967 and 1973.

TOP SCORERS

1	Dimitar Berbatov	48
2	Hristo Bonev	47
3	Hristo Stoichkov	37
4	Emil Kostadinov	26
5	Petar Zhekov	25
=	Ivan Kolev	25
7	Atanas Mihaylov	23
8	Nasko Sirakov	23
9	Dimitar Milanov	20
10	Georgi Asparukhov	19

MAYOR WITH NO HAIR

Balding **Yordan Letchkov** headed the winning goal against holders and defending champions Germany in the 1994 FIFA World Cup quarter-final in the United States. At the time, he played for German club Hamburg. He later became mayor of Sliven, the Bulgarian town where he was born in July 1967.

HRISTO'S HISTORY

Hristo Stoichkov, born in Plovdiv, Bulgaria, on 8 February 1968, shared the 1994 FIFA World Cup Golden Boot, awarded to the tournament's top scorer, with Russia's Oleg Salenko. Both scored six times, though Stoichkov became the sole winner of that year's European Footballer of the Year award. Earlier that same year, he had combined up-front with Brazilian Romario to help Barcelona reach the final of the UEFA Champions League. Earlier in his career he was banned for a year after a brawl during the 1985 Bulgarian cup final between CSKA Sofia and Levski Sofia. Stoichkov won trophies with clubs in Bulgaria, Spain, Saudi Arabia and the United States before retiring as a player in 2003.

HEAD BOY

Bulgaria's most-capped player is **Borislav Mikhailov**, born in Sofia on 12 February 1963, who sometimes wore a wig while playing and later had a hair transplant. After retiring in 2005, he was appointed president of the Bulgarian Football Union. His father Bisser was also a goalkeeper and Boris's own son, Nikolay, signed for Liverpool in 2007. All three have played for Levski Sofia.

CROATIA

Croatia's distinctive red-and-white chequered jersey has become one of the most recognized in world football – just ask England. Croatia broke English hearts not once but twice in the UEFA Euro 2008 qualifying tournament. First Croatia beat England 2-0 in Zagreb and then they shocked them 3-2 at Wembley to secure qualification. Croatia's subsequent march to the quarter-finals at UEFA Euro 2008 confirmed their status as a football power.

BILIC BEAT

Shortly after becoming Croatia manager, the guitar-playing **Slaven Bilic** and his rock band released a single, "Vatreno Ludilo" ("Fiery Madness"), which recalled the team's progress during the 1998 FIFA World Cup and went to No. 1 in the Croatian charts. Fashion-conscious Bilic also sports a diamond-studded earring.

TOP SCORERS

1	Davor Suker	45
2	Darijo Srna	18
=	Eduardo da Silva	18
4	Goran Vlaovic	15
5	Niko Kovac	14
6	Ivica Olic	13
7	Zvonimir Boban	12
=	Ivan Klasnic	12
9	Mladen Petric	11
10	Robert Prosinecki	10
=	Alen Boksic	10
=	Bosko Balaban	10
=	Niko Kranjcar	10

HAPPY OPENINGS

Few national teams have been as successful in their infancy as Croatia. Formerly part of Yugoslavia, in their very first senior competition as an independent country, UEFA Euro 96, Croatia reached the quarter-finals, then came third at the 1998 FIFA World Cup, where they became known as the "golden generation". Since becoming eligible to participate in 1993, Croatia qualified for every FIFA World Cup, except for 2010, and missed only one UEFA European Championship.

GOOD AND BAD

Croatia's joint highest-scoring victories were the 7-0 wins over Andorra in 2006 and Australia in 1998. Croatia's worst defeat in the modern era was a 5-1 loss to England in London, in September 2009, during the qualifiers for the FIFA World Cup.

SUPER SUKER

Striker Davor Suker won the Golden Boot for being top scorer at the FIFA World Cup in 1998, scoring six goals in seven games as Croatia finished third. His strikes included the opening goal in Croatia's 2-1 semi-final defeat to eventual champions France, and the winner in a 2-1 triumph over Holland in the third-place play-off. Suker, by far his country's leading scorer of all time, had hit three goals at the UEFA European Championship in 1996 – including an audacious long-distance lob over Denmark goalkeeper Peter Schmeichel.

DEER DARIJO

Darijo Srna is Croatia's second-top-scorer of all time despite playing many games as a right-back or wing-back. He has a tattoo on his calf in the shape of a deer, the Croatian word for which is "srna". He also has a tattoo on his chest – the name of his brother Igor, who has Down's syndrome and to whom he dedicates each goal he scores.

THE KIDNEYS ARE ALL RIGHT

Striker Ivan Klasnic returned to international duty with Croatia despite suffering kidney failure in early 2007. A first attempt at a transplant failed when his body rejected a kidney donated by his mother, but follow-up surgery – using a kidney from his father – proved successful. He recovered enough to play for Croatia again in March 2008 and represented his country in that summer's UEFA European Championship, scoring twice – including a winning goal against Poland.

FAMILY AFFAIR

Niko Kranjcar is the son of former Croatian coach Zlatko Kranjcar, but it wasn't always an easy affiliation. "Two days before he became Croatia's head coach everyone said I should get a call-up," Niko once said. "Then when Dad picked me for UEFA Euro 2004 suddenly it was because I was his son." No such problems for the **Kovac brothers, Robert and Niko**, both of whom are part of Croatian footballing folklore. The siblings were born in Berlin but are proud Croats. Both brothers have now hung up their boots at international level, though Robert went on for a year after Niko retired from Croatian duty.

TOP CAPS

1	Dario Simic	100
2	Robert Kovac	84
3	Niko Kovac	83
4	Robert Jarni	81
5	Stipe Pletikosa	79
6	Josip Simunic	76
7	Darijo Srna	73
8	Davor Suker	69
=	Ivica Olic	69
10	Aljosa Asanovic	62

EXPORT SPECIALISTS

Nearly all of Croatia's national team squad play for overseas clubs. Of the 23 selected against Romania in February 2009, only five of the squad were home-based.

DINAMO THE POWER

Dinamo Zagreb is the most popular club in the country, claiming between 33 and 36 per cent of the population supporting them. The club controversially changed its name to HAK-Gradanski in 1992 and another name change was made the following year to Croatia Zagreb. These were widely seen as political moves and were never accepted by the club's true fans, who kept calling it Dinamo in their chants and on banners.

CZECH REPUBLIC

The most successful of the former Eastern Bloc countries, as Czechoslovakia they finished as runners-up in the 1934 and 1962 FIFA World Cup™ competitions, and then shocked West Germany in a penalty shoot-out to claim the UEFA European Championship in 1976. Playing as the Czech Republic since 1994, they came agonizingly close to victory at UEFA Euro 96, and lost out in the semi-finals at UEFA Euro 2004. Recent times have been tougher, and although one of Europe's stronger nations the Czechs did not qualify for the 2010 FIFA World Cup™.

CHIP WITH EVERYTHING

One of the most famous penalties ever taken was Antonin Panenka's decisive spot-kick for Czechoslovakia against West Germany in the final of the 1976 UEFA European Championship, giving the Czechs victory in the shoot-out. Despite the tension, and the responsibility resting on him, Panenka cheekily chipped the ball into the middle of the goal – as goalkeeper Sepp Maier dived to the side. That style of spot-kick is now widely known as a "Panenka", and has been replicated by the likes of France's Zinedine Zidane, in the 2006 FIFA World Cup final.

senior debut against Belgium and struck ten goals in ten successive internationals. He scored six goals in each of the 2000, 2004 and 2008 UEFA European Championship qualifying campaigns. He began his career with Sparta Prague, who converted him from goalkeeper to goalscorer. Then, in Belgium, he was top scorer with Lokeren, before scoring 42 goals in two league title-winning campaigns with Anderlecht. Later, with Borussia Dortmund in Germany, he once went in goal after Jens Lehmann was sent off and kept a clean sheet – having scored in the first half.

POPULAR KAREL

UEFA Euro 96 gave the frizzy-haired **Karel Poborsky** the perfect platform to take his career to new heights as he helped the Czech Republic reach the final and then sealed a dream move to Manchester United. His lob against Portugal in the quarter-finals was rated as one of the finest opportunist goals in the tournament's history. His 118 appearances is a record for his country.

CECH CAP

Goalkeeper **Petr Cech** has worn a protective cap while playing ever since suffering a fractured skull during an English Premier League match in October 2006. He later added a chin protector after a facial operation following a training accident.

TOP CAPS

(Czechoslovakia and Czech Republic)

1	Karel Poborsky	118
2	Jan Koller	91
=	Pavel Nedved	91
4	Zdenek Nehoda	90
5	Pavel Kuka	87
6	Jiri Nemec	84
7	Vladimir Smicer	81
8	Marek Jankulovski	79
9	Milan Baros	78
=	Tomas Ujfalusi	78

PASSING THE PUC

The final of the 1934 FIFA World Cup was the first to go into extra-time, with Czechoslovakia ultimately losing 2-1 to hosts Italy despite taking a 76th-minute lead through Antonin Puc. Puc was Czechoslovakia/the Czech Republic's top international scorer from when he retired in 1938 until he was passed, first by Jan Koller, 67 years later, and, latterly, by Milan Baros.

WALK-OUT

Belgium's 1920 victory in the Olympic Games was overshadowed when Czechoslovakia walked off the pitch after half an hour in protest following what they saw as biased refereeing. Czechoslovakia are the only team to have been disqualified in the history of Olympic football.

THE CANNON COLLECTS

Pavel Nedved's election as European Footballer of the Year in 2003 ended an impatient wait for fans in the Czech Republic who had seen a string of outstanding players overlooked since Josef Masopust had been honoured back in 1962. Masopust, a midfield general, had scored the opening goal in the FIFA World Cup final that year before Brazil hit back to win 3-1 in the Chilean capital of Santiago. Years later, Masopust was remembered by Pele and nominated as one of his 125 greatest living footballers. At club level, Masopust won eight Czechoslovak league titles with Dukla Prague, the army club. He was also the winner, in 1962, of the first Czech Golden Ball as domestic footballer of the year. It was another day and in another age. Masopust was presented with his award before the kick-off of a European Cup quarter-final with Benfica – with a minimum of fuss. Years later, Masopust said: "Eusebio just shook hands with me, I put the trophy in my sports bag and went home on the tram."

GOING FOR A SONG

Army club Dukla Prague were immortalized by British rock band Half Man Half Biscuit with their song: "All I Want For Christmas is a Dukla Prague Away Kit".

UNLUCKY SEVEN?

Karel Bruckner steered the Czech Republic to the semi-finals of UEFA Euro 2004 in Portugal and retired after the 2008 finals. He had been in charge for seven years. His subsequent comeback as Austria coach was short-lived, however: he lasted only seven months.

TOP SCORERS

1	Jan Koller	55
2	Milan Baros	38
3	Antonin Puc	35
4	Zdenek Nehoda	31
5	Pavel Kuka	29
6	Oldrich Nejedly	28
=	Josef Silny	28
8	Vladimir Smicer	27
9	Adolf Scherer	22
=	Frantisek Svoboda	22

LATE WINNER

For years, **Oldrich Nejedly** was honoured "only" as joint top scorer at the 1934 FIFA World Cup, with four for runners-up Czechoslovakia. In 2006, 16 years after his death, FIFA revised the tally, awarding him a previously disputed goal, which brought his total to five goals, making him top scorer. He also netted twice at the 1938 tournament, in which the Czechs reached the quarter-finals.

DENMARK

Denmark have been playing international football since 1908, but it was not until the mid-1980s that they became competitive at the game's major tournaments. The country's crowning moment came in 1992 when, after being called up as a replacement just ten days before the start of the tournament, they walked away with the UEFA European Championship crown, shocking defending world champions West Germany 2-0 in the final. They may not have been able to repeat that success, but remain a significant player in the world game.

TOP CAPS

1	Peter Schmeichel	129
2	Jon Dahl Tomasson	112
3	Thomas Helveg	108
4	Michael Laudrup	104
5	Morten Olsen	102
6	Martin Jorgensen	99
=	Dennis Rommedahl	99
8	Thomas Sorensen	90
9	John Sivebaek	87
10	Jan Heintze	86

STRANDED ON 99

Midfielder **Martin Jorgensen** became the first Danish footballer to play at three different FIFA World Cups when he captained the side at the 2010 tournament, after also featuring in 1998 and 2002. His decision to retire from the national team after the South Africa event, and the team's failure to make the second round, meant he ended his Denmark career one cap short of a century. The 2010 finals also took winger Dennis Rommedahl to 99 international appearances.

LEADERSHIP STYLE

Morten Olsen captained Denmark at the 1986 FIFA World Cup. After he retired from playing in 1989, he switched to coaching, first at club level with Brondby, FC Koln and Ajax Amsterdam, before taking on the job as Danish national coach in 2000.

GOLDEN GLOVES

Peter Schmeichel was rated as the world's best goalkeeper in the early 1990s, winning many club honours with Manchester United and, famously, the UEFA European Championship with his native Denmark.

PENALTY PERSISTENCE

Jon Dahl Tomasson became the first Danish player in five attempts to miss a FIFA World Cup penalty, when his shot was saved by Japan's Eiji Kawashima in a 2010 first-round match. Tomasson scored from the rebound, but his team still lost 3-1 to be eliminated from the competition. The penalty was the 200th awarded in FIFA World Cup history, while the goal was Tomasson's 52nd for Denmark, equalling Poul Nielsen's national record. Tomasson's tally came in 112 appearances, while Nielsen's were scored in just 38 matches between 1910 and 1925.

TRENDSETTER

Nils Middelboe, who represented Denmark at three different Olympic Games, was the first ever goalscorer for the national football team. Then, in 1913, he moved abroad to play for Chelsea, becoming Denmark's first player to play in England and the first of many foreign players with the West London club.

CHRISTIAN YOUTH

Denmark fielded the youngest player at the 2010 FIFA World Cup: 18-year-old Ajax midfielder **Christian Eriksen**, who came on as substitute against Holland and Japan. He had made his international debut against Austria in March 2010, becoming Denmark's fourth-youngest international of all time.

EXPORT SPECIALISTS

Danish footballers have long been coveted by foreign clubs. The first player to sign a professional contract abroad was Carl "Skomar" (Shoemaker) Hansen, who was bought by Rangers in 1921. Later Danish players were mainly sold to clubs in England, Germany, Holland and Belgium. Allan Simonsen became internationally known while playing for Borussia Monchengladbach in the 1970s. He won the UEFA Cup in 1975 and 1979, and was voted 1977 European Footballer of the Year.

TOP SCORERS

1	Poul Nielsen	52
=	Jon Dahl Tomasson	52
3	Pauli Jorgensen	44
4	Ole Madsen	42
5	Preben Elkjaer-Larsen	38
6	Michael Laudrup	37
7	Henning Enoksen	29
8	Michael Rohde	22
=	Ebbe Sand	22
10	Brian Laudrup	21
=	Flemming Povlsen	21
=	Allan Simonsen	21

THE UNEXPECTED IN 1992

Few football fans are ever likely to forget June 1992, Denmark's finest hour, when their team managed to win the UEFA European Championship. Denmark had not qualified for the final round in Sweden, but ten days before the opening match UEFA asked them to take the place of Yugoslavia, who were thrown out of the tournament in the wake of international sanctions over the Balkan War. The Danes had come second in their qualifying group, behind Yugoslavia, and they took over their spot at the tournament proper. Expectations were minimal, but then the inconceivable happened. Relying heavily on goalkeeper Peter Schmeichel, his defence, and the creative spark of Brian Laudrup, Denmark crafted one of the biggest shocks in modern football history by winning the tournament, culminating in a 2-0 victory over world champions Germany. Their victory was all the more remarkable in that Brian's brother Michael, their finest player, quit during the qualifying competition after falling out with coach Richard Moller Nielsen. He revived his international career in 1993, only for Denmark to fail to qualify for the subsequent FIFA World Cup in the United States.

QUICK DRAW

Ebbe Sand scored the fastest FIFA World Cup goal ever scored by a substitute, when he netted a mere 16 seconds after coming on to the pitch in Denmark's clash against Nigeria at the 1998 FIFA World Cup.

SLICED AND CURED

Denmark's 6-1 defeat of Uruguay in the 1986 FIFA World Cup finals first-round group stage in Neza, Mexico, ranks among the country's greatest victories. Sadly, Denmark's adventure was ended by Spain in the last 16.

BROTHERS IN ARMS

Brian (left) and Michael Laudrup are among the most successful footballing brothers of modern times. As well as making a combined 186 international appearances, they played across Europe at club level. Michael (104 caps, 37 goals) played in Italy with Lazio and Juventus and in Spain with Barcelona and Real Madrid. Brian (82 caps, 21 goals) starred in Germany with Bayer Uerdingen and Bayern Munich, Italy with Fiorentina and Milan, Scotland for Rangers and England for Chelsea.

GREECE

There is no argument about Greece's proudest footballing moment – their shock triumph at the 2004 UEFA European Championship, one of the game's greatest international upsets. Guided by their long-serving German coach Otto Rehhagel, it was only the Greeks' second appearance at a UEFA Euro finals – while the 2010 tournament in South Africa marked just their second qualification for a FIFA World Cup™.

SIMPLY THEO BEST

Theodoros "Theo" Zagorakis – born near Kavala on 27 October 1971 – was captain of Greece when they won the UEFA European Championship in 2004 and the defensive midfielder was also given the prize for the tournament's best player. He is the most-capped Greek footballer of all time, with 120 caps. But it was not until his 101st international appearance – 10 years and five months after his Greek debut – that he scored his first goal for his country, in a FIFA World Cup qualifier against Denmark, in February 2005. He retired from international football after making a 15-minute cameo appearance against Spain in August 2007.

TOP SCORERS

1	Nikos Anastopoulos	29
2	Angelos Charisteas	24
3	Dimitris Saravakos	22
4	Mimis Papaioannou	21
5	Theofanis Gekas	20
6	Nikos Machlas	18
7	Demis Nikolaidis	17
8	Panagiotis Tsalouchidis	16
9	Giorgos Sideris	14
10	Nikos Liberopoulos	13

PARTY CRASHERS

Shock UEFA Euro 2004 winners Greece became the first team to beat both the holders and the hosts on the way to winning either a UEFA European Championship or FIFA World Cup. In fact, they beat hosts Portugal twice – in both the tournament's opening game and the final, with a quarter-final victory over defending champions France in between.

ALL WHITE NOW

The surprise triumph at UEFA Euro 2004 brought a major change to Greek international football – they switched the national team's kit from blue to white. The former colours had been used since the Hellenic Football Federation was formed in 1926 but the success of Otto Rehhagel's men in their second kit prompted a permanent change of colours.

HONESTY PAYS

Greece's 500th goal in international football was scored by Demis Nikolaidis at Manchester's Old Trafford in October 2001, giving them an unexpected 2–1 lead away to England in a final 2002 FIFA World Cup qualifier – although David Beckham would go on to equalize with a famous last-minute free-kick. In March the following year, striker Nikolaidis was formally acclaimed by the International Committee for Fair Play for admitting to the referee that he handled the ball when scoring for AEK Athens in the final of the Greek Cup. His team still won the match, and the trophy.

TOP CAPS

1	Theodoros Zagorakis	120
2	Angelos Basinas	100
3	Stratos Apostolakis	96
=	Giorgios Karagounis	96
4	Antonios Nikopolodis	90
6	Angelos Charisteas	85
7	Dimitris Saravakos	78
8	Stelios Giannakopoulos	77
=	Tasos Mitropoulos	77
10	Panagiotis Tsalouchidis	76

DIMI MORE

Striker **Dimitrios Salpingidis** not only struck the only goal of Greece's 2010 FIFA World Cup qualifying play-off against Ukraine, sealing their place in South Africa. He also then became the first Greek ever to score at a FIFA World Cup, with a 44th-minute deflected strike in the 2-1 Group B triumph over Nigeria.

MIGHTY MOUSTACHE

Nikos Anastopoulos is the Greek national team's all-time leading scorer, with 29 goals from 74 international appearances. One of those strikes was Greece's only goal of their first major tournament, the 1980 UEFA European Championship – a header against defending champions Czechoslovakia. Anastopoulos was known as "Moustakias", meaning "The Mustachio'd One".

FAMILIAR FOES

Greece's two appearances at a FIFA World Cup have both involved first-round games against Argentina and Nigeria. Their other opponents were Bulgaria, in 1994, and South Korea 16 years later. Argentina won both matches against Greece, 4-0 and 2-0 respectively, but while Nigeria won 2-0 in 1994 the Greeks gained some revenge with a 2-1 triumph in 2010.

BACK DOWN WITH A BUMP

Three countries have failed to qualify for the FIFA World Cup two years after winning the UEFA European Championship – Czechoslovakia (who took the title in 1976), Denmark (1992) and Greece (2004). Otto Rehhagel's Greece team got their 2006 FIFA World Cup qualification campaign off to the worst possible start, losing 2–1 to minnows Albania just two months after being crowned shock European champions. His side had also lost their first two matches of qualifying for UEFA Euro 2004, but reached the tournament after winning their final six.

SECONDS OUT

Greece, in 2008, were the first defending UEFA European Championship holders to fail to win a single point at the following tournament, losing all three Group D matches at UEFA Euro 2008 – though they did take the lead, with their only goal of the tournament, in a 2-1 defeat to eventual champions Spain.

SIXTEEN–YEAR WAIT

After failing to find the net during all three games at the 1994 FIFA World Cup finals – the only European country to exit that World Cup without scoring – Greece finally opened their account when they next qualified, in 2010. A 2-1 win over Nigeria gave them their first goals – and first points. But despite that victory, thanks to **Vasileios Torosidis**'s decisive goal, defeats to South Korea and Argentina meant Otto Rehhagel's men failed to make the second round.

KING OTTO

German coach **Otto Rehhagel** became the first foreigner to be voted "Greek of the Year" in 2004, after leading the country to glory at that year's UEFA European Championship. He was also offered honorary Greek citizenship. His nine years in charge after being appointed in 2001 made him Greece's longest-serving international manager. The UEFA Euro 2004 triumph was the first time a country coached by a foreigner had triumphed at either the UEFA European Championship or FIFA World Cup. Rehhagel was aged 65 at UEFA Euro 2004, making him the oldest coach to win the UEFA European Championship – though that record was taken off him four years later, when 69-year-old Luis Aragones lifted the trophy with Spain.

HUNGARY

For a period from the 1950s, Hungary boasted the most fearsome national team in the world. Club giants such as Honved and Ferencvaros... ...World Cup... ...semi-finals... ...and the crown... ...loss to West Germany in the final and Hungary's dominating fortunes on the world stage have never been the same again.

TOP SCORERS

1	Ferenc Puskas	84
2	Sandor Kocsis	75
3	Imre Schlosser-Lakatos	59
4	Lajos Tichy	51
5	Gyorgy Sarosi	42
6	Nandor Hidegkuti	39
7	Ferenc Bene	36
8	Gyula Zsengeller	32
=	Tibor Nyilasi	32
10	Florian Albert	31

TOP CAPS

1	Jozsef Bozsik	101
2	Laszlo Fazekas	92
3	Gyula Grosics	86
4	Ferenc Puskas	85
5	Imre Garaba	82
6	Sandor Matrai	81
7	Ferenc Sipos	77
8	Laszlo Balint	76
=	Ferenc Bene	76
=	Mate Fenyvesi	76

GOING FOREIGN

Englishman Jimmy Hogan was a hero in Hungary for coaching the virtues of pure football in the 1920s. He was even the Hungarian Federation's guest of honour following the 1953 victory over England. The value of new ideas from abroad was still being maintained into the new century under Erwin Koeman, one of Holland's UEFA European champions in 1988.

TURNING POINT

The turning point in Hungary's football history came with the futile 1956 revolt against Communist rule, which saw captain Ferenc Puskas and many of his national team-mates flee the country. He was only allowed to return from his Spanish self-exile to visit his family long after his retirement from playing.

LOWEST OF THE LOW

When things in Hungary are bad, they are said to be "beka segge alatt" ("under the belly of a frog"). Football was held to have reached that point when the national team, in the 1980s, began a long sad sequence of failing to qualify for all the major tournament finals.

GOLDEN HEAD

Sandor Kocsis, top scorer in the 1954 FIFA World Cup finals with 11 goals, was so good in the air he was known as "The Man with the Golden Head". In 68 internationals he scored an incredible 75 goals, including a record seven hat-tricks. His tally included two decisive extra-time goals in the 1954 FIFA World Cup semi-final against Uruguay, when Hungary had appeared to be on the brink of defeat.

GALLOPING MAJOR

Ferenc Puskas was one of the greatest footballers of all time, scoring a remarkable 84 goals in 85 international matches for Hungary and 514 goals in 529 matches in the Hungarian and Spanish leagues. Possessing the most lethal left-foot shot in the history of football, he was known as the "Galloping Major" – by virtue of his playing for the army team Honved before joining Real Madrid and going on to play for Spain. During the 1950s he was top scorer and captain of the legendary "Mighty Magyars" (the nickname given to the Hungarian national team), as well as of the army club Honved.

HUNGARY FOR IT

Hungary's 6-3 win over England at Wembley in 1953 remains one of the most significant international results of all time. Hungary became the first team from outside the British Isles to beat England at home, a record that had stood since 1901. The Hungarians had been undefeated for three years and had won the Olympic tournament the year before, while England were the so-called "inventors" of football. The British press dubbed it "The Match of the Century". In the event, the match revolutionized the game in England, Hungary's unequivocal victory exposing the naivete of English football tactics. England captain Billy Wright later summed up the humiliation by saying: "We completely underestimated the advances that Hungary had made, and not only tactically. When we walked out at Wembley ... I looked down and noticed that the Hungarians had on these strange, lightweight boots, cut away like slippers under the ankle bone. I turned to big Stan Mortensen and said: 'We should be all right here, Stan, they haven't got the proper kit.'"

EUROPEAN PIONEERS

While Argentina's match against Uruguay in July 1902 was the first international outside the British Isles, Hungary's 5-0 defeat to Austria in Vienna three months later was Europe's first between two non-UK sides. Ten of Hungary's first 16 internationals were against Austria, with the Hungarians winning four, drawing one and losing five. In total, Hungary have won 66, drawn 30 and lost 40 against their Austrian neighbours.

GLORIOUS FAILURE

Hungary were runaway favourites to win the 1954 FIFA World Cup in Switzerland. They arrived for the finals having been unbeaten for four years. In the first round they thrashed West Germany 8-3, despite finishing with ten men after skipper Ferenc Puskas injured an ankle.

GOODISON LESSON

In the 1966 FIFA World Cup, Hungary gave Brazil a footballing lesson at Goodison Park, running out 3-1 winners before their progress was stopped by the Soviet Union in the quarter-finals. It was Brazil's first defeat in the FIFA World Cup since the 1954 quarter-finals, when they had lost 4-2 to ... Hungary.

YEARS OF PLENTY

Hungary's dazzling line-up of the early 1950s was known as the "Aranycsapat" – or "Golden Team". They set a record for international matches unbeaten, going 31 consecutive games without defeat between May 1950 and their July 1954 FIFA World Cup final loss to West Germany – a run that included clinching Olympic gold at Helsinki in Finland in 1952. That 31-match tally has been overtaken since only by Brazil and Spain. Hungary in the 1950s also set a record for most consecutive games scoring at least one goal – 73 matches – while their average of 5.4 goals per game at the 1954 FIFA World Cup remains an all-time high for the tournament.

HIGH FLYERS

1938 – Hungary reach the FIFA World Cup final in France, losing 4-2 to Italy.

1953 – Hungary become the first team from outside the British Isles to beat England at home, winning 6-3 at Wembley.

1954 – Hungary reach the FIFA World Cup final in Switzerland and, despite being odds-on favourites, lose 3-2 to West Germany.

1964 – Hungary reach the semi-finals of UEFA European Championship in Spain.

1965 – Ferencvaros become Hungary's first, and to date only, European club winner, lifting the Inter-Cities Fairs (UEFA) Cup.

1972 – Hungary reach the semi-finals of UEFA European Championships in Belgium, before losing 1-0 to the Soviet Union.

1986 – The last time Hungary qualify for the FIFA World Cup finals – in Mexico.

Tamas Hajnal
Centre Midfield,
Vice Captain,
34 Caps, 4 Goals

NORTHERN IRELAND

Northern Ireland have played as a separate country since 1921 (before that there had been an all-Ireland side). They have qualified for the FIFA World Cup™ finals on three occasions: in 1958 (when they became the smallest country to reach the quarter-final stage), 1982 (when they reached the second round) and 1986.

GEORGE BEST

One of the greatest players never to grace a FIFA World Cup, **George Best** (capped 37 times by Northern Ireland) nevertheless won domestic and European honours with Manchester United – including both a European Champions Cup medal and the European Footballer of the Year award in 1968. He also played in the United States, Hong Kong and Australia before his "final" retirement in 1984.

GIANT JENNINGS

Pat Jennings's record 119 appearances for Northern Ireland also stood at one stage as an international record. The former Tottenham Hotspur and Arsenal goalkeeper made his international debut – aged just 18 – against Wales on 15 April 1964, and played his final game in the 1986 FIFA World Cup, against Brazil, on his 41st birthday.

AWARD–WINNING FANS

The Amalgamation of Northern Ireland Football Supporters' Clubs was awarded the 2006 Brussels International Supporters' Award for its work with the Irish Football Association to tackle sectarianism in football.

OH DANNY BOY

Northern Ireland's captain at the 1958 FIFA World Cup was Tottenham Hotspur's cerebral **Danny Blanchflower** – the first twentieth-century captain of an English club to win both the league and FA Cup in the same season, in 1960–61. When asked the secret of his national team's success in 1958, he offered the explanation: "Our tactic is to equalize before the others have scored." More famously, he offered the philosophy: "The great fallacy is that the game is first and foremost about winning. It's nothing of the kind. The game is about glory. It's about doing things in style, with a flourish, about going out and beating the other lot, not waiting for them to die of boredom."

AGE OLD QUESTION

Sam Johnston is the youngest player to have played for any Ireland national team. He was 15 years and 154 days old when he turned out for the old combined team (before the founding of the Irish Free State) in 1882. He also scored in his second game, making him Ireland's youngest-ever goalscorer, too.

"PETER THE GREAT"

Former Manchester City and Derby County striker **Peter Doherty**, one of the most expensive players of his era, won the English league and FA Cup as a player, and earned 19 caps for Northern Ireland in a career interrupted by World War Two. His late goal to earn a 2-2 draw in 1947 ensured Northern Ireland avoided defeat against England for the first time. As manager, he led Northern Ireland to the quarter-finals of the 1958 FIFA World Cup – Northern Ireland remain the smallest country ever to reach that stage of the competition. They were defeated 4-0 by France, who went on to finish third.

TOP SCORERS

1	David Healy	35
2	Colin Clarke	13
=	Billy Gillespie	13
4	Gerry Armstrong	12
=	Joe Bambrick	12
=	Iain Dowie	12
=	Jimmy Quinn	12
8	Billy Bingham	10
=	Johnny Crossan	10
=	Jimmy McIlroy	10
=	Peter McParland	10

TOP CAPS

1	Pat Jennings	119
2	Mal Donaghy	91
3	Sammy McIlroy	88
4	Keith Gillespie	86
5	Maik Taylor	83
6	David Healy	80
7	Jimmy Nicholl	73
8	Aaron Hughes	71
=	Michael Hughes	71
10	David McCreery	67

HERO HEALY

Northern Ireland's record goalscorer **David Healy** has scored more than double the amount of international goals than the next highest player on the list. He scored two goals on his debut against Luxembourg on 23 February 2000, and scored all three as Northern Ireland stunned Spain 3-2 in a qualifier for UEFA Euro 2008 on 6 September 2006.

YOUNG GUN

Norman Whiteside became the then-youngest player at a FIFA World Cup finals (beating Pele's record) when he represented Northern Ireland in Spain in 1982 aged 17 years and 41 days. He went on to win 38 caps, scoring nine goals – before injury forced his retirement aged just 26.

HOME OWNERSHIP

Northern Ireland remain the reigning holders of the British Home Championship, a title contested annually by England, Scotland, Wales and Northern Ireland from 1883–84 to 1983–84. The last tournament ended with all four teams level on four points, after each winning once, drawing once and losing once – but Billy Bingham's Northern Ireland were the only side with a positive goal difference.

BINGHAM'S DOUBLE

Billy Bingham was a key player on the right wing in Northern Ireland's 1958 FIFA World Cup run, and managed the national side to FIFA World Cup qualification in 1982 and 1986 – the only time the country has made it to consecutive tournaments.

NORWAY

Although they played their ~~first~~ [match] against ~~Sweden, in 1908 and qualified~~ for ~~the~~ ~~World Cup™, it would take~~ ~~and the introduction of~~ ~~football, before Norway~~ ~~major international~~ ~~In such competitions, he~~ ~~they have never progressed beyond~~ ~~the second round, but Norway~~ ~~retains the distinction of~~ ~~being the only nation in~~ ~~history never to have~~ ~~lost to Brazil.~~

BRAZIL RESISTANCE

Norway are the only nation never to have lost – so far – to Samba kings Brazil, enjoying a record of two victories and two draws. Their most memorable match against Brazil came in the first round of the 1998 FIFA World Cup, when Norway triumphed 2-1 against a side who would go on to reach that year's final. Norway actually went a goal down, but came back to win thanks to strikes in the last seven minutes from **Tore Andre Flo** and Kjetil Rekdal.

WIN OF THE YEAR

Norway's defeat of Germany in February 2009 was their first since the 1936 Olympic success. All the more remarkable was that Germany had only recently finished as UEFA Euro 2008 runners-up, while Norway had not won a competitive game for a year. The historic winner was scored in the 63rd minute by Christian Grindheim from a low cross from **Morten Gamst Pedersen**.

DRILLO'S PAD

Known by the nickname "Drillo", Egil Olsen was renowned for knowing the precise height of every significant mountain on earth. An aggressive anti-smoker, he never drove anywhere while manager at Wimbledon, always walking to the training ground, often in his boots.

YOUR BOYS TOOK A HELL OF A BEATING

Bjorge Lillelien's famous commentary after Norway beat England 2-1 in a qualifier for the 1982 FIFA World Cup remains one of the iconic moments of European football. A commentator from 1957 until just before his death from cancer in 1987, he concentrated on winter sports and football. Roughly translated, it sounded as follows: "Lord Nelson, Lord Beaverbrook, Sir Winston Churchill, Sir Anthony Eden, Clement Attlee, Henry Cooper, Lady Diana, Maggie Thatcher, can you hear me? Your boys took a hell of a beating." Although the commentary was for Norwegian radio, it soon made its way to an English audience and has achieved cliché status. In 2002, Lillelien's words were designated the greatest piece of sports commentary ever by the *Observer* newspaper's sports supplement. Such is its place in British sporting culture, parodies of the commentary have been written to celebrate a vast array of domestic sporting victories.

BIG JOHN

Centre-forward **John Carew** has an un-Norwegian-sounding name because he is half-Gambian. The number seven figures prominently in his career. He has had seven clubs (including loan deals) and was the seventh Aston Villa player to score a league hat-trick – in a 4-1 win over Newcastle United in 2007–08. He was also Norway's first black player.

TOP CAPS

1	Thorbjorn Svenssen	104
2	Henning Berg	100
3	Erik Thorstvedt	97
4	Oyvind Leonhardsen	86
=	John Arne Riise	86
6	Kjetil Rekdal	83
7	John Carew	82
8	Erik Mykland	78
9	Svein Grondalen	77
=	Steffen Iversen	77

TOP SCORERS

1	Jorgen Juve	33
2	Einar Gundersen	26
3	Harald Hennum	25
4	Tore Andre Flo	23
=	Ole Gunnar Solskjaer	23
5	John Carew	22
=	Gunnar Thoresen	22
7	Steffen Iversen	21
8	Jan Age Fjortoft	20
9	Odd Iversen	19
=	Oyvind Leonhardsen	19
=	Olav Nilsen	19

THE MIGHTY THOR

Norway's 4-0 defeat to Nordic neighbours Denmark in their own capital Oslo, in September 1961, can't have been a very happy occasion for home fans – but it did mark a century of international appearances for Norwegian centre-back Thorbjorn Svenssen. He became only the second footballer to play 100 games for his country, following in the footsteps of England's Billy Wright, who reached the landmark just two years earlier.

BOOT CAMPER

Egil Olsen, one of Europe's most eccentric coaches, was signed up for a surprise second spell as national manager when Norway put their faith in the direct-football specialist along the road towards the 2010 FIFA World Cup finals in South Africa – 15 years after he had led the unfancied Scandinavians to the 1994 finals. That had been Norway's first finals appearance since 1938 and they followed it up by beating Brazil in the first round in France in 1998, making a hero out of the man in Wellington boots who guided his country to an impressive No. 2 in FIFA's official rankings. Before answering his country's call for a second stint as manager, Olsen's last job had been as manager of Iraq but he left after only three months in charge. Remarkably, in his first match back at the helm for Norway, he masterminded a 1-0 win away to Germany with his route-one tactics. But life was not quite as happy for Olsen during his time at Wimbledon in the 1999–2000 Premier League season. The Norwegian, a firm believer in sports science, imposed a zonal marking system, which he was convinced would work. Critics held it responsible for Wimbledon's collapse in the second half of the season.

ERIK THE VIKING

Erik Thorstvedt's career at Tottenham Hotspur could not have got off to a worse possible start. Less than five minutes into his debut against Nottingham Forest, he dropped the ball to gift Nigel Clough the opening goal. Despite the blunder, Thorstvedt became hugely popular and earned himself the nickname "Erik the Viking".

1936 AND ALL THAT

Norway's victory over Germany in the 1936 Olympic Games in Berlin, three years after Adolf Hitler came to power, was a political as well as a sporting milestone. The crowd, Hitler among its number, also included his henchmen Goebbels, Goering and Hess. Germany lost 2-0 and Hitler, who had never seen an international match before, left early in a huff.

POLAND

The history of Polish football is extremely tumultuous. The national team have been at the top of world football and at the bottom. They had their golden era from the 1970s to the early 1980s and then had to wait until 2006 to return to the World Cup finals. They also reached the European Championship for the first time in 2008 and will co-host the tournament (with Ukraine) in 2012.

COOL KEEPER

What is it with Polish goalkeepers? The country's outfield players may not be household names worldwide, but Jerzy Dudek (Liverpool), Artur Boruc (Celtic), **Lukasz Fabianski** (Arsenal) and Tomasz Kuszczak (Manchester United) have all played significant roles at four of Britain's most successful clubs. Lukasz Zaluska, heading from Dundee United to Celtic, may prove the next in line.

SUPER ERNEST

Ernest Wilimowski wrote his name into FIFA World Cup history in 1938 when he scored four goals but still finished on the losing side. Poland went down 6-5 after extra-time to Brazil in a first-round tie in Strasbourg.

TOP CAPS

1	Grzegorz Lato	100
2	Kazimierz Deyna	97
3	Jacek Krzynowek	96
=	Jacek Bak	96
5	Michal Zewlakow	94
6	Wladyslaw Zmuda	91
7	Antoni Szymanowski	82
8	Zbigniew Boniek	80
9	Wlodzimierz Lubanski	75
10	Tomasz Waldoch	74

STAR SIGN LEO

Leo Beenhakker became the first foreigner to coach Poland when he took charge in July 2006. In a career spanning more than 30 years, Beenhakker has coached Holland and Saudi Arabia, as well as Trinidad and Tobago. He also won three Spanish league titles with Real Madrid from 1987–89 and two Dutch league titles with Ajax in 1980 and 1990. The silver-haired Dutchman underlined his workaholic reputation in the spring of 2009 by taking up an extra role as consultant back home with Feyenoord.

POLE DANCING

Three is Poland's lucky football number. The years 1974 and 1982 stand out in the annals of the country's sport because, on both occasions, the Poles came third at the FIFA World Cup. In 1974, with their lightning speed and team chemistry, they were almost unstoppable after upsetting England in qualifying. Memorably, when they played hosts West Germany, the pitch was half-flooded and the Poles, who needed a win to reach the final, wanted the game postponed. Instead, in miserably wet conditions, Gerd Muller scored a late German winner. In 1982, in Spain, only Grzegorz Lato, Andrzej Szarmach, Marek Kusto and Wladyslaw Zmuda remained from the 1974 squad. But the exciting mix of veterans and youngsters were no match for Italy in the semi-finals, losing 2-0.

BLACK HISTORY

Poland has long been rocked by a string of corruption scandals involving referees, players, club officials and federation members. The crisis was exacerbated by the appalling condition of many stadiums, financial problems and hooliganism. In 2001 the government intervened and Poland were very nearly banned from international competition by FIFA, which forbids any form of governmental intervention.

TOP SCORERS

1	Wlodzimierz Lubanski	48
2	Grzegorz Lato	45
3	Kazimierz Deyna	41
4	Ernest Pol	39
5	Andrzej Szarmach	32
6	Gerard Cieslik	27
7	Zbigniew Boniek	24
8	Ernest Wilimowski	21
9	Dariusz Dziekanowski	20
10	Roman Kosecki	19
=	Eusebiusz Smolarek	19

PUNCTUALITY PUNISHMENT

Kazimierz Gorski was the coach – once-capped as a player – who led Poland to third place at the 1974 FIFA World Cup, having won gold at the Olympics in Munich, Germany, two years earlier. While winning a reputation for closeness with his players, Gorski could also be ruthless – key player Adam Musial was dropped from the team for a second-round game against Sweden at the 1974 tournament as punishment for turning up 20 minutes late to training. Poland still won the game, 1-0.

O COME, O COME, EMMANUEL

Poland were the first European country to qualify for the 2002 FIFA World Cup in South Korea and Japan, largely thanks to the eight goals scored by striker **Emmanuel Olisadebe** – setting a Polish record for a FIFA World Cup qualifying campaign. Nigerian-born Olisadebe had been awarded Polish citizenship during a successful four-year stint at Polonia Warsaw. He was actually given special permission by the president of Poland to become a citizen a year before completing the official qualification period.

FIVE ASIDE

Poland had five different goalscorers when they beat Peru 5-1 at the 1982 FIFA World Cup: **Wlodzimierz Smolarek**, Grzegorz Lato, Zbigniew Boniek, Andrzej Buncol and Wlodzimierz Ciolek. The feat was not repeated until Phillip Cocu, Marc Overmars, Dennis Bergkamp, Pierre van Hooijdonk and Ronald de Boer gave Holland a 5-0 victory over South Korea at the 1998 FIFA World Cup.

BONIEK

Zbigniew Boniek, arguably the best player Poland has ever produced, earned a place among football's legends for his role in the country's progress to third place at the 1982 FIFA World Cup. However, his absence from the tournament's semi-final will go down as one of the great "what ifs" of the competition. Robbed of their star forward through suspension, could Poland have upset both Italy and the odds and reached the final? Instead they lost 2-0.

LATO'S MISSION

Grzegorz Lato, one of Poland's finest-ever players, became president of the country's football federation in 2008, promising to clean up the sport as Poland gears up to co-host the 2012 UEFA European Championships with Ukraine. "I am determined to change the image of Polish football, to make it transparent and pure," said Lato, a legend in the 1970s and '80s and the top scorer at the 1974 FIFA World Cup (with seven goals).

PORTUGAL

Portugal's first experience of international competition almost ended in triumph. Inspired by Eusebio, they marched through to the semi-finals of the 1966 FIFA World Cup™, only to lose to eventual champions England. A standout performance in the 1984 UEFA European Championship apart, more than 30 years would pass before Portugal enjoyed such giddy heights again. A "golden" generation of players arrived on the scene and since the turn of the century Portugal have become a consistent force on the world football stage.

⚽ TOP CAPS

1	LUIS Filipe Madeira FIGO	127
2	FERNANDO Manuel Silva COUTO	110
3	RUI Manuel Cesar COSTA	94
4	Pedro Miguel Resendes "PAULETA"	88
5	SIMAO Pedro Fonseca SABROSA	85
6	JOAO Manuel VIEIRA PINTO	81
7	VITOR Manuel Martins BAIA	80
8	RICARDO Alexandre Martins PEREIRA	79
9	Nuno Miguel Soares "NUNO GOMES"	77
10	CRISTIANO RONALDO dos Santos Aveiro	76

⚽ GOODISON GLORY

At the 1966 FIFA World Cup Portugal beat North Korea 5-3 in an incredible quarter-final at Everton's Goodison Park. The sensational Eusebio spurred an amazing comeback after the Koreans had gone 3-0 ahead in the first 25 minutes. He scored four goals to take Portugal to the semi-finals in their first-ever FIFA World Cup appearance. Despite the tears that flowed after defeat to eventual winners England, Portugal rallied to claim third place with a **2-1 victory over the Soviet Union**.

⚽ TOP SCORERS

1	Pedro Miguel Resendes "PAULETA"	47
2	EUSEBIO da Silva Ferreira	41
3	LUIS Filipe Madeira FIGO	32
4	Nuno Miguel Soares "NUNO GOMES"	29
5	RUI Manuel Cesar COSTA	26
6	JOAO Manuel VIEIRA PINTO	23
=	CRISTIANO RONALDO dos Santos Aveiro	23
8	Tamagnini Baptista "NENE"	22
=	SIMAO Pedro Fonseca SABROSA	22
10	Rui Manuel Trinidade JORDAO	15
=	Fernando Baptista de Seixas PEYROTEO de Vasconcelo	15

⚽ CLOUD NINE

Scoring nine goals in one match against Leca, eight goals in one match against Boavista, six goals in a game three times, five goals in a game 12 times and four goals in a game 17 times, Fernando Baptista Peyroteo is one of the most prolific goalscorers in world football history. He scored an astonishing 330 goals in 197 Portuguese league games (1.68 goals a game) between 1937 and 1949, and 15 goals in just 20 games for the national side.

THE BLACK PANTHER

Born in Mozambique, **Eusebio** da Silva Ferreira was named Portugal's "Golden Player" to mark UEFA's 50th anniversary in 2004. Signed by Benfica in 1960 at the age of 18, he scored a hat-trick in only his second game – against Santos in a friendly tournament in Paris – outshining the opponents' young star, Pele. He helped Benfica win the second of their European Cups in 1962, was named European Footballer of the Year in 1965, and led Portugal to third place in the 1966 FIFA World Cup, finishing the tournament as top scorer with nine goals. A phenomenal striker, Eusebio scored 320 goals in 313 appearances in the Portuguese league, won the first European Golden Boot in 1968 (and earned a second in 1973). His 41 goals for Portugal – in 64 matches – has been bettered only by Pauleta, who scored 47, but in 24 more appearances.

AT SIXES AND SEVENS

Six different players were on the scoresheet in Portugal's 7-0 victory over North Korea at the 2010 FIFA World Cup: Raul Meireles, Simao, Hugo Almeida, Tiago (who scored twice), Liedson and captain Cristiano Ronaldo. That tally has only been outdone by the seven who shared Yugoslavia's nine goals without reply against Zaire at the 1974 FIFA World Cup. The goals by Simao and **Cristiano Ronaldo** meant they emulated Pauleta in scoring for Portugal at two separate FIFA World Cups.

CRISTIANO RONALDO

Cristiano Ronaldo dos Santos Aveiro got his second name because his father was a great fan of US President Ronald Reagan. Despite growing up a Benfica fan, Ronaldo began his career with local rivals Sporting before moving to Manchester United in 2003. He enjoyed a fantastic season in 2008, winning the Premier League, the Champions League, the Golden Boot in the Premier League and Europe, and capping it all by becoming the second Portuguese player (after Luis Figo) to win the FIFA World Player of the Year award. He became the most expensive footballer ever when Real Madrid paid £80 million to sign him from Manchester United in 2009.

THE FAMOUS FIVE

Eusebio, Mario Coluna, Jose Augusto, Antonio Simoes, and Jose Torres were the "Fabulous Five" in Benfica's 1960s Dream Team, who made up the spine of the Portuguese national side at the 1966 FIFA World Cup. Coluna (the "Sacred Monster"), scored the vital third goal in the 1961 European Cup final and captained the national side in 1966. Jose Augusto, who scored two goals in the opening game against Hungary, went on to manage the national side and later the Portuguese women's team. Antonio Simoes (the "Giant Gnome" – just 1.58 metres/5ft 3in tall) made his debut for Portugal and Benfica in 1962, aged just 18. Jose Torres – the only one of the five not to win the European Cup (though he played in the defeats in both 1963 and 1968) – scored the winner against Russia in the 1966 third-place match, and went on to manage the national side to their next appearance at the FIFA World Cup finals in 1986.

KOREA OPPORTUNITIES

Portugal scored seven goals in four matches at the 2010 FIFA World Cup, all against North Korea in a 7-0 Group G trouncing. It was the joint third-biggest winning margin in a FIFA World Cup finals. Added to the 5-3 triumph over them in a 1966 quarter-final, it means almost one-third of Portugal's 39 FIFA World Cup goals have been scored against North Korea.

CALLING ON CARLOS

The 2010 FIFA World Cup in South Africa was the first time **Carlos Queiroz** had failed to lead a Portugal side into at least the semi-finals of a FIFA competition. He had previously been in charge of Portugal's "Golden Generation" sides who won the FIFA World Under-20 Cup in 1989 and 1991, and also the team finishing third at the 1989 FIFA World Under-17 Cup. But in his second spell as coach of the Portugal senior team, he could only reach the second round of the 2010 FIFA World Cup, keeping three clean sheets out of three in the first round but then losing 1-0 to Spain.

REP. OF IRELAND

It took a combination of astute management and endless searching through ancestral records before the Republic of Ireland finally qualified for the finals of a major tournament, at the 20th time of asking. But ever since Jack Charlton took the team to UEFA Euro 88, Ireland have remained one of Europe's most dangerous opponents.

KEANE CARRY-ON

Roy Keane stormed out of Ireland's preparation for the 2002 FIFA World Cup in Japan and Korea, heading home before the tournament had even started. Keane's career with Ireland began against Chile on 22 May 1991. He played in all four Ireland's matches at the 1994 FIFA World Cup in the United States, including the shock 1-0 defeat of Italy. Originally appointed captain by Mick McCarthy, Keane returned to the Irish set-up after McCarthy resigned – but announced his international retirement after Ireland failed to qualify for the 2006 FIFA World Cup. His final game was a 1-0 defeat to France on 7 September 2005.

STEVE STAUNTON

Ireland's then record cap holder was made captain for the 2002 FIFA World Cup after Roy Keane's sensational walkout. **Steve Staunton** went on to manage Ireland from 2006–07 but was replaced after he failed to guide the team to the finals of the 2008 UEFA European Championships. Staunton's record for Irish international appearances has since been overtaken by two players he selected often when he was coach: goalkeeper Shay Given and versatile left-back/midfielder **Kevin Kilbane**.

CROKE PARK

Croke Park is the traditional Dublin home of the Gaelic Athletic Association and banned "foreign" sports ... until Ireland were given special permission to play their qualifiers for UEFA Euro 2008 there while their traditional home, Lansdowne Road, was being renovated.

CHAMPION CHARLTON

Jack Charlton became a hero after he took Ireland to their first major finals in 1988, defeating England 1-0 in their first game at the UEFA European Championship. Even better was their first FIFA World Cup finals two years later, where the unfancied Irish lost out only to hosts Italy in the quarter-finals.

GILES PILES UP THE JOBS

Jack Charlton is Ireland's longest-serving manager, with nine years in the job between 1986 and 1995. But Johnny Giles's stint as boss, between 1973 and 1980, also deserves recognition, since he was still playing club football throughout his reign – for Leeds United, West Bromwich Albion, Philadelphia Fury and finally Shamrock Rovers. Despite his national team duties, that seven-year stint included being a key member of Leeds's 1973–74 English league championship squad and serving as player-manager of both West Brom and Rovers.

CAPTAIN ALL–ROUND

Johnny Carey not only captained Matt Busby's Manchester United to the English league title in 1952, he also captained both Northern Ireland (nine caps) and later the Republic of Ireland (27 caps). He went on to manage the Republic of Ireland between 1955 and 1967

MORE FOR MOORE

Paddy Moore was the first player ever to score four goals in a FIFA World Cup qualifier when Ireland came from behind to draw 4-4 with Belgium on 25 February 1934. Don Givens became the only Irishman to equal Moore's feat when he scored all four as Ireland beat Turkey in October 1975.

HOORAY FOR RAY

Ray Houghton may have been born in Glasgow and spoke with a Scottish accent, but he scored two of Ireland's most famous goals. A header gave the Republic a shock 1–0 win over England at UEFA Euro 88 in West Germany and, six years later, his long-range strike was the only goal of the game against eventual finalists Italy, in the first round of the 1994 FIFA World Cup in the USA.

ED BROOKES

Bohemians striker Ed Brookes scored Ireland's first hat-trick just one year after the Football Association of Ireland's recognition from FIFA in a 3-1 win over the United States in June 1924.

CROSSING THE CODES

Cornelius "Con" Martin was a Gaelic footballer whose passion for soccer resulted in his expulsion from the Gaelic Athletic Association. His versatility meant he was as good at centre-half as he was in goal, both for club (Aston Villa) and country. He played both in goal and outfield for the fledgling Irish national team, scoring a penalty in the 2-0 victory over England at Goodison Park in 1949 – in what was England's first home defeat to a non-British opponent.

TOP CAPS

#	Player	Caps
1	Shay Given	103
=	Kevin Kilbane	103
3	Steve Staunton	102
4	Robbie Keane	99
5	Niall Quinn	91
6	Tony Cascarino	88
7	Paul McGrath	83
8	Damien Duff	82
9	Packie Bonner	80
10	Ray Houghton	73

TOP SCORERS

#	Player	Goals
1	Robbie Keane	43
2	Niall Quinn	21
3	Frank Stapleton	20
4	John Aldridge	19
=	Tony Cascarino	19
=	Don Givens	19
7	Noel Cantwell	14
8	Gerry Daly	13
=	Jimmy Dunne	13
10	Ian Harte	11

ROMANIA

The history of Romanian football is littered with a series of bright moments – they were one of four countries (with Brazil, France and Belgium) to appear in the first three editions of the FIFA World Cup™ – followed by significant spells in the doldrums – since 1938 they have qualified for the finals of the tournament only four times in 14 attempts. The country's football highlight came in 1994 when, inspired by Gheorghe Hagi, they reached the quarter-finals of the FIFA World Cup™.

A GOOD NAME

Gheorghe Popescu was a Romanian international defender, born in 1918, who went on to great success as manager of Steaua Bucharest before becoming president of the Romanian Football Association. Gheorghe "Gica" Popescu – no relation – was also a Romanian international defender, born in 1967, who won 115 caps and a string of European club titles, including the now-defunct Cup-Winners' Cup, the UEFA Cup, as well as domestic leagues and cups in Holland, Spain, Romania and Turkey.

WIN SOME, LOSE SOME…

Romania enjoyed a great start to their first-ever game in the first-ever FIFA World Cup when Adalbert Desu scored in the first minute. Romania won 3-1 in the match, which saw Peru's Placido Galindo become the first player to be sent off in a FIFA World Cup on 54 minutes. Only 300 spectators – the lowest recorded attendance for a FIFA World Cup finals match – witnessed the drama.

THE "HERO OF SEVILLE"

Helmuth Duckadam, the "Hero of Seville", will always be remembered for saving four consecutive penalties as Steaua Bucharest became the first Eastern European side to win the European Cup, beating Barcelona in a shoot-out in 1986. A rare blood disease forced him to retire from the game in 1991, after which he became a stopper of a different kind as a major in the Romanian Border Police.

TERRIFIC TRIO

Gheorghe Hagi, **Florin Raducioiu** and **Ilie Dumitrescu** lit up the FIFA World Cup in the United States in 1994. Together they scored nine of Romania's ten goals (Raducioiu four, Hagi three, Dumitrescu two). All three successfully converted their penalties in the quarter-final shoot-out against Sweden, but misses from Dan Petrescu and Miodrag Belodedici sent the Romanians crashing out. All three made big-money moves for the following 1994–95 season: Hagi went from Brescia to Barcelona, Dumitrescu from Steaua Bucharest to Tottenham Hotspur, and Raducioiu went from warming the bench at Milan to the first team at Espanyol.

YELLOW PERIL

Despite topping Group G ahead of England, Colombia and Tunisia at the 1998 FIFA World Cup, Romania's players of that tournament might perhaps be best-remembered for the collective decision to dye their hair **blond** ahead of their final first-round game. The newly bleached Romanians struggled to a 1-1 draw against Tunisia, before being knocked out 1-0 by Croatia in the second round.

TOP SCORERS

1	Gheorghe Hagi	35
2	Iuliu Bodola	31
3	Adrian Mutu	29
4	Anghel Iordanescu	26
5	Viorel Moldovan	25
6	Ladislau Boloni	23
7	Rodion Camataru	22
8	Dudu Georgescu	21
=	Florin Raducioiu	21
10	Stefan Dobay	20
=	Ilie Dumitrescu	20

TOP CAPS

1	Dorinel Munteanu	134
2	Gheorghe Hagi	125
3	Gheorghe Popescu	115
4	Ladislau Boloni	108
5	Dan Petrescu	95
6	Bogdan Stelea	91
7	Michael Klein	90
8	Marius Lacatus	84
9	Mircea Rednic	83
10	Silviu Lung	77

HOW MANY?

Striker Rodion Camataru may have scored 22 goals in 75 games for Romania, but he is best remembered for controversially winning the European Golden Boot in the 1986–87 season. Camataru's impressive tally of 44 goals remains the second-highest total ever for the Romanian league, but suspicions were raised when it emerged that 18 of these goals came in the final six games of the season. The competition was later suspended and resurfaced only a decade later with a complex new formula for rating the difficulty level of different European leagues.

PAYING THE PENALTY

Romania were knocked out of consecutive FIFA World Cup finals on penalties. In 1990, after a dull 0-0 draw, they lost out 5-4 on penalties to the Republic of Ireland. They went one better in 1994, reaching the quarter-finals, but lost 5-4 on penalties again – this time to Sweden. Their only penalty shoot-out victories have come against lowly opposition in minor tournaments – 5-3 against China in the "Great Wall Cup" in 1985 and 4-2 against Georgia in the 2000 Cyprus Cup.

CENTURY MAN

Gheorghe Hagi, Romania's "Player of the [20th] Century", scored three goals and was named in the Team of the Tournament in the 1994 FIFA World Cup in the United States, where Romania lost out on penalties to Sweden after a 2-2 draw in the quarter-finals. Hagi made his international debut in 1983, aged just 18, scored his first goal aged 19 (in a 3-2 defeat by Northern Ireland) and remains Romania's top goalscorer with 35 goals in 125 games. Despite retiring from international football after the 1998 FIFA World Cup, Hagi couldn't resist answering his country's call to play in UEFA Euro 2000. Sadly, two yellow-card offences in six minutes in the quarter-final against Italy meant Hagi's final bow on the international stage saw him receive a red card – and leave the field to take an early bath. Farul Constanta, in Hagi's hometown, named their stadium after him in 2000 – but fans stopped referring to it as such after he took the manager's job at rivals Timisoara.

MAJOR TOURNAMENTS

FIFA WORLD CUP™: 7 appearances – quarter-finals 1994
UEFA EUROPEAN CHAMPIONSHIP: 4 appearances – quarter-finals 2000
FIRST INTERNATIONAL: Yugoslavia 1 Romania 2 (Belgrade, Yugoslavia, 8 June 1922)
BIGGEST WIN: Romania 9 Finland 0 (Bucharest, Romania, 14 October 1973)
BIGGEST DEFEAT: Hungary 9 Romania 0 (Budapest, Hungary, 6 June 1948)

MUTU MUTED

Romania have been unfortunate to see arguably their finest player of the 21st century so far banned from the game not just once but twice, for failing drugs tests. The first was a private test carried out on **Adrian Mutu** by his club employers Chelsea in September 2004, which showed traces of cocaine and provoked the English side into sacking him. He was also banned for seven months but did manage to rehabilitate his career in Italy, for Juventus and then Fiorentina. Mutu then tested positive, however, for an outlawed anti-obesity drug, in January 2010, and received a nine-month ban in April that year. He remains the Romania national team's third-highest scorer of all time, with a tally which includes a strike against Italy at the 2008 UEFA European Championship. Romania have only lost once when Mutu has scored.

RUSSIA

Before the break-up of the Soviet Union, the
Soviet Union (USSR) was among the powerhouses
of world football, winning the inaugural UEFA
European Championship in 1960, striking gold
at the 1956 and 1988 Olympic tournaments, and
qualifying for the FIFA World Cup™ finals on
all but two occasions (1974 and 1978).
Playing as Russia since August 1992, though,
the good times have eluded them
– they were UEFA Euro 2008
semi-finalists, but then failed
to advance from the
qualifying play-offs
to reach the FIFA
World Cup
2010™.

TOP SCORERS
(Russia only)

1	Vladimir Beschastnykh	26
2	Valeri Karpin	17
3	Andrei Arshavin	16
4	Alexandr Kerzhakov	15
=	Roman Pavlyuchenko	15
=	Dmitri Sychev	15
7	Igor Kolyvanov	12
8	Sergei Kiriakov	10
=	Aleksandr Mostovoi	10
10	Dmitri Radchenko	9

IMPRESSIVE ED START

Eduard Streltsov celebrated becoming the
Soviet Union's youngest-ever international
by scoring a hat-trick in his debut against
Sweden in June 1956, at the age of 17 years
and 340 days. He scored another three in his
second game, against India. He helped the
USSR win Olympic gold in Melbourne in 1958,
but his career was interrupted by five years in
a labour camp following a disputed conviction
for rape. Russia's youngest post-Soviet
international is goalkeeper Igor Akinfeev, 18
years and 20 days old when he made his
debut in a 3-2 defeat to Norway in April 2004.

TOP CAPS
(Russia only)

1	Viktor Onopko	109
2	Valeri Karpin	72
3	Vladimir Beschastnykh	71
4	Sergei Semak	61
5	Sergei Ignashevich	56
6	Dmitry Alenichev	55
=	Yuri Nikiforov	55
=	Alexei Smertin	55
9	Dmitry Khokhlov	53
10	Andrei Arshavin	51

MONEY MAN

Roman Abramovich, the commodities billionaire behind Chelsea's 21st-century
success, has also been instrumental in the resurgence of Russian football at all
levels – including the key step of importing Dutchman Guus Hiddink to manage
the national side. In 2008, Hiddink took Russia to the semi-finals of the UEFA
European Championship (their best post-Soviet performance), where they lost
3-0 to eventual winners Spain. Abramovich also sponsors the "National Academy
of Football" in Russia, which helps build training facilities and pitches to support
youth football throughout the country.

MAJOR TOURNAMENTS

FIFA WORLD CUP™: 9 appearances (7 as USSR, 2 as Russia) – fourth, 1966
UEFA EUROPEAN CHAMPIONSHIP: 9 appearances (5 as USSR, 1 as CIS 1992, 3 as Russia) – winners 1960 (USSR), semi-finals 2008 (Russia)
FIRST INTERNATIONAL:
Russian Empire: Finland 2 Russian Empire 1 (Stockholm, Sweden, 30 June 1912)
USSR: USSR 3 Turkey 0 (Moscow, 16 November 1924) (final international: Cyprus 0 USSR 3, Larnaca, 13 November 1991)
CIS: USA 0 CIS 1 (Miami, USA, 25 January 1992) (final international: Scotland 3 CIS 0, Norrkoping, Sweden, 18 June 1992)
Russia: Russia 2 Mexico 0 (Moscow, 16 August 1992)
BIGGEST WIN:
USSR: USSR 11 India 1 (Moscow, 16 September 1955); Finland 0 USSR 10 (Helsinki, 15 August 1957)
CIS: El Salvador 0 CIS 3 (San Salvador, 29 January 1992)
Russia: San Marino 0 Russia 7 (San Marino, 7 June 1995)
BIGGEST DEFEAT:
Russian Empire: Germany 16 Russian Empire 0 (Stockholm, Sweden, 1 July 1912)
USSR: England 5 USSR 0 (London, 22 October 1958)
CIS: Mexico 4 CIS 0 (Mexico City, 8 March 1992)
Russia: Portugal 7 Russia 1 (Lisbon, 13 October 2004)

CAPPING IT ALL

Viktor Onopko, despite being born in the Ukraine, played all his career for the CIS and Russian national football teams. The first of Onopko's 113 international caps (the first four for the CIS) came in a 2-2 draw against England in Moscow on 29 April 1992. He played in the 1994 and 1998 FIFA World Cups, as well as the UEFA European Championship in 1996. He was due to join the squad for the UEFA European Championship in 2004 but missed out through injury. Onopko's club career, spanning 19 years, took him to Shakhtar Donetsk, Spartak Moscow, Real Oviedo, Rayo Vallecano, Alania Vladikavkaz and FC Saturn. He was Russian footballer of the year in 1993 and 1994.

SUPER STOPPER

FIFA declared **Lev Yashin** to be the finest goalkeeper of the 20th century – naturally, he made it into their Century XI team, too. In a career spanning 20 years, Yashin played 326 league games for Dynamo Moscow – the only club side he ever played for – and won 78 caps for the Soviet Union, conceding on average less than a goal a game (only 70 in total). With Dynamo, he won five Soviet championships and three Soviet cups, the last of which came in his final full season in 1970. He saved around 150 penalties in his long career, and kept four clean sheets in his 12 World Cup matches. Such was Yashin's worldwide reputation, Chilean international Eladio Rojas was so excited at scoring past the legendary Yashin in the 1962 FIFA World Cup that he gave the surprised keeper a big hug with the ball still sitting in the back of the net. Yashin was nicknamed the "Black Spider" for his distinctive black jersey and his uncanny ability to get a hand, arm, leg or foot in the way of shots and headers of all kinds. In 1963, Yashin became the first, and so far only, keeper to be named European Footballer of the Year, the same year in which he won his fifth Soviet championship and starred for the Rest of the World XI in the English FA's Centenary Match at Wembley.

PUTTING ON THE STYLE

Coach Guus Hiddink picked **Andrei Arshavin** in his Russia squad for the 2008 UEFA European Championship, despite knowing the playmaker would miss the first two of three group games due to suspension. Arshavin had been sent off for a petulant kick at an opponent, in the closing moments of the final qualifier against Andorra. But he proved his worth with starring roles in Russia's first-round victory over Sweden and their 3-1 quarter-final triumph over Holland. Arshavin, who later joined English club Arsenal from 2008 UEFA Cup holders Zenit St Petersburg, is not just a world-class footballer and one of his country's leading scorers, but also a talented draughts player – and a university graduate, having completed a diploma in fashion design.

GOLDEN BOY

Igor Netto captained the USSR national side to their greatest successes: gold at the 1956 Olympics in Melbourne and victory in the first-ever UEFA European Championship in France in 1960. Born in Moscow in 1930, Netto was awarded the Order of Lenin in 1957, and became an ice hockey coach after retiring from football.

SCOTLAND

A country with a vibrant domestic league and a rich football tradition – it played host to the first-ever international football match, against England, in November 1872 – Scotland have never put in the performances on the international stage to match their lofty ambitions. There have been moments of triumph, such as an unexpected victory over Holland at the 1978 FIFA World Cup™, but far too many moments of despair. They have not qualified for the finals of a major tournament since 1998.

TOP SCORERS

1	Kenny Dalglish	30
=	Denis Law	30
3	Hughie Gallacher	24
4	Lawrie Reilly	22
5	Ally McCoist	19
6	Bob Hamilton	15
=	James McFadden	15
8	Maurice Johnston	14
9	Bob McColl	13
10	John Collins	12
=	Alan Gilzean	12
=	Billy Steel	12
=	Andy Wilson	12

KING KENNY

Kenny Dalglish is Scotland's joint-top international goalscorer (with Denis Law) and remains the only player to have won more than a century of caps for the national side, with 102 in total – 11 more than the next highest cap-winner, goalkeeper Jim Leighton. Despite growing up a Rangers fan (he was born in Glasgow on 4 March 1951), Dalglish made his name spear-heading Celtic's domestic dominance in the 1970s, winning four league titles, four Scottish Cups and one League Cup. He then went on to become a legend at Liverpool, winning a hat-trick of European Cups (1978, 1981 and 1984) and leading the side as player-manager to their first-ever league and cup double in 1986. He later joined Herbert Chapman and Brian Clough as one of the few managers to lead two different sides to the league title – guiding Blackburn Rovers to the summit of English football in 1994–95. For Scotland, Dalglish scored in both the 1978 and 1982 FIFA World Cup finals, netting the first goal in the famous 3-2 victory over eventual runners-up Holland in the 1978 group stages. He played his last international in 1986.

THE LAWMAN

Denis Law is joint top scorer for Scotland with Kenny Dalglish, scoring 30 goals in only 55 games compared with the 102 it took Dalglish to do the same. Law twice scored four goals in a match for Scotland. First against Northern Ireland on 7 November 1962, helping win the British Home Championships. He repeated the feat against Norway in a friendly on 7 November 1963. Law clearly enjoyed playing against Norway, having grabbed a hat-trick in Bergen just five months earlier.

DON'T COME HOME TOO SOON

Scotland have never made it past the initial stages of the finals of an international tournament. They've gone out of the FIFA World Cup on goal difference three times: to **Brazil in 1974**, to eventual runners-up Holland (on goals scored) in 1978 and to the Soviet Union in 1982.

ROOM FOR ONE MORE?

Hampden Park, Scotland's national stadium, boasts the record for the highest-ever football attendance in Europe. The crowd was so huge no one can be quite sure how many squeezed in to watch Scotland v England in 1937, though the official figure is usually quoted as 149,415. Scotland won the British Home Championship tie 3-1, though they ended runners-up to Wales in the overall tournament.

ONE TEAM IN TALLINN

When Scotland travelled to Estonia for a FIFA World Cup qualifier in October 1996, there was only one team in it – literally. The hosts refused to play in protest at kick-off time being brought forward by almost four hours, following a Scottish complaint about the floodlights. At the newly scheduled time, Scotland sent 11 men on to the field at the Kadrioru Stadium in Tallinn, even though there were no opponents. After Billy Dodds and John Collins had dutifully kicked off, Yugoslav referee Miroslav Radoman blew his whistle and formally abandoned the game. FIFA later ordered the game to be replayed in neutral Monaco. It ended goalless, and Scotland went on to reach the 1998 FIFA World Cup in France.

NEW BALLS PLEASE

Lanarkshire-born forward Andy Wilson scored 12 goals in 12 official international football fixtures for Scotland from February 1920 to April 1923, but spent most of his club career across the border – playing for Middlesbrough, Chelsea and Queens Park Rangers, before spending his last two seasons at French club Nimes. He also represented England at bowls.

TOP CAPS

1	Kenny Dalglish	102
2	Jim Leighton	91
3	Alex McLeish	77
4	Paul McStay	76
5	Tom Boyd	72
6	Christian Dailly	67
7	Willie Miller	65
=	David Weir	65
9	Danny McGrain	62
10	Richard Gough	61
=	Ally McCoist	61

UNOFFICIAL WORLD CHAMPIONS

One of the victories most cherished by Scotland fans is the **3-2 triumph** over arch-rivals and reigning world champions England, in April 1967 at Wembley – the first time Sir Alf Ramsey's team had lost since clinching the 1966 FIFA World Cup. Scotland's man of the match that day was ball-juggling left-half/midfielder Jim Baxter, while it was also the first game in charge for Scotland's first full-time manager, Bobby Brown. Less fondly recalled is Scotland's 9-3 trouncing by the same opposition at the same stadium in April 1961, which made unfortunate goalkeeper Frank Haffey the butt of a popular joke that did the rounds across the border in England: "What's the time? Nearly 10 past Haffey." The game was Haffey's second – and last – for Scotland.

I HAVEN'T FELT THIS GOOD SINCE ARCHIE GEMMILL SCORED AGAINST HOLLAND

Archie Gemmill scored Scotland's greatest goal on the world stage in the surprise 3-2 victory over Holland at the 1978 FIFA World Cup. He jinked past three defenders before chipping the ball neatly over Dutch goalkeeper Jan Jongbloed. Amazingly, in 2008, this magical moment was turned into a dance in the English National Ballet's "The Beautiful Game".

GONE TOO SOON

The late Celtic legend **Tommy Burns** (16 December 1956–15 May 2008), in addition to a clean sweep of winners' medals from the domestic Scottish game and eight caps, holds the dubious honour of being Scotland's shortest-reigning manager. Taking over as caretaker after Berti Vogts resigned, his single game in charge was a dispiriting 4-1 defeat to Sweden. Burns went on to help chart the national team's mini-revival as assistant to Walter Smith from 2004–07.

SERBIA

The former Yugoslavia was one of the strongest football nations in eastern Europe. They reached the FIFA World Cup™ semi-finals in 1930 and 1962, they were also runners-up in the UEFA European Championships of 1960 and 1968. In addition, Yugoslavia's leading club, Red Star Belgrade, remain the only team from eastern Europe to win the European Cup, when they beat Marseille on penalties in the 1991 final.

MAGIC DRAGAN

Yugoslavia's greatest player was Red Star left winger **Dragan Dzajic**, who later went on to become the club's president. He made his international debut at 18, won a national record 85 caps and scored 23 goals. The most important was his last-minute winner against world champions England in the 1968 UEFA European Championship semi-final in Florence, which took Yugoslavia to the final against Italy. Pele said of Dzajic: "He's a real wizard. I'm sorry he's not Brazilian."

SAVICEVIC STRIKES

Dejan Savicevic is Serbia's greatest player of the modern era. The attacking midfielder was a key member of **Red Star Belgrade**'s 1991 European Cup-winning team. He also inspired them to three consecutive championships. He moved on to Milan and starred as his new club beat Barcelona 4-0 in the 1994 European Cup final. He created the opening goal, then crashed home a 35-yard volley. Savicevic later became a prominent supporter of the drive for Montenegrin independence from Serbia and has been credited with playing an influential role in the referendum vote on 21 May 2006 that led to the establishment of a separate Montenegrin state.

TOP CAPS

1	Savo Milosevic	102
2	Dejan Stankovic	91
3	Dragan Stojkovic	84
4	Predrag Mijatovic	73
5	Slavisa Jokanovic	64
=	Sinisa Mihajlovic	64
7	Mladen Krstajic	59
=	Zoran Mirkovic	59
9	Darko Kovacevic	58
10	Dejan Savicevic	56

YUGOSLAVIA HIT BY BOYCOTT

The rivalry between Serbia and Croatia was apparent even in the early days of the old federation. Yugoslavia reached the last four of the inaugural FIFA World Cup in 1930. But they did so without any Croat players, who boycotted the squad for the finals in protest at the new federal association headquarters being located in the Serb capital, Belgrade.

TOP SCORERS

1	Savo Milosevic	37
2	Predrag Mijatovic	28
3	Dejan Savicevic	19
4	Mateja Kezman	17
5	Nikola Zigic	16
6	Dragan Stojkovic	15
7	Dejan Stankovic	14
8	Slavisa Jokanovic	10
=	Darko Kovacevic	10
=	Danko Lazovic	10

STAN'S THE MAN

Dejan Stankovic can claim to have been the first man to play for three separate nation states at different FIFA World Cups: Yugoslavia in 1998, Serbia and Montenegro in 2006 and Serbia – as captain – in 2010. The versatile midfielder came into the tournament in South Africa after a treble-winning season with Inter Milan – winning the Italian championship, the Italian cup and the UEFA Champions League.

SANTRAC LASTS LONGEST

Slobodan Santrac was the first manager of the "new" Yugoslavia. He served the longest term too, between 1994 and 1998, winning 26 of his 43 games in charge. Since Santrac's departure, Serbia have employed Milan Zivadinovic, Vujadin Boskov (twice), Ilija Petkovic (twice), Milovan Doric, Ivan Curkovic, Dejan Savicevic (twice), Spanish coach Javier Clemente, Miroslav Dukic and current manager **Radi Antic**.

MILORAD'S MILESTONE

The first man to captain and then coach his country at the FIFA World Cup was Milorad Arsenijevic, who captained Yugoslavia to the semi-finals at the inaugural tournament in Uruguay in 1930 and then managed their squad in Brazil 20 years later.

THE WHITE EAGLES

The national team of former Yugoslavia were nicknamed "Plavni" ("Blues") because of their shirt colour. However, Serbia decided to change their colours after Montenegro voted to become independent. They went for red, not blue. The team asked supporters for a new nickname. The broadcaster B92 proposed "Beli Orlovi" ("White Eagles"), taken from the double-headed white eagle on Serbia's national flag. The name was adopted by both the Serb fans and the national association. The national team is now known as "Beli Orlovi" and the Under-21 side is called "Orlici" ("Eaglets").

GOING IT ALONE

After Serbia and Montenegro competed at the 2006 FIFA World Cup, the 2010 tournament was the first featuring Serbia alone following Montenegro's independence. Topping their qualifying group ahead of France, Radomir Antic's Serbian side failed to make it through to the knockout stages in South Africa, despite a single-goal victory over Group D rivals Germany. A Serbian working for an opposing team was partly to blame – Milovan Rajevac was coach of the Ghana side that beat Serbia 1-0 in their first first-round match. Serbia conceded penalties due to inexplicable handballs in their two opening matches of the finals – Zdravko Kuzmanovic was the culprit against Ghana, and **Nemanja Vidic** (for which he was shown a yellow card) against Germany. Ghana converted their kick to win 1-0, but Germany missed theirs and lost by the same score.

SWEDEN

Eleven appearances at the FIFA World Cup™ finals (with a best result of second, as tournament hosts, in 1958) and three Olympic medals (including gold in London in 1948), bear testament to Sweden's rich history on the world football stage. Recent success has been harder to find, however, with semi-final appearances at the 1992 UEFA European Championship (again as hosts) and the FIFA World Cup 1994™ the country's best performances in recent years.

GRE–NO–LI OLYMPIC AND ITALIAN GLORY

Having conquered the world by leading Sweden to gold in the 1948 Olympics in London, Gunnar Gren, Gunnar Nordahl and Nils Liedholm were snapped up by AC Milan. Their three-pronged "Gre-No-Li" forward line led the Italian giants to their 1951 scudetto win. Nordahl, who topped the Serie A scoring charts five times between 1950 and 1955, remains Milan's all-time top scorer with 221 goals in 268 games. Gren and Liedholm went on to appear for the Swedish national team in the 1958 FIFA World Cup – where they finished runners-up.

ONE MORE ENCORE, AGAIN!

One of the most famous and decorated Swedish footballers of modern times, **Henrik Larsson** (a star on the club scene with both Celtic and Barcelona) quit international football after the 2002 FIFA World Cup ... and again after the 2006 FIFA World Cup in Germany. He then made a further comeback in the 2010 FIFA World Cup qualifiers. With 37 goals in his 106 appearances, including five in his three FIFA World Cups, fans and officials clamoured for his return each time he tried to walk away. Sweden's failure to qualify for the tournament in 1998 meant that a record-equalling 12 years elapsed between Larsson's first FIFA World Cup finals goal against Bulgaria in 1994 and his last – so far! – with his dramatic equalizer in the 2-2 group-round draw with England in 2006.

TOP CAPS

1	Thomas Ravelli	143
2	Roland Nilsson	116
3	Bjorn Nordqvist	115
4	Niclas Alexandersson	109
5	Anders Svensson	107
6	Henrik Larsson	106
7	Olof Mellberg	101
8	Patrik Andersson	96
9	Orvar Bergmark	94
10	Teddy Lucic	86

TOP–STOPPER RAVELLI

Thomas Ravelli kept goal for Sweden a record 143 times – conceding 143 goals. He saved two penalties in a shoot-out against Romania in the 1994 FIFA World Cup quarter-final to send Sweden into the last four, where they lost 1-0 to Brazil. Sweden went on to finish third, and were also the tournament's highest scorers with 15 goals in all – four more than eventual champions Brazil. Sweden's tally included five for Kennet Andersson, four for Martin Dahlin and three for Tomas Brolin.

ONE–MINUTE WONDERS

Sweden's Magnus Erlingmark can claim to have the shortest FIFA World Cup finals career – amounting to nothing more than his appearance as an 89th-minute substitute against Russia, in the first round of the 1994 tournament. His only rival for the unenviable record is Bulgaria's Petar Mikhtarski, another 89th-minute replacement that summer, in his country's second-round victory over Mexico.

JUST GETTING BYE

Sweden only needed to play one match to reach the last four at the 1938 FIFA World Cup, thanks to a first-round bye when scheduled opponents Austria were annexed by Germany and withdrew. When the Swedes were finally called into action, they made up for lost time by thrashing Cuba 8-0, including hat-tricks by both Tore Keller and Gustav Wetterstrom. But they lost their semi-final 5-1 to eventual runners-up Hungary, despite being given the lead by Arne Nyberg after just 35 seconds.

GOTHENBURG FLY THE FLAG

Under Sven-Goran Eriksson, IFK Gothenburg became the first Swedish team to win a European tournament when, in 1982, they crushed Hamburg 4-0 on aggregate in the UEFA Cup final.

MANAGER SWAP

The most successful manager Sweden ever had was Englishman **George Raynor**, who led them to Olympic gold in London in 1948 and steered Sweden to third place and the runners-up spot in the 1950 and 1958 FIFA World Cups respectively. Raynor got one over on the country of his birth when Sweden became only the second foreign side to win at Wembley, with a 3-2 victory over England in 1959. Working in the opposite direction, in 2001 Sven-Goran Eriksson left Serie A side Lazio to become England's first foreign coach. He led the side to three consecutive quarter-finals – in the FIFA World Cups of 2002 and 2006 and the 2004 UEFA European Championship in between. Eriksson, however, failed to lead England to a win over his home country, recording three draws (1-1 in a friendly, 2001; 1-1 in a 2002 FIFA World Cup group game; 2-2 in a 2006 FIFA World Cup group game) and one defeat (0-1 in a friendly, 2004).

LOSING LOSERS

Despite losing to Nottingham Forest in the final of the 1979 European Cup, Malmo contested the World Club Cup in 1979 after the English side declined the invitation. Sadly, Malmo ended as runners-up again, losing out on away goals to Olimpia Asuncion from Paraguay.

AS LONG AS WE BEAT THE DANES

In 1931, Sweden's record goalscorer, Sven Rydell, became the first footballer to be awarded the prestigious Svenska Dagbladet gold medal for scoring two goals in a 3-1 victory over Denmark in the Nordic Championship. Rydell scored 49 goals in 43 games for Sweden (1.14 per match) – including seven hat-tricks and two four-goal hauls – and his tournament tally of six goals was instrumental in Sweden winning the bronze medal in the 1924 Olympics in Paris. His daughter, Ewa Rydell, carried on the family's Olympic tradition when she competed as a gymnast in 1960 and 1964.

Zlatan Ibrahimovic
Striker, 62 caps, 22 goals

TOP SCORERS

1	Sven Rydell	49
2	Gunnar Nordahl	43
3	Henrik Larsson	37
4	Gunnar Gren	32
5	Kennet Andersson	31
6	Marcus Allback	30
7	Martin Dahlin	29
8	Agne Simonsson	27
9	Tomas Brolin	26
10	Per Kaufeldt	23

AGE SHALL NOT WEARY THEM

Aged 33 years and 159 days, Tore Keller is the oldest hat-trick scorer in FIFA World Cup finals history – scoring three of Sweden's eight without reply against Cuba in the quarter-finals of the 1938 tournament. Nils Liedholm, part of Sweden's 1948 Olympic gold medal-winning team, became the oldest player, at 35, to score in a FIFA World Cup final itself, as Sweden lost 5-2 to Brazil in 1958

BROTHERS IN ARMS

The Nordahl brothers – Bertil, Knut and Gunnar – all won gold medals with Sweden in the 1948 Olympics football tournament. All three went on to play in Italy: Bertil with Atalanta, Knut with Roma, while Gunnar became a goalscoring legend at AC Milan before also turning out for Roma. Twins Thomas and Andreas Ravelli continued the brotherly tradition, winning 143 and 41 caps for Sweden respectively.

EMERGENCY MAN

Goalkeeper Karl-Oskar "Rio-Kalle" Svensson, who played in the bronze and silver medal-winning sides at the 1950 and 1958 FIFA World Cups, held down a job as a fire fighter in Helsingborg. He holds the unenviable record of having conceded the most goals in the Swedish top division – 575 in 349 games.

SWITZERLAND

Switzerland set a record in 2006 when they became the first side in FIFA World Cup™ finals history to depart the tournament without conceding a goal. It sums up the country's football history: despite three FIFA World Cup™ quarter-final appearances (in 1934, 1938 and 1954 – the latter as tournament hosts), Switzerland has failed to establish itself on the international football stage. The country co-hosted the 2008 UEFA European Championship, with Austria, and is better known as being the home of both FIFA and UEFA.

CLEAN SHEET WIPE–OUT

The Swiss national team made history in 2006 by becoming the first – and to date only – team to exit the FIFA World Cup without conceding a single goal in regulation time. However, in the shoot-out defeat to Ukraine in the second round, following a goalless 120 minutes, they failed to score a single penalty and lost 3-0. Despite being beaten three times in the shoot-out, goalkeeper **Pascal Zuberbuhler**'s performances in Germany earned him a Swiss record for consecutive clean sheets at an international tournament.

TOP SCORERS

1	Alexander Frei	40
2	Kubilay Turkyilmaz	34
3	Max Abegglen III	34
4	Andre Abegglen II	29
=	Jacques Fatton	29
6	Adrian Knup	26
7	Josef Hugi II	23
8	Charles Antenen	22
9	Lauro Amado	21
=	Stephane Chapuisat	21

TOP CAPS

1	Heinz Hermann	117
2	Alain Geiger	112
3	Stephane Chapuisat	103
4	Johann Vogel	94
5	Hakan Yakin	83
6	Patrick Muller	81
7	Severino Minelli	80
8	Andre Egli	79
=	Ciriaco Sforza	79
10	Alexander Frei	77

CHAMPION CHAPPI

Stephane "Chappi" Chapuisat – the third man to make 100 appearances for Switzerland – was the first Swiss player to win a UEFA Champions League medal when he led the line for Borussia Dortmund in their 3-1 victory over Juventus in 1997. But his most significant contribution in the final was to make way for Lars Ricken, whose goal with his first touch put the game beyond Juventus. Stephane's father, Pierre-Albert Chapuisat, was also a successful Swiss international – earning 34 caps for the national side in the 1970s and 1980s – but he failed to reach the heights of Stephane, who would later add both the Club World Cup and the Swiss super league (while playing for Grasshoppers) to his winners' medal collection.

LLAMA FARMER FREI–ING HIGH

After being compared to a llama by an angry Swiss sports press for spitting at Steven Gerrard at UEFA Euro 2004, Alexander Frei, Switzerland's all-time top scorer, adopted a llama at Basel zoo as part of his apology to the nation.

VALON OFF

Valon Behrami became the first Swiss player ever sent off at a FIFA World Cup, when the winger was shown a red card 31 minutes into their 1-0 defeat by Chile in a 2010 first-round encounter. He was punished for elbowing Chile's Arturo Vidal.

SWISS GUARD

Switzerland set a FIFA World Cup record in 2010 when they completed nine hours and 10 minutes without conceding a goal, including the 2006 tournament and passing a mark set by Italy. They then held out for a further nine minutes before conceding to Chile's Mark Gonzalez. Ottmar Hitzfeld's men lost that Group H match 1-0 and would fail to advance to the second round – despite conceding no other goals in their three group games.

ONE MAN LEAGUE

Heinz Hermann, in addition to being Switzerland's most-capped player, won the Swiss player of the year trophy an incredible five seasons in a row between 1984 and 1988.

ADMIRABLE GELSON

Switzerland shocked European champions and pre-tournament favourites Spain by beating them 1-0 in their first Group H game at the 2010 FIFA World Cup. Midfielder **Gelson Fernandes** scored the only goal at Durban's Moses Mabhida stadium. Yet Spain enjoyed 63 per cent of possession, having 24 shots compared with Switzerland's eight and 12 corners to Switzerland's three. The victory was Switzerland's first over Spain in 19 attempts.

THE ORIGINAL BOLT

Karl Rappan did so much for Swiss football – including founding its first national football fan club – that it is often forgotten that he was Austrian. After a moderately successful career as a player and coach in Austria, Rappan achieved lasting fame as an innovative manager in Switzerland, leading the national side in the 1938 and 1954 FIFA World Cups, as well as securing league titles and cups as manager of Grasshopper-Club, FC Servette and FC Zurich. He developed a flexible tactical system – which allowed players to switch positions depending on the situation and putting greater pressure on their opponents. This revolutionary new idea became known as the "Swiss bolt", and helped the unfancied hosts defeat Italy on the way to the quarter-finals of the 1954 FIFA World Cup, before losing out to Rappan's home country, Austria. An early advocate of a European league, Rappan eventually settled for the simpler knockout tournament, the Intertoto Cup, which he helped devise and launch in 1961. Rappan was, until Kobi Kuhn, Switzerland's longest-serving and statistically most successful manager, with 29 victories in 77 games in charge.

"MERCI KOBI"

Former Swiss international player and manager, **Jakob "Kobi" Kuhn**, was left close to tears as his players unfurled a "thank you" banner at the end of his final game as Swiss national manager – the 2-0 victory over Portugal in the final group game of UEFA Euro 2008. How times have changed for Kuhn: while now a much-loved elder statesmen of the Swiss game, when Kuhn was just 22 years old, he was sent home from the 1966 FIFA World Cup for missing a curfew. He was then banned from the national side for a year. The shoe was on the other foot when Kuhn had to send Alexander Frei home from UEFA Euro 2004 after the centre-forward spat at England's Steven Gerrard. Kuhn spent most of his playing career, where he was described as playing "with honey in his boots", with FC Zurich, winning six league titles and five Swiss Cups. He played 63 times for the national side, scoring five goals. He then worked his way up through the ranks of the Swiss national team, leading first the Under-18s, then the Under-21s and finally the senior national team. He retired, aged 64, with a record of 32 victories, 18 draws and 23 defeats in 73 matches as Swiss coach.

TURKEY

Galatasaray's penalty shoot-out success over Arsenal in the 2000 UEFA Cup final signalled a changing fortune for Turkish football. Prior to that night in Copenhagen, Turkey had qualified for the FIFA World Cup™ only once, in 1950, when they withdrew, and had otherwise consistently underachieved on the world stage. Since 2000, however, Turkish fans have had plenty to cheer about, including a third-place finish at the 2002 FIFA World Cup™ in Japan and South Korea, and a semi-final appearance at the 2008 UEFA European Championship.

HAT–TRICK HERO

Turkey captain **Tuncay Sanli** became the first Turkish player to score a hat-trick in the UEFA Champions League when he scored all of Fenerbahce's goals in their 3-0 defeat of Manchester United in Istanbul in 2004. He has also notched up two hat-tricks for the national side, against Switzerland on 16 November 2005 (final score 4-2) and in another 4-2 victory, this time over Austria, on 19 November 2008.

OLD GOLD

The last FIFA World Cup "golden goal" was scored by Turkey substitute Ilhan Mansiz, in the 94th minute of their 2002 quarter-final against Senegal – giving his side a 1-0 win, on their way to finishing third overall. The "golden goal" rule was abandoned ahead of the 2006 FIFA World Cup, which went back to two guaranteed 15-minute periods of extra-time if a knockout fixture ended level after 90 minutes.

QUICK OFF THE MARK

Hakan Sukur scored the fastest-ever FIFA World Cup finals goal – taking only 11 seconds to score Turkey's first goal in their third-place play-off match against South Korea at the 2002 FIFA World Cup. Turkey went on to win the game 3-2 to claim third place, their finest-ever performance in the competition. His total of 51 goals (in 112 games) is more than double his nearest competitor in the national team ranking. His first goal came in only his second appearance, as Turkey beat Denmark 2-1 on 8 April 1992. He went on to score four goals in a single game twice – in the 6-4 win over Wales on 20 August 1997 and in the 5-0 crushing of Moldova on 11 October 2006.

GUESS WHO'S BACK?

Rustu Recber doesn't know the meaning of the word "quit". Less than a year after retiring from international football after UEFA Euro 2008, Turkey's highest-capped player came out of retirement to join the national team once more in the qualifying campaign for the 2010 FIFA World Cup in South Africa. This was not his first international comeback – for UEFA Euro 2008, Rustu had been relegated to the bench, but played in the quarter-final against Croatia after first-choice keeper Volkan Demirel was sent off in the final group game. Rustu was the hero of the penalty shoot-out, saving from Mladen Petric to send Turkey through to their first-ever UEFA European Championship semi-final, where they lost to Germany. Back in 1993, Rustu came back from an even more devastating set-back after he was seriously injured in a car crash that resulted in the death of a friend. The accident also scuppered a potential move to Besiktas, although he went on to star for Fenerbahce, winning five Turkish league titles in 12 years with them. With his distinctive pony-tail and charcoal-black war paint, Rustu has always stood out, but perhaps never more so than as a star performer in Turkey's third-place performance at the 2002 FIFA World Cup finals. He was elected into the Team of the Tournament and was named FIFA's Goalkeeper of the Year.

MAJOR TOURNAMENTS

FIFA WORLD CUP™: 2 appearances – 3rd place 2002
UEFA EUROPEAN CHAMPIONSHIP: 3 appearances – semi-finals 2008
FIRST INTERNATIONAL: Turkey 2 Romania 2 (Istanbul, 26 October 1923)
BIGGEST WIN: Turkey 7 Syria 0 (Ankara, 20 November 1949)
Turkey 7 Korea Republic 0 (Geneva, Switzerland, 20 June, 1954)
Turkey 7 San Marino 0 (Istanbul, 10 November 1996)
BIGGEST DEFEAT: Poland 8 Turkey 0 (Chorzow, 24 April 1968)
Turkey 0 England 8 (Istanbul, 14 November 1984)
England 8 Turkey 0 (London, 14 October 1987)

FATIH TERIM

Having coached Galatasaray to their UEFA Cup triumph in 2000, **Fatih Terim** put a disappointing year and a half in Italy with Fiorentina and AC Milan behind him to lead Turkey in their amazing run to the 2008 UEFA European Championship semi-finals. Defeat to Portugal in the opening game left the Turks with an uphill task, but stunning successive comebacks against Switzerland and the Czech Republic took them through to the quarter-finals. A 119th-minute goal seemed to have clinched the tie for Croatia, but, as the Croatian players celebrated, "Emperor" Fatih urged his players to get up, pick the ball out of the net and fight on to the very end. They did just that, and Semih Senturk's improbable equalizer took the match to penalties. The semi-final against Germany provided yet another rollercoaster ride, but this time there was no answer to the Germans' last-minute winner. When Fatih said "there is something special about this team" few could disagree.

TOP SCORERS

1	Hakan Sukur	51
2	Tuncay Sanli	22
3	Lefter Kucukandonyadis	21
4	Metin Oktay	19
=	Cemil Turan	19
6	Nihat Kahveci	17
7	Zeki Riza Sporel	15
8	Arif Erdem	11
=	Saglam Ertugrul	11
10	Tanju Colak	9

TOP CAPS

1	Rustu Recber	119
2	Hakan Sukur	112
3	Bulent Korkmaz	102
4	Tugay Kerimoglu	94
5	Alpay Ozalan	90
6	Ogun Temizkanoglu	76
7	Tuncay Sanli	74
8	Abdullah Ercan	71
9	Oguz Cetin	70
10	Emre Belozoglu	69

THREE'S THE CHARM

Turkey's record victory is 7-0 – a winning margin they've managed three times: against Syria (1949), South Korea (1954) and San Marino (1996). However, they've also lost 8-0 on three separate occasions – to Poland in 1968, and twice to England: in 1984, when Bryan Robson scored a hat-trick, and again at Wembley in 1987, when Gary Lineker claimed three.

COCA–COLA COLIN

England failed to qualify, but there were two English-born footballers at the 2008 UEFA European Championship – Italy's Simone Perrotta, born just outside Manchester, and the East Londoner formerly called **Colin Kazim-Richards** but known in his adopted homeland of Turkey as Kazim-Kazim. He qualified for Turkey through his mother. Before signing for Turkish giants Fenerbahce in June 2007, he had only played for unfashionable English clubs Bury, Brighton and Hove Albion and Sheffield United. When Brighton bought him from Bury, the transfer fee was paid by Coca-Cola thanks to a competition won by a Brighton fan – meaning Kazim-Richards was duly nicknamed "The Coca-Cola Kid".

UKRAINE

Ukraine has been a stronghold of football in eastern Europe for many years. A steady flow of talent from Ukrainian clubs with a rich European pedigree, such as Dynamo Kiev, provided the Soviet national team with many standout players in the years before independence. Since separating from the Soviet Union in 1991, Ukraine has become a football force in its own right, qualifying for the FIFA World Cup™ for the first time in 2006, reaching the quarter-finals.

MAJOR TOURNAMENTS

FIFA WORLD CUP™: 1 appearance – quarter-finals (2006)
FIRST INTERNATIONAL: Ukraine 1 Hungary 3 (Uzhhorod, Ukraine, 29 April 1992)
BIGGEST WINS: Ukraine 6 Azerbaijan 0 (Kiev, Ukraine, 15 August 2006)
Andorra 0 Ukraine 6 (Andorra la Vella, Andorra, 14 October 2009)
BIGGEST DEFEATS: Croatia 4 Ukraine 0 (Zagreb, Croatia, 25 March 1995)
Spain 4 Ukraine 0 (Leipzig, Germany, 14 June 2006)

CUP–WINNING KIEV

The Soviet Union might have made a big impression at the 1974 FIFA World Cup – after all, the nucleus came from the Dynamo Kiev side who would win both the European Cup-Winners' Cup (against Ferencvaros) and then the European Supercup (against Bayern Munich) the following year. However, the Soviet government refused to send the team to Chile for the second leg of a Europe/South America qualifying play-off because the match was due to be played in the Estadio Nacional in Santiago ... which had been used as a concentration camp during the military coup that saw the overthrow of communist president Salvador Allende.

PENALTY KING

Oleksandr Shovkovskyi, who holds Dynamo Kiev's appearance record (with more than 300), is the third-highest-capped player (with 86, behind only Andriy Shevchenko and Anatoliy Tymoschuk) for the Ukraine national side. He is best remembered for two saves in the penalty shoot-out against Switzerland that took Ukraine to the FIFA World Cup quarter-finals in Germany in 2006. It had all looked very different at the start of 2006: he broke his collarbone in a friendly before the start of the Ukrainian season and feared he might not be able to make it to the finals at all. In the event, he made a full recovery in just two months to make his mark in Ukraine's biggest result to date on the international stage.

HARD START

With the newly independent Ukraine unable to register with FIFA in time for the qualifying rounds for the 1994 FIFA World Cup, many of their stars opted to play for Russia and went to the finals in the United States representing that country. Andrei Kanchelskis, Viktor Onopko, Sergei Yuran and Oleg Salenko could all have played for the new Ukraine side, but decided not to. Ukraine then failed to qualify for an international tournament until the 2006 FIFA World Cup in Germany, where they lost 3-0 in the quarter-finals to eventual winners Italy.

SUPER SHEVA

In 2004, **Andriy Shevchenko** became the third Ukrainian to win the Ballon D'Or – the first to do so, in 1975, was his 2006 FIFA World Cup coach Oleg Blokhin (second was Igor Belanov in 1986). Shevchenko was the first to win the award since Ukraine's independence from the Soviet Union. Born on 29 September 1976, he was a promising boxer as a youngster, before deciding to focus on football full-time. He has won trophies at every club he's played for, including five titles in a row with Dynamo Kiev, the Serie A and the Champions League with AC Milan, and even two cups in his "disappointing" time at Chelsea. Shevchenko is Ukraine's highest-capped player and leading goalscorer, with 45 goals in 96 games. This includes two at the 2006 FIFA World Cup, where Shevchenko captained his country in their first-ever appearance at a major finals.

LEADING FROM THE FRONT

Oleg Blokhin, Ukraine's manager on their first appearance at the FIFA World Cup finals in 2006, made his name as a star striker with his hometown club Dynamo Kiev. Born on 5 November 1952, in the days when Ukraine was part of the Soviet Union, Blokhin scored a record 211 goals in another record 432 appearances in the USSR national league. He also holds the caps and goals records for the USSR, with 42 goals in 112 games. He led Kiev to two triumphs in the European Cup-Winners' Cup in 1975 and 1986, scoring in both finals, and winning the European Footballer of the Year trophy for his exploits in 1975. Always an over-achiever, Blokhin became the first manager to lead Ukraine to the finals of an international tournament, at the 2006 FIFA World Cup in Germany, where they lost out to eventual winners Italy 3-0 in the quarter-finals after knocking out Switzerland in the second round – also on penalties. Blokhin was renowned for his speed – when Olympic gold medallist Valeriy Borzov trained the Kiev squad in the 1970s, Blokhin recorded a 100 metres time of 11 seconds, just 0.46 seconds slower than Borzov's own 1972 medal-winning run.

REBROV REBORN

Serhiy Rebrov, who retired in 2009, was Andriy Shevchenko's dynamic strike partner for both club and country. The forward pair starred for Dynamo Kiev in the late 1990s before making big-money moves across Europe. Like Shevchenko at Chelsea, Rebrov struggled in London, first at Tottenham Hotspur and then at West Ham United. But after returning to Ukraine in 2005, he earned a late-career recall to the international team – and scored a memorable long-range strike against Saudi Arabia at the 2006 FIFA World Cup. Having dropped back into midfield, he then crossed the border and helped outsiders Rubin Kazan win their first Russian league title in 2008. But Rebrov, a keen amateur radio "ham", remains the Ukrainian Premier League's all-time leading scorer, with 125 goals in 268 games.

TOP SCORERS

1	Andriy Shevchenko	45
2	Serhiy Rebrov	15
3	Sergiy Nazarenko	11
4	Andriy Vorobey	9
=	Andriy Gusin	9
6	Timerlan Huseinov	8
7	Maksym Kalinichenko	7
=	Oleg Gusev	7
9	Viktor Leonenko	6
=	Ruslan Rotan	6
=	Andriy Voronin	6

EUROS IN UKRAINE

The 69,000-capacity **Olympic Stadium** in Kiev was scheduled to stage the final of the 2012 UEFA European Championship, a tournament being co-hosted by Ukraine and Poland. The stadium, originally opened in 1923, has been rebuilt and renovated several times since then, and takes its current name from its role in the 1980 Summer Olympics. Although the Games were mostly played in Moscow, Kiev was the setting for seven matches in the Olympic football tournament.

TOP CAPS

1	Andriy Shevchenko	96
2	Anatoliy Tymoschuk	95
3	Oleksandr Shovkovskyi	86
4	Serhiy Rebrov	75
5	Andriy Gusin	71
6	Andriy Vorobey	68
7	Andriy Nesmachnyi	67
8	Vladyslav Vashchuk	63
9	Andriy Voronin	61
10	Olexandr Golovko	58

WALES

In a land where rugby union remains the national obsession, Wales have struggled to impose themselves on the world of international football. Despite having produced a number of hugely talented players, Wales have only ever played once in the finals of a major tournament – at the 1958 FIFA World Cup™ finals in Sweden.

BRICKS TO BRILLIANCE

Goalkeeper **Neville Southall** made the first of his record 92 appearances for Wales in a 3-2 win over Northern Ireland on 27 May 1982. The former hod-carrier and bin man kept 34 clean sheets in 15 years playing for Wales and won the English Football Writers' Player of the Year in 1985 thanks to his performances alongside Welsh captain Kevin Ratcliffe at Everton. In his final match for Wales on 20 August 1997, he was substituted halfway through a 6-4 defeat against Turkey in Istanbul.

RUSH FOR GOAL

Ian Rush is Wales's leading goalscorer, with 28 goals in 73 games. His first came in a 3-0 win over Northern Ireland on 27 May 1982; he scored the 28th and final goal in a 2-1 win over Estonia in Tallinn in 1994.

WHERE'S OUR GOLDEN BOY?

One of the most skilful and successful players never to appear at the FIFA World Cup, **Ryan Giggs** somehow missed 18 consecutive friendlies for Wales.

HAT–TRICK HERO

Welsh striker **Robert Earnshaw** holds the remarkable record of having scored hat-tricks in all four divisions of English football, the FA Cup, the League Cup, as well as scoring three for the national team against Scotland on 18 February 2004.

TOP CAPS

1	Neville Southall	92
2	Gary Speed	85
3	Dean Saunders	75
4	Peter Nicholas	73
=	Ian Rush	73
6	Mark Hughes	72
=	Joey Jones	72
8	Ivor Allchurch	68
9	Brian Flynn	66
10	Andy Melville	65

TOP SCORERS

1	Ian Rush	28
2	Trevor Ford	23
=	Ivor Allchurch	23
4	Dean Saunders	22
5	Craig Bellamy	17
6	Mark Hughes	16
=	Cliff Jones	16
8	John Charles	15
9	Robert Earnshaw	14
=	John Hartson	14

HOME CHAMPIONS

Wales won the Home Championship (an annual competition played between England, Ireland, Scotland and Wales between 1883 and 1984) on 12 occasions, seven outright and five shared.

MATCH RECORDS

Wales's record victory is an 11-0 win over Ireland at Wrexham on 3 March 1888; their 9-0 defeat to Scotland on 23 March 1878 remains their worst loss.

YOUNG DRAGON

Gareth Bale became the youngest player to play for Wales when he came on as sub against Trinidad and Tobago on 27 May 2006 aged 16 years and 315 days.

BORDER DISPUTES

Wales only ever won once in 16 matches at Wembley, beating England 1-0 in May 1977 thanks to Leighton James's 44th-minute goal. But they will get another chance in September 2011, after being drawn in the same group as their English neighbours in qualifiers for the 2012 UEFA European Championship. Including other grounds, Wales have inflicted more home defeats on England than any country except for Scotland – eight in all, compared to Scotland's 18. England have lost five times at home to Germany/West Germany.

GOSH, IT'S TOSH

Current Wales manager – and published poet – John Toshack scored 12 goals in 40 games for his country, in a playing career that also brought him three league championships, one European Cup and two UEFA Cups with Liverpool. After retiring, he coached Swansea City all the way from England's fourth to first division in four seasons, and later served two spells in charge at Real Madrid. During the first, he won the 1989–90 La Liga championship with a team that scored a Spanish-record 107 goals in 38 games. Toshack lasted just 41 days as Wales manager in 1994, but has lasted rather longer since returning to the post in September 2004.

CAUGHT ON CAMERA

Pioneer movie-makers Sagar Mitchell and James Kenyon captured Wales v Ireland in March 1906, making it the first filmed international football match.

GIGANTE BUONO

Welsh legend **John Charles**, who was never booked or sent off, was nicknamed "The Gentle Giant" by fans at Juventus, where he won three league titles and two Italian cups. In 1958, he capped off a Player-of-the-Year season with Juve by playing with Wales at the FIFA World Cup. However, he missed the 1-0 quarter-final defeat to Brazil through injury.

KEEPING UP WITH THE JONESES

Cliff Jones, left-winger for Wales at the 1958 FIFA World Cup and for Tottenham Hotspur's league and cup "Double" winners in 1961, was part of a Welsh footballing dynasty. His father Ivor Jones had previously played for Wales, as did Ivor's brother Bryn. Cliff's cousin Ken, a goalkeeper, was another member of the 1958 FIFA World Cup squad, but never actually played for his country.

OTHER TEAMS EUROPE

For the major European football powers, a qualifying campaign for one of the game's major international tournaments would not be the same without an awkward trip to one of the former Eastern Bloc countries or the chance of a goal-fest against the likes of San Marino or Luxembourg. For these countries' players, the thrill of representing their nation is more important than harbouring dreams of world domination.

SELVA SERVICE

San Marino, with a population of under 30,000, is the smallest country to be a member of UEFA. Striker **Andy Selva** is not only San Marino's top scorer, with eight goals, but also the only player to score more than once in recorded senior internationals for the country.

BEGINNERS' LUCK

Slovakia were the only qualifiers who were making their first FIFA World Cup Finals appearance at the 2010 tournament – and also became the first European debutants in 12 years to avoid defeat in their opening game. Slovakia drew 1-1 with New Zealand and were only denied victory by a stoppage-time equalizer. Spain defeated the two previous European debutants, Ukraine 4-0 in 2006 and Slovenia 3-1 in 2002.

UNDERDOGS HAVE THEIR DAY

Slovenia were the only one of the four unseeded teams to win their UEFA qualifying play-off to reach the 2010 FIFA World Cup, beating Russia on away goals. Slovenia went 2-0 down in the first leg, in Moscow, only for substitute Nejc Pecnik to score a crucial away goal two minutes from time. Zlatko Dedic then scored the only goal of the second leg, in Maribor, levelling the score on aggregate and putting them through by the slimmest of margins. With a population of just two million, Slovenia became the smallest nation represented at the 2010 finals. Just 429 of the country's citizens were registered professional footballers.

OWN GOAL WOES

The man whose goal sent Slovakia to their first-ever FIFA World Cup finals actually played for Poland – it was defender **Seweryn Gancarczyk**'s own goal that gave Slovakia a 1-0 win in October 2009, in their final, decisive Group 3 game of the 2010 qualifiers. Also in the same campaign, Georgian captain **Kakha Kaladze** went one better – or worse – in a Group 8 match against Italy. He put the ball past his own goalkeeper twice in 12 minutes, giving Italy a 2-0 win in September 2009 after three games without a goal. Adding insult to injury for Georgia, Kaladze played his club football for Italy's AC Milan. At least Kaladze avoided the fate of Germinal Ekeren defender Stan van den Buys, who scored a hat-trick of own goals in a Belgian league match against Anderlecht in January 1995. His team lost 3-2.

GIVING IT UP

Lithuania and Estonia did not bother playing their final group game against each other in the 1934 FIFA World Cup qualifying competition. Sweden had already guaranteed themselves top spot, and the sole finals place available, by beating Lithuania 2-0 and Estonia 6-2.

BEYOND THE IRON CURTAIN

The break-up of the Soviet Union in 1990 led to 15 new footballing nations, though initially Russia played on at the 1992 UEFA European Championship as CIS, or the Commonwealth of Independent States – without the involvement of Estonia, Latvia and Lithuania. In the coming years, UEFA and FIFA approved the creation of separate teams for Russia, Armenia, Azerbaijan, Belarus, Estonia, Georgia, Kazakhstan, Kyrgyzstan, Latvia, Lithuania, Moldova, Tajikstan, Turkmenistan, Ukraine and Uzbekistan. Upheavals in the early 1990s would also fragment the former Yugoslavia into Croatia, Serbia, Bosnia-Herzegovina, Macedonia, Slovenia and Montenegro, while Czechoslovakia split into Slovakia and the Czech Republic.

YEAR AFFILIATED TO FIFA

Albania:	1932
Andorra:	1996
Austria:	1905
Belarus:	1992
Bosnia-Herzegovina:	1996
Cyprus:	1948
Estonia:	1923
Faroe Islands:	1988
Finland:	1908
Georgia:	1992
Greece:	1927
Iceland:	1947
Israel:	1929
Kazakhstan:	1994
Latvia:	1922
Liechtenstein:	1974
Luxembourg:	1910
Macedonia:	1994
Malta:	1959
Moldova:	1994
Montenegro:	2007
San Marino:	1988
Slovakia:	1994
Slovenia:	1992

FORLORN BOURG

If at first you don't succeed, try and try again – but poor Luxembourg have valiantly tried and failed to qualify for 17 consecutive World Cups. The only time they were not involved was the very first in 1930, when there was no qualification tournament and Luxembourg were not invited to the finals. The country has only ever recorded three victories in FIFA World Cup qualifiers: 4-2 at home to Portugal in October 1961, 2-0 at home to Turkey in October 1972, and 2-1 away to Switzerland in September 2008, when **Alphonse Leweck** scored a late winner.

THE FULL MONTE

Montenegro became the 208th and latest country to be recognized by FIFA, not long after Serbia and Montenegro had competed in the 2006 FIFA World Cup. But the new nation did not become a FIFA or UEFA member in time to compete in qualifiers for the 2008 UEFA European Championships and had to wait until the 2010 FIFA World Cup campaign for their first competitive match – a 2-2 draw at home to Bulgaria, in September 2008.

TRAVELLING MEN

Israel looked like qualifying for the 1958 FIFA World Cup without kicking a ball, because scheduled opponents Turkey, Indonesia and Sudan refused to play them. But FIFA ordered them into a two-legged play-off against a European side – which Israel lost 4-0 on aggregate to Wales. Israel were unfortunate again in the 2006 FIFA World Cup qualifiers, ending the campaign unbeaten – yet failing even to make the play-offs, finishing third in their group behind France and Switzerland. Coach Avram Grant later went on to manage Chelsea, losing the 2008 Champions League final on penalties to Manchester United. Israel hosted, and won, the 1964 Asian Nations Cup, and qualified for the 1970 FIFA World Cup through a combined Asia/Oceania qualifying competition, but are now members of the European Federation.

SLO STARTERS

The only country to beat Italy on their way to winning the 2006 FIFA World Cup were Slovenia, who triumphed 1-0 in an October 2004 qualifier, thanks to a late goal by centre-back **Bostjan Cesar**. However, Slovenia still missed out on the finals.

MORE SIND AGAINST

Austria's star player **Matthias Sindelar** refused to play for a new, merged national team when Germany annexed Austria in 1938. Sindelar, born in modern-day Hungary in February 1903, was the inspirational leader of Austria's so-called Wunderteam of the 1930s. He scored 27 goals in 43 games for Austria, who went 14 internationals unbeaten between April 1931 and December 1932, won the 1932 Central European International Cup and silver at the 1936 Olympics. During a special reunification match between the Austrian and German teams in Vienna in April 1938, Sindelar disobeyed orders and scored a spectacular solo goal. Austria went on to win 2-0 in a game which might have been expected to end in a diplomatic draw. Sindelar was mysteriously found dead from carbon monoxide poisoning in his Vienna apartment in January 1939.

THE GUD SON

Iceland striker **Eidur Gudjohnsen** made history on his international debut away to Estonia in April 1996, by coming on as a substitute for his own father, Arnor Gudjohnsen. Eidur was 17 at the time, his father 34 – though both were disappointed they did not get to play on the pitch at the same time. The Icelandic Football Association thought they would get a chance to do so in Iceland's next home game, but Eidur was ruled out by an ankle injury and the opportunity never arose again.

BROKEN–DOWN KARHAN

Slovakia's defensive midfielder **Miroslav Karhan** helped his country qualify for the 2010 FIFA World Cup, taking his appearances tally to a national record 95. But an Achilles tendon injury meant the team captain was ruled out of the tournament itself.

HAPPY ELVIR

Elvir Bolic holds the caps and goals record for Bosnia-Herzegovina, scoring 24 times in 52 games since the country began playing internationals in 1996. His was also the strike that ended Manchester United's 40-year unbeaten record at home in European competition: it was the only goal of the game for Turkish side Fenerbahce during a Champions League tie at Old Trafford in October 1996.

TOP KAT

Srecko Katanec has twice quit as an international coach after falling out with his star player. In 2002, he led Slovenia to their first FIFA World Cup finals, where temperamental captain and playmaker Zlatko Zahovic was sent home in disgrace after a tantrum. Tearful Katanec quit after his country's first-round elimination, allowing Zahovic to return to the side. Katanec later took over as Macedonia coach, but resigned in April 2008 after falling out with skipper Goran Pandev.

VITAL ASTAFJEVS

Midfielder Vitalijs Astafjevs put Latvia on the map when he became, temporarily at least, the most-capped European footballer of all time, with 158 appearances for his country – including three at the 2004 UEFA European Championship. He also scored 16 goals for his country. Astafjevs made his international debut in 1992, the year the Latvian national football team was revived after independence following the break-up of the Soviet Union, and was still playing for his country at the age of 38 in November 2009, when a friendly against Honduras allowed him to overtake Estonian Martin Reim's record and become the most-capped European footballer. Reim scored 14 goals in 156 games for Estonia between 1992 and 2007.

MOST INTERNATIONAL APPEARANCES

Albania:	Foto Strakosha	73
Andorra:	Oscar Sonejee	83
Austria:	Andreas Herzog	103
Belarus:	Aliaksandr Kulchiy	83
Bosnia-Herz.:	Elvir Bolic	55
Cyprus:	Ioannis Okkas	97
Estonia:	Martin Reim	157
Faroe Islands:	Oli Johannesen	83
Finland:	Jari Litmanen	132
Georgia:	Levan Kobiashvili	87
Greece:	Theo Zagorakis	120
Iceland:	Runar Kristinsson	106
Israel:	Arik Benado	95
Kazakhstan:	Ruslan Baltiev	73
Latvia:	Vitalijs Astafjevs	162
Liechtenstein:	Mario Frick	92
Luxembourg:	Jeff Strasser	96
Macedonia:	Goce Sedloski	100
Malta:	David Carabott	122
Moldova:	Radu Rebeja	74
Montenegro:	Vakasin Poleksic	21
San Marino:	Damiano Vannucci	53
Slovakia:	Miroslav Karhan	96
Slovenia:	Zlatko Zahovic	80

ROBERT THE HERO

Slovakia's **Robert Vittek** became only the fourth player from a country making their FIFA World Cup debut to score as many as four goals in one tournament, at the 2010 event in South Africa. He hit one against New Zealand, two against defending champions Italy, and a late penalty in a second-round defeat to Holland. The previous three players to do so were Portugal's Eusebio in 1966, Denmark's Preben Elkjaer Larsen in 1986 and Croatia's Davor Suker in 1998. Vittek's last-minute penalty against Holland made him Slovakia's all-time leading scorer, overtaking former Sparta Prague and Middlesbrough striker Szilard Nemeth.

DARK ERA

Macedonian striker **Darko Pancev** had to wait 15 years to receive his European Golden Boot award for the 1990–91 season, when he scored 34 goals for European Cup winners Red Star Belgrade. Organizers originally suspended the competition between 1991 and 1996, due to disagreements about goal tallies in Cyprus – but eventually agreed to hand Pancev his prize in August 2006. The unlucky European top scorers from 1992 to 1996 were Scotland's Ally McCoist (twice), Welshman David Taylor, Armenian Arsen Avetisyan and Georgian Zviad Endeladze.

KEEPING COUSINS

Two of Slovenia's three goalkeepers at the 2010 FIFA World Cup were cousins – 25-year-old first-choice **Samir Handanovic** and back-up Jasmin Handanovic, seven years older. Despite Slovenia's first-round elimination, Samir was widely acclaimed for his three displays – having already been described by 2006 FIFA World Cup-winning Italian Gianluigi Buffon as one of the best goalkeepers in Italy. After joining Italian club Udinese, Samir Handanovic made his Serie A debut just three days after his international debut in November 2004. The two games brought mixed fortunes for the 20-year-old – he conceded four goals and was sent off in Udinese's 5-4 win over Lecce, but kept a clean sheet for Slovenia in a goalless draw with Slovakia.

MOST INTERNATIONAL GOALS

Albania:	Alban Bushi	14
Andorra:	Ildefons Lima	7
Austria:	Toni Polster	44
Belarus:	Maxim Romaschenko	20
Bosnia-Herz.:	Elvir Bolic	24
Cyprus:	Michalis Konstantinou	29
Estonia:	Andres Oper	36
Faroe Islands:	Rogvi Jacobsen	10
Finland:	Jari Litmanen	31
Georgia:	Shota Arveladze	26
Iceland:	Eidur Gudjohnsen	24
Israel:	Mordechai Spiegler	25
Kazakhstan:	Ruslan Baltiev	13
Latvia:	Maris Verpakovskis	26
Liechtenstein:	Mario Frick	14
Luxembourg:	Leon Mart	16
Macedonia:	Goran Pandev	23
Malta:	Michael Mifsud	24
Moldova:	Serghei Clescenco	11
Montenegro:	Mirko Vucinic	9
San Marino:	Andy Selva	8
Slovakia:	Szilard Nemeth	22
Slovenia:	Robert Vittek	23

TU–WHIT TWO–NIL

Finland's adopted lucky mascot is an eagle-owl called "Bubi" that occasionally swoops down on the Helsinki Olympic Stadium during international matches – making his debut during a 2-0 UEFA European Championship qualifier win over Belgium in June 2007 and holding up the game for several minutes as he flew about the pitch and perched on goalposts. The eagle owl was later voted the Finnish capital's "Resident of the Year".

HIGH LIFE

At 64°09'N, Reykjavik, in Iceland, is the northernmost city to host a FIFA World Cup match – though so far only in qualifiers. The northernmost FIFA World Cup finals venue is Sandviken in Sweden, at 60°37'N – while Christchurch in New Zealand (43°32'S) holds the record for southernmost FIFA World Cup venue, with the finals record held by Mar del Plata in Argentina (38°01'S).

BOHEMIAN RHAPSODY

Striker **Josef "Pepi" Bican** is, for many Austrian fans, the most prolific goalscorer of all time. Some authorities put his total tally in officially recognized matches at 805 goals, higher in the rankings than Romario, Pele and Gerd Muller. Bican played for Austrian clubs Rapid Vienna and Admira in the 1930s, but the bulk of his strikes came for Czech-based Slavia Prague between 1937 and 1948. He also scored 19 goals in 19 games for Austria from 1933 to 1936, before switching citizenship and hitting 21 in 14 matches for Czechoslovakia between 1938 and 1949. Although he reached the semi-finals of the 1934 FIFA World Cup with Austria, an administrative error meant he was not registered with his new country in time for the 1938 tournament. He also played one international match for a representative Bohemia and Moravia side in 1939, scoring a hat-trick.

BARREN SPELLS

Seven European teams have failed to score a single goal during a FIFA World Cup qualifying campaign: Liechtenstein (across eight games ahead of the 2002 tournament), San Marino (eight games in 1998), Malta (six games in 1978), and 10 games in 2010, Cyprus (four games in 1966), Israel (four games in 1954), Finland (three games in 1938) and Lithuania (one game in 1934).

KOREN VALUES

Captain **Robert Koren** gave Slovenia their first FIFA World Cup Finals win with the only goal of the game against Algeria, in Group C at the 2010 tournament. But as in 2002, they were unable to qualify for the second round after then drawing 2-2 with the USA and losing 1-0 to England. Koren went into the tournament without a club, having just been released by England's promoted West Bromwich Albion.

LAT'S ENTERTAINMENT

After Austria, who had finished top of their qualifying group, were annexed by Germany prior to the 1938 FIFA World Cup, **Latvia** – who had finished as runners-up behind the Austrians – hoped to take their place, but were overlooked and the tournament went ahead with 15 teams instead of 16. After spending the years between 1940 to 1991 as part of the Soviet Union, Latvia finally qualified for their first major finals in 2004, defeating Turkey in a play-off to reach the UEFA European Championship finals.

RECORD WINS

Albania:	5-0 v Vietnam (A, December 2003);
	6-1 vs Cyprus (H, August 2009)
Andorra:	2-0 v Belarus (H, April 2000);
	2-0 v Albania (H, April 2002)
Austria:	9-0 v Malta (H, April 1977)
Belarus:	5-0 v Lithuania (H, June 1998)
Bosnia-Herzegovina:	7-0 v Estonia (H, September 2008)
Cyprus:	5-0 v Andorra (H, November 2000)
Estonia:	6-0 v Lithuana (H, July 1928)
Faroe Islands:	3-0 v San Marino (H, May 1995)
Finland:	10-2 v Estonia (H, August 1922)
Georgia:	7-0 v Armenia (H, March 1997)
Greece:	8-0 v Syria (H, November 1949)
Iceland:	9-0 v Faroe Islands (H, July 1985)
Israel:	9-0 v Chinese Taipei (A, March 1988)
Kazakhstan:	7-0 v Pakistan (H, June 1997)
Latvia:	8-0 v Estonia (A, August 1942)
Liechtenstein:	4-0 v Luxembourg (A, October 2004)
Luxembourg:	6-0 v Afghanistan (A, July 1948)
Macedonia:	11-1 v Liechtenstein (A, November 1996)
Malta:	7-1 v Liechtenstein (H, March 2008)
Moldova:	5-0 v Pakistan (A, August 1992)
Montenegro:	3-0 v Kazakhstan (H, May 2008)
San Marino:	1-0 v Liechtenstein (H, April 2004)
Slovakia:	7-0 v Liechtenstein (H, September 2004);
	7-0 v San Marino (H, October 2007);
	7-0 v San Marino (H, June 2009)
Slovenia:	7-0 v Oman (A, February 1999)

RECORD DEFEATS

Albania:	0-12 v Hungary (A, September 1950)
Andorra:	1-8 v Czech Republic (A, June 2005);
	0-7 v Croatia (A, October 2006)
Austria:	1-11 v England (H, June 1908)
Belarus:	0-5 v Austria (A, June 2003)
Bosnia-Herzegovina:	0-5 v Argentina (A, May 1998)
Cyprus:	0-12 v West Germany (A, May 1969)
Estonia:	2-10 v Finland (A, August 1922)
Faroe Islands:	0-7 v Yugoslavia (A, May 1991);
	0-7 v Romania (A, May 1992);
	0-7 v Norway (H, August 1993);
	1-8 v Yugoslavia (H, October 1998)
Finland:	0-13 v Germany (A, September 1940)
Georgia:	0-5 v Romania (A, April 1996);
	1-6 v Denmark (A, September 2005)
Greece:	1-11 v Hungary (A, March 1938)
Iceland:	2-14 v Denmark (A, August 1967)
Israel*:	1-7 v Egypt (A, March 1934);
	1-7 v Germany (A, February 2002)
Kazakhstan:	0-6 v Turkey (H, June 2006);
	0-6 v Russia (A, May 2008)
Latvia:	0-12 v Sweden (A, May 1927)
Liechtenstein:	1-11 v Macedonia (H, November 1996)
Luxembourg:	0-9 v England (H, October 1960);
	0-9 v England (A, December 1982)
Macedonia:	0-5 v Belgium (H, June 1995)
Malta:	1-12 v Spain (A, December 1983)
Moldova:	0-6 v Sweden (A, June 2001)
Montenegro:	0-4 v Romania (A, May 2008)
San Marino:	0-13 v Germany (H, September 2006)
Slovakia:	0-6 v Argentina (A, June 1995)
Slovenia:	0-5 v France (A, October 2002)

* Played under the British Mandate of Palestine.

NO–SCORE ANDORRA

Since playing their first international on New Year's Day 1996 – a 6-1 home defeat to Estonia – Andorra have won only three matches, two of them friendlies. Their only competitive triumph was a 1-0 success over Macedonia in an October 2004 FIFA World Cup qualifying match, when left-back **Marc Bernaus** struck the only goal of the game. Perhaps their lack of strength should come as no surprise – the principality is the sixth-smallest country in Europe, with a population of just 71,822 and they have played their most high-profile games, against England, across the Spanish border in Barcelona.

GEORGIA ON MY MIND

Dynamo Tbilisi, from Georgia, and Zalgiris Vilnius, from Lithuania, played out a 2-2 draw in May 1990 in a game later categorized as an international match between the clubs' two countries. The fixture is now regarded as Georgia's first international, even though the country did not become independent from Russia for another 11 months.

VLAD ALL OVER

Three relatives named Vladimir Weiss – different generations of the same family – have represented their country in international football, with two of them featuring at the 2010 FIFA World Cup. The first Vladimir won a footballing silver medal with Czechoslovakia at the 1964 Olympics, before his son **Vladimir** played for the same country at the 1990 FIFA World Cup. This second Vladimir then led Slovakia to the 2010 tournament as coach, picking his Manchester City winger son – yet another **Vladimir** – for three of the team's four matches. The first Vladimir made three appearances for Czechoslovakia, including the 1964 Olympics final in which he scored an own goal as Hungary triumphed 2-1. The second Vladimir won 19 caps for Czechoslavakia and 12 for Slovakia, and the third ended the 2010 FIFA World Cup with 12 but still aged only 20. The coach described their 3-2 victory over holders Italy at the 2010 FIFA World Cup as the second happiest day of his life – only beaten by the day his son was born.

SOUTH AMERICA

South America provided the first hosts of the FIFA World Cup™ and the first winners in the shape of Uruguay and claims nine successes in total (Brazil five, Argentina and Uruguay two each). It also boasts fans with a unique cultural tradition whose magic can turn a football match into a carnival.

ARGENTINA

Copa America champions on 14 occasions, FIFA Confederations Cup winners in 1992, Olympic gold medallists in 2004 and 2008 and, most treasured of all, FIFA World Cup™ winners in 1978 and 1986: no country has won as many international titles as Argentina. The country has a long and rich football history (the first Argentine league was contested in 1891) and has produced some of the greatest footballers ever to have played the game.

FRINGE PLAYERS

Daniel Passarella was a demanding captain when he led his country to glory at the 1978 World Cup. He was the same as coach. After taking over the national side in 1994, he refused to pick anyone unless they had their hair cut short – and ordered striker Claudio Caniggia to get rid of his "girl's hair".

A ROUND DOZEN

Argentina were responsible for the biggest win in Copa America history, when five goals by Jose Manuel Moreno helped them thrash Ecuador 12-0 in 1942. Moreno won league titles in Argentina, Mexico, Chile and Colombia.

WORTH WAITING FOR

Argentina's national stadium, "El Monumental" in Buenos Aires, hosted its first game in 1938. But the original design was not completed until 20 years later – largely thanks to the £97,000 River Plate received for a transfer fee from Juventus for Omar Sivori. The stadium is a must-see stop on the itinerary of many global football tourists, for the "Superclasico" derby between hosts River Plate and cross-city rivals Boca Juniors.

BOTTOMS UP

Perhaps the most predictable thing about **Diego Maradona**'s spell as Argentina's coach has been its unpredictability. He was banned from football for two months for his foul-mouthed criticism of journalists after his side finally clinched a place at the 2010 FIFA World Cup. The prospect of being abused did not deter hordes of journalists from flocking to his press conferences in South Africa, meaning attendance had to be made ticket-only. Eccentric elements of his squad's World Cup training sessions included Maradona puffing on cigars while issuing instructions – or bending over and inviting players to aim shots at his backside.

BEGINNER'S LUCK

The youngest FIFA World Cup coach was Juan Jose Tramutola, just 27 years and 267 days old when Argentina opened their 1930 campaign by beating France 1-0. Argentina went on to reach the final, only to lose 4-2 to Uruguay – with both sides providing their own choice of ball for each of the halves.

NUMBERS GAME

Argentina's FIFA World Cup squads of 1978 and 1982 were given numbers based on alphabetical order, rather than positions, which meant the No. 1 shirt was worn by midfielders Norberto Alonso in 1978 and Osvaldo Ardiles in 1982. The only member of the 1982 squad whose shirt number broke the alphabetical order was No. 10, Diego Maradona.

THE KIDS ARE ALL RIGHT

Argentina's youngsters have won the FIFA World Under-20 Championship a record six times, most recently in 2005 and 2007. Sergio Aguero and Mauro Zarate scored the goals in a 2-1 final win over the Czech Republic, when Canada hosted the tournament in 2007.

MASCH OF THE DAY

Diego Maradona picked 107 different players for Argentina in matches ahead of the 2010 FIFA World Cup. But captain **Javier Mascherano** could be in no doubt he had the faith of his manager. Maradona insisted: "My team is Mascherano and 10 more." The defensive midfielder had previously been part of Argentina's Olympics-winning teams in both 2004 and 2008, the first male footballer since 1928 to collect two Olympic gold medals.

SUPER BOLATTI

Argentina fans had to wait until just six minutes from the end of their final qualifying match for the goal confirming they would be at the 2010 FIFA World Cup. Midfield substitute Mario Bolatti scored the winning goal that gave Argentina automatic qualification and condemned opponents Uruguay to a play-off against Costa Rica.

CHINA IN YOUR HAND

In an unusual move, the two 2008 Olympics football finalists Argentina and Nigeria were allowed to take two drinks breaks during the match, which was watched by 89,102 spectators. The game was played in stifling heat in Chinese host city Beijing. **Angel Di Maria** scored the only goal for Argentina, allowing them to retain the title they won in Athens – for the first time – four years earlier.

DO YOU COME HERE OFTEN?

Argentina and Uruguay have played each other more often than any other two nations – 177 matches, including the first international played outside the UK, in 1902. Argentina won that one, 6-0, in the Uruguayan capital Montevideo and have led the way ever since – winning 81 games, compared to Uruguay's 53, with 43 draws.

MAJOR TOURNAMENTS

FIFA WORLD CUP™: 15 appearances – Winners (2) 1978, 1986

COPA AMERICA: 38 appearances – Winners (14) 1921, 1925, 1927, 1929, 1937, 1941, 1945, 1946, 1947, 1955, 1957, 1959, 1991, 1993

CONFEDERATIONS CUP: Three appearances – Winners (1) 1993

FIRST INTERNATIONAL: Uruguay 2 Argentina 3 (Montevideo, Uruguay, 16 May 1901)

BIGGEST WIN: Argentina 12 Ecuador 0 (Montevideo, Uruguay, 22 January 1942)

BIGGEST DEFEAT: Czechoslovakia 6 Argentina 1 (Helsingborg, Sweden, 15 June 1958); Bolivia 6 Argentina 1, La Paz, Bolivia, 1 April 2009

GLOBAL GLORY

The old Intercontinental Cup, contested by the club champions of Europe and South America until 2004, was won most often by Argentine sides, who triumphed nine times. Boca Juniors took three titles, Independiente two, with single successes for Estudiantes, Racing Club, River Plate and Velez Sarsfield.

SUPER MARIO

Mario Kempes, who scored twice in the 1978 FIFA World Cup final and won the Golden Boot, was the only member of Cesar Menotti's squad who played for a non-Argentine club. Playing for Valencia, he had been the Spanish league's top scorer for the previous two seasons.

TOP SCORERS

1	Gabriel Batistuta	56
2	Hernan Crespo	36
3	Diego Maradona	34
4	Luis Artime	24
5	Leopoldo Luque	22
=	Daniel Passarella	22
7	Jose Sanfilippo	21
=	Herminio Masantonio	21
9	Mario Kempes	20
10	Norberto Mendez	19
=	Jose Manuel Moreno	19
=	Rene Pontoni	19

IN THE CUP FOR TOTTINGHAM

After Argentina won the FIFA World Cup for the first time in 1978, Osvaldo Ardiles and Ricardo Villa crossed the Atlantic to Europe and both joined English club Tottenham Hotspur, where they both played a major role in the club's 1981 FA Cup final appearance. Ardiles was granted a solo line in the club's Cup final song, "Ossie's Dream"; Villa went one better, scoring the spectacular solo winner against Manchester City in a replay at Wembley.

SPOT–KICK FLOP

If at first you don't succeed, try and try again – unfortunately Martin Palermo missed all three penalties he took during Argentina's 1999 Copa America clash with Colombia. The first hit the crossbar, the second flew over the bar, and the third was saved. Colombia won the match 3-0.

WINNING TOUCH

Midfielder Marcelo Trobbiani played just two minutes of FIFA World Cup football – the last two minutes of the 1986 final, after replacing winning goalscorer Jorge Burruchaga. Trobbiani touched the ball once, a backheel. The former Boca star ended his international career with 15 caps and one goal to his name.

SECOND TIME LUCKY

Luisito Monti is the only man to play in the FIFA World Cup finals for two different countries. The centre-half, born in Buenos Aires on 15 May 1901 but with Italian family origins, was highly influential in Argentina's run to the 1930 final. They lost the game 4-2 to Uruguay – after Monti allegedly received mysterious pre-match death threats. Following a transfer to Juventus the following year, he was allowed to play for Italy and was on the winning side when they beat Czechoslovakia in the 1934 final. Another member of the 1934 team was Raimundo Orsi, who had also played for Argentina before switching sides in 1929.

DIVINE DIEGO

To many people **Diego Armando Maradona** is the greatest footballer the world has ever seen, better even than Pele. The Argentine legend, born in Lanus on 30 October 1960, first became famous as a ball-juggling child during half-time intervals at Argentinos Juniors matches. He was distraught to be left out of Argentina's 1978 FIFA World Cup squad and was then sent off for retaliation at the 1982 tournament. Maradona, as triumphant Argentina captain in Mexico in 1986, scored the notorious "Hand of God" goal and then a spectacular individual strike within five minutes of each other in a quarter-final win over England. He again captained Argentina to the final in 1990, in Italy – the country where he inspired Napoli to Serie A and UEFA Cup success. He was thrown out of the 1994 FIFA World Cup finals in disgrace after failing a drugs test. Maradona captained Argentina 16 times in FIFA World Cup matches, a record, and was surprisingly appointed national coach in 2008, despite scant previous experience as a manager.

FITTER, JAVIER

Javier Zanetti is Argentina's most-capped player, with 136 international appearances – despite being surprisingly left out of Jose Pekerman's squad for the 2006 FIFA World Cup finals. He returned to the team under Alfio Basile, to overtake Roberto Ayala's record caps tally. Zanetti, who can play at full-back or in midfield, has also played more Serie A matches than any other non-Italian. But he missed out on the FIFA World Cup again in 2010, when he and Esteban Cambiasso were left out by Diego Maradona despite helping Internazionale win the Italian league, the Italian Cup and the UEFA Champions League in 2009–10.

THE ANGEL GABRIEL

Gabriel Batistuta, nicknamed "Batigol" and Argentina's all-time leading scorer, is the only man to have scored hat-tricks in two separate FIFA World Cups. He scored the first against Greece in 1994 and the second against Jamaica four years later. Hungary's Sandor Kocsis, France's Just Fontaine and Germany's Gerd Muller each scored two hat-tricks in the same FIFA World Cup. Batistuta, born in Reconquista on 1 February 1969, also set an Italian league record during his time with Florentina, by scoring in 11 consecutive Serie A matches at the start of the 1994–95 season.

LEO BRAVO

Despite some sparkling performances, **Lionel Messi** somehow failed to score in five games at the 2010 FIFA World Cup. But he did enjoy the achievement of becoming Argentina's youngest-ever captain, when he wore the armband for their final group game against Greece, as regular skipper Javier Mascherano was rested. Before the tournament, coach Diego Maradona had told of struggling to track down Barcelona star Messi on the phone, saying: "He is more difficult to get hold of than US President Barack Obama."

TOP CAPS

1	Javier Zanetti	136
2	Roberto Ayala	115
3	Diego Simeone	106
4	Oscar Ruggeri	97
5	Diego Maradona	91
6	Ariel Ortega	87
7	Gabriel Batistuta	78
8	Juan Pablo Sorin	76
9	Americo Gallego	73
=	Juan Sebastian Veron	73

SAINTED PALERMO

Veteran striker **Martin Palermo** waited 10 years between international appearances before being called up again by his former Boca Juniors team-mate Diego Maradona in 1999. He justified the surprise recall with a stoppage-time winner in the penultimate qualifier against Peru, prompting Maradona to take a celebratory dive in rain-sodden mud on the touchline and then hail "the miracle of St Palermo". Palermo then became his country's oldest-ever FIFA World Cup scorer, at the 2010 tournament in South Africa. He was 36 years and 227 days old when he came on as a substitute in the first round against Greece and completed the scoring in a 2-0 victory – a year and 358 days older than Maradona was when scoring against the same country 16 years earlier.

BRAZIL

No country has captured the soul of the game to the same extent as Brazil. The country's distinctive yellow-shirted and blue-shorted players have thrilled generations of football fans, have produced some of the game's greatest moments, and no FIFA World Cup™ tournament would be the same without them. Brazil – the nation that gave birth to Pele, Garrincha, Zico, Ronaldo and Kaka – are the only team to have appeared in the finals of every FIFA World Cup™, and have won the competition a record-breaking five times.

EXTRA CONTINENTAL

Until 2010, Brazil was the only country to have won the FIFA World Cup outside of its own continent – which it has achieved on three occasions, in 1958 in Sweden, in the United States in 1994 and in Japan/Korea in 2002.

CLOSE ENCOUNTERS

Brazil have been involved in many memorable games. Their 3-2 defeat to Italy in 1982 is regarded as one of the classic games in FIFA World Cup finals history. Paolo Rossi scored all three of Italy's goals with Brazil coach Tele Santana much criticized for going all out in attack when only a 2-2 draw was needed. Brazil's 1982 squad, with players such as **Socrates**, Zico and **Falcao**, is considered one of the greatest teams never to win the tournament. In 1994, a 3-2 win over Holland in the quarter-finals – their first competitive meeting in 20 years – was just as thrilling, with all the goals coming in the second half.

OPENING ACTS

Brazil have played in more FIFA World Cup opening matches than any other country, with nine, though this includes tournaments up to 1962 when all teams played their first matches at the same time. Next come Mexico, whose 2010 opener against South Africa was their seventh. Brazil last opened a FIFA World Cup as holders in 1998, when they beat Scotland 2-1 in the Stade de France, Saint-Denis.

FIERCEST RIVALS

Brazil's oldest club classic is Fluminense versus Botafogo in Rio de Janeiro. The clubs faced each other for the first time on 22 October 1905, when Fluminense won 6-0. One particular match stirred a controversy that lasted 89 years. The two teams disagreed on the result of the 1907 championship, whose title was disputed up to 1996 ... when they finally decided to share it.

BRAZIL'S RECORD

FIFA WORLD CUP™	19 appearances (every finals)
Matches (97)	W67, D15, L15, GF210, GA88
Winners (5)	1958, 1962, 1970, 1994, 2002
Runners-up (2)	1950, 1998
Third place (2)	1938, 1978
Fourth place (1)	1974
COPA AMERICA	32 appearances
Winners (8)	1919, 1922, 1949, 1989,
	1997, 1999, 2004, 2007
CONFEDERATIONS CUP	Six appearances
Winners (3)	1997, 2005, 2009
FIRST INTERNATIONAL	Argentina 3 Brazil 0
	(Buenos Aires, 20 September 1914)
BIGGEST WIN	Brazil 14 Nicaragua 0
	(Mexico City, 17 October 1975)
HEAVIEST DEFEAT	Uruguay 6 Brazil 0
	(Chile, 18 September 1920)

LAND OF FOOTBALL

No country is more deeply identified with football success than Brazil, who have won the FIFA World Cup a record five times – in 1958, 1962, 1970, 1994 and 2002. They are also the only team never to have missed a FIFA World Cup finals and are favourites virtually every time the competition is staged. After winning the trophy for a third time in Mexico in 1970, Brazil kept the **Jules Rimet Trophy** permanently. Sadly, it was stolen from the federation's headquarters in 1983 and was never recovered. Brazilians often refer to their country as "o país do futebol" ("the country of football"). It is the favourite pastime of youngsters, while general elections are often held in the same year as the FIFA World Cup, with critics arguing that political parties try to take advantage of the nationalistic surge created by football and bring it into politics. Charles Miller, the son of a Scottish engineer, is credited with bringing football to Brazil in 1894. Yet the sport would only truly become Brazilian when blacks were able to play at the top level in 1933. At first, because of the game's European origin, it was the sport of Brazil's urban white elite. However, it quickly spread among the urban poor as Brazilians realized the only thing they needed to play was a ball, which could be substituted inexpensively with a bundle of socks, an orange, or even a cloth filled with paper.

CAPTAIN TO COACH

Brazil's 1994 FIFA World Cup-winning captain **Dunga** was appointed national coach in 2006 despite having no previous management experience. He led the team to 2007 Copa America and 2009 FIFA Confederations Cup success. But he lost his job after Brazil were knocked out of the 2010 FIFA World Cup in a 2-1 quarter-final defeat to Holland. Dunga – real name Carlos Caetano Bledorn Verri, but widely known by the Portuguese for "Dopey" – had already faced criticism back home for his team's defensive style and decisions not to take Ronaldinho, Adriano or Alexandre Pato to South Africa.

1966 AND ALL THAT

Brazil's preparation for the 1966 FIFA World Cup in England was affected by political influences. All the major clubs wanted their players included in the squad to increase their transfer value. In the final months of preparation, coach **Vicente Feola** was working with a squad of 46, of whom only 22 would go to England. This caused unrest among the players and Brazil failed to progress beyond the group stages – one of their worst-ever performances.

BLOWING HOT AND COLD

A rare FIFA World Cup to be played in winter conditions put Brazil through more extremes than most, in South Africa in 2010. The *Selecao* opened their campaign in 3°C conditions at Johannesburg's Ellis Park stadium, though later faced Portugal in 25°C heat on the coast, in Durban.

BLACK DIAMOND

Leonidas da Silva, who died aged 90 in 2004, is widely credited with being the first player to perfect the bicycle kick. Top scorer at the 1938 FIFA World Cup – including four goals in a single game against Poland – he was left out of the team in the semi-finals. It turned out to be a big mistake by then Brazil manager, Ademar Pimenta, as Brazil were knocked out by Italy. Apparently, when he scored his final goal against Poland, Leonidas was shoe-less, grounds for the referee to invalidate the goal. Cleverly, Leonidas splashed his feet into the dark mud and the referee could not tell he was not wearing any shoes!

TOP CAPS

1	Cafu	142
2	Roberto Carlos	125
3	Claudio Taffarel	101
4	Djalma Santos	98
5	Ronaldo	97
6	Lucio	96
7	Gilmar	94
8	Gilberto Silva	93
9	Pele	92
=	Rivelino	92

LEADING BRAZILIAN FIFA WORLD CUP™ MARKSMEN

1	Ronaldo	(top scorer in 2002)	15
2	Pele		12
3	Ademir	(top scorer in 1950)	9
=	Jairzinho	(the only player to score in every game played at a FIFA World Cup, in 1970)	9
=	Vava	(joint-top scorer in 1962)	9
6	Leonidas	(top scorer in 1938)	8
=	Rivaldo		8
7	Careca		7
8	Bebeto		6
=	Rivelino		6

TOP SCORERS

1	Pele	77
2	Ronaldo	62
3	Romario	55
4	Zico	52
5	Bebeto	39
6	Rivaldo	34
7	Jairzinho	33
8	Ademir	32
=	Ronaldinho	32
=	Tostao	32

THE KING

Pele is considered by many as the greatest player of all time, a sporting icon *par excellence* and not only for his exploits on the pitch. When, for instance, he scored his 1,000th goal, Pele dedicated it to the poor children of Brazil. He began playing for Santos at the age of 15 and won his first FIFA World Cup two years later, scoring twice in the final. Despite numerous offers from European clubs, the economic conditions and Brazilian football regulations at the time allowed Santos to keep hold of their prized asset for almost two decades, until 1974. All-time leading scorer of the Brazilian national team, he is the only footballer to be a member of three FIFA World Cup-winning teams. Despite being in the Brazilian squad at the start of the 1962 tournament, an injury suffered in the second match meant he was not able to play on and, initially, he missed out on a winner's medal. However, FIFA announced in November 2007 that he would be awarded a medal retrospectively. After the disastrous 1966 tournament, when Brazil fell in the first round, Pele said he did not wish to play in the FIFA World Cup again. He was finally talked round and ended up, in 1970, playing a key role in what is widely considered as one of the greatest sides ever. Since his retirement in 1977, Pele has been a worldwide ambassador for football, as well undertaking various acting roles and commercial ventures.

KAKA KEEPS FAITH

Brazilian playmaker **Kaka** collected a FIFA World Cup winners' medal in 2002 despite playing just 25 minutes of football in the tournament, as a first-round substitute against Costa Rica. But he was fortunate to be playing for his country at all, after almost being paralysed by a diving-board accident at the age of 18. His recovery helped strengthen his devout Christian faith. He went on to become FIFA World Footballer of the Year in 2007 – the same year he inspired AC Milan to UEFA Champions League glory. He was briefly the world's most expensive player in 2009 when Real Madrid paid £56 million to sign him from AC Milan. Kaka was less successful in the FIFA World Cups of 2006 and 2010, going out in the quarter-finals each time. He was shown a red card in the 2010 first-round match against the Ivory Coast.

WHITHER RONALDO?

Only one person knows exactly what happened to **Ronaldo** in the hours before the 1998 FIFA World Cup final – the man himself. He sparked one of the biggest mysteries in FIFA World Cup history when his name was left off the teamsheet before the game, only for it to reappear just in time for kick-off. It was initially reported that Ronaldo had an ankle injury, and then a upset stomach. Finally team doctor Lidio Toledo revealed the striker had been rushed to hospital after suffering a convulsion in his sleep, but that he had been cleared to play after neurological and cardiac tests. The most dramatic account came from Ronaldo's roommate Roberto Carlos. "Ronaldo was scared about what lay ahead. The pressure had got to him and he couldn't stop crying," said the legendary full-back. "At about four o'clock, he became ill. That's when I called the team doctor and told him to get over to our room as fast as he could."

TWO NAMES, TWO COUNTRIES

Playing for two countries is not allowed nowadays, but **Jose Altafini**, the third-highest scorer in the history of Italy's Serie A who had dual nationality, played international football for both Brazil and Italy. In Brazil he was nicknamed "Mazzola" for his striking resemblance to the former Torino forward Valentino Mazzola. He played in the 1958 FIFA World Cup for Brazil, though not in the latter stages of the tournament, and then switched to Italy for the 1962 event. The Italians preferred to call him by his real name.

SEVENTIES ICONS

No country has scored as many FIFA World Cup goals – nor shared them around so many different players – as Brazil. Their nine goals at the 2010 tournament took their overall tally to 210. New additions to their FIFA World Cup goal-getting ranks that summer were striker **Luis Fabiano** and centre-back Juan, respectively Brazil's 70th and 71st World Cup scorers.

URUGUAY

Uruguay was the first country to win a FIFA World Cup™, and they remain the smallest – boasting a population of under four million. Yet their footballers won the game's greatest prize in both 1930 and 1950, the second time shocking hosts and favourites Brazil. Until a fourth-place finish at the FIFA World Cup™ 2010, recent times had been less productive, though only Argentina can match Uruguay's 14 triumphs in the Copa America.

TOP SCORERS

1	Hector Scarone	31
2	Diego Forlan	29
3	Angel Romano	28
4	Oscar Miguez	27
5	Sebastian Abreu	26
6	Pedro Petrone	24
7	Carlos Aguilera	23
8	Fernando Morena	22
9	Jose Piendibene	20
10	Severino Varela	19

HAPPY ANNIVERSARY

A so-called "Mundialito", or "Little World Cup", was staged in December 1980 and January 1981 to mark the 50th anniversary of the FIFA World Cup – and, as in 1930, Uruguay emerged triumphant. The tournament was meant to involve all six countries who had previously won the tournament, though 1966 champions England turned down the invitation and were replaced by 1978 runners-up Holland. Uruguay beat Brazil 2-1 in the final, a repeat of the scoreline from the two teams' final match of the 1950 FIFA World Cup. The Mundialito-winning Uruguay side was captained by goalkeeper **Rodolfo Rodriguez**, still his country's most capped player, and coached by Roque Maspoli, who had played in goal in that 1950 final.

FORLAN HERO

Diego Forlan was the stand-out Uruguayan star of the 2010 FIFA World Cup. He scored five goals – including three from outside the penalty area, making him the first player to do so at a FIFA World Cup since Germany's Lothar Matthaus in 1990. He also hit the crossbar with a long-range free-kick, the final touch of Uruguay's 3-2 defeat to Germany in the third-place play-off. Forlan went into the 2010 tournament having just scored a late winner for Atletico Madrid, against Fulham, in the 2009–10 UEFA Europa League final. Uruguay's fourth-placed finish in South Africa meant Diego fared better than his father Pablo, who played in the Uruguay team knocked out in the first round of the 1974 FIFA World Cup.

DIFFERENT BALL GAME

Uruguay were the inaugural hosts – and the first winners – of the FIFA World Cup in 1930, having won football gold at the Olympics of 1924 in Paris and 1928 in Amsterdam. Among the players who won all three of those titles was forward Hector Scarone, who remains Uruguay's all-time top scorer with 31 goals in 52 internationals. They beat arch-rivals Argentina 4-2 in the 1930 final, in a game which used two different footballs – Argentina's choice in the first half, in which they led 2-1, before Uruguay's was used for their second-half comeback.

TOP CAPS

1	Rodolfo Rodriguez	79
2	Fabian Carini	74
3	Enzo Francescoli	72
4	Diego Forlan	69
=	Alvaro Recoba	69
6	Pablo Gabriel Garcia	68
=	Angel Romano	68
8	Carlos Aguilera	65
9	Jorge Barrios	61
=	Paolo Montero	61

TEACHER KNOWS BEST

Uruguay were the last of 32 teams to clinch qualification for the 2010 FIFA World Cup, needing a play-off against Central America contenders Costa Rica. But despite finishing fifth in the 10-team South America league table, Uruguay went on to finish fourth at the tournament itself – higher than all their continental rivals, including Brazil and Argentina. Their manager throughout qualifying and in South Africa was former schoolteacher **Oscar Washington Tabarez**, nicknamed "The Maestro" and also the man in charge when Uruguay had reached the second round of the 1990 FIFA World Cup.

LUCKY LUIS

Striker **Luis Suarez** made a dramatic intervention in his own penalty area in the last moments of Uruguay's quarter-final against Ghana at the 2010 FIFA World Cup in South Africa. He handled the ball on the line, preventing a certain Ghana goal, in the last minute of extra-time. After receiving a straight red card, he was distraught as he headed down the tunnel at Johannesburg's Soccer City stadium – only to dance in delight when Asamoah Gyan's penalty crashed into the crossbar. After the match finished 1-1, Uruguay won 4-2 on penalties, though they were without the suspended Suarez for the semi-final against Holland. Suarez was widely condemned for his actions but did receive some solace from his Ajax Amsterdam club-mate Maarten Stekelenburg. The Dutch goalkeeper sent Suarez a text message congratulating him on his "save".

TRAVEL SICKNESS

Despite winning the 1930 FIFA World Cup, Uruguay turned down the chance to defend their crown four years later, when the tournament was held in Italy. Uruguayan football authorities were unhappy that only four European countries had made the effort to travel to Uruguay and take part in 1930.

BOYS IN BLUE

Uruguay's 6-0 home defeat to neighbours Argentina, in Montevideo on 20 July 1902, was the first international match outside the UK – and it remains Uruguay's heaviest loss. The two countries have played each other a further 176 times in official internationals – a world record. Uruguay won 53 of those, Argentina 80, with 43 draws. Before an agreed kit-swap in 1910, Uruguay would often wear vertical light-blue and white stripes and arch-rivals Argentina would don pale-blue shirts.

FOUNDING FATHER

Uruguayan journalist Hector Rivadavia Gomez was the leading figure behind the formation of the South American football confederation, CONMEBOL – which was agreed by Uruguay, Brazil, Chile and Argentina on 9 July 1916. The date marked the 100th anniversary of Argentina's independence.

PLAY-OFF REGULARS

Uruguay have been involved in the FIFA World Cup qualifying play-offs for the last three tournaments: 2002, 2006 and 2010. They beat Australia in the showdown for 2002, lost to the same country four years later, then saw off Costa Rica 2-1 on aggregate for the right to compete at the 2010 competition in South Africa. **Dario Silva**, who scored Uruguay's first goal in the 3-1 aggregate victory over Australia in November 2001, had to have his right leg amputated five years later following a car crash.

OTHER TEAMS SOUTH AMERICA

EMPTY VICTORY

Chile reached the 1974 FIFA World Cup finals thanks to a walkover against the Soviet Union, in a qualifying play-off. The USSR, a Communist state, refused to play in Santiago's Estadio Nacional because it had been used as a detention camp by the regime of Chilean dictator Augusto Pinochet. Despite there being no opposition, Chile's players kicked off in an empty stadium, scored in an unguarded net and were awarded the win by the referee.

TIM'S TIME

Peru were coached at the 1982 FIFA World Cup by Tim, who had been waiting an unprecedented 44 years to return to the FIFA World Cup finals – after playing once as striker for his native Brazil in the 1938 tournament.

NATIONAL STADIUMS

Bolivia:
Estadio Hernando Siles,
La Paz (45,000 capacity)

Chile:
Estadio Nacional,
Santiago (63,379)

Colombia:
Estadio El Campin,
Bogota (48,600)

Ecuador:
Estadio Olimpico Atahualpa,
Quito (40,948)

Paraguay:
Estadio Defensores
del Chaco, Asuncion (36,000)

Peru:
Estadio Nacional,
Lima (45,574)

Venezuela:
Estadio Polideportivo
de Pueblo Nuevo,
San Cristobal (38,755)

HAPPY ANNIVERSARY

Chile went exactly 48 years between victories at a FIFA World Cup. Their long wait ended in South Africa in 2010 as **Jean Beausejour** (No. 15) scored the only goal of their Group H game against Honduras on 16 June. On 16 June 1962, when they were the tournament's hosts, Chile overcame Yugoslavia in the third-place play-off, also 1-0 (Eladio Rojas scoring). They suffered seven defeats and six draws in between. The win in Nelspruit was also Chile's first FIFA World Cup victory outside of South America.

SIX AND OUT

Bolivia and El Salvador have both played the most FIFA World Cup finals matches without managing to win even once – six each. At least Bolivia did achieve a goalless draw against South Korea in 1994. But they went a record five successive FIFA World Cup finals matches without scoring a goal, across the 1930 and 1994 tournaments, before **Erwin Sanchez** put an end to their barren spell in a 3-1 defeat to Spain in their final 1994 fixture. The unwanted record was equalled at the 2010 FIFA World Cup, by both Honduras and New Zealand. Honduras drew twice and lost once in 1982, then drew once and lost twice in 2010. New Zealand lost all three matches in 1982 then drew all three in 2010.

HOME SECURITY

Colombia are the only country to go through a Copa America tournament without conceding a goal, when they hosted and won the cup for the first and only time in 2001. Their striker **Victor Aristazabal** ended the tournament as top scorer, with six goals, but the only goal of the final against Mexico came from defender Ivan Cordoba. Colombia's hosting rights were put in jeopardy due to security fears – they prompted Argentina to withdraw – but after pondering a move to Venezuela, South American football's governing body, CONMEBOL, decided to keep it in Colombia.

CONTINENTAL CONQUESTS

Chile and Paraguay each won 10 matches during the South American qualifiers for the 2010 FIFA World Cup – more than any other of their CONMEBOL rivals, including table-toppers Brazil who only managed nine. The 2010 qualification campaign was the first time Paraguay broke the 30-point barrier under the current 10-team, 18-match format.

EVERYONE OUT

Nineteen players were sent off when Uruguay played Chile in June 1975 – ten Chileans and nine Uruguayans. Referee Sergio Vasquez, a Chilean, was later suspended and fined for losing control.

A FIRST FOR ECUADOR

LDU Quito, based in the Ecuador capital, became the first and to date only team from the country to claim an international title when they won the Copa Libertadores in 2008. They beat Brazilian side Fluminense 3-1 on penalties in the final – after the two legs had ended 5-5 on aggregate. LDU went on to lose to Manchester United in the final of the FIFA Club World Cup later in the year.

TOP CAPS: CHILE

1	Leonel Sanchez	84
2	Nelson Tapia	73
3	Alberto Fouilloux	70
=	Marcelo Salas	70
5	Fabian Estay	69
=	Ivan Zamorano	69
7	Javier Margas	63
8	Miguel Ramirez	62
9	Clarence Acuna	61
10	Juan Carlos Letelier	57

HIGH LIFE

Bolivia and Ecuador play their home internationals at higher altitudes than any other teams on earth. Bolivia's showpiece Estadio Hernando Siles stadium, in the capital La Paz, is 3,637 metres (11,932ft) above sea level, while Ecuador's main Estadio Olimpico Atahualpa, in Quito, sits 2,800 metres (9,185ft) above sea level. Opposing teams have complained that the rarefied nature of the air makes it difficult to breathe, let alone play, but a FIFA ban on playing competitive internationals at least 2,500 metres (8,200ft) above sea level, first introduced in May 2007, was amended a month later adjusting the limit to 3,000 metres (9,840ft) and allowing Estadio Hernando Siles to be used as a special case. The altitude ban was suspended entirely in May 2008. FIFA had changed its mind after protests by Bolivia, Ecuador and other affected nations Colombia and Peru. Other campaigners to overturn the law included Argentina legend Diego Maradona. He may have regretted his decision. In March 2009 **Bolivia scored a 6-1 home win against Argentina** in a FIFA World Cup qualifier. The Argentina coach was ... Maradona.

TOP GOALS: CHILE

1	Marcelo Salas	37
2	Ivan Zamorano	34
3	Caros Caszely	29
4	Leonel Sanchez	23
5	Jorge Aravena	22
6	Juan Carlos Letelier	18
=	Humberto Suazo	18
8	Enrique Hormazabal	17
9	Jaime Ramirez Banda	12
=	Alberto Fouilloux	12
=	Hugo Eduardo Rubio	12

ABOVE–PAR PARAGUAY

In their eighth appearance at a FIFA World Cup, Paraguay topped their first-round group for the first time in 2010. Not only that, they went on to reach a later stage of the tournament than ever before, the quarter-finals, before narrowly losing 1-0 to Spain. Their penalty shoot-out victory over Japan in the second round (**Oscar Cardozo**, No. 7 converting the decisive kick) meant four South American countries made the quarter-finals – outnumbering the three European nations for the first time. That said, there were no quarter-finals in 1930, 1950, 1974, 1978 or 1982.

LUCKY LEO

Leonel Sanchez holds the Chilean record for international appearances, scoring 23 goals in 84 games. But he was lucky to remain on the pitch for one of them – escaping a sending-off despite punching Italy's Mario David in the face during their so-called "Battle of Santiago" clash at the 1962 FIFA World Cup. Sanchez, a left-winger born in Santiago on 25 April 1936, finished the tournament as one of six players sharing the Golden Boot – he, Brazilians Garrincha and Vava, Russian Valentin Ivanov, Yugoslavian Drazan Jerkovic and Hungarian Florian Albert all scored four.

ELITE CUB

Peru forward **Teofilo Cubillas** became the first player to twice end a FIFA World Cup finals with at least five goals – he scored five apiece in 1970 and 1978, though failed to win the Golden Boot on either occasion. Germany's Miroslav Klose emulated the achievement by scoring five in 2002 and the same tally four years later, the same year he picked up the Golden Boot award.

MOST INTERNATIONAL GOALS

Bolivia	Joaquin Botero	20
Chile	Marcelo Salas	37
Colombia	Adolfo Valencia	31
Ecuador	Agustin Delgado	31
Paraguay	Jose Saturnino Cardozo	25
Peru	Teofilo Cubillas	26
Venezuela	Giancarlo Maldonado	19

MOST INTERNATIONAL CAPS

Bolivia	Luis Cristaldo	93
	Marco Sandy	93
Chile	Leonel Sanchez	84
Colombia	Carlos Valderrama	111
Ecuador	Ivan Hurtado	167
Paraguay	Carlos Gamarra	110
Peru	Roberto Palacios	122
Venezuela	Jose Manuel Rey	109

TOP GOALS: PARAGUAY

1	Jose Saturnino Cardozo	25
2	Roque Santa Cruz	21
3	Julio Cesar Romero	13
=	Saturnino Arrua	13
5	Carlos Gamarra	12
=	Gerardo Rivas	12
7	Miguel Angel Benitez	11
8	Salvador Cabanas	10
=	Aurelio Gonzalez	10
=	Carlos Humberto Paredes	10
=	Juan Bautista Villalba	10

RENE HIGUITA

Eccentric goalkeeper **Rene Higuita** managed to score three goals for his country and also performed a famous, and acrobatic, "scorpion kick" save at Wembley in September 1995, hurling himself into the air and flicking away a Jamie Redknapp shot with the heels of both feet. He played for Colombia at the 1990 FIFA World Cup, but missed the 1994 FIFA World Cup finals due to a seven-month jail sentence for his involvement in a kidnapping and then tested positive for cocaine in November 2004.

WE HAPPY THREE

The first player to be named South American Footballer of the Year three times was not Pele, Garrincha or Diego Maradona, but Chilean centre-back Elias Figueroa, who took the prize in three consecutive years between 1974 and 1976 while playing for Brazilian club Internacional. The only players to emulate such a hat-trick were Brazil's Zico, in 1977, 1981 and 1982, and Argentina forward Carlos Tevez, in 2003, 2004 and 2005. Two more Chileans have won the award: Marcelo Salas in 1997 and Matias Fernandez in 2006. Outside of Brazil and Argentina, the most winners of the prize have come from Chile and Paraguay, with five apiece – Paraguay's were Romerito (1985), Raul Vicente Amarilla (1990), Jose Luis Chilavert (1996), Jose Cardozo (2002) and Salvador Cabanas (2007).

IVAN THE ADMIRABLE

Ecuador defender Ivan Hurtado is South America's most-capped footballer, playing 168 games since making his debut in 1992, including five goals. He was one of Ecuador's most influential stars at their first FIFA World Cup finals, in 2002. Hurtado captained them as they reached the second round four years later.

MEDELLIN MURDER

Tragic Colombian defender Andres Escobar, 27, was shot dead outside a Medellin bar two days after scoring an own goal in a 1994 FIFA World Cup first-round match against the United States. Colombia lost the game 2-1 and were eliminated from a tournament some observers – including Pele – had tipped them to win.

DURBAN LEGEND

Mark Gonzalez, Chile's winning goalscorer against Switzerland at the 2010 FIFA World Cup in South Africa, could have been eligible to play for the host country instead. He was born in Durban, South Africa, on 10 July 1984, as his Chilean international footballer father Raul was playing club football there at the time. But Mark moved to Chile 10 years later and has been playing international football for the land of his family since 2003. Gonzalez was denied a return to Durban for any of Chile's four matches at the 2010 tournament, which all took place in other host cities.

TOP CAPS: PARAGUAY

1	Carlos Gamarra	110
2	Denis Caniza	99
3	Roberto Acuna	97
4	Celso Ayala	85
5	Jose Saturnino Cardozo	82
6	Roberto Fernandez	78
=	Justo Villar	78
8	Juan Bautista Torales	77
9	Paulo Da Silva	76
10	Roque Santa Cruz	75

SAFE HANDS OSCAR

Keeping clean sheets for Colombia all the way through the 2001 Copa America was **Oscar Cordoba**, who went on to become his country's most-capped goalkeeper – with 73 appearances between 1993 and 2006.

CANIZA CAN DO

Centre-back and captain **Denis Caniza**, 36, became the first Paraguayan to play at four different FIFA World Cups, with his one appearance against New Zealand during the 2010 tournament. He has also now played more FIFA World Cup matches than any other Paraguayan, taking his tally to 12 – and his total cap count to 99. Caniza had retired from international football after the 2006 FIFA World Cup, but was persuaded to return by new coach Gerardo Martino the following year.

SALAS DAYS

Chile's all-time leading scorer Marcelo Salas formed a much-feared striking partnership with Ivan Zamorano during the late 1990s and early 21st century. Salas scored four goals as Chile reached the second round of the 1998 FIFA World Cup in France despite not winning a game. The Temuco-born striker spent two years in international retirement, from 2005 to 2007, but returned for the first four games of qualification for the 2010 FIFA World Cup. His contribution included both Chile goals in a 2-2 draw with Uruguay on 18 November 2007, but his international career ended for good three days later, with a 3-0 defeat to Paraguay.

AFRICA

Africa has been one of the great contributors to world football with a stream of outstanding players even before nations such as Cameroon, Nigeria and later Ivory Coast and Ghana began to make their mark on the international scene. The continent became the focus of world football attention in 2010 when its fans welcomed the FIFA World Cup™ finals to the Rainbow Nation of South Africa.

NORTH AFRICA FIFA WORLD CUP™ RECORDS

FAWZI'S FIRST

Abdelrahman Fawzi became the first African footballer to score at a FIFA World Cup, when he pulled a goal back for Egypt against Hungary in the first round of the 1934 tournament – then scored an equalizer eight minutes later, to make it 2-2 at half-time. Egypt went on to lose the match 4-2, and would not return to the finals for another 56 years.

PLAY–OFF PIQUE

Morocco's qualification for the 1970 FIFA World Cup ended a 36-year African exile from the finals. No African countries played at the 1966 FIFA World Cup in Africa, with 16 possible candidate countries all boycotting the event because FIFA wanted the top African team to face a side from Asia or Oceania in a qualification play-off.

AGELESS ALI

Tunisian goalkeeper **Ali Boumnijel** played in all three of his country's games at the 2006 FIFA World Cup – making him the oldest player to feature in Germany that summer, as well as only the fifth man over the age of 40 to play at a FIFA World Cup. Boumnijel conceded six goals in those three matches, against Saudi Arabia (two, in a 2-2 draw), Spain (three, in a 3-1 defeat) and Ukraine (one, in a 1-0 loss).

REDS IN A ROW

When Antar Yahia was sent off for a second bookable offence, three minutes into stoppage-time of Algeria's 1-0 defeat to the USA at the 2010 FIFA World Cup, it was not only the latest red card shown in any World Cup game not featuring extra-time. It also meant at least one player had been sent off on eight consecutive days of the 2010 tournament – a record run for any FIFA World Cup.

ANTAR THE STAR

Antar Yahia had been the hero of Algeria's 2010 FIFA World Cup qualifying campaign, scoring the winning goal in a play-off against arch-rivals Egypt. The defender was actually born in France, in 1982, and played for the French under-18s before switching to Algeria in 2004, scoring on his debut for the country's under-23s.

SUDDEN DEATH IN SUDAN

As if the North African rivalry between Algeria and Egypt were not intense enough, qualifiers for the 2010 FIFA World Cup pitted them against one another not once, not twice – but three times. A 2-0 win for Egypt against Algeria – including a stoppage-minute goal by Emad Moteab – in their scheduled second qualifier meant they ended the final African phase level on points, goal difference and goals scored. A one-off play-off match, hosted in neutral Sudan, was held – and Algeria's **Antar Yahia** (right) scored the only goal of the game, taking Algeria to the finals for the first time in 24 years. Both countries' governments felt compelled to call for calm, amid allegations that the Algerian team bus and Egyptian fans had come under attack ahead of the crucial matches.

MOROCCAN ROLL

Morocco remain the only North African country to reach the second round of a FIFA World Cup, though they were knocked out, 1-0, by eventual finalists West Germany. It was in Mexico in 1986 that Morocco were the first African team to top a FIFA World Cup group, finishing above England, Poland and Portugal. Crucial was their 3-1 victory over Portugal in their final group game, following goalless draws against the other two teams – including an England side who lost captain Bryan Robson to a dislocated shoulder and vice-captain Ray Wilkins to a red card. **Abderrazak Khairi** scored two of the goals against ..... Portugal, while Lothar Matthaus's winning strike for Germany came with just three minutes remaining.

NORTH AFRICAN COUNTRIES' BEST FIFA WORLD CUP™ PERFORMANCES

ALGERIA: First round 1982, 1986, 2010
EGYPT: First round 1934, 1990
MOROCCO: Second round 2006
TUNISIA: First round 1978, 1998, 2002, 2006

NORTH AFRICAN COUNTRIES' FIFA WORLD CUP™ QUALIFICATIONS

ALGERIA: 3 (1982, 1986, 2010)
EGYPT: 2 (1934, 1990)
MOROCCO: 4 (1970, 1986, 1994, 1998)
TUNISIA: 4 (1978, 1998, 2002, 2006)

NORTH AFRICA: TOP FIFA WORLD CUP™ GOALSCORERS

Salah Assad (Algeria) 2
Salaheddine Bassir (Morocco) 2
Abdelrahman Fawzi (Egypt) 2
Abdeljalil Hadda (Morocco) 2
Abderrazak Khairi (Morocco) 2

NO WAITING GAME

Morocco's 2-1 defeat to Saudi Arabia in 1994 was one of the last two games to be played simultaneously at a FIFA World Cup, without falling on a final match-day of a group. Belgium were beating Holland 1-0 at the same time, with every team in Group F having still one game to play. At later tournaments, every match has been played separately until the climactic two fixtures of any group.

HOMEGROWN HERO

Of the six African countries at the 2010 FIFA World Cup, Algeria's was the only squad with an African coach – **Rabah Saadane**, in his fifth separate stint in charge since 1981. He previously led his country to the 1986 FIFA World Cup in Mexico, where they were also eliminated in the first round. Along with Honduras, the Algeria team of 2010 were one of only two countries failing to score a single goal. However, they did concede just twice in their three games: 1-0 defeats to Slovakia and the USA, and a surprise goalless draw with England – Algeria's first-ever FIFA World Cup clean sheet.

MOKHTAR RUNS AMOK

Egypt had to play only two matches to qualify for the 1934 FIFA World Cup, becoming the first African representatives at the tournament. Both games were against a Palestine side under the British mandate – and the Egyptians won both games handsomely, 7-1 in Cairo and 4-1 in Palestine. Captain and striker Mahmoud Mokhtar scored a hat-trick in the first leg, a brace in the second. Turkey were also meant to contest qualifiers against the two sides, but withdrew, leaving the path to the finals free for Egypt.

TUNISIA IN TUNE

Tunisia became the first African team to win a match at a FIFA World Cup finals, when they beat Mexico 3-1 in Rosario, Argentina, in 1978 – thanks to goals from Ali Kaabi, Nejib Ghommidh and Mokhtar Dhouib. While they share with Morocco the North African record of reaching four different FIFA World Cups, they are the only nation from that part of the continent to qualify for three finals in a row – in 1998, 2002 and 2006. Among the players to feature in all three tournaments were 2006 captain Riadh Bouazizi, Hatem Trabelsi and **Radhi Jaidi**. ....

GOING UP IN FLAMES

Key CAF documents were initially kept at the Sudan Football Association's HQ in Khartoum, but within just a few months of the federation's founding, a blaze broke out there and destroyed them – prompting the CAF to set up official home in the Egyptian capital Cairo instead.

FOUNDING FATHERS

The Confederation of African Football was officially established by a meeting in the Sudanese capital Khartoum, in the city's Grand Hotel on 7 February 1957 – three days before the first Africa Cup of Nations kicked off in the same city. Representatives of Sudan, South Africa, Ethiopia and Egypt were present at the first assembly, and Egypt's Abdel Aziz Salem became CAF's first president.

HITTING THE TOP 10

Egypt's record-breaking third successive Africa Cup of Nations triumph in February 2010 helped propel them to 10th place in the official FIFA rankings. Nigeria are the only African country to have reached any higher, hitting fifth in April 1994.

OFFICIAL INFLUENCE

The first African to referee a FIFA World Cup final was Morocco's **Said Belqola**, who controlled the 1998 climax in which hosts France beat Brazil 3-0. Perhaps his most notable moment was sending off France's **Marcel Desailly** in the 68th minute – brandishing only the third red card to be shown in a FIFA World Cup final. Belqola was 41 at the time. He died from cancer just under four years later.

FEELING FINE AT 15

They may have escaped early their 21-0 trouncing by Libya in 1966, but Oman had to endure the entire 90 minutes of the second-biggest beating by an African side – and, again, it was a North African country doling out the punishment. Sudan saw off the unfortunate Omanis 15-0 in September 1965, though they were only equalling a scoreline set by Egypt, against Laos, in November 1963.

NORTH AFRICA: SELECTED TOP GOALSCORERS

ALGERIA: **Abdelhafid Tasfaout 34**
EGYPT: **Hossam Hassan 69**
LIBYA: **Tarik El Taib 14**
MOROCCO: **Salaheddine Bassir 25**
SUDAN: **Haytham Tambal 26**
TUNISIA: **Francileudo Santos 22**

SORE LOSERS

Libya could claim the record for highest-scoring victory by an African side, having racked up a 21-0 lead over Oman during the Arab Nations Cup in April 1966. But the Oman players walked off with 10 minutes remaining, in protest at Libya being awarded a penalty, and played no further part in the competition. Libya's goal tally included nine for Ahmed Ben Suwed, seven for Ali Al-Baski and four for Mahmoud Al-Jahani. Mahmoud Zand got the other. Ahmed Ben Suwed and Ali Al-Baski subsequently scored five apiece in a 13-0 trouncing of North Yemen – yet still Libya only ended the tournament in third place, after losing their semi-final to hosts Iraq.

HALFWAY TO A HUNDRED

Amr Zaki and **Ahmad Fathy** scored the goals as the Confederation of African Football celebrated their 50th anniversary with a friendly between Egypt and Sweden in February 2007 – and a 2-0 victory for the reigning African champions.

HEAD-TO-HEAD

The international career of Algeria's leading scorer **Abdelhafid Tasfaout** came to an end at the 2002 Africa Cup of Nations – though it could have been a lot worse. Tasfaout was knocked out by a collision with Mali defender Boubacar Diarra which caused him to swallow his tongue, prompting fears he might not even survive – though, thankfully, he did recover. Tasfaout, who played French league football for six years, scored 34 goals in 62 games for Algeria between 1990 and 2002.

NORTH AFRICA: SELECTED TOP APPEARANCES

ALGERIA: Mahieddine Meftah 107
EGYPT: Ahmed Hassan 173
LIBYA: Tarik El Taib 77
MOROCCO: Abdelmajid Dolmi 124
SUDAN: Haitham Mustafa 102
TUNISIA: Sadok Sassi 110

NEW TUNISIAN

Tunisia's all-time top scorer was not born there – in fact, he did not even visit the place until his late teens. But Brazilian-born **Francileudo Santos** eventually accepted Tunisian citizenship at the age of 24 in 2004, four years after completing a two-year spell at the country's leading club Etoile du Sahel. Within weeks of officially turning Tunisian, he was helping his new nation not only host but win the 2004 Africa Cup of Nations – scoring four goals, including the opener in the final against Morocco. A knee injury restricted him to just 11 minutes' action at the FIFA World Cup two years later, but he recovered to reclaim his place in the Tunisian first 11 and now boasts a tally of 22 international goals in 40 games.

MAD FOR 'MADIBA'

Apart from the Dutch and Spanish sides competing in the 2010 FIFA World Cup final, one of the star attractions in Johannesburg's Soccer City stadium on 11 July 2010 was South Africa's legendary former president **Nelson Mandela**. The frail 91-year-old – known affectionately by his tribal name of "Madiba" – was driven on to the pitch before the game in a golf cart and given a rapturous reception by the crowd. It marked his one and only public appearance at the tournament. Mandela had hoped to attend the opening ceremony and game on 11 June, but was mourning the death of his 13-year-old great-granddaughter in a car crash the previous evening. He had been a high-profile presence at the FIFA vote in 2004 which awarded South Africa hosting rights for 2010.

GOING FOR A SONG

Two players have been sent off at two separate FIFA World Cups: Cameroon's Rigobert Song, against Brazil in 1994 and Chile four years later, and France's Zinedine Zidane – red-carded against Saudi Arabia in 1998 and against Italy in the 2006 final. Song's red card against Brazil made him the youngest player to be dismissed at a FIFA World Cup – he was just 17 years and 358 days old. Song, born in Nkanglikock on 1 July 1976, is Cameroon's most-capped player, with 137 appearances – including winning displays in the 2000 and 2002 finals of the Africa Cup of Nations. He has been joined in the national team by his nephew, Arsenal utility player Alexandre Song Billong.

LIONS TAMED

Cameroon's third and final game at the 2010 FIFA World Cup, a 2-1 defeat to Holland, made them the first African country to play as many as 20 FIFA World Cup matches. But there was little to celebrate this time around – the "Indomitable Lions", coached by Frenchman Paul Le Guen, had already become the first team eliminated from the 2010 competition.

SUB–SAHARAN AFRICAN COUNTRIES' BEST FIFA WORLD CUP™ PERFORMANCES

ANGOLA: First round 2006
CAMEROON: Quarter-finals 1990
GHANA: Quarter-finals 2010
IVORY COAST: First round 2006, 2010
NIGERIA: Second round 1994, 1998
SENEGAL: Quarter-finals 2002
SOUTH AFRICA: First round 1998, 2002, 2010
TOGO: First round 2006
ZAIRE/CONGO DR: First round 1974

JOLLY ROGER

Cameroon striker **Roger Milla**, famous for dancing around corner flags after each goal, became the FIFA World Cup's oldest scorer against Russia in 1994 – aged 42 years and 39 days. He came on as substitute during that tournament with his surname handwritten, rather than printed, on the back of his shirt. Milla, born in Yaounde on 20 May 1952, had retired from professional football for a year before Cameroon's president, Paul Biya, persuaded him to join the 1990 FIFA World Cup squad. His goals in that tournament helped him win the African Footballer of the Year award for an unprecedented second time – 14 years after he had first received the trophy. He finally ended his international career after the 1994 FIFA World Cup in the United States, finishing with 102 caps and 28 goals to his name.

SUB–SAHARAN AFRICAN COUNTRIES' FIFA WORLD CUP™ QUALIFICATIONS

CAMEROON: 6 (1982, 1990, 1994, 1998, 2002, 2010)
NIGERIA: 4 (1994, 1998, 2002, 2010)
SOUTH AFRICA: 3 (1998, 2002, 2010)
GHANA: 2 (2006, 2010)
IVORY COAST: 2 (2006, 2010)
ANGOLA: 1 (2006)
SENEGAL: 1 (2002)
TOGO: 1 (2006)
ZAIRE/CONGO DR: 1 (1974)

BROTHERS AT ARMS

Two Boateng brothers were on the pitch at the same time when Germany played Ghana at the 2010 FIFA World Cup – but on opposing sides, a FIFA World Cup first. Jerome was playing left-back for Germany, while elder half-brother **Kevin-Prince** was in the Ghana midfield – having officially switched nationality just a month before the tournament. Both were born in the German capital Berlin, and have the same German mother but different Ghanaian fathers. Kevin-Prince had an extra effect on the 2010 FIFA World Cup in South Africa, through his tackle on German captain Michael Ballack in the May 2010 FA Cup final in England. Ballack was so badly injured that he had to be substituted and missed the World Cup altogether.

HORN OF AFRICA

Colombian pop star Shakira sang the official 2010 FIFA World Cup anthem, which she performed at both an official tournament-opening concert and the closing ceremony. But perhaps an even more distinctive sound that summer was the din of the vuvuzelas – the plastic horns that have been a feature of South African football matches since the 1980s and were a must-have for many fans attending FIFA World Cup fixtures. Some players – including Argentina's Lionel Messi and Portugal's Cristiano Ronaldo – complained that the constant drone was distracting, though others such as England's Jamie Carragher and Holland's Wesley Sneijder spoke up in the horns' defence. FIFA and the South African tournament organizers resisted calls for the instruments to be banned, while some television channels made technical arrangements to turn down the vuvuzelas' volume.

HENRI AND IVORY

The Ivory Coast were widely considered unfortunate to go out in the first round of their first FIFA World Cup, in 2006, having been drawn in the "group of death" alongside Argentina and Holland. A side starring **Didier Drogba**, Didier Zokora and brothers Kolo and Yaya Toure was managed by Frenchman Henri Michel, who was coaching at a fourth FIFA World Cup with a fourth different country. He had previously led France in 1986, Cameroon in 1994 and Morocco in 1998. Only Bora Milutinovic and Carlos Alberto Parreira have taken more different teams to FIFA World Cups. The same "group of death" nickname was given to the Ivory Coast's group in 2010, when they faced Brazil, Portugal and North Korea, and again finished third.

RATOMIR GETS IT RIGHT

Ghana went through four different managers during qualifiers for the 2006 FIFA World Cup, with Serbian coach Ratomir Dujkovic finally clinching the country a place at the finals for the very first time. He led them through the whole of 2005 unbeaten, winning a FIFA prize for being the most-improved team of the year. Ghana were the only African country to make it through the first round of both the 2006 and 2010 FIFA World Cups, despite having the youngest average age of any squad each time. They were again coached by a Serb in 2010, this time Milovan Rajevac.

SUB–SAHARAN AFRICAN COUNTRIES: TOP FIFA WORLD CUP™ GOALSCORERS

Roger Milla (Cameroon) 5
Asamoah Gyan (Ghana) 4
Papa Bouba Diop (Senegal) 3
Samuel Eto'o (Cameroon) 3
Daniel Amokachi (Nigeria) 2
Emmanuel Amunike (Nigeria) 2
Shaun Bartlett (South Africa) 2
Henri Camara (Senegal) 2
Aruna Dindane (Ivory Coast) 2
Didier Drogba (Ivory Coast) 2
Patrick Mboma (Cameroon) 2
Benni McCarthy (South Africa) 2
Sulley Muntari (Ghana) 2
Francois Omam-Biyik (Cameroon) 2

'BAFANA BAFANA' BACK 'BAGHANA BAGHANA'

Despite missing injured midfielder Michael Essien, Ghana were the only African side to survive the first round of the 2010 FIFA World Cup – and received exuberant support from home fans in South Africa as they reached the quarter-finals. Ghana's footballers, traditionally known as the "Black Stars", were renamed "Africa's Stars" by some – or "BaGhana BaGhana", playing on South Africa's nickname "Bafana Bafana", which means "The Boys, The Boys".

SUB-SAHARAN AFRICA NATIONAL RECORDS

⚽ FIFTEEN LOVE

Fifteen-year-old Samuel Kuffour became the youngest footballer to win an Olympic medal when Ghana took bronze at the 1992 Olympics in Barcelona – 27 days before his 16th birthday.

⚽ EAGLETS SOAR

The first African country to win an official FIFA tournament was Nigeria, when their "Golden Eaglets" beat Germany 2-0 in the final of the 1985 World Under-17 Championships.

⚽ ANGOLAN GOALS

Angola lost their first match against former colonial masters Portugal 6-0 in 1989. Their second meeting, 12 years later, was abandoned as Portugal led 5-1, after Angola had four players sent off and another, Helder Vicente, carried off injured.

⚽ SUB-SAHARAN AFRICA: SELECTED TOP GOALSCORERS

ANGOLA: Akwa 36
BOTSWANA: Dipsy Selolwane 11
CAMEROON: Samuel Eto'o 44
GHANA: Abedi "Pele" Ayew 33
IVORY COAST: Didier Drogba 43
MOZAMBIQUE: Tico-Tico 27
NAMIBIA: Gervatius Uri Khob 12
NIGERIA: Rashidi Yekini 37
SENEGAL: Henri Camara 31
SOUTH AFRICA: Benni McCarthy 32
SWAZILAND: Sibusiso Dlamini 26
ZIMBABWE: Peter Ndlovu 38

⚽ SUB-SAHARAN AFRICA: SELECTED TOP APPEARANCES

ANGOLA: Akwa 80
BOTSWANA: Dipsy Selolwane 34
CAMEROON: Rigobert Song 135
GHANA: Abedi "Pele" Ayew 73
IVORY COAST: Didier Zokora 78
MOZAMBIQUE: Dario 88
NAMIBIA: Johannes Hindjou 69
NIGERIA: Mudashiru Lawal 86
SENEGAL: Henri Camara 99
SOUTH AFRICA: Aaron Mokoena 99
SWAZILAND: Mlungisi Ngubane 91
ZIMBABWE: Peter Ndlovu 100

⚽ KNOCKED OUT ON PENALTIES

Botswana goalkeeper and captain Modiri Marumo was sent off in the middle of a penalty shoot-out against Malawi in May 2003, after punching the opposing goalkeeper Philip Nyasulu in the face. Botswana defender Michael Mogaladi had to go in goal for the rest of the shoot-out, which Malawi won 4-1.

GENEROUS GEORGE

In 1995 Liberia's George Weah became the first African to be named FIFA World Player of the Year, an award that recognized his prolific goalscoring exploits for Paris Saint-Germain and AC Milan. That same year he added the European Footballer of the Year and African Footballer of the Year prizes to his collection. Weah not only captained his country, but often funded the team's travels – though he remains the only FIFA World Player of the Year whose country has never qualified for a FIFA World Cup. After retiring in 2003 after 60 caps and 22 international goals, he moved into politics and ran unsuccessfully for the Liberian presidency in 2005.

DRAMATIC TURNAROUNDS

Ghana managed to concede three goals in a minute to world champions Germany in an April 1993 friendly. Ghana had been 1-0 up with 20 minutes left, before losing the game 6-1. In the 1989 FIFA World Youth Championships, Nigeria were 4-0 down with 25 minutes left in their quarter-final against the Soviet Union – but hit back to draw 4-4 before winning 5-3 on penalties.

UNFULFILLED PROMISE

Zambia have never qualified for a FIFA World Cup, but caused a sensation when they beat Italy 4-0 in a group game at the 1988 Olympics in Seoul. **Kalusha Bwalya** scored a hat-trick and later revealed the Italians had rudely snubbed his team before the game – but were pleading for autographs afterwards. Tragedy struck on 27 April 1993. Zambia were in a strong position to reach the 1994 FIFA World Cup but lost their coach and 18 of their players when the military plane carrying them crashed in Gabon on its way to a qualifier in Senegal, killing everyone on board. Olympic hero Bwalya had missed the flight because he was playing for Dutch team PSV Eindhoven at the time.

HEAD OVER HEELS

Augustine "Jay-Jay" Okocha was famous not only for his dazzling free-kicks, but also for the acrobatic somersaults he performed when celebrating goals – a skill he shared with Nigerian team-mates Julius Aghahowa and Obafemi Martins. Okocha, whose clubs included Fenerbahce, Paris Saint-Germain and Bolton Wanderers, was a member of his country's 1996 Olympic gold medal-winning team.

SOUTH LONDON SOUTH AFRICANS

English club Charlton Athletic featured four South African-born players in the 1950s – though **Eddie Firmani** would play three internationals for Italy, while John Hewie earned 19 caps for Scotland. Firmani went on to play for Sampdoria, Internazionale and Genoa, becoming the first man to score a century of league goals in both England and Italy.

ASIA & OCEANIA

South Korea made history in 2002 – sharing with Japan the first co-hosting of the first FIFA World Cup™ in Asia. Their footballers also became the first Asian team to reach the semi-finals of the FIFA World Cup™ where they lost to Germany before losing again, narrowly, to Turkey in the third-place play-off. The Koreans could truly claim to have put Asia on the world football map.

AUSTRALIA

Victims, perhaps, of an overcomplicated qualifying system that has limited the country's FIFA World Cup™ finals appearances, and hampered by its geographical isolation that, in the early years, saw other sports prosper in the country at football's expense, it has taken many years for Australia to establish itself on the world football map. However, driven by a new generation of players, many based with top European clubs, the Socceroos delivered for the first time at the 2006 FIFA World Cup™. They are the No. 1 ranked team in Asia.

AUSTRALIA'S SHOOT–OUT RECORD

Australia are the only team to reach the FIFA World Cup finals via a penalty shoot-out – in the final qualifying play-off in November 2005. They had lost the first leg 1-0 to Uruguay in Montevideo. Marco Bresciano's goal levelled the aggregate score, which remained 1-1 after extra-time. Goalkeeper **Mark Schwarzer** made two crucial saves as Australia won the shoot-out 4-2, with John Aloisi scoring the winning spot-kick.

TOP CAPS

1	Alex Tobin	87
2	Paul Wade	84
3	Mark Schwarzer	78
4	Tony Vidmar	76
5	Brett Emerton	75
6	Scott Chipperfield	68
7	Peter Wilson	64
8	Attila Abonyi	61
9	John Kosmina	60
=	Stan Lazaridis	60

TOP SCORERS

1	Damian Mori	29
2	John Aloisi	27
3	Attila Abonyi	25
=	John Kosmina	25
4	Tim Cahill	21
=	Archie Thompson	21
5	David Zdrilic	20
6	Graham Arnold	19
9	Ray Baartz	18
10	Gary Cole	17
=	Brett Emerton	17
	Aurelio Vidmar	

SOCCEROOS MAKE IT AT LAST

The Australian national team – nicknamed the "Socceroos" – have been buoyed by massive support over the past decade. Their FIFA World Cup battles – culminating in a run to the last 16 in the 2006 finals – have established football among the nation's most popular sports. For many years, the game had languished behind cricket, the two rugby codes and Aussie rules football in the public imagination. Football had been kept alive by immigrants – first from Britain, then by arrivals from Italy, Greece and the former Yugoslavia. But the nation rallied round for the 1998 FIFA World Cup qualifying play-off final against Iran, which the Socceroos lost on away goals. Four years later, Australia lost another play-off, this time to Uruguay, 3-1 on aggregate.

LUCKY NUMBER

The No. 2 shirt is the only one to have been on the field for Australia for all 900 minutes of their three FIFA World Cup campaigns. In 1974 it was worn by Doug Utjesenovic and in both 2006 and 2010 by Lucas Neill.

HIDDINK'S DUAL ROLE

Guus Hiddink is Australia's most successful coach, despite running the team for only 12 matches. He steered them through the qualifying play-offs, then guided them to the last 16 of the 2006 FIFA World Cup finals. The Dutchman, who had guided South Korea to the semi-finals of the 2002 tournament, played a dual role during the 2005–06 season, coaching the Dutch champions PSV Eindhoven as well as the Socceroos. He resigned after Australia's dramatic last-16 defeat by Italy to become coach of Russia in the 2010 FIFA World Cup qualifiers and then Turkey.

CAHILL MAKES HISTORY

Tim Cahill netted Australia's first-ever FIFA World Cup finals goal when he scored an 84th-minute equalizer against Japan in Kaiserslautern on 12 June 2006. Cahill added another five minutes later and John Aloisi struck in stoppage time to give the Socceroos a 3-1 win – their only victory in the finals. Australia later lost 2-0 to Brazil and drew 2-2 with Croatia to qualify from their group.

AVOIDING UNNECESSARY FUSS

After needing play-offs to reach the 1974 and 2006 FIFA World Cups, qualifying for the 2010 event proved much less stressful for Australia. They conceded only one goal in eight unbeaten games during the final round of Asian Football Confederation qualifiers, topping their group. They became only the third team to confirm their place – following hosts South Africa, and just a few hours after AFC rivals Japan.

AUSTRALIA RECORDS

Honours: Oceania champions 1980, 1996, 2000, 2004
First international: v New Zealand (lost 3-1), Auckland, 17 June 1922
Biggest win: 31-0 v American Samoa, Sydney, 11 April 2001
Biggest defeat: 7-0 v Croatia, Zagreb, 6 June 1998

BET ON BRETT

Brett Holman's goal against Ghana, in a 1-1 draw at the 2010 tournament, made him Australia's youngest marksman at a FIFA World Cup. He was 26 years 84 days old at the time, 105 days younger than Tim Cahill had been when striking against Japan in 2006. Holman added to his tally five days later, when Australia beat Serbia 2-1. Cahill himself was also on the scoresheet, though goal difference meant Australia failed to reach the second round.

DEUTSCHLAND UBER ALLES

After competing at the 1974 and 2006 tournaments in Germany, Australia's first FIFA World Cup Finals match to be played elsewhere came in 2010 in South Africa ... against Germany, who won 4-0.

OLD ALLEGIANCES STILL MATTER

Many Australian-born players chose to play for their parents' countries rather than for Australia – Joey Didulica, Anthony Seric and Josip Simunic (Croatia), Sasa Ognenovski (Macedonia) and Sasa Ilic (Serbia). Simunic even played for Croatia against Australia in the 2006 FIFA World Cup finals – and was famously sent off after being shown three yellow cards by English referee Graham Poll. Bologna-born Italy striker Christian Vieri grew up in Australia, but his Aussie-born brother Max represented the Socceroos.

KEWELL THE TOPS

Harry Kewell (born on 22 September 1978) is widely regarded as Australia's best-ever player. The left winger has scored 13 goals in 39 international appearances, including the equalizer against Croatia that took Australia to the last 16 of the 2006 FIFA World Cup finals. Kewell has enjoyed a successful club career with Leeds United, Liverpool and Galatasaray. He is also the only Australian-born player to gain a Champions League winner's medal, with Liverpool in 2005. He endured an unhappier time at the 2010 FIFA World Cup, when he lasted just 22 minutes before being red-carded for handball against Ghana – the 150th sending-off in the history of the finals.

OTHER ASIAN COUNTRIES

The lesser-known Asian footballing nations represent the true backwaters of world football. These may well be the countries in which true football obsession has yet to take hold, but competition between, and achievements by, these teams are no less vibrant. The regions are the home to many of the game's record-breakers – from the most goals in a single game to the most career appearances – and some of these records may never be broken.

JAPAN TOP SCORERS

1	Kunishige Kamamoto	75
2	Kazuyoshi Miura	55
3	Hiromi Hara	37
4	Takuya Takagi	27
5	Kazushi Kimura	26
6	Shunsuke Nakamura	24
7	Naohiro Takahara	23
8	Masashi Nakayama	21
9	Teruki Miyamoto	18
10	Atsushi Yanagisawa	17
=	Yuji Nakazawa	17
=	Shinji Okazaki	17

SAUDIS MAKE FLYING START

Saudi Arabia reached the last 16 in their first FIFA World Cup finals appearance in 1994. Saeed Owairan's winner against Belgium enabled them to finish level on points with Holland at the top of Group F. **Sami Al-Jaber** and Fuad Amin had scored in a 2-1 win over Morocco, after the Saudis lost their opening game 2-1 to Holland. They went down 3-1 to Sweden in the last 16. Substitute Fahad Al-Ghesheyan scored in the 85th minute after the Swedes led 2-0. Kennet Andersson grabbed Sweden's decisive third goal three minutes later. The Saudis have failed to advance beyond the group stages in their three subsequent appearances.

THREE AND IN

Japan's 3-1 Group E victory over Denmark in Bloemfontein at the 2010 FIFA World Cup made them the first Asian side to score three times in one World Cup match since North Korea's 5-3 defeat to Portugal in their 1966 quarter-final. Japan's goals came from **Keisuke Honda**, Yasuhito Endo and Shinji Okazaki. Honda and Endo both scored directly from free-kicks, the first time a team has managed such a double in one FIFA World Cup game since Yugoslavia managed three when beating Zaire 9-0 in 1974.

HAPPIER TRAVELLERS

Both South Korea and Japan achieved their first-ever FIFA World Cup victories on foreign soil at the 2010 tournament in South Africa – and both teams reached the knockout stages for the first time away from home as well. South Korea beat Greece 2-0 before losing 2-1 to Uruguay in the second round, while Japan fell to Paraguay on penalties at the same stage after wins over Cameroon and Denmark in their first-round group.

RANK OUTSIDERS

North Korea only narrowly lost their first game of the 2010 FIFA World Cup, 2-1 to Brazil – **Ji Yun-Nam** scoring late on for the Koreans. The match was between the tournament's highest- and lowest-ranked qualifying teams. Brazil were in first place in the FIFA rankings, while North Korea were 105th.

JAPAN TOP CAPS

1	Masami Ihara	122
2	Yoshikatsu Kawaguchi	116
3	Yuji Nakazawa	109
4	Yasuhito Endo	98
=	Shunsuke Nakamura	98
6	Kazuyoshi Miura	89
7	Alessandro dos Santos	82
=	Junichi Inamoto	82
9	Satoshi Tsunami	78
10	Hidetoshi Nakata	77

MOST APPEARANCES IN THE FIFA WORLD CUP™ FINALS

South Korea	8	(1954, 1986, 1990, 1994, 1998, 2002, 2006, 2010)
Japan	4	(1998, 2002, 2006 2010)
Saudi Arabia	4	(1994, 1998, 2002, 2006)
Australia	3	(1974*, 2006*, 2010)
Iran	3	(1978, 1998, 2006)
New Zealand	2	(1982*, 2010*)
North Korea	2	(1966, 2010)
China	1	(2002)
Indonesia**	1	(1938)
Iraq	1	(1986)
Israel	1	(1970)
Kuwait	1	(1982)
United Arab Emirates	1	(1990)

* Qualified as member of Oceania Confederation
** Played as Dutch East Indies

AN UNWANTED RECORD

South Korea hold an unwanted record for the most goals conceded in one finals tournament. They let in 16 in 1954 – in just two games. They were overwhelmed by Hungary 9-0, before Turkey trounced them 7-0. No wonder their heroic goalkeeper **Hong Duk-Yung** looked shaken.

IRAN STOP AT 19

Iran hold the record for the highest score in an Asian zone FIFA World Cup qualifier. They thrashed Guam 19-0 in Tabriz on 24 November 2000. **Karim Bagheri** scored six goals and Ali Karimi four. Future national coach Ali Daei and Farhad Majidi both netted three. This was two goals better than Iran's previous highest qualifying win – 17-0 against the Maldives on 2 June 1997, when Bagheri scored seven times. Two days after their 19-goal thrashing, Guam crashed 16-0 to Tajikistan.

PALESTINE THE PIONEERS

Palestine, then under British rule, were the first Asian team to enter the FIFA World Cup qualifiers. They lost 7-1 away to Egypt on 16 March 1934. They lost the return match at home on 6 April, 4-1. Four years later, they were eliminated by Greece, who won 3-1 in Tel Aviv and 1-0 at home.

CHINA YET TO REALIZE POTENTIAL

China, the world's most populous nation, have qualified just once for the FIFA World Cup finals, in 2002. They topped their final qualifying group by eight points from the United Arab Emirates, but coach Bora Milutinovic's team slumped in the finals, failing to score a goal in defeats by Costa Rica (2-0), Brazil (4-0) and Turkey (3-0).

ON THE UP

The best Asian countries have become familiar figures at recent FIFA World Cup finals tournaments. Co-hosts South Korea and Japan both gave a good account of themselves in 2002 – with the South Koreans achieving Asia's best-ever finish, losing in the semi-finals. Saudi Arabia and Iran have been powerful forces, too, and the Asian Federation was strengthened by new members, Australia, after 2006. North Korea set the standard for Asian hopefuls in 1966 when they reached the quarter-finals in their first tournament appearance. They overcame teams from Asia, Africa and Oceania to qualify, beating Australia 9-2 on aggregate in a final play-off. Asia had four guaranteed places at the 2010 finals in South Africa, with the chance of a fifth but Bahrain, the fifth-placed team in the qualifiers, lost a play-off to Oceania winners New Zealand.

NAKATA BLAZES THE TRAIL

Hidetoshi Nakata ranks among Japan's best-ever players. The midfielder set up all three goals in a 3-2 FIFA World Cup qualifying playoff win over Iran in November 1997. Nakata moved to Perugia in Italy after the 1998 finals, becoming the first Japanese player to star in Europe, and won a Serie A championship medal with Roma in 2001. He started in three FIFA World Cup finals tournaments, making ten appearances and scored one goal – the second in a 2-0 win over Tunisia that took Japan to the last 16 in 2002. Nakata won 77 caps and scored 11 goals.

AI–DEAYEA CAPS THEM ALL

Saudi goalkeeper Mohamed Al-Deayea had to choose between football and handball as a youngster. He was persuaded by his elder brother Abdullah to pick football. He made 181 appearances for his country, the first coming against Bangladesh in 1990, the last against Belgium in May 2006. He also appeared in the FIFA World Cup finals tournaments of 1994, 1998 and 2002. He played his last finals game in a 3-0 defeat by the Republic of Ireland on 11 June 2002 and was recalled to the squad for the 2006 finals, although he did not play.

STAR PARK

Team captain **Park Ji-Sung**'s 52nd-minute strike against Greece on 12 June 2010 made him the first South Korean to score at three separate FIFA World Cup finals. It also meant he joined countryman Ahn Jung-Hwan and Saudi Arabia's Sami Al-Jaber on three FIFA World Cup goals apiece, more than any other Asian footballer.

HONG SETS FIFA WORLD CUP™ RECORD

South Korea defender **Hong Myung-Bo** was the first Asian player to appear in four consecutive FIFA World Cup finals tournaments. He played all three games as South Korea lost to Belgium, Spain and Uruguay in 1990. He scored twice in three appearances in 1994 – his goal against Spain sparking a Korean fightback from 2-0 down to draw 2-2. In 1998, he started all three group games as South Korea were eliminated at the group stage. Four years later, on home soil, he captained South Korea to fourth place in the finals, the best-ever performance by an Asian team. Hong's total of 16 appearances in the FIFA World Cup finals is also a record for an Asian player. He later became coach of the South Korea Under-20 squad.

ASIAN FOOTBALLER OF THE YEAR

Year	Player	Country
1988	Ahmed Radhi	Iraq
1989	Kim Joo-Sung	South Korea
1990	Kim Joo-Sung	South Korea
1991	Kim Joo-Sung	South Korea
1992	not awarded	
1993	Kazuyoshi Miura	Japan
1994	Saeed Owarain	Saudi Arabia
1995	Masami Ihara	Japan
1996	Khodadad Azizi	Iran
1997	Hidetoshi Nakata	Japan
1998	Hidetoshi Nakata	Japan
1999	Ali Daei	Iran
2000	Nawaf Al Temyat	Saudi Arabia
2001	Fan Zhiyi	China
2002	Shinji Ono	Japan
2003	Mehdi Mahdavikia	Iran
2004	Ali Karimi	Iran
2005	Hamad Al-Montashari	Saudi Arabia
2006	Khalfan Ibrahim	Qatar
2007	Yasser Al-Qahtani	Saudi Arabia
2008	Server Djeparov	Uzbekistan
2009	Yasuhito Endo	Japan

SOUTH KOREA TOP CAPS

1	Hong Myung-Bo	136
2	Lee Woon-Jae	131
3	Yoo Sang-Chul	123
4	Cha Bum-Kun	121
5	Lee Young-Pyo	122
6	Kim Tae-Young	104
7	Hwang Seon-Hong	103
8	Kim Nam-Il	100
9	Park Ji-Sung	96
10	Choi Soon-Ho	95
=	Ha Seok-Joo	95

THE JONG TURNING

North Korea's star striker at the 2010 FIFA World Cup, **Jong Tae-Se**, sobbed when their anthem was played before the first game against Brazil, but he had never actually visited the country he was playing for. Jong was born in Japan, where he continues to play his club football for Kawasaki Frontale, and has parents who are South Korean citizens. But he chose to pursue his family right to a North Korean passport.

PAK STRIKE MAKES HISTORY

North Korea's **Pak Doo Ik** earned legend status by scoring the goal that eliminated Italy from the 1966 FIFA World Cup finals. The shockwaves caused by the victory were comparable to those caused by the United States' 1-0 win over England in 1950. Pak netted the only goal in the 42nd minute at Middlesbrough on 19 July. North Korea thus became the first Asian team to reach the quarter-finals. Pak, an army corporal, was promoted to sergeant after the victory and later became a gymnastics coach.

SOUTH KOREA TOP SCORERS

1	Cha Bum-Kun	55
2	Hwang Seon-Hong	50
3	Choi Soon-Ho	30
4	Huh Jung-Moo	29
4	Kim Do-Hoon	29
6	Choi Yong-Soo	27
6	Lee Tae-Ho	27
8	Lee Dong-Gook	25
9	Lee Young-Moo	24
=	Park Sung-Hwa	24

KIM'S TREBLE SUCCESS

South Korea midfielder Kim Joo-Sung is the only player to have won the Asian Footballer of the Year award three times – and in successive years – between 1989 and 1991. He played in three FIFA World Cup finals tournaments, but his side never advanced beyond the group stage. He won 77 caps, scoring 14 goals, and was one of the first South Korean players to move abroad, joining Bundesliga side Bochum in 1992 and staying for two seasons.

ASIA PRESSES ON

The best Asian players have become famous around the world over the past decade. FIFA's decision to expand the World Cup finals – and allocate more places to Asian teams – gave those stars the chance to shine on an international stage. Hidetoshi Nakata, Japan's general of the 1998 finals, led the way to success in Europe, soon followed by his colleague Shinji Ono to Feyenoord, and, more recently, by midfielder Shunsuke Nakamura. Iran's top scorer, Ali Daei, made a name for himself in Germany with Hertha Berlin while Iranian winger, or midfielder, Mehdi Mahdavikia was twice voted "Player of the Year" by Hamburg's supporters. South Korean midfielder Park Ji-Sung won the UEFA Champions League with Manchester United and was a semi-finalist with PSV Eindhoven, alongside international team-mate Lee Young-Pyo.

A LONG JOURNEY FOR A BEATING

The first Asian country to play in a FIFA World Cup finals was Indonesia, who as the Dutch East Indies played in France in 1938. The tournament was a straight knockout and, on 5 June in Reims, Hungary beat them 6-0, with goals from Gyorgy Sarosi, Gyula Zsengeller (two each), Vilmos Kohut and Geza Toldi.

OWAIRAN'S MAGIC GOAL

Saudi Arabia forward Saeed Owairan scored the finest goal of the 1994 FIFA World Cup finals. He dribbled for more than 50 yards, beating five challenges, to hit the winner against Belgium on 29 June. His goal helped the Saudis to reach the last 16 in their finals debut. Owairan scored 24 goals in 50 matches for Saudi Arabia between 1991 and 1998.

AL-JABER TO THE FORE

Saml Al-Jaber (born on 11 December 1972 in Riyadh) became only the second Asian player to appear in four FIFA World Cup finals tournaments when he started against Tunisia in Munich on 14 June 2006. He scored in a 2-2 draw, his third goal in nine appearances at the finals. Al-Jaber played only one game in 1998 before he was rushed to hospital with a burst appendix, which ruled him out of the competition. He became Saudi Arabia's record scorer, with 44 goals in 163 matches.

YOU'RE BARRED

The penalty shoot-out between Japan and Paraguay in the second round in 2010 was the first in FIFA World Cup history that did not feature at least one European country. The shoot-out was the first of the 2010 tournament and the 21st overall. Paraguay won 5-3 on penalties after the match had ended goalless after extra-time. Japanese full-back **Yuichi Komano** was the only taker to miss, hitting the bar with his spot-kick.

HUGE FOLLOWING FOR FOOTBALL IN CHINA

China's national team boasts a massive fan base – as was demonstrated when they reached the FIFA World Cup finals for the only time in 2002. Between their qualification on 19 October 2001 and their opening game of the finals against Costa Rica on 4 June 2002, an estimated 170 million new TV sets were sold throughout China! TV audiences for the team's three matches regularly topped 300 million, even though China lost all three matches and failed to score a goal.

LOCAL COACHES MAKE THEIR MARK

Three more native-born Asian national team coaches have been named Asia's Coach of the Year. The first, in 2001, was **Nasser Al-Johar**, who steered Saudi Arabia through to the 2002 FIFA World Cup finals, two points clear of Iran in the decisive qualifying group. Adnan Hamad followed him three years later, leading Iraq to the Asian Cup quarter-finals, little more than a year after the US invasion. The 2007 winner was Uzbekistan's Rauf Inileyev, who guided his country to the 2007 Asian Cup quarter-finals, beating China 3-0 on the way.

HIGHEST ... AND LOWEST

The highest attendance for an Asian team in a home FIFA World Cup qualifier was the 130,000 who watched Iran draw 1-1 with Australia in the Azadi Stadium, Tehran, on 22 November 1997. The game was the first leg of a final playoff for the last place in the 1998 finals. Iran advanced on away goals after drawing the second leg 2-2 in Melbourne. The lowest attendance was the "crowd" of 20 that turned out for Turkmenistan's 1-0 win over Taiwan, played in Amman, Jordan, on 7 May 2001.

TAKE TWO FOR TAKESHI

Japan have opened three of their four FIFA World Cup finals campaigns on that same date, 14 June – losing 1-0 to Argentina in 1998, beating Tunisia 2-0 in 2002 and beating Cameroon 1-0 in 2010. Former international defender Takeshi Okada was Japan's coach for both the 1998 and 2010 competitions. Three foreign coaches had been in charge in between – Frenchman Philippe Troussier, Brazilian Zico and Bosnian Ivica Osim.

PAK CARRIES THE FLAME

North Korea's hero of the 1966 FIFA World Cup finals, **Pak Doo Ik,** is still much admired by his countrymen. He was chosen as one of the 56 people to carry the Olympic torch across North Korea on its way to the 2008 Beijing Olympics. He was also the oldest – a sprightly 70.

TROUSSIER STEERS JAPAN TO VICTORY

Paris-born **Philippe Troussier** was named Asia's Coach of the Year in 2000 after leading Japan to a 1-0 victory over Saudi Arabia in the Asian Cup final in Lebanon. He also steered the Japanese to their best-ever FIFA World Cup finish on home soil in 2002, when they lost 1-0 to Turkey in the last 16. But that achievement was overshadowed by Hiddink's success with South Korea.

178 ASIA & OCEANIA

ASIAN CUP WINNERS

The Asian Cup is Asia's continental championship

Year	Winners
1956	South Korea
1960	South Korea
1964	Israel
1968	Iran
1972	Iran
1976	Iran
1980	Kuwait
1984	Saudi Arabia
1988	Saudi Arabia
1992	Japan
1996	Saudi Arabia
2000	Japan
2004	Japan
2007	Iraq

DOUBLE AGENT

Although North Korea's Kim Myong-Won usually plays as a striker, he was named as one of three goalkeepers in the country's 23-man squad for the 2010 FIFA World Cup. FIFA told North Korea he would only be able to play in goal, rather than outfield, though he failed to make it on to the pitch in any form during his country's three Group G matches.

CHINA'S 4X4

Four teams carry the name of China. The China national team receives most attention, but Hong Kong (a former British colony) and Macau (a former Portuguese colony) both retain their autonomous status for football – as Hong Kong China and Macau China respectively. Meanwhile, the independent island state of Taiwan competes in the FIFA World Cup and other competitions as Chinese Taipei.

HIDDINK THE SOUTH KOREAN HERO

Dutchman Guus Hiddink is the most successful coach in Asian international football history. He had steered PSV Eindhoven to European Cup victory in 1996 and Holland to fourth place in the 1998 FIFA World Cup finals, before he took charge of the South Korea squad on 20 December 2000. He said: "When I arrived, the team was very conservative." He decided on a faster, more attacking approach, experimenting in friendlies, because South Korea had automatically qualified as co-hosts. Korean fans and media were not convinced, but hoped their team would at least reach the last 16. They did even better. Hiddink's team topped their group with wins over Poland and Portugal, eliminated Italy with a goal in the last minute of extra-time, then reached the semi-finals with a shoot-out victory over Spain. They lost 1-0 to Germany, then 3-2 in the third-place play-off to Turkey. Fourth place was still the highest-ever finish achieved by an Asian team at the finals. Hiddink became the first foreigner to be made an honorary South Korean citizen and the stadium at Gwangju was renamed in his honour.

THE ISRAEL ISSUE

Israel is, geographically, an Asian nation. It hosted – and won – the Asian Cup in 1964. But, over the years, many Asian confederation countries refused to play Israel on political grounds. When Israel reached the 1970 FIFA World Cup finals they came through a qualifying tournament involving two Asian nations – Japan and South Korea – and two from Oceania – Australia and New Zealand. In 1989, Israel topped the Oceania group, but lost a final play-off to Colombia for a place in the 1990 finals. They switched to the European zone qualifiers in 1992 and have been a full member of the European federation, UEFA, since 1994.

SOVIET REPUBLICS FIND NEW HOME

The break-up of the former Soviet Union swelled the ranks of the Asian Confederation in the early 1990s. Former Soviet republics Kazakhstan, Kyrgyzstan, Tajikistan, Turkmenistan and Uzbekistan all joined in 1994, though the Kazaks switched to UEFA in 2002. **Uzbekistan** have been the most successful, reaching the Asian Cup quarter-finals in 2007. Australia are the AFC's the 46th – and newest – members, entering the confederation on 1 January 2006, a few months after East Timor had become the 45th.

OCEANIA

Football in Oceania can claim some of the most eye-catching football statistics – though not necessarily in a way many there would welcome, especially the long-suffering goalkeepers from minnow islands on the end of cricket-style scorelines. The departure to the Asian Football Confederation of Australia, seeking more testing competition, was a morale blow – but benefited New Zealand out on the pitch. The finals tournament of the 2010 FIFA World Cup™ was the first to feature both Australia and New Zealand.

KAREMBEU THE FIFA WORLD CUP WINNER

Christian Karembeu, born in New Caledonia, is the only FIFA World Cup winner to come from the Oceania region. He started for France in their 3-0 final victory over Brazil on 12 July 1998. The defensive midfielder had earlier begun against Denmark (group), Italy (quarter-finals) and Croatia (semi-finals). He played 53 times for France, scoring one goal, and was also a double European Champions League Cup winner with Real Madrid in 1998 in 2000.

TOP CAPS: NEW ZEALAND

1	Ivan Vicelich	69
2	Simon Elliott	66
3	Vaughan Coveny	64
4	Ricki Herbert	61
5	Chris Jackson	60
6	Brian Turner	59
7	Duncan Cole	58
=	Steve Sumner	58
9	Chris Zoricich	57
10	Ceri Evans	56

LATE DANE

After losing all three of their games at the 1982 tournament, centre-back **Winston Reid**'s stoppage-time header against Slovakia in their 2010 opener gave New Zealand a 1-1 draw – and their first-ever point at a FIFA World Cup. Reid had only made his New Zealand debut less than a month earlier, having lived in Denmark since the age of ten and taken up Danish citizenship.

BAD LUCK OF THE DRAW

Despite featuring at only their second-ever FIFA World Cup – and first since 1982 – New Zealand did not lose a game in South Africa in 2010. They drew all three first-round matches, against Slovakia, Italy and Paraguay. The three points were not enough to secure a top-two finish in Group F, but third-placed New Zealand did finish above defending world champions Italy. The only other three teams to have gone out despite going unbeaten in their three first-round group games were Scotland in 1974, Cameroon in 1982 and Belgium in 1998.

PIERRE'S PERFECT START

The very first goal of the 2010 FIFA World Cup was scored, in qualifying, by New Caledonia's Pierre Wajoka – the only strike of an August 2007 match against Tahiti, the country of his birth.

TOP SCORERS: NEW ZEALAND

1	Vaughan Coveny	28
2	Steve Sumner	22
3	Brian Turner	21
4	Jock Newall	17
=	Shane Smeltz	17
6	Keith Nelson	16
7	Grant Turner	15
8	Darren McClennan	12
=	Michael McGarry	12
=	Wynton Rufer	12

RETURNING RICKI

Ricki Herbert is the only footballer from New Zealand to reach a FIFA World Cup twice – he played left-back at the 1982 tournament in Spain, then coached the country to what is only their second World Cup, in 2010. Qualification second time around came courtesy of a play-off win over Asian Football Confederation representatives Bahrain – though the New Zealand football authorities have been pondering whether to follow Australia in defecting from Oceania and joining the AFC. Herbert, born in Auckland in 1961, combined qualifying for the 2010 FIFA World Cup with coaching New Zealand-based club Wellington Phoenix, who play in Australia's A-League.

ISRAEL GIVEN A GO

Oceania's best hope of reaching the 1990 FIFA World Cup bizarrely rested with Israel, who contested a play-off against Colombia during a brief stint as "temporary" OFC member country – having been snubbed by other continents. Having seen off both Australia and New Zealand, Israel then lost the play-off, 1-0 on aggregate, to the South Americans. Two years later Israel was integrated into UEFA.

LOCAL RIVALRY

An "AFC–OFC" contest has been staged twice – with Asian sides prevailing both times. A showdown in 2001 between AFC Asian Cup or Asian Games winners against the OFC Nations Cup champions saw Japan defeat Australia 3-0. Two years later, New Zealand lost to Iraq by the same scoreline. The challenge has not been staged since.

GETTING AWAY WITH IT

New Zealand-born footballers who have opted to play international football for Australia instead include Archie Thompson. He was the scorer of an international-record 13 goals in his adopted country's 31-0 trouncing of American Samoa in April 2001. But the tables were turned when German-born, Australian-raised Shane Smeltz chose to represent New Zealand, the country where he spent much of his childhood. Smeltz scored New Zealand's goal in their 1-1 draw with Italy at the 2010 FIFA World Cup, in the South African city of Nelspruit.

LAUGHING ALL THE WAY TO THE BANK

New Zealand went to the 2010 FIFA World Cup with four amateur players in their 23-man squad. Midfielder **Andy Barron**, who works as an investment adviser at a bank in Wellington, even made it on to the pitch as a stoppage-time substitute against reigning world champions Italy.

BUSY NICKY

Nicky Salapu was the unfortunate goalkeeper who conceded an international-record 31 times, as his American Samoa team lost 31-0 to Australia in April 2001. Just two days earlier, Australia had crushed Tonga 22-0. Passport problems meant American Samoa were denied several of their best players for the Australia game and included three 15-year-olds in a line-up that had an average age of just 18. Depite this, they managed to keep the game goalless ... for the first 10 minutes. In his eight international appearances, Salapu conceded 91 goals – with just one in his opposite number's net, scored by Natia Natia, in a 9-1 defeat to Vanuatu in May 2004. Midfielder Natia's goal was American Samoa's first in a FIFA World Cup qualifier. The country's only victory, over Wallis and Futana in 1983, came before they were officially recognized by FIFA in 1998. Wallis and Futana – a tiny Polynesian island, a French colony, 800km west of American Samoa – remain unrecognized by world football's governing body.

THE WHITE STUFF

New Zealand's national football team is known as the "All-Whites" – not just a recognition of their kit colours, but also a counterpoint to the "All-Blacks" nickname of the country's more famous and successful rugby union side.

CONCACAF

Football is enthusiastically followed in many parts of the Caribbean, Central and North American region of the world game. Mexican fans have long been among the most colourful followers of FIFA World Cup™ action, all the way back to the inaugural finals in 1930. Mexico was also, in 1970 and 1986, the first country to host the finals on two occasions.

MEXICO

Mexico may well be the powerhouse of the CONCACAF region and are regular qualifiers for the FIFA World Cup™ – they did not play in the finals of the tournament on just three occasions (1934, 1974 and 1982) – but they have always struggled to impose themselves on the international stage. Two FIFA World Cup™ quarter-final appearances (both times as tournament hosts, in 1970 and 1986) represent their best performances to date. A football-mad nation expects more.

TOP CAPS

1	Claudio Suarez	178
2	Pavel Pardo	148
3	Jorge Campos	131
4	Alberto Garcia Aspe	127
5	Ramon Ramirez	121
=	Cuauhtemoc Blanco	121
7	Gerardo Torrado	118
8	Oswaldo Sanchez	99
9	Rafael Marquez	94
10	Carlos Hermosillo	90

TOP SCORERS

1	Jared Borgetti	46
2	Cuauhtemoc Blanco	39
3	Carlos Hermilloso	35
=	Luis Hernandez	35
5	Enrique Borja	31
6	Zague	30
7	Luis Flores	29
=	Luis Garcia	29
=	Hugo Sanchez	29
10	Benjamin Galindo	28

MAKING HIS MARQUEZ

Rafael Marquez set a FIFA World Cup appearance record for Mexico when playing in the 2010 second-round defeat to Argentina. That game took him to 12 games in the competition, one more than former goalkeeper Antonio Carbajal and also two other members of the 2010 squad – forward Cuauhtemoc Blanco and midfielder Gerardo Torrado.

MEXICO RECORDS

First international: won 3-2 v Guatemala, Guatemala City, 1 January 1923
Biggest win: 13-0 v Bahamas, Toluca, 28 April 1987
Biggest defeat: 8-0 v England, Wembley, 10 May 1961
CONCACAF champions: 1965, 1971, 1977, 1993, 1996, 1998, 2003
Confederations Cup winners: 1999

HERNANDEZ HEADS THE FINALS LIST

Luis Hernandez's four goals in 1998 make him Mexico's highest-ever scorer in a FIFA World Cup finals tournament. Hernandez netted twice in Mexico's 3-1 group win over South Korea. His last-minute equalizer also earned them a 2-2 draw against Holland. Hernandez, nicknamed "The Matador", gave his side the lead against Germany in the last 16, before late goals by Jurgen Klinsmann and Oliver Bierhoff eliminated the Mexicans.

YET TO MAKE THEIR MARK

Mexico may have played in the finals of 14 FIFA World Cup tournaments, but they have been serial underachievers, advancing to the quarter-finals only twice – both times when they were tournament hosts (in 1970 and 1986). They lost 4-1 to runners-up Italy in Toluca in 1970. Sixteen years later – after the finals were enlarged – they beat Bulgaria 2-0 in the last 16, before losing a shoot-out to West Germany in Monterrey after a 0-0 draw. Mexico have been eliminated at the last-16 stage in each of the last five World Cup finals, by Bulgaria on penalties, after a 1-1 draw (1994), 2-1 by Germany in 1998, 2-0 by the United States in 2002, and twice by Argentina, 2-1, after extra-time, in 2006, and 3-1 in 2010. Mexico were among the 13 participants in the inaugural FIFA World Cup in 1930. They have since been one of the strongest teams in the CONCACAF region, qualifying for the finals on 11 occasions. But they failed to progress beyond the group stage in 1930, 1950, 1954, 1958, 1962 and 1966 and once went 13 games without a win in the finals, until a 3-1 defeat of Czechoslovakia in 1962.

FAMILY SPLIT

Winger **Giovani dos Santos** was distraught when Mexico's 30-man preliminary squad was reduced to 23 for the 2010 FIFA World Cup – though not for the obvious reason. He actually made the cut, and played in all four of Mexico's matches, but his brother Jonathan dos Santos was left out by coach Javier Aguirre.

ROSAS NETS HISTORIC PENALTY

Mexico's Manuel Rosas scored the first penalty ever awarded in the FIFA World Cup finals when he converted a 42nd-minute spot-kick in his country's match against Argentina in 1930. Rosas scored again in the 65th minute, but it was too little too late for the Mexicans: they crashed to a 6-3 defeat.

LITTLE PEA FROM A POD

Javier Hernandez's goal for Mexico against France, in Polokwane on 17 June 2010 made him the third generation of his family to play at a FIFA World Cup. Hernandez – nicknamed "Chicharito", or "Little Pea" – is the son of Javier Hernandez who reached the quarter-finals with Mexico in 1986 and the grandson of Tomas Balcazar, a member of the country's 1954 squad. Balcazar also scored against France at his FIFA World Cup – and like his grandson was aged 22 when he did so.

MEXICO BEATS EARTHQUAKE

Mexico stepped in to host the 1986 FIFA World Cup finals after the original choice, Colombia, pulled out in November 1982. FIFA chose Mexico as the replacement venue because of its stadiums and infrastructure, still in place from the 1970 finals. The governing body turned down rival bids from Canada and the United States. Mexico had to work overtime to be ready for the finals, after the earthquake of 19 September 1985, which killed an estimated 10,000 people in central Mexico and destroyed many buildings in Mexico City.

THIRD TIME UNLUCKY

Mexico have played Argentina three times at a FIFA World Cup finals, and have been beaten each time. They went down 6-3 in the first round of the inaugural tournament in 1930, and lost second-round ties in 2006, 2-1 – after extra-time – and 3-1 four years later.

AGUIRRE IN CHARGE AGAIN

Mexico coach **Javier Aguirre** has had two spells in charge. Aguirre, known as "The Basque" because of his ancestry, guided Mexico to the last 16 in 2002. He returned in place of Sven-Goran Eriksson on 3 April 2009, after the Swede was sacked following Mexico's 3-1 defeat by Honduras in a FIFA World Cup qualifier for South Africa 2010. Aguirre announced his resignation after Mexico were eliminated from the 2010 tournament by Argentina.

SUAREZ SETS OUTFIELD RECORD

Mexico defender **Claudio Suarez** is the world's most-capped outfield player, with 178 caps. He ranks second only to Saudi Arabia goalkeeper Mohamed Al-Deayea, who has 181 caps. Suarez – nicknamed "The Emperor" – played in all of Mexico's four games in 1994 and 1998. He missed the 2002 finals because of a broken leg, but was included in the squad for the 2006 finals at the age of 37, although he did not play.

UNITED STATES

Some of the game's biggest names – from Pele to David Beckham – may well have graced the United States' domestic league over the years, and the country may well be one of only 15 countries to have been granted the honour of hosting a FIFA World Cup™, but football is still very much a minority sport in the world's most powerful country. However, following a series of impressive performances on the world stage, the hope is that the situation will soon change.

TOP SCORERS

1	Landon Donovan	45
2	Eric Wynalda	34
3	Brian McBride	30
4	Joe-Max Moore	24
5	Bruce Murray	21
6	Clint Dempsey	19
7	DaMarcus Beasley	17
=	Earnie Stewart	17
9	Cobi Jones	15
10	Marcelo Balboa	13
=	Hugo Perez	13

LANDON HOPE AND GLORY

The USA's all-time leading scorer **Landon Donovan** was the undoubted star of their 2010 FIFA World Cup campaign. He scored three goals in four matches, including a stoppage-time winner against Algeria that meant his side finished top of Group C. His four displays at the tournament meant he has now featured in 13 FIFA World Cup matches for the USA, two ahead of compatriots Earnie Stewart and Cobi Jones. His successful penalty in a second-round defeat to Ghana also made him the USA's all-time top scorer in the competition, with five goals – one more than 1930 hat-trick hero Bert Patenaude.

ARENA'S MEN REACH LAST EIGHT

The US's best performance in the modern FIFA World Cup finals came in 2002 when they reached the last eight. Coach Bruce Arena's side beat Portugal 3-2, drew 1-1 with South Korea and lost 3-1 to Poland to qualify in second place from Group D. **Brian McBride** and Landon Donovan scored in a 2-0 win over Mexico in the last 16. They lost 1-0 to Germany in the quarter-finals. The squad featured many players with European experience – **Brad Friedel**, Kasey Keller, Claudio Reyna, McBride, Donovan, DaMarcus Beasley and Cobi Jones. Arena was later succeeded by his assistant Bob Bradley after the US were eliminated at the group stage of the 2006 finals in Germany.

CAGLIURI'S SHOT MAKES HISTORY

The US's FIFA World Cup qualifying win in Trinidad, on 19 November 1989, is regarded as a turning point in the country's football history. The team included just one full-time professional, Paul Cagliuri, of (West) German second division club Meppen. He scored the only goal of the game with a looping shot after 31 minutes to take the US to their first finals for 40 years. The Trinidad goalkeeper, Michael Maurice, claimed to have been blinded by the sun. The victory raised the profile of the team hugely, despite their first-round elimination in the 1990 finals. It also provided the impetus for the professional organization of the national squad. Cagliuri said: "It was the single most important game we ever won."

BOB'S YOUR FATHER

Coach **Bob Bradley**'s USA team were surprise winners of Group C at the 2010 FIFA World Cup, a place above seeded favourites England. This was the first time the country had topped their first-round group since the very first FIFA World Cup in 1930. Bradley picked his son **Michael** for all four USA games at the 2010 tournament, and the midfielder rewarded his father's faith by scoring a late equalizer in the 2-2 Group C draw with Slovenia.

DEMPSEY'S DOUBLE

Clint Dempsey became only the second USA international to score at two different FIFA World Cups when his long-range shot was fumbled into the net by England goalkeeper Robert Green in their 1-1 draw in Rustenburg at the 2010 tournament. Dempsey had previously scored in a 2-1 defeat to Ghana, in the first round in Germany four years earlier. The first American to achieve the feat was striker Brian McBride, who netted against Iran in 1998 and winners against Portugal and Mexico in 2002. Dempsey's feat was emulated by Landon Donovan – a goalscorer against Poland and Mexico in 2002 and against Slovenia, Algeria and Ghana in 2010.

RECORD–BREAKERS

FIFA's choice of the United States to host the 1994 finals was controversial. Critics pointed to US's poor international record, and the lack of a national professional league. But the US made it as far as the last 16, thanks to a 2-1 win over Colombia, before losing 1-0 to eventual winners Brazil. In addition, the total attendance of 3,587,538 set a record for the finals.

ENGLAND STUNNED BY GAETJENS

The US's 1-0 win over England on 29 June 1950 ranks among the biggest surprises in FIFA World Cup history. England, along with hosts Brazil, were joint favourites to win the trophy. The US had lost their last seven matches, scoring just two goals. **Joe Gaetjens** scored the only goal, in the 37th minute, diving to head Walter Bahr's cross past goalkeeper Bert Williams. England dominated the game, but US keeper Frank Borghi made save after save. Defeats by Chile and Spain eliminated the US at the group stage, but their victory over England remains the greatest result in the country's football history.

TEAM AMERICA'S BRIEF EXPERIMENT

Governing body US Soccer entered the US national side in the NASL as "Team America" for one season in 1983. The experiment was soon dropped when the side finished bottom of the table. Team America struggled from the start because many of the top players preferred to stay with their own clubs. They were rarely able to field a settled side either.

TOP CAPS

#	Name	Caps
1	Cobi Jones	164
2	Jeff Agoos	134
3	Marcelo Balboa	128
4	Landon Donovan	127
5	Claudio Reyna	112
6	Paul Cagliuri	110
7	Eric Wynalda	106
8	Kasey Keller	102
9	Earnie Stewart	101
10	Tony Meola	100
=	Joe-Max Moore	100

SUPERPOWER IN WAITING

The United States are one of the most consistent national teams of the modern era. They have played in the last six FIFA World Cup finals, qualifying five times and hosting the 1994 tournament. They were quarter-finalists in South Korea/Japan in 2002, losing 1-0 to Germany. The US have a proud FIFA World Cup history. They finished third in the inaugural competition in 1930. Twenty years later, they sprang one of the biggest shocks in the history of the finals when they beat joint favourites England 1-0 in Belo Horizonte. But soccer in the US has traditionally been overshadowed by American football, baseball and basketball. After the demise of the North American Soccer League (NASL) in 1984, the US lacked even a national professional league. The turning point was the US's 1-0 victory in Trinidad that took them to the FIFA World Cup finals in 1990 for the first time in 40 years. The 1994 finals added further impetus – and the start of Major League Soccer in 1996 led to the development of a succession of players for the national team. Many – such as Landon Donovan, Clint Dempsey, Brad Friedel, Claudio Reyna and DaMarcus Beasley – have also played for European clubs.

CONCACAF OTHER TEAMS

Mexico and the United States (with 23 FIFA World Cup™ finals appearances between them) are undoubtedly the powerhouses of the CONCACAF region. Of the other teams to make up the football nations in North and Central America and the Caribbean, only three countries (Costa Rica in 1990, 2002 and 2006), El Salvador (1970 and 1982) and Honduras (1982 and 2010) have qualified for the FIFA World Cup™ finals on more than one occasion.

PAVON ... AND ON ... AND ON

Striker **Carlos Pavon**, the only man to play a century of games for Honduras, scored seven goals in their qualifiers to reach the 2010 FIFA World Cup – their first finals since 1982. Yet the veteran, then aged 36, played just 60 minutes of the tournament itself. Pavon, nicknamed "The Shadow", has played club football in seven different countries: Honduras, Mexico, Spain, Italy, Colombia, Guatemala and the United States, where he starred alongside David Beckham for the Los Angeles Galaxy.

COSTA RICA KEEP BATTLING

Costa Rica, spearheaded by **Paulo Wanchope**, have been the most successful of Mexico's Central American neighbours at the FIFA World Cup finals. They qualified in 1990, 2002 and 2006, and reached the last 16 at that first attempt, beating Scotland 1-0 and Sweden 2-1 in their group. They were knocked out by Czechoslovakia, 4-1. In 2002, they beat China 2-0 and drew 1-1 with Turkey but went home after losing 5-2 to Brazil. They again departed at the group stage in 2006, losing all three matches. El Salvador qualified twice, in 1970 and 1982 – but lost all six of their matches, including a 10-1 defeat by Hungary in 1982. Honduras have also qualified twice but gone out in the first round both times. In 1982, they drew 1-1 with Spain and Northern Ireland, but lost 1-0 to Yugoslavia. They didn't score a goal in 2010, losing to Chile and Spain before drawing with Switzerland.

CANADA'S SOLE APPEARANCE

Canada reached the FIFA World Cup finals for the only time in 1986, beating Honduras and Costa Rica in the final CONCACAF qualifying group, but they lost all three games and failed to score a goal. They were beaten by France (1-0), Hungary (2-0) and the Soviet Union (2-0).

HIGHEST ATTENDANCE

The biggest crowd ever to watch a CONCACAF team play at home was the 119,853 people who saw Mexico lose 2-0 to Brazil in a friendly at the Aztec Stadium, Mexico City, on 7 July 1968.

COSTA RICA WIN WITHOUT A CROWD

The lowest-ever attendance for a CONCACAF FIFA World Cup qualifier was for the Costa Rica–Panama game on 26 March 2005. FIFA ordered the game, staged at the Saprissa Stadium in San Jose, to be played behind closed doors after missiles were thrown at visiting players and the match officials when Mexico won there 2-1 on 9 February. The game was known as "the ghost match". Costa Rica beat Panama 2-1, thanks to a **Roy Myrie** goal in the first minute of stoppage time.

CONCACAF TEAMS IN THE FIFA WORLD CUP™ FINALS

Appearances made by teams from the CONCACAF region at the FIFA World Cup finals

1	Mexico	14
2	US	9
3	Costa Rica	3
4	El Salvador	2
=	Honduras	2
6	Canada	1
=	Cuba	1
=	Haiti	1
=	Jamaica	1
=	Trinidad & Tobago	1

PROUD RECORD

The CONCACAF confederation can boast of having had at least one representative in every FIFA World Cup finals. Mexico and the United States entered the first finals in 1930 – and the US reached the semi-finals before losing to Argentina. Since then, these two have dominated the qualifying competition. Mexico have played in a total of 14 finals tournaments; the USA have in nine, and all of the last six. Other countries have challenged them recently. Costa Rica's third appearance and Trinidad & Tobago's debut at the 2006 FIFA World Cup gave CONCACAF a record four representatives at one tournament. And, at the 2010 FIFA World Cup, Honduras made their second finals appearance.

REGGAE BOYZ STEP UP

In 1998, Jamaica became the first team from the English-speaking Caribbean to reach the FIFA World Cup finals. The "Reggae Boyz", as they were nicknamed, included several players based in England. They were eliminated at the group stage, despite beating Japan 2-1 in their final game with two goals by **Theodore Whitmore**. They had earlier lost 3-1 to Croatia and 5-0 against Argentina.

BROTHERS IN ARMS

Honduras became the first team to field not one, not two, but three siblings at a FIFA World Cup, when they picked defender **Johnny** (left), midfielder **Wilson** (right) and striker **Jerry** (middle) **Palacios** in the 2010 squad. Jerry was a last-minute call-up, as replacement for injured Julio Cesar de Leon. Tottenham Hotspur defensive midfielder Wilson Palacios was perhaps the most famous and acclaimed player in the first Honduras side to reach a FIFA World Cup in 28 years. Like the 1982 side, though, Reinaldo Rueda's men went three games without a win or even a goal. An older brother, Milton Palacios, played 14 times as a defender for Honduras between 2003 and 2006 but was not in the running for the 2010 squad.

CUBA SHOW THE WAY

In 1938, Cuba became the first island state of the CONCACAF region to reach the FIFA World Cup quarter-finals. They drew 3-3 with Romania after extra-time in the first round, then won the replay 2-1 with goals by Hector Socorro and Carlos Oliveira after trailing at half-time. They were thrashed 8-0 by Sweden in the last eight. Haiti were the next Caribbean island to play in the finals, in 1974. They lost all three group games, 3-1 to Italy, 7-0 against Poland and 4-1 to Argentina.

PALACIOS FAMILY PAIN

Another of the Palacios brothers, the youngest, Edwin, was mourned by all the three siblings who went to the 2010 FIFA World Cup. He had been kidnapped in 2007, and his remains were found 18 months later. After hearing the tragic news, Wilson Palacios sat in reception all night in the hotel where Tottenham Hotspur were preparing for a Saturday match, reluctant to disturb anyone – to the amazement of sympathetic manager Harry Redknapp, who found him patiently waiting there in the morning.

TRINIDAD'S FIRST TIME

Trinidad & Tobago reached the FIFA World Cup finals for the first time in 2006 after a marathon qualifying competition that ended with their 1-0 play-off victory in Bahrain. The team, nicknamed the "Socca Warriors", held Sweden 0-0 in their opening game, but lost 2-0 to England and 2-0 to Paraguay.

RUEDA AWAKENING

Colombian-born coach Reinaldo Rueda was granted Honduran citizenship after leading his adopted country to the 2010 FIFA World Cup. The players were also granted an open-top bus tour through the capital Tegucigalpa and an audience with the president after a successful end to CONCACAF qualifiers.

PART 3: EUROPEAN CHAMPIONSHIP

UEFA, the European federation, was founded during the 1954 FIFA World Cup in Switzerland and initially set itself the task of creating a championship for national teams. Many of the major European nations – such as Italy, West Germany and England – refused to take part in the initial competition, launched in 1958, because their national associations feared fixture congestion. So the first finals, featuring four nations, were staged in France and saw the Soviet Union end up as first winners after defeating Yugoslavia in the final in the original Parc des Princes in the south-west of Paris. Now the map of Europe has changed so remarkably that, while UEFA's membership has more than doubled, the Soviet Union and Yugoslavia no longer exist.

The Soviets also reached the second finals in 1964, but lost their crown in the final against their Spanish hosts in the Estadio Bernabeu in Madrid. Spain's playmaker, Luis Suarez, from Italy's Internazionale, thus became the first player to win the European Championship and the European Cup in the same season. In the tournament's early years, the qualifying system was based on a simple two-legged knockout system, but this was amended to a group-based format and then, in 1980, the finals were expanded to eight nations. That year saw West Germany win for a second time, having previously triumphed in 1972. In 1996, they extended their record to three titles after beating the Czech Republic with a golden goal in extra-time at Wembley. By then the finals had been expanded again to 16 teams and history was made in 2000 when Belgium and Holland organized the first co-hosted finals. Austria and Switzerland repeated the "trick" in 2008, when Spain won their first major international trophy since their 1964 European Championship success.

Austria-Swiss

Fernando Torres celebrates Spain's 2008 European Championship triumph in Vienna – after scoring the winning goal against Germany in the final.

EUROPEAN CHAMPIONSHIP QUALIFIERS

The European Championship qualifying competition has become a huge event in its own right, with 50 teams having competed for places alongside hosts Austria and Switzerland at Euro 2008. How times have changed. There was one two-legged qualifying round for the 1960 competition, to reduce the 17 entrants to 16, and none for the 1964 tournament, which saw teams meet each other on a home-and-away basis in the first round. A full-scale qualifying competition was first launched for the 1968 finals, with eight groups of four and one group of three. The number of qualifiers increased in size again during the 1990s as several new associations joined UEFA after the break-ups of the Soviet Union and Yugoslavia and entered the championship for the first time.

HEALY POSTS GOAL RECORD

Northern Ireland forward **David Healy** (born in Killyleagh on 5 August 1979) set a new scoring record with 13 goals in the Euro 2008 qualifiers. His tally included hat-tricks against Spain and Liechtenstein. Healy beat the previous record of 12 goals, netted by Croatia's Davor Suker in the qualifiers for Euro 96. Ole Madsen of Denmark scored 11 goals before the finals tournament in 1964, but qualifying groups were not introduced until two years later.

IRISH VICTORY NOT ENOUGH

West Germany's 1-0 defeat by Northern Ireland in Hamburg on 11 November 1983 was their first-ever home loss in the qualifying competition, but their 2-1 win over Albania in Saarbrucken four days later enabled them to pip Northern Ireland on goal difference for a place in the 1984 finals.

IRISH STAGE FIRST QUALIFIER

The first qualifying game in European Championship history was played on 5 April 1959, when the Republic of Ireland beat Czechoslovakia 2-0 in Dublin. Seventeen teams entered the inaugural competition, so the total had to be reduced to 16 for the first round. The Czechs went through 4-2 on aggregate, after winning the second leg in Bratislava 4-0 on 10 May.

GERMANS RUN UP 13

Germany's 13-0 win in San Marino on 6 September 2006 was the biggest victory margin in qualifying history. **Lukas Podolski** (4), Miroslav Klose (2), Bastian Schweinsteiger (2), Thomas Hitzlsperger (2), Michael Ballack, Manuel Friedrich and Bernd Schneider scored the goals. The previous biggest win was Spain's 12-1 rout of Malta in 1983.

BRITS STAY HOME TO QUALIFY

The four British teams used the Home International Championship of 1966–67 and 1967–68 as a qualifying group for the 1968 finals. FIFA World Cup holders England went through but, at their own request, the British teams have been drawn separately for each subsequent qualifying competition.

EAST AND WEST COME TOGETHER

East and West Germany were originally drawn to face each other in the Group 5 qualifiers for Euro '92, but the country was officially reunified in October 1990, so a reunified team entered an international competition as "Germany" for the first time since the 1938 FIFA World Cup finals.

GERMANY'S WEMBLEY WONDER NIGHT

West Germany's greatest-ever team announced their arrival at Wembley on 29 April 1972, when they beat England 3-1 in the first leg of the European Championship quarter-finals. Uli Hoeness, Gunter Netzer and Gerd Muller scored the goals. West Germany went on to win the trophy, beating the Soviet Union 3-0 in the final. Their team at Wembley was: Sepp Maier; Horst Hottges, Georg Schwarzenbeck, Franz Beckenbauer, Paul Breitner; Jurgen Grabowski, Herbert Wimmer, Gunter Netzer, Uli Hoeness; Sigi Held, Gerd Muller. Eight of them played in West Germany's 1974 FIFA World Cup final win over Holland.

FLOWERS OPENS ENGLAND'S ACCOUNT

England, Italy and West Germany did not enter the first European Championship. England and Italy entered the 1964 competition, but the West Germans stayed out until the qualifiers for the 1968 finals. England took their bow with a 1-1 draw against France at Hillsborough, Sheffield, on 3 October 1962. **Ron Flowers** scored their goal from a penalty. They were eliminated after France won the second leg 5-2 in Paris. Italy beat Turkey, 6-0 at home and 1-0 away.

APPEARANCES IN THE FINALS TOURNAMENT

10	West Germany/Germany
9	Soviet Union/CIS/Russia
8	Holland
	Spain
7	Czech Republic/Czechoslovakia
	Denmark
	England
	France
	Italy
5	Portugal
	Yugoslavia
4	Belgium
	Romania
	Sweden
3	Croatia
	Greece
	Switzerland
	Turkey
2	Bulgaria
	Hungary
	Scotland
1	Austria
	Latvia
	Norway
	Poland
	Republic of Ireland
	Slovenia

FAROES BEGIN WITH A BANG

The Faroe Islands played their qualifier on 12 September 1990 – and began with a shock 1-0 win over Austria at Landskrona, Sweden. Torkil Nielsen scored the only goal of the game. Austria coach Josef Hickersberger was sacked after the defeat. That was the Faroes' only win: they finished bottom of their group, which also included Yugoslavia, Denmark and Northern Ireland.

PANCEV FORCED TO MISS OUT

Yugoslavia's **Darko Pancev** (born in Skopje on 7 September 1965) was top scorer in the qualifiers for Euro 1992 with ten goals. Yugoslavia topped qualifying Group Four, but they were banned from the finals because of their country's war in Bosnia, so Pancev never had the chance to shine. After the break-up of the Yugoslav federation, he went on to become the star player for the new nation of Macedonia.

ANDORRA, SAN MARINO STRUGGLE

Minnows Andorra and San Marino each have yet to win a match in the qualifying competition. Andorra have lost all their 30 games, with a goal difference of six against 88. San Marino have lost all their 46 games, with a goal difference of six against 200!

DUTCH EDGE FIRST PLAY-OFF

The first-ever qualifying play-off was held on 13 December 1995 at Liverpool when Holland beat the Republic of Ireland 2-0 to clinch the final place at Euro 96. **Patrick Kluivert** scored both Dutch goals.

THREE OFF AS CZECHS ADVANCE

Czechoslovakia's 3-1 semi-final win over Holland in Zagreb, on 16 June 1976, featured a record three red cards. The Czechs' Jaroslav Pollak was dismissed for a second yellow card – a foul on Johan Neeskens – after an hour. Neeskens followed in the 76th minute for kicking **Zdenek Nehoda**. Wim van Hanegem became the second Dutchman dismissed, for dissent, after Nehoda scored the Czechs' second goal with six minutes of extra-time left.

DENMARK'S UNEXPECTED TRIUMPH

Denmark were unlikely winners of Euro 1992. They had not even expected to take part after finishing behind Yugoslavia in their qualifying group, but they were invited to complete the final eight when Yugoslavia were barred for security fears following the country's collapse. Goalkeeper **Peter Schmeichel** was their hero – in the semi-final shoot-out win over Holland and again in the final against Germany, when goals by John Jensen and Kim Vilfort earned Denmark a 2-0 win.

SPAIN REFUSE TO MEET SOVIETS

Political rivalries wrecked the planned clash between Spain and the Soviet Union in the 1960 quarter-finals. The fascist Spanish leader, General Francisco Franco, refused to allow Spain to go to the communist Soviet Union – and banned the Soviets from entering Spain. The Soviet Union were handed a walkover on the grounds that Spain had refused to play. Franco relented four years later, allowing the Soviets to come to Spain for the finals. He was spared the embarrassment of presenting the trophy to them, however, as Spain beat the Soviet Union 2-1 in the final.

GERMANS DOMINATE AS COMPETITION TAKES OFF

In 50 years, the European Championship has grown to become the most important international football tournament, after the FIFA World Cup finals. Only 17 teams entered the first competition, won by the Soviet Union in 1960. Fifty took part in qualifying for the right to join hosts Austria and Switzerland at the 2008 finals. Germany (formerly West Germany) have dominated the tournament, even though they did not enter the first two competitions. They have won three times and finished runners-up on three more occasions. France and Spain have each triumphed twice. Denmark, in 1992, and Greece, in 2004, have been the tournament's surprise winners. Meanwhile, some of Europe's most famous teams have underachieved. Italy have won the trophy only once, on home soil in 1968; whereas England have never even reached the final – their best finish was third place in 1968.

DOMENGHINI RESCUES ITALY

The most controversial goal in the history of the final came on 8 June 1968. Hosts Italy were trailing 1-0 to Yugoslavia with ten minutes left. The Yugoslavs seemed still to be organizing their wall when Angelo Domenghini curled a free-kick past goalkeeper Ilja Pantelic for the equalizer. Yugoslavia protested but the goal was allowed to stand. Italy won the only replay in finals history 2-0, two days later, with goals from Gigi Riva and Pietro Anastasi.

FRANCE BOAST PERFECT RECORD

France, on home soil in 1984, are the only side to win all their matches since the finals expanded beyond four teams. They won them without any shoot-outs, too, beating Denmark 1-0, Belgium 5-0 and Yugoslavia 3-2 in their group, Portugal 3-2 after extra-time in the semi-finals and Spain 2-0 in the final.

CZECHS WIN LONGEST SHOOT-OUT

The longest penalty shoot-out in finals history came in the 1980 third-place play-off between hosts Italy and Czechoslovakia, in Naples on 21 June. The Czechs won 9-8, following a 1-1 draw. After eight successful spot-kicks each, Czech goalkeeper **Jaroslav Netolicka** saved Fulvio Collovati's kick.

FRANCE STRIKE, WITHOUT STRIKERS

France still hold the record for the most goals scored by one team in a finals tournament, 14 in 1984. Yet only one of those goals was netted by a recognized striker – **Bruno Bellone**, who hit the second in their 2-0 final win over Spain. France's inspirational captain, Michel Platini, supplied most of the French firepower, scoring an incredible nine goals in five appearances. He hit hat-tricks against Belgium and Denmark and a last-gasp winner in the semi-final against Portugal. Midfielders Alain Giresse and Luis Fernandez chipped in with goals in the 5-0 win over Belgium. Defender Jean-Francois Domergue gave France the lead against Portugal in the semi-finals, and added another in extra-time after Jordao had put Portugal 2-1 ahead.

GERMANS SET RECORD MARGIN

West Germany's 3-0 win over the Soviet Union in 1972 remains the biggest margin of victory in any final. **Gerd Muller** netted the opening goal in the 27th minute. Midfielder Herbert Wimmer added the Germans' second after 52 minutes and Muller completed the rout six minutes later. All of the past four finals (1996, 2000, 2004 and 2008) have been settled by one-goal margins.

PORTUGAL SPURN HOME ADVANTAGE

In 2004, Portugal became the first host nation to reach the final since France 20 years earlier. They were also the first hosts to lose the final, going down 1-0 to Greece in Lisbon on 4 July. France (1984) and Spain (1964) had previously become European champions on home soil.

TOP TEAM SCORERS IN THE FINALS

1960	Yugoslavia	6
1964	Spain, Soviet Union, Hungary	4
1968	Italy	4
1972	West Germany	5
1976	West Germany	6
1980	West Germany	6
1984	France	14
1988	Holland	8
1992	Germany	7
1996	Germany	10
2000	France, Holland	13
2004	Czech Republic	9
2008	Spain	12

BIGGEST WINS IN THE FINALS

Holland 6, Yugoslavia 1, 2000
France 5, Belgium 0, 1984
Denmark 5, Yugoslavia 0, 1984
Sweden 5, Bulgaria 0, 2004

EUROPEAN CHAMPIONSHIP WINNERS

3 West Germany/Germany (1972, 1980, 1996)
2 France (1984, 2000)
  Spain (1964, 2008)
1 Soviet Union (1960)
  Czechoslovakia (1976)
  Italy (1968)
  Holland (1998)
  Denmark (1992)
  Greece (2004)

DELLAS TIMES IT RIGHT FOR GREECE

Greece scored the only "silver goal" victory in the history of the competition in the Euro 2004 semi-finals. (The silver goal rule meant that a team leading after the first period of extra-time won the match.) Traianos Dellas headed Greece's winner seconds before the end of the first period of extra-time against the Czech Republic in Porto on 1 July. Both golden goals and silver goals were abandoned for Euro 2008, and drawn knockout matches reverted to being decided over the full 30 minutes of extra-time, and penalties if necessary.

TOSS FAVOURS HOSTS ITALY

Italy reached the 1968 final on home soil thanks to the toss of a coin. It was the only game in finals history decided in such fashion. Italy drew 0-0 against the Soviet Union after extra-time in Naples on 5 June 1968. The Soviet captain, Albert Shesternev, made the wrong call at the toss – so Italy reached the final where they beat Yugoslavia.

EUROPEAN CHAMPIONSHIP PLAYER RECORDS

⚽ KADLEC FATHER AND SON

Czech defenders Miroslav and Michal Kadlec are the only father and son to have played in the finals. Miroslav (born on 22 June 1964 in Uherkse Hradiste) captained the Czech Republic side that finished as runners-up to Germany at Euro 96. He also scored the winning penalty in the semi-final shoot-out against France. Michal (born on 13 December 1984 in Vyskov) made his first appearance as an 80th-minute substitute for Jaroslav Plasil in the Group A game against Turkey in Geneva on 15 June 2008.

⚽ BROTHERS IN ARMS

Four pairs of brothers went to Euro 2000: Gary and Phil Neville (England), Frank and Ronald de Boer (Holland), Daniel and Patrik Andersson (Sweden) and Belgium's Emile and Mbo Mpenza.

⚽ BIERHOFF NETS FIRST "GOLDEN GOAL"

Germany's **Oliver Bierhoff** scored the first golden goal in the history of the tournament when he hit the winner against the Czech Republic in the Euro 96 final at Wembley on 30 June. (The golden goal rule meant the first team to score in extra-time won the match.) Bierhoff netted in the fifth minute of extra-time. His shot from 20 yards deflected off defender Michal Hornak and slipped through goalkeeper Petr Kouba's fingers.

⚽ SCIFO THE YOUNGEST

The youngest player to feature in a game at the finals was Belgium midfielder **Enzo Scifo**. He was 18 years 115 days when he appeared in his country's 2-0 win over Yugoslavia on 13 June 1984 and started in all three of Belgium's group games.

⚽ SUAREZ GAINS FIRST DOUBLE

The first man to earn winners' medals in the European Championship and the European Cup in the same season was Spain's **Luis Suarez**. He helped Spain beat the Soviet Union 2-1 in the final on 21 June 1964. A few weeks earlier, Suarez had been in the Internazionale team that beat Real Madrid 3-1 in the European Cup final. Four players were in both PSV Eindhoven's 1988 European Cup final victory over Benfica and Holland's Euro 88 final defeat of Russia. Nicolas Anelka won the Champions League with Real Madrid in 2000 and was in the France squad that won Euro 2000, but he did not appear in the final.

⚽ KIRICHENKO NETS QUICKEST GOAL

The fastest goal in the history of the finals was scored by Russia forward Dmitri Kirichenko. He netted after just 68 seconds to give his side the lead against Greece on 20 June 2004. Russia won 2-1, but Greece still qualified for the quarter-finals – and went on to become shock winners. The fastest goal in the final was Spain midfielder Jesus Pereda's sixth-minute strike in 1964, when Spain beat the Soviet Union 2-1.

⚽ TOP SCORERS IN FINALS HISTORY

1	Michel Platini (France)	9
2	Alan Shearer (England)	7
3	Nuno Gomes (Portugal)	
	Thierry Henry (France)	
	Patrick Kluivert (Holland)	
	Ruud van Nistelrooy (Holland)	6
7	Milan Baros (Czech Republic)	
	Jurgen Klinsmann (W Germany/Germany)	
	Marco van Basten (Holland)	
	Zinedine Zidane (France)	5

MOST GAMES PLAYED IN THE FINALS

16	Edwin van der Sar	(Holland)
	Lilian Thuram	(France)
14	Luis Figo	(Portugal)
	Nuno Gomes	(Portugal)
	Karel Poborsky	(Czech Republic)
	Zinedine Zidane	(France)

MATTHAUS MIRRORS TOURNAMENT GROWTH

The career of Lothar Matthaus straddles the growth of the European Championship. He appeared in four tournaments between 1980 and 2000. He missed Euro 92 because of injury and stayed at home for Euro 96 after falling out with coach Berti Vogts and skipper Jurgen Klinsmann. He had made his entry as a 19-year-old substitute for Bernd Dietz in West Germany's 3-2 group win over Holland in Naples on 14 June 1980. That was the first tournament which involved eight teams and two groups rather than the previous four semi-finalists. He ended his association with the championship at the age of 39, playing for a reunited Germany as they were eliminated 3-0 by Portugal at Euro 2000. By now the tournament had expanded to include 16 teams in four groups. Despite featuring in four tournaments, Matthaus made only 11 appearances in total. He did, however, enter the tournament when it was taking its first steps to expansion and left it when the European Championship had become second only to the FIFA World Cup as football's most important international competition.

PORTUGAL TRIO BANNED FOR THE LONGEST

The longest suspensions in the history of the finals were handed out to three Portugal players after their Euro 2000 semi-final defeat by France. Zinedine Zidane's "Golden Goal" penalty infuriated the Portuguese, who surrounded referee Gunter Benko and assistant Igor Sramka. The three Portuguese players – **Abel Xavier**, Nuno Gomes and Paulo Bento – were banned for "physically and verbally intimidating" the officials. Xavier was suspended from European football for nine months. Gomes, who was also sent off, was banned for eight months. Bento received a six-month suspension.

ILYIN GOAL MAKES HISTORY

Anatoly Ilyin of the Soviet Union scored the first goal in Championship proper history when he netted after four minutes against Hungary on 29 September 1958. A crowd of 100,572 watched the USSR win 3-1 in the Lenin Stadium, Moscow. The Soviet Union went on to win the first final, in 1960.

ARAGONES THE VETERAN COACH

Luis Aragones, Spain's coach in 2008, is the oldest boss of a European champion team. Aragones (born in Madrid on 28 July 1938) was 29 days short of his 70th birthday when Spain beat Germany 1-0 in the final on 29 June. That was his last match in charge. He had taken over the national team after Euro 2004.

VONLANTHEN BEATS ROONEY RECORD

The youngest scorer in finals history was Switzerland midfielder **Johan Vonlanthen.** He was 18 years 141 days when he netted in their 3-1 defeat by France on 21 June 2004. He beat the record set by England forward Wayne Rooney four days earlier. Rooney was 18 years 229 days when he scored the first goal in England's 3-0 win over the Swiss.

TOP SCORERS IN THE FINALS

1960:	Francois Heutte (France)	2
	Milan Galic (Yugoslavia)	
	Valentin Ivanov (Soviet Union)	
	Drazan Jerkovic (Yugoslavia)	
	Slava Metreveli (Soviet Union)	
	Viktor Ponedelnik (Soviet Union)	
1964:	Ferenc Bene (Hungary)	2
	Dezso Novak (Hungary)	
	Jesus Pereda (Spain)	
1968:	Dragan Dzajic (Yugoslavia)	2
1972:	Gerd Muller (West Germany)	4
1976:	Dieter Muller (West Germany)	4
1980:	Klaus Allofs (West Germany)	3
1984:	Michel Platini (France)	9
1988:	Marco van Basten (Holland)	5
1992:	Dennis Bergkamp (Holland)	3
	Tomas Brolin (Sweden)	
	Henrik Larsen (Denmark)	
	Karlheinz Riedle (Germany)	
1996:	Alan Shearer (England)	5
2000:	Patrick Kluivert (Holland)	5
	Savo Milosevic (Yugoslavia)	
2004:	Milan Baros (Czech Republic)	5
2008:	David Villa (Spain)	4

EURO 2012 UNDER WAY

Euro 2012 – which features 24 teams for the first time – will be co-hosted by Poland and Ukraine. The opening match will be staged at Poland's National Stadium in Warsaw. Ukraine will host the final, at the Olympic Stadium, Kiev. The other Polish venues are in Gdansk, Poznan and Wroclaw. The Ukrainian venues are at Lviv, Kharkiv and Donetsk.

RECORD FINAL CROWD AT THE BERNABEU

The record attendance for a European Championship final was the 120,000 who saw Spain beat the Soviet Union 2-1 at the Estadio Santiago Bernabeu in Madrid on 21 June 1964.

DUTCH TAKE TO THE WATER

Holland celebrated their 1988 triumph in unusual style. The team paraded on a barge through the canals of Amsterdam. A crowd estimated at more than one million greeted them – and many houseboats moored on the canals were damaged by happy fans dancing on their roofs!

GREEKS HAND ALBANIA WALKOVER

When Greece were drawn against Albania in the first round of the 1964 tournament, the Greeks immediately withdrew, handing Albania a 3-0 walkover win. The countries had technically been at war since 1940. The Greek government did not formally lift the state of war until 1987, although diplomatic relations were re-established in 1971.

ELLIS BLOWS THE WHISTLE

English referee **Arthur Ellis** took charge of the first European Championship final between the Soviet Union and Yugoslavia in 1960. Ellis had also refereed the first-ever European Cup final, between Real Madrid and Reims, four years earlier. After he retired from football, he became the "referee" on the British version of the Europe-wide game show *It's a Knock-out*.

THE "ITALIAN JOB"

The 1968 finals in Italy were used as the backdrop to a famous English-language film – *The Italian Job*, starring Michael Caine – about a British gang who use the cover of the finals to stage a daring gold robbery in Turin. The film was released in England on 2 June 1969.

NAMES ON THEIR SHIRTS

Players wore their names as well as their numbers on the back of their shirts for the first time at Euro 92. They had previously been identified only by numbers.

ITALY HOSTS TWICE

Italy were the first country to host the finals twice – in 1968 and 1980. They were awarded the finals in 1968 in recognition of the 60th anniversary of the Italian football federation. Belgium have also hosted the finals twice: first, alone, in 1972, and then in partnership with Holland for Euro 2000.

FINALS HOSTS

1960 France
1964 Spain
1968 Italy
1972 Belgium
1976 Yugoslavia
1980 Italy
1984 France
1988 West Germany
1992 Sweden
1996 England
2000 Holland and Belgium
2004 Portugal
2008 Austria and Switzerland

LOW COUNTRIES START DUAL TREND

In 2000, Belgium and Holland began the trend for dual hosting the European Championship finals – it was the first time the tournament was staged in more than one country. The opening game was Belgium's 2-1 win over Sweden in Brussels on 10 June. The final was staged in Rotterdam on 2 July. Austria and Switzerland jointly hosted Euro 2008. The opening game was Switzerland's 1-0 defeat by the Czech Republic in Basel on 7 June. The final was staged in Vienna on 29 June.

THUNDERSTORM HAMPERS SEMI–FINAL COVERAGE

Euro 2008 TV viewers missed much of the dramatic finale to Germany's 3-2 semi-final win over Turkey because of a television blackout. A thunderstorm and high winds in Vienna – where TV operations were based – meant the loss of pictures for several minutes. TV viewers missed both Miroslav Klose's goal that gave Germany a 2-1 lead, and Semih Senturk's equalizer. But coverage was resumed just in time for **Philipp Lahm's** stoppage-time winner.

EURO 2008 IN THE INTERNET AGE

The Internet became a massive conduit for public interest for the Euro 2008 finals. More than 105 million surfers from more than 200 countries visited the dedicated site www.Euro2008.com. The biggest volume of traffic – around 15 per cent – came from the United Kingdom. The greatest number of daily hits was 4.9 million.

TOP TEN TEAMS IN FINALS MATCHES

Team	Pld	W	D	L	F	A
West Germany/Germany	38	19	10	9	55	39
Holland	32	17	8	7	55	32
France	28	14	7	7	46	34
Spain	30	13	9	8	38	31
Portugal	23	12	4	7	34	22
Italy	27	11	12	4	27	18
Czechoslovakia/Czech Republic	25	11	5	9	36	32
Soviet Union/CIS/Russia	27	11	5	11	31	36
England	23	7	7	9	31	28
Denmark	24	6	6	12	26	38

CHAMPIONSHIPS BECOME AN EXTRAVAGANZA

The European Championship attracts more media attention than any other football tournament except for the FIFA World Cup finals and one can only imagine the shock when TV pictures from the Euro 2008 semi-final between **Germany and Turkey** were disrupted by bad weather. Once the finals featured four teams and lasted for a few days; now they include 16 teams and the competition has become a three-week extravaganza. The party will last even longer in 2012 when 24 teams will contest the tournament in Poland and Ukraine for the first time. TV viewing figures will almost certainly set new records, while new media – such as the Internet – will play an ever-increasing role in the coverage.

SPAIN'S RECORD TV AUDIENCE

Spain's Euro 2008 final win over Germany attracted the largest television audience in the country's history. More than 14 million homes tuned in to the game, and hundreds of thousands more fans watched on giant public screens in squares and parks. The final was shown live in 231 countries around the globe.

JET travel has had a revolutionary effect on international sports competition over the past 50 years, but the difficulties of organizing major events in the first half of the 20th century did have some positive effects. FIFA's founding membership in 1904 was entirely European, and though South American nations – such as Brazil, Argentina and Uruguay – were not slow in signing up, the opportunities available to them to play against their European cousins were scarce. Occasional European teams, usually clubs, made sporadic tours to South America, but the time taken and disruption caused by long sea journeys meant that, for example, only four European national teams went to Uruguay to play in the inaugural FIFA World Cup in 1930, and they all sailed on the same vessel.

The South Americans thus had to organize their own international competitions, which led directly to the creation in 1916 of the South American Championship, now known as the Copa America. Communications not being what they are today, even then organization was a far from simple matter – hence many of the initial championships are now considered "unofficial". Further problems arose over competition scheduling which, in later years, often meant that countries were unable to secure the release of their finest players who were contracted to clubs in Europe. The issue of such a player exodus was a particular problem for Argentina in the late 1950s. They won the South American title in 1957 and were considered favourites to win the FIFA World Cup the following year. By then, however, they had lost all their inspirational inside-forward trio – Humberto Maschio, Antonio Valentin Angelillo and Enrique Omar Sivori – to Italian clubs. Eventually the club versus country issue was resolved by FIFA's enforcement of a unified international calendar, which recognized the priority status of the Copa America.

Brazil celebrate victory at the 2007 Copa America – with their minds also fixed on their role as FIFA World Cup hosts in 2014.

PA AMERICA

COPA AMERICA TEAM RECORDS

LITTLE NAPOLEON

In 1942, Ecuador and their goalkeeper Napoleon Medina conceded more goals in one tournament than any other team, when they let in 31 goals across six games – and six defeats. Three years later he and his team-mates finally managed to keep a clean sheet, in a goalless draw against Bolivia – but still managed to let in another 27 goals in their five other matches.

COLLECTIVE RESPONSIBILITY

Brazil's players shared the goalscoring duties on their way to the 1997 Copa America title, finishing with a record ten scorers: Ronaldo (five goals), Leonardo and Romario (three apiece), Denilson, Djalminha and Edmundo (two each) and Aldair, Dunga, Flavio Conceicao and **Ze Roberto** (one each).

COPA AMERICA WINNERS

1916	Uruguay (league format)
1917	Uruguay (league format)
1919	Brazil 1 Uruguay 0
1920	Uruguay (league format)
1921	Argentina (league format)
1922	Brazil 3 Paraguay 1
1923	Uruguay (league format)
1924	Uruguay (league format)
1925	Argentina (league format)
1926	Uruguay (league format)
1927	Argentina (league format)
1929	Argentina (league format)
1935	Uruguay (league format)
1937	Argentina 2 Brazil 0
1939	Peru (league format)
1941	Argentina (league format)
1942	Uruguay (league format)
1945	Argentina (league format)
1946	Argentina (league format)
1947	Argentina (league format)
1949	Brazil 7 Paraguay 0
1953	Paraguay 3 Brazil 2
1955	Argentina (league format)
1956	Uruguay (league format)
1957	Argentina (league format)
1959	Argentina (league format)
1959	Uruguay (league format)
1963	Bolivia (league format)
1967	Uruguay (league format)
1975	Peru 4 Colombia 1 (on aggregate, after three games)
1979	Paraguay 3 Chile 1 (on aggregate, after three games)
1983	Uruguay 3 Brazil 1 (on aggregate, after two games)
1987	Uruguay 1 Chile 0
1989	Brazil (league format)
1991	Argentina (league format)
1993	Argentina 2 Mexico 1
1995	Uruguay 1 Brazil 1 (Uruguay won 5-3 on penalties)
1997	Brazil 3 Bolivia 1
1999	Brazil 3 Uruguay 0
2001	Colombia 1 Mexico 0
2004	Brazil 2 Argentina 2 (Brazil won 4-2 on penalties)
2007	Brazil 3 Argentina 0

HOSTING RIGHTS BY COUNTRY

Argentina	8	(1916, 1921, 1925, 1929, 1937, 1946, 1959, 1987)
Uruguay	7	(1917, 1923, 1924, 1942, 1956, 1967, 1995)
Chile	6	(1920, 1926, 1941, 1945, 1955, 1991)
Peru	6	(1927, 1935, 1939, 1953, 1957, 2004)
Brazil	4	(1919, 1922, 1949, 1989)
Ecuador	3	(1947, 1959, 1993)
Bolivia	2	(1963, 1997)
Paraguay	1	(1999)
Colombia	1	(2001)
Venezuela	1	(2007)

EXTRA TIME

The longest match in the history of the Copa America was the 1919 final between Brazil and Uruguay. It lasted 150 minutes, 90 minutes of regular time plus two extra-time periods of 30 minutes each.

HOW IT STARTED

The first South American "Championship of Nations", as it was then known, was held in Argentina from 2–17 July 1916, during the country's independence centenary commemorations. The tournament was won by Uruguay, who drew with Argentina in the last match of the tournament. It was an inauspicious beginning. The 16 July encounter had to be abandoned at 0-0 when fans invaded the pitch and set the wooden stands on fire. The match was continued at a different stadium the following day and still ended goalless ... but Uruguay ended up topping the mini-league table and were hailed the first champions. Isabelino Gradin was the inaugural tournament's top scorer. The event also saw the foundation of the South American federation CONMEBOL, which took place a week into the competition on 9 July 1916. From that point on the tournament was held every two years, though some tournaments are now considered to have been unofficial.

SUB-STANDARD

During the 1953 Copa America, Peru were awarded a walkover win when Paraguay tried to make one more substitution than they were allowed. Would-be substitute Milner Ayala was so incensed, he kicked English referee Richard Maddison and was banned from football for three years. Yet Paraguay remained in the tournament and went on to beat Brazil in the final – minus, of course, the disgraced Ayala.

ROTATING RIGHTS

The Campeonato Sudamericano de Selecciones was rebaptized the Copa America from 1975. Between then and 1983 there was no host nation, before CONMEBOL adopted the policy of rotating the right to host the Copa America among the ten member confederations. The first rotation was complete after Venezuela hosted the 2007 edition, with Argentina lined up to play host for the ninth time in 2011.

HISTORY MEN

The Copa America is the world's oldest surviving international football tournament, having been launched in 1916 when the participating nations were Argentina, Bolivia, Brazil, Chile, Colombia, Ecuador, Paraguay, Peru, Uruguay and Venezuela. In 1910, an unofficial South American championship had been won by Argentina, who beat Uruguay 4-1 in the decider – though the final match had been delayed a day after rioting fans burnt down a stand at the Gimnasia stadium in Buenos Aires.

FALLEN ANGELS

Argentina's 1957 Copa America-winning forward trio of Humberto Maschio, Omar Sivori and Antonio Valentin Angelillo became known by the nickname "the angels with dirty faces". At least one of them scored in each of the side's six matches – Maschio finished with nine, Angelillo eight and Sivori three. Argentina's most convincing performance was an opening 8-2 win over Colombia, in which Argentina had scored four goals and missed a penalty within the first 25 minutes. The dazzling displays made Argentina, not eventual winners Brazil, favourites for the following year's FIFA World Cup. Before then, however, Maschio, Sivori and Angelillo had all been lured away to Europe by Italian clubs and the Argentine federation subsequently refused to pick them for the trip to Sweden for the FIFA World Cup. Sivori and Maschio ultimately made it to the FIFA World Cup, in 1962. However, to fury back home, they did so wearing not the light blue-and-white stripes of Argentina, but the Azzurri blue of their newly adopted Italy.

CONSISTENT COLOMBIANS

In 2001, Colombia, who went on to win the trophy for the first and only time in their history, became the only country to go through an entire Copa America campaign without conceding a single goal. They scored 11 goals themselves, more than half of them from six-goal tournament top scorer **Victor Aristazabal**. Keeping the clean sheets was goalkeeper Oscar Cordoba, who had previously spent much of his international career as back-up to the eccentric Rene Higuita. Just a month earlier, Cordoba had won the South American club championship, the Copa Libertadores, with Argentine side Boca Juniors.

TRIUMPHS BY COUNTRY

Uruguay 14 (1916, 1917, 1920, 1923, 1924, 1926, 1935, 1942, 1956, 1959, 1967, 1983, 1987, 1995)
Argentina 14 (1921, 1925, 1927, 1929, 1937, 1941, 1945, 1946, 1947, 1955, 1957, 1959, 1991, 1993)
Brazil 8 (1919, 1922, 1949, 1989, 1997, 1999, 2004, 2007)
Peru 2 (1939, 1975)
Paraguay 2 (1953, 1979)
Bolivia 1 (1963)
Colombia 1 (2001)

MORE FROM MORENO

Argentina were not only responsible for the Copa America's biggest win, but also the tournament's highest-scoring game, when they put 12 past Ecuador in 1942 – to no reply. Jose Manuel Moreno's five strikes in that game included the 500th goal in the competition's history. Moreno, born in Buenos Aires on 3 August 1916, ended that tournament as joint top scorer with team-mate Herminio Masantonio – hitting seven goals. Both men ended their international careers with 19 goals for their country, though Moreno did so in 34 appearances – compared to Masantonio's 21. Masantonio scored four in the Ecuador thrashing.

FAMILIAR FACES

Uruguay have made the most appearances (40), followed by Argentina (38), Chile (35), Paraguay (33), Brazil (32) and Peru (28). Argentina has hosted the Copa America the most times – eight, followed by **Uruguay** (seven) and Chile (six).

COPA AMERICA PLAYER RECORDS

FROG PRINCE

Chilean goalkeeper Sergio Livingstone holds the record for most Copa America appearances, with 34 games, across the 1941, 1942, 1945, 1947, 1949 and 1953 tournaments. Livingstone, nicknamed "The Frog", was voted player of the tournament in 1941 – becoming the first goalkeeper to win the award – and might have played even more Copa America matches had he not missed out on the 1946 competition. Livingstone, born in Santiago on 26 March 1920, spent almost his entire career in his home country – save for a season with Argentina's Racing Club in 1943–44. Overall, he made 52 appearances for Chile between 1941 and 1954, before retiring and becoming a popular TV journalist and commentator.

OVERALL TOP SCORERS

1	Norberto Mendez (Argentina)	17
=	Zizinho (Brazil)	17
3	Teodoro Fernandez (Peru)	15
=	Severino Varela (Uruguay)	15
5	Ademir (Brazil)	13
=	Jair da Rosa Pinto (Brazil)	13
=	Gabriel Batistuta (Argentina)	13
=	Jose Manuel Moreno (Argentina)	13
=	Hector Scarone (Uruguay)	13

CHILE'S ILL FORTUNE

The first Copa America own goal was scored by Chile's Luis Garcia, giving Argentina a 1-0 win in 1917, in the second edition of the tournament. Even more unfortunately for Chile, Garcia's strike was the only goal by one of their players throughout the tournament – making Chile the first team to fail to score a single goal in a Copa America competition.

LOW-KEY JOSE

The first-ever Copa America goal, in 1916, was scored by Jose Piendibene – setting Uruguay on the way to a 4-0 triumph over Chile. But he is not thought to have marked the moment with any great extravagance – Piendibene, renowned for his sense of fair play, made a point of not celebrating goals, to avoid offending his opponents.

MOST GAMES PLAYED

1	Sergio Livingstone (Chile)	34
2	Zizinho (Brazil)	33
3	Leonel Alvarez (Colombia)	27
4	Carlos Valderrama (Colombia)	27
5	Alex Aguinaga (Ecuador)	25
6	Claudio Taffarel (Brazil)	25
7	Teodoro Fernandez (Peru)	24
8	Angel Romano (Uruguay)	23
9	Djalma Santos (Brazil)	22
10	Claudio Suarez (Mexico)	22

REPEATING THE FEAT

Uruguay's **Pedro Petrone** (in 1923 and 1924) and **Gabriel Batistuta** of Argentina (in 1991 and 1995) are the only players to finish as top scorers in the Copa America on two occasions. Batistuta made his Argentina debut just a few days before the 1991 Copa America, in which his starring performances – including a decisive goal in the final – helped him win a transfer from Boca Juniors to Italy's Fiorentina.

MAGIC ALEX

When Alex Aguinaga lined up for Ecuador against Uruguay in his country's opening game at the 2004 event, he became only the second man to take part in eight different Copa Americas – joining legendary Uruguayan goalscorer Angel Romano. Aguinaga, a midfielder born in Ibarra on 9 July 1969, played a total of 109 times for his country – 25 of them in the Copa America, a competition that yielded four of his 23 international goals. His Copa America career certainly began well: Ecuador went undefeated for his first four appearances, at the 1987 and 1989 events, but his luck had ran out by the time his Ecuador career was coming to an end: he lost his final seven Copa America matches.

START TO FINISH

Colombia playmaker Carlos Valderrama and defensive midfielder **Leonel Alvarez** played in all 27 of their country's Copa America matches between 1987 and 1995, winning ten, drawing ten and losing seven – including third-place finishes in 1987, 1993 and 1995. Valderrama's two Copa America goals came in his first and final appearances in the competition – in a 2-0 victory over Bolivia in 1987 and a 4-1 thrashing of the United States eight years later.

REGULAR GUEST

Of the non-South Americans invited to take part in the Copa America, Mexico's **Claudio Suarez** has appeared the most – 22 games across five tournaments from 1993 to 2004. Suarez, the world's most-capped outfield footballer, was ever-present during Mexico's run to the 1993 final, but missed the 2001 event, when they finished runners-up, to rest before crucial FIFA World Cup qualifiers – only to break his leg just before the 2002 FIFA World Cup itself.

FANTASTIC FIVES

Four players have scored five goals in one Copa America game: Hector Scarone in Uruguay's 6-0 win over Bolivia in 1926; Juan Marvezzi in Argentina's 6-1 win over Ecuador in 1941; Jose Manuel Moreno in Argentina's 12-0 win over Ecuador in 1942; and Evaristo de Macedo in Brazil's 9-0 win over Colombia in 1957.

PELE'S INSPIRATION

Brazilian forward **Zizinho** jointly holds the all-time goalscoring record for the Copa America, along with Argentina's Norberto Mendez. Both men struck 17 goals, Zizinho across six tournaments and Mendez three – including the 1945 and 1946 tournaments, which featured both men. Mendez was top scorer once and runner-up twice and won championship medals on all three occasions, while Zizinho's goals helped Brazil take the title only once, in 1949. Zizinho, Pele's footballing idol, would emerge from the 1950 FIFA World Cup as Brazil's top scorer and was also voted the tournament's best player – but was forever traumatized by the hosts' surprise defeat to Uruguay that cost Brazil the title. On 16 July every year, the anniversary of the match, Zizinho would take his phone off the hook, because people would still call asking him how Brazil lost. He missed out on a place in Brazil's 1958 FIFA World Cup squad, when selectors instead opted for a promising 17-year-old striker – that childhood fan, Pele. The following year, Pele finished as Copa America top scorer for the first and only time, with eight goals.

SUCCESSFUL INVADERS

Only two foreign coaches have led a country to Copa America glory – Brazilian Danilo Alvim, whose Bolivian side won in 1963, and Englishman Jack Greenwell, Peru coach in 1939. Alvim, who won the tournament as a centre-half with Brazil in 1949, not only coached Bolivia to their one and only Copa America triumph – he did it by beating his native land 5-4 in the final match.

HOME COMFORTS

Uruguay have a unique record in remaining unbeaten in 38 Copa America games on home turf, all played in the country's capital Montevideo – comprising 31 wins, seven draws. The last tournament match they hosted was both a draw and a win – 1-1 against Brazil in 1995, with Uruguay emerging as champions, 5-3 on penalties after Fernando Alvez saved Tulio's penalty.

INVITED GUESTS

1993 **Mexico (runners-up), United States**

1995 **Mexico, United States (fourth)**

1997 **Costa Rica, Mexico (third)**

1999 **Japan, Mexico (third)**

2001 **Costa Rica, Honduras (third), Mexico (runners-up)**

2004 **Costa Rica, Mexico**

2007 **Mexico (third), United States**

MULTI–TASKING

Argentina's **Guillermo Stabile** not only holds the record for most Copa America triumphs as coach – he trounces all opposition. He led his country to the title on no fewer than six occasions – in 1941, 1945, 1946, 1947, 1955 and 1957. No other coach has lifted the trophy more than twice. Stabile coached Argentina from 1939 to 1960, having been appointed at the age of just 34. He lasted for 123 games in charge, winning 83 of them – and still managed to coach three clubs on the side at different times throughout his reign. He remained as Red Star Paris manager during his first year in the Argentina role, then led Argentine club Huracan for the next nine years – before leading domestic rivals Racing Club from 1949 to 1960. Stabile's Argentina may have, unusually, missed out on Copa America success in 1949, but that year brought the first of three Argentina league championships in a row for Stabile's Racing Club.

CAPTAIN CONSISTENT

Uruguay's 1930 World Cup-winning captain **Jose Nasazzi** is the only footballer to be voted player of the tournament at two different Copa America tournaments. Even more impressively, he achieved the feat 12 years apart – first taking the prize in 1923, then again in 1935. He was a Cup winner in 1923, 1924, 1926 and 1935. Nasazzi also captained Uruguay to victory in the 1924 and 1928 Olympic Games and in the 1930 World Cup.

ONE−NIL TO THE ANYONE

Perhaps predictably, the most common scoreline in Copa America history is the 1-0 win – the result on no fewer than 106 occasions, most recently when **Javier Mascherano**'s first goal for Argentina saw off Paraguay in the 2007 group stage.

POINTS WIN PRIZES

If every Copa America win were awarded three points, with one for a draw, Argentina would emerge from the tournament's history with the most per game – an average 2.1 points per match, ahead of Brazil's 1.89 and Uruguay's 1.82. The only country to still go without a single Copa America match victory is Japan, who failed to triumph in three matches when invited to take part – for the first and, so far, only time – in the 1999 competition.

FINE HOST

Argentina has hosted more tournaments than any other South American country, followed by Uruguay (seven), Chile (six) and Peru (also six). Despite hosting the final play-off game in 1975, Venezuela remained the last South American country not to host a full tournament until 2007.

WRONG JUAN

It took 21 years, but Uruguay's Juan Emilio Piriz became the first Copa America player sent off, against Chile in 1937 – the first of 170 dismissals so far. Some 127 of those disgraced players have had a red card flourished in their face, since FIFA introduced the card system for referees in 1970.

SEEING RED

Brazil may have the worst FIFA World Cup disciplinary record, but neighbours Uruguay assume that unenviable position in the Copa America. Uruguayan players have been sent off 30 times, followed by Argentina and Peru on 22 dismissals apiece, Brazil (19), Venezuela (18), Chile (15), Bolivia and Paraguay (11 each), Colombia, Ecuador and Mexico (nine each), and Honduras and Japan (one each). Only Costa Rica and the US have, so far, made their way through Copa America participations with eleven men on the field throughout.

TROPHY−WINNING COACHES

6 Guillermo Stabile (Argentina 1941, 1945, 1946, 1947, 1955, 1957)

2 Alfio Basile (Argentina 1991, 1993)
Juan Carlos Corazzo (Uruguay 1959, 1967)
Ernesto Figoli (Uruguay 1920, 1926)

1 Jorge Pacheco and Alfredo Foglino (Uruguay 1916)
Ramon Platero (Uruguay 1917)
Pedro Calomino (Argentina 1921)
Lais (Brazil 1922)
Leonardo De Lucca (Uruguay 1923)
Ernesto Meliante (Uruguay 1924)
Americo Tesoriere (Argentina 1925)
Jose Lago Millon (Argentina 1927)
Francisco Olazar (Argentina 1929)
Raul V Blanco (Uruguay 1935)
Manuel Seoane (Argentina 1937)
Jack Greenwell (Peru 1939)
Pedro Cea (Uruguay 1942)
Flavio Costa (Brazil 1949)
Manuel Fleitas Solich (Paraguay 1953)
Hugo Bagnulo (Uruguay 1956)
Victorio Spinetto (Argentina 1959)
Danilo Alvim (Bolivia 1963)
Marcos Calderon (Peru 1975)
Ranulfo Miranda (Paraguay 1979)
Omar Borras (Uruguay 1983)
Roberto Fleitas (Uruguay 1987)
Sebastiao Lazaroni (Brazil 1989)
Hector Nunez (Uruguay 1995)
Mario Zagallo (Brazil 1997)
Wanderlei Luxemburgo (Brazil 1999)
Francisco Maturana (Colombia 2001)
Carlos Alberto Parreira (Brazil 2004)
Dunga (Brazil 2007)

PART 5:
AFRICA CUP OF NATIONS

THE AFRICAN governing football confederation – Confederation Africaine de Football (or CAF) – is three years younger than UEFA, yet their cross-continental tournament, the Africa Cup of Nations, kicked off before the first European Championship. Formed on 8 February 1957, the CAF announced the first championship just three days later.

Egypt's ultimate triumph in that inaugural tournament set an appropriate pattern – the "Pharaohs" have won a record number of championships overall (seven) – but the competition has changed, and progressed, plenty since then.

Only three teams entered in 1957, but 45 nations will be vying for 14 qualification spots at the next event, in 2012, alongside already qualified co-hosts Equatorial Guinea and Gabon. The global prominence of the Africa Cup of Nations has also grown, especially as the spotlight falls on major African stars taking time off from European club duties every other January. There have been mounting calls for the competition to be moved to the middle of the year, to avoid disrupting European league seasons, but these have been rejected for climatic and seasonal reasons.

Whatever the place in the calendar, the trophy – now in its third physical incarnation – will always be contested with vivacious skills and fierce local pride. There have been more different winners of the ACN than of any other continental championship, with glory being shared among 13 separate nations – including Africa's largest three countries, Sudan, Algeria and Congo DR, as well as mid-sized entrants such as Cameroon, Morocco, the Ivory Coast and early standard-setters Ghana.

And extra significance was achieved when the preliminary rounds for the 2010 event were integrated into Africa's FIFA World Cup 2010™ qualification competition.

Egypt's seventh victory in the Africa Cup of Nations in 2010 – a 1-0 victory over Ghana in the final – was small consolation for the nation's failure to qualify for the 2010 FIFA World Cup.

TEST OF ENDURANCE

The Ivory Coast have won the two highest-scoring penalty shoot-outs in full international history – they beat Ghana 11-10 over 24 penalties in the 1992 Africa Cup of Nations final, and Cameroon 12-11, over the same number of kicks, in the quarter-finals of the 2006 Africa Cup of Nations.

GHANA AGAIN

Ghana's "Black Stars" became the first country to reach the final of four consecutive Africa Cup of Nations, lifting the trophy in 1963 and 1965 and finishing runners-up in 1968 and 1970. They have now reached eight finals in all – a tally matched only by Egypt. The two countries have also staged the tournament four times apiece.

SIX-YEAR ITCH

Hocine Achiou's 86th-minute goal not only gave Algeria a highly prized 2-1 victory over old rivals Egypt in 2004. His strike also marked the last time Egypt lost an Africa Cup of Nations match, before embarking upon a record-breaking 19-game unbeaten run that included triumphs at the 2006, 2008 and 2010 tournaments. That run included a 4-0 victory over Algeria in a 2010 Africa Cup of Nations semi-final – a game which ended with the Algerians reduced to eight men after three red cards.

BAFANA BAFANA

The Africa Cup of Nations has been won by its hosts on 11 separate occasions – including three times by Egypt and twice by Ghana. But perhaps the most surprising host-country triumph was South Africa's in 1996. The country had returned to international football only four years earlier, post-apartheid, when an 82nd-minute penalty by Theophilus "Doctor" Khumalo gave them a win over Cameroon on 7 July 1992. In February 1996, substitute Mark Williams scored both goals against Tunisia as South Africa won the Africa Cup of Nations trophy – lifted by white captain **Neil Tovey**, and handed over by the country's president Nelson Mandela, in Johannesburg's Soccer City stadium. South Africa were not even meant to be hosts, but stepped in for original choice Kenya who were stripped of staging rights after falling behind on new stadium-building.

REIGNING PHARAOHS

Egypt dominate the Africa Cup of Nations records. They won the first tournament, in 1957, having been helped by a bye to the final when semi-final opponents South Africa were disqualified, and have emerged as champions another six times since – more than any other country. Their victories in the last three tournaments – 2006, 2008 and 2010 – make them the only country to lift the trophy three times in a row. They have also qualified for a record 22 tournaments, playing 84 matches – 10 more than nearest challenger Nigeria. Egypt have won 45 matches in all, followed by Nigeria on 39, Ghana on 37 and Cameroon on 36.

UNLUCKY LOSERS

Five countries have qualified for the Africa Cup of Nations without yet winning a single game in the finals. Mauritius and Tanzania have played three unsuccessful games apiece, while Namibia have gone six without a win, Benin seven and Mozambique 10. Zaire, or the Democratic Republic of Congo, have lost more Africa Cup of Nations fixtures than anyone else – 25 defeats from 56 games, followed by Ivory Coast's 24 out of 68 and Egypt's 24 out of 84.

EQUATORIAL DEBUTANTS

Equatorial Guinea will take part in an Africa Cup of Nations finals for the first time in 2012 – thanks to co-hosting the tournament, along with Gabon. Equatorial Guinea have never managed to qualify for the tournament before, while Gabon have only reached the finals four times previously. The 2012 competition will be only the second to be shared between host nations. Libya has been awarded the right to host the Africa Cup of Nations, for a second time, in 2013 – though Nigeria has been installed as first reserve should any problems arise in 2012 or 2013.

TOURNAMENT TRIUMPHS

- 7 Egypt (1957, 1959, 1986, 1998, 2006, 2008, 2010)
- 4 Ghana (1963, 1965, 1978, 1982)
  Cameroon (1984, 1988, 2000, 2002)
- 2 Zaire/Congo DR (1968, 1974)
  Nigeria (1980, 1994)
- 1 Algeria (1990)
  Congo (1972)
  Ethiopia (1962)
  Ivory Coast (1992)
  Morocco (1976)
  South Africa (1996)
  Sudan (1970)
  Tunisia (2004)

TOURNAMENT APPEARANCES

- 22 Egypt
- 19 Ivory Coast
- 18 Ghana
- 17 Cameroon, Nigeria
- 15 Zaire/Congo DR
- 14 Algeria, Tunisia, Zambia
- 13 Morocco
- 10 Senegal
- 8 Ethiopia, Guinea, South Africa
- 7 Burkina Faso, Sudan
- 6 Angola, Congo, Mali, Togo
- 5 Gabon, Kenya, Uganda
- 4 Mozambique
- 3 Benin, Malawi
- 2 Liberia, Libya, Namibia, Sierra Leone, Zimbabwe
- 1 Mauritius, Rwanda, Tanzania

FOUR SHAME

Hosts **Angola** were responsible for perhaps the most dramatic collapse in Africa Cup of Nations history, when they threw away a four-goal lead in the opening match of the 2010 tournament. Even more embarrassingly, they were leading 4-0 against Mali with just 11 minutes left, in the capital Luanda's Estadio 11 de Novembro. Mali's final two goals, by Barcelona's Seydou Keita and Boulogne's Mustapha Yatabare, were scored deep into stoppage-time. Mali failed to make it through the first round, while Angola went out in the quarter-finals.

FASHION POINTS

Cameroon were docked six FIFA World Cup qualifying points by FIFA after wearing a forbidden one-piece kit for the 2004 Africa Cup of Nations. They won the points back on appeal.

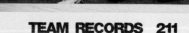

STAR STRUCK

Gabon's Chiva Star Nzigou became the Africa Cup of Nations' youngest-ever player when he took the field against South Africa in January 2000, aged 16 years and 91 days. Gabon lost the game 3-1 and finished bottom of Group B without a win from three games.

REVOLUTION #9

No player has scored more goals in one Africa Cup of Nations than Zaire's Mulamba Ndaye's nine during the 1974 tournament. Three months later he was sent off at the FIFA World Cup in West Germany, as his team crashed to a 9-0 defeat against Yugoslavia.

PROLIFIC POKOU

Ivory Coast striker Laurent Pokou scored a record five goals in one Africa Cup of Nations match, as his side trounced Ethiopia 6-1 in the first round of the 1968 tournament. He finished top scorer at that tournament, and the following one – though ended both without a winners' medal. Only modern-day Cameroon star Samuel Eto'o has overtaken his overall Africa Cup of Nations tally of 14 goals.

FAMILIAR FACES

Cameroon's **Rigobert Song** has appeared at more Africa Cup of Nations tournaments than any other player – eight competitions in all, in 1996, 1998, 2000, 2002, 2004, 2006, 2008 and 2010. His 35 consecutive matches in the Africa Cup of Nations is also unsurpassed. He won the trophy in 2000 and 2002 and captained Cameroon to the final in 2008 – though it was his error in that match that helped set up Egypt's winning goal. Ivory Coast goalkeeper Alain Gouamene played at seven tournaments from 1988 to 2000.

TOURNAMENT TOP SCORERS

1957	Mohamed Diab El-Attar (Egypt)	5
1959	Mahmoud Al-Gohari (Egypt)	3
1962	Abdelfatah Badawi (Egypt) Mengistu Worku (Ethiopia)	3
1963	Hassan El-Shazly (Egypt)	6
1965	Ben Acheampong (Ghana) Kofi Osei (Ghana) Eustache Mangle (Ivory Coast)	3
1968	Laurent Pokou (Ivory Coast)	6
1970	Laurent Pokou (Ivory Coast)	8
1972	Salif Keita (Mali)	5
1974	Mulamba Ndaye (Zaire)	9
1976	Keita Aliou Mamadou 'N'Jo Lea' (Guinea)	4
1978	Opoku Afriyie (Ghana) Segun Odegbami (Nigeria) Philip Omondi (Uganda)	3
1980	Khaled Al Abyad Labied (Morocco) Segun Odegbami (Nigeria)	3
1982	George Alhassan (Ghana)	4
1984	Taher Abouzaid (Egypt)	4
1986	Roger Milla (Cameroon)	4
1988	Gamal Abdelhamid (Egypt) Lakhdar Belloumi (Algeria) Roger Milla (Cameroon) Abdoulaye Traore (Ivory Coast)	2
1990	Djamel Menad (Algeria)	4
1992	Rashidi Yekini (Nigeria)	4
1994	Rashidi Yekini (Nigeria)	5
1996	Kalusha Bwalya (Zambia) Mark Williams (South Africa)	5
1998	Hossam Hassan (Egypt) Benni McCarthy (South Africa)	7
2000	Shaun Bartlett (South Africa)	5
2002	Julius Aghahowa (Nigeria) Patrick Mboma (Cameroon) Rene Salomon Olembe (Cameroon)	5
2004	Francileudo Santos (Tunisia) Frederic Kanoute (Mali) Patrick Mboma (Cameroon) Youssef Mokhtari (Morocco) Jay-Jay Okocha (Nigeria)	4
2006	Samuel Eto'o (Cameroon)	5
2008	Samuel Eto'o (Cameroon)	5
2010	Mohamed Nagy 'Gedo' (Egypt)	5

⚽ GOAL RUSH RASHIDI

Rashidi Yekini is Nigeria's all-time leading scorer, with 37 goals in 70 games between 1984 and 1998. Perhaps his most significant strike came against Bulgaria in 1994, Nigeria's first-ever goal at a FIFA World Cup. They won 3-0 and reached the second round. Yet more tangible glory came when Yekini finished top scorer as Nigeria won the 1994 Africa Cup of Nations, 14 years after their only previous triumph in the tournament.

⚽ NO HASSLE FOR HASSAN

Egypt's **Ahmed Hassan** not only became the first footballer to play in the final of four different Africa Cup of Nations in 2010 – he also became the first to collect his fourth winners' medal. Earlier in the same tournament, his appearance in the quarter final against Cameroon gave him his 170th cap – a new Egyptian record. Hassan marked the game with three goals – one in his own net and two past Cameroon goalkeeper Carlos Kameni – although one appeared not to cross the line.

⚽ OPENING GOAL

The first Africa Cup of Nations goal was a penalty scored by Egypt's Raafat Ateya in the 21st minute of their 2-1 semi-final win over Sudan in 1957. But his team-mate Mohamed Diab El-Attar would soon take over – he not only scored Egypt's second goal that day, but all four goals in the final against Ethiopia.

⚽ WRONG KIND OF LUCK

Thomas Nkono, Cameroon's goalkeeper at the 1982 and 1990 FIFA World Cups, was arrested moments before his country's Africa Cup of Nations semi-final against hosts Mali in 2002. Nkono, in his role as goalkeeping coach, was accused of sprinkling "black magic" charms on the pitch. Cameroon won the match 3-0, then beat Senegal 3-2 on penalties in the final after the match had ended in a 0-0 stalemate.

AFRICA CUP OF NATIONS ALL–TIME TOP SCORERS

1	Samuel Eto'o (Cameroon)	18
2	Laurent Pokou (Ivory Coast)	14
3	Rashidi Yekini (Nigeria)	13
4	Hassan El-Shazly (Egypt)	12
5	Hossam Hassan (Egypt)	11
=	Patrick Mboma (Cameroon)	11
7	Kalusha Bwalya (Zambia)	10
=	Ahmed Hassan (Egypt)	10
=	Mulamba Ndaye (Zaire)	10
=	Francileudo Santos (Tunisia)	10
=	Joel Tiehi (Ivory Coast)	10
=	Mengistu Worku (Ethiopia)	10

⚽ SAM THE MAN

Cameroon's Samuel Eto'o, who made his full international debut – away to Costa Rica on 9 March 1997 – one day short of his 16th birthday, is the Africa Cup of Nations' all-time leading goalscorer. He was part of Cameroon's victorious teams in 2000 and 2002, but had to wait until 2008 to pass Laurent Pokou's 14-goal Africa Cup of Nations record. That year's competition took his overall tally to 16 goals – only for the former Real Madrid and Barcelona striker, now with Italy's Internazionale, to add another two in 2010. In 2005, Eto'o became the first player to be named African Footballer of the Year three years running. He has also won an Olympic Games gold medal with Cameroon in 2000 and the UEFA Champions League three times, with Barcelona in 2006 and 2009 – scoring in both finals – and Inter in 2010.

AFRICA CUP OF NATIONS: FINALS

1957	(Host country: Sudan) Egypt 4 Ethiopia 0
1959	(Egypt) Egypt 2 Sudan 1
1962	(Ethiopia) Ethiopia 4 Egypt 2 (aet)
1963	(Ghana) Ghana 3 Sudan 0
1965	(Tunisia) Ghana 3 Tunisia 2 (aet)
1968	(Ethiopia) Zaire/Congo DR 1 Ghana 0
1970	(Sudan) Sudan 1 Ghana 0
1972	(Cameroon) Congo 3 Mali 2
1974	(Egypt) Zaire/Congo DR 2 Zambia 2
Replay:	Zaire/Congo DR 2 Zambia 0
1976	(Ethiopia) Morocco 1 Guinea 1 (Morocco win mini-league system)
1978	(Ghana) Ghana 2 Uganda 0
1980	(Nigeria) Nigeria 3 Algeria 0
1982	(Libya) Ghana 1 Libya 1 (aet; Ghana win 7-6 on penalties)
1984	(Ivory Coast) Cameroon 3 Nigeria 1
1986	(Egypt) Egypt 0 Cameroon 0 (aet; Egypt win 5-4 on penalties)
1988	(Morocco) Cameroon 1 Nigeria 0
1990	(Algeria) Algeria 1 Nigeria 0
1992	(Senegal) Ivory Coast 0 Ghana 0 (aet; Ivory Coast win 11-10 on penalties)
1994	(Tunisia) Nigeria 2 Zambia 1
1996	(South Africa) South Africa 2 Tunisia 0
1998	(Burkina Faso) Egypt 2 South Africa 0
2000	(Ghana & Nigeria) Cameroon 2 Nigeria 2 (aet; Cameroon win 4-3 on penalties)
2002	(Mali) Cameroon 0 Senegal 0 (aet; Cameroon win 3-2 on penalties)
2004	(Tunisia) Tunisia 2 Morocco 1
2006	(Egypt) Egypt 0 Ivory Coast 0 (aet; Egypt win 4-2 on penalties)
2008	(Ghana) Egypt 1 Cameroon 0
2010	(Angola) Egypt 1 Ghana 0

TIME TO SAY GOODBYE?

Former Yugoslavia international **Vahid Halilhodzic** was perhaps predictably upset and angry to be fired as Ivory Coast coach after their quarter-final exit to Algeria at the 2010 Africa Cup of Nations. His team had conceded a stoppage-time equalizer and an extra-time winner, though it was his only defeat in 24 matches in charge. Yet he found himself replaced by Sven-Goran Eriksson ahead of the 2010 FIFA World Cup in South Africa. Other coaches who have been sacked in the short period between an Africa Cup of Nations and a FIFA World Cup include Henri Michel, by Tunisia in 2002, and Nigeria's Shaibu Amodu in both 2002 and 2010.

INTERNATIONAL EXILE

South Africa were disqualified from the four-team Africa Cup of Nations in 1957 after refusing to pick a multi-racial squad.

GEDO BLASTER

Egypt's hero in 2010 was Mohamed Nagy, better known by his nickname "Gedo" – Egyptian Arabic for "Grandpa". He scored the only goal of the final, against Ghana, his fifth of the tournament, giving him the Golden Boot. Yet he did all this without starting a single game. He had to settle for coming on as a substitute in all six of Egypt's matches, playing a total of 135 minutes in all. Gedo – born in Damanhur on 3 October 1984 – made his international debut only two months earlier, and had played just two friendlies for Egypt before the tournament proper.

TOGO'S TRAGIC FATE

Togo were the victims of tragedy shortly before the 2010 Africa Cup of Nations kicked off – followed by expulsion from the event. The team's bus was fired on by Angolan militants three days before their first scheduled match, killing three people: the team's assistant coach, press officer and bus driver. The team returned home to Togo for three days of national mourning, and were then thrown out of the competition by the CAF as punishment for missing their opening game against Ghana. Togo were later expelled from the 2012 and 2014 competitions, but this sanction was overturned on appeal in May 2010.

UNFINISHED BUSINESS

Beware – if you go to see Nigeria play Tunisia, you may not get the full 90 minutes. Nigeria were awarded third place at the 1978 Africa Cup of Nations after the Tunisian team walked off after 42 minutes of their play-off, with the score at 1-1. They were protesting about refereeing decisions, but thus granted Nigeria a 2-0 victory by default. Oddly enough, it had been Nigeria walking off when the two teams met in the second leg of a qualifier for the 1962 tournament. Their action came when Tunisia equalized after 65 minutes. The punishment was a 2-0 win in Tunisia's favour – putting them 3-2 ahead on aggregate.

ON AND OFF THE FIELD

The only man to win the Africa Cup of Nations as both player and manager is Egypt's **Mahmoud El-Gohary**, top scorer and medal-winner at the 1959 tournament and in charge of the squad lifting the trophy 39 years later. His four separate stints as Egyptian national coach also included taking the team to the 1990 World Cup finals. Egypt's 2010 triumph was a record-equalling third for manager Hassan Shehata – who, as a striker, had finished in third place with Egypt in 1974 and fourth in 1980. Charles Gyamfi, who played for Ghana from 1950 to 1961, coached his national side to success at the 1963, 1965 and 1982 finals.

TUNED IN TO SUDAN

The 1970 Africa Cup of Nations in Sudan marked the first time the tournament was televised. Ghana reached the final for an unprecedented fourth time in a row, but lost 1-0 to the hosts.

RECENT AFRICA CUP OF NATIONS–WINNING COACHES

1988	Claude Le Roy (Cameroon)
1990	Abdelhamid Kermali (Algeria)
1992	Yeo Martial (Ivory Coast)
1994	Clemens Westerhof (Nigeria)
1996	Clive Barker (South Africa)
1998	Mahmoud El-Gohary (Egypt)
2000	Pierre Lechantre (Cameroon)
2002	Winfried Schafer (Cameroon)
2004	Roger Lemerre (Tunisia)
2006	Hassan Shehata (Egypt)
2008	Hassan Shehata (Egypt)
2010	Hassan Shehata (Egypt)

LOCK DEFENCE

Liberia's military leader Samuel Doe threatened to jail the national team if they lost at an Africa Cup of Nations qualifier to Gambia in December 1980 – a game that also doubled up as a FIFA World Cup qualifier. The players escaped punishment by achieving a 0-0 draw, though neither side went on to reach either the Africa Cup of Nations or the 1982 FIFA World Cup.

TREBLE DENIED

Egyptian playmaker Mohamed Aboutrika struck the decisive penalty in the 2006 final shoot-out against the Ivory Coast, then scored the only goal against Cameroon at the climax of the 2008 competition – but missed out through injury in 2010. Aboutrika, a philosophy graduate who was born in Giza on 7 November 1978, has won the nickname "The Smiling Assassin" for his ruthless goalscoring and cheery appearance.

CUP FOR KEEPS

The 2012 Africa Cup of Nations will feature a new trophy, after **Egypt's third consecutive triumph in 2010** allowed them to keep the cup for good. The new design will actually be the fourth different ACN prize – the first was given to Ghana for keeps in 1978, after they became the first country to win the competition three separate times. The second was retained in 2000 by Cameroon, as they too became three-time winners.

PART 6:
OTHER FIFA TOURNAMENTS

FOOTBALL at the highest level is not only about the most high-profile superstars, but also about the working investment of a myriad of enthusiasts at grassroots level across the world. Regional confederations organize international championships for players in a wide range of age groups. In 1977, FIFA extended its own worldwide development programme with the launch of the FIFA World Youth Cup. The first finals were hosted by Tunisia and the Soviet Union beat Mexico in the final. Later, in 1985, came the FIFA U-17 World Cup. Simultaneously, the Olympic Games football tournament was converted into an Under-23 event with, initially, an exception for teams in the finals to field up to three over-age players.

The establishment of such events at the pinnacle of the world game encouraged all the regional confederations to create matching tournaments of their own so that their teams could qualify for a place on the big stage. A flood of outstanding players first made headlines in the age-group system. Most notable among these players was Diego Maradona, who led Argentina to victory in Japan in the FIFA World Youth Cup in 1979. Seven years later, in 1986 in Mexico, he was his country's winning captain and inspiration at the FIFA World Cup. Women's championships were organized in response to the rapid acceleration of interest in the game and, in 2000, FIFA stepped into the senior club sphere too, with the launch of what is now the established, annual FIFA Club World Cup.

Brazil, with captain and match-winner Lucio holding the trophy, celebrate after winning the 2009 FIFA Confederations Cup final against the USA in South Africa.

FIFA U-20 WORLD CUP

First staged in 1977 in Tunisia and known as the FIFA Youth World Championship until 2005, the FIFA U-20 World Cup is the world championship of football for players under the age of 20 and has featured some of the game's most notable names. Staged on a bi-annual basis, the tournament's most successful team has been Argentina, who have lifted the trophy on six occasions.

FULL HOUSES

The 2009 tournament saw record crowds – and those crowds saw more goals than in any previous FIFA Under-20 World Cup. Some 1,295,586 fans attended the 52 games, at seven venues across five Egyptian cities, meaning the average attendance was 24,915 per match. The overall tally exceeded the 1,195,299 attending the tournament in Canada two years earlier – but the average crowd of 36,099 for the 32 games in Mexico in 1983 remains a record too. A total of 167 goals were scored during the 2009 competition, two more than in Malaysia 12 years earlier. The Egypt contest had 3.21 goals per game, marginally higher than Malaysia's 3.17. Poor Tahiti helped keep the goal-rate high – they conceded 21 goals in three group games in Egypt, while failing to score themselves.

SUPER SUB

The Soviet Union became the first winners of the FIFA Under-20 World Cup when they beat hosts Mexico 9-8 on penalties after a 2-2 draw in the 1977 final. Their shoot-out hero was substitute goalkeeper Yuri Sivuha, who had replaced Aleksandre Novikov during extra-time. It remains the only time the Soviet Union won the event, though their striker **Oleg Salenko**, a future 1994 FIFA World Cup Golden Boot winner, took the top scorer award in 1989, with five goals. Two years later, fellow Soviet Sergei Sherbakov also finished top scorer, also with five goals, although his full international career was less successful. He played only twice for Ukraine before injuries suffered in a car accident in 1993 left him in a wheelchair.

DOMINANT DOMINIC

Ghana became the first African country to lift the trophy when they upset Brazil in the 2009 final – despite playing 83 of the 120 minutes with just 10 men, following Daniel Addo's red card. The final finished goalless, one of only two games in which **Dominic Adiyiah** failed to score. He ended the tournament as top scorer with eight goals and also won the Golden Ball prize for best player. Immediately afterwards a further reward was a transfer from Norway's Fredrikstad to Italy's AC Milan. The Silver Ball went to Brazil's Alex Teixeira, even though it was his missed penalty, when the final shoot-out went to sudden death, which handed Ghana victory.

LISBON LIONS

In 1991, Portugal became the first hosts to win the tournament with a team that became known as the country's "Golden Generation", featuring Luis Figo, Rui Costa, Joao Pinto, Abel Xavier and Jorge Costa. Portugal's winning squad was coached by **Carlos Queiroz**, who would later manage the full national side twice, with spells in charge at Real Madrid and as assistant at Manchester United in between. Their penalty shoot-out win over Brazil in the final was played at Benfica's iconic Estadio da Luz in the capital Lisbon. In 2001, Argentina became the second team to lift the trophy on home territory.

WAITING GAME

Nigeria were originally scheduled to host the 1995 tournament, but were replaced by Qatar due to concerns about human rights issues – and Nigeria were not even permitted to participate in the competition. The country was finally granted hosting rights for the event four years later. The 2011 edition of the FIFA Under-20 World Cup will be held in Colombia.

SAVIOUR SAVIOLA

Javier Saviola has scored more goals in one FIFA Under-20 World Cup than any other player – he managed 11 in seven games at the 2001 competition, as his side Argentina went on to beat Ghana in the final, with Saviola scoring his team's three unanswered goals. Saviola, born on 11 December 1981 in Buenos Aires, was playing for River Plate at the time but joined Barcelona for £15 million not long afterwards – before later signing for the Spanish side's arch-rivals Real Madrid. When Pele picked his 125 "greatest living footballers" for FIFA in March 2004, 22-year-old Saviola was the youngest player on the list.

CAPTAIN MARVELS

Two men have lifted both the FIFA Under-20 World Cup and the FIFA World Cup as captain: Brazil's Dunga (in 1983 and 1994) and Argentina's Diego Maradona (in 1979 and 1986). Many had expected Maradona to make Argentina's full squad for the 1978 FIFA World Cup but he missed out on selection. He showed his potential by being voted best player at the 1979 youth tournament in Japan.

TOURNAMENT HOSTS AND FINAL RESULTS

1977 (Host: Tunisia) USSR 2 Mexico 2 (ael: USSR win 9-8 on penalties)
1979 (Japan) Argentina 3 USSR 1
1981 (Australia) West Germany 4 Qatar 0
1983 (Mexico) Brazil 1 Argentina 0
1985 (USSR) Brazil 1 Spain 0 (aet)
1987 (Chile) Yugoslavia 1 West Germany 1 (aet: Yugoslavia win 5-4 on penalties)
1989 (Saudi Arabia) Portugal 2 Nigeria 0
1991 (Portugal) Portugal 0 Brazil 0 (aet: Portugal win 4-2 on penalties)
1993 (Australia) Brazil 2 Ghana 1
1995 (Qatar) Argentina 2 Brazil 0
1997 (Malaysia) Argentina 2 Uruguay 1
1999 (Nigeria) Spain 4 Japan 0
2001 (Argentina) Argentina 3 Ghana 0
2003 (United Arab Emirates) Brazil 1 Spain 0
2005 (Holland) Argentina 2 Nigeria 1
2007 (Canada) Argentina 2 Czech Republic 1
2009 (Egypt) Ghana 0 Brazil 0 (aet: Ghana win 4-3 on penalties)

WHAT A MESSI

Lionel Messi was the star of the show for Argentina in 2005, and not just for scoring both his country's goals in the final – both from the penalty spot. He achieved a hat-trick by not only winning the Golden Boot for top scorer and Golden Shoe for best player, but also by captaining his side to the title. This feat was emulated two years later by compatriot Sergio Aguero, who scored once in the final against the Czech Republic, before team-mate Mauro Zarate struck a late winner. Three other men have finished as both top scorer and as the tournament's best player (as voted by journalists) – Brazil's Geovani in 1983, Argentina's Javier Saviola in 2001 and Dominic Adiyiah of Ghana in 2009.

TOURNAMENT TOP SCORERS

Year	Player	Goals
1977	Guina (Brazil)	4
1979	Ramon Diaz (Argentina)	8
1981	Ralf Loose (West Germany), Roland Wohlfarth (West Germany), Taher Amer (Egypt), Mark Koussas (Argentina)	4
1983	Geovani (Brazil)	6
1985	Gerson (Brazil), Balalo (Brazil), Muller (Brazil), Alberto Garcia Aspe (Mexico), Monday Odiaka (Nigeria), Fernando Gomez (Spain), Sebastian Losada (Spain)	3
1987	Marcel Witeczek (West Germany)	7
1989	Oleg Salenko (USSR)	5
1991	Sergei Sherbakov (USSR)	5
1993	Ante Milicic (Australia), Adriano (Brazil), Gian (Brazil), Henry Zambrano (Colombia), Vicente Nieto (Mexico), Chris Faklaris (USA)	3
1995	Joseba Etxeberria (Spain)	7
1997	Adailton Martins Bolzan (Brazil)	10
1999	Mahamadou Dissa (Mali), Pablo (Spain)	5
2001	Javier Saviola (Argentina)	11
2003	Fernando Cavenaghi (Argentina), Dudu (Brazil), Daisuke Sakata (Japan), Eddie Johnson (USA)	4
2005	Lionel Messi (Argentina)	6
2007	Sergio Aguero (Argentina)	7
2009	Dominic Adiyiah (Ghana)	8

SIX APPEAL

Argentina have won the FIFA Under-20 World Cup the most times, winning six times, most recently in 2005 and 2007. Brazil have won four times, Portugal twice, with one success apiece for Germany, Spain, the Soviet Union, Yugoslavia and Ghana. The only final Argentina have contested, but lost, came against arch-rivals Brazil, in 1983, when Geovani struck the only goal.

FIFA U-17 WORLD CUP

First staged in China in 1985, when it was known as the FIFA Under-16 World Championship, the age limit was raised from 16 to 17 in 1991 and the competition became known as the FIFA U-17 World Cup from 2007. Staged on a bi-annual basis, the 2009 edition of the event was staged in Nigeria, the defending champions, who, along with Brazil, are the tournament's most successful countries, with three wins each.

WHOSE SHOE?

Sani Emmanuel can boast of being top scorer while also voted best player, after starring in Nigeria's run to the 2009 final – though that last match was the only one he started. He was awarded the Golden Ball for his performances, but had to settle for the Silver Shoe prize – despite scoring five goals, the same tally as Golden Shoe winner Borja. The Spanish striker took the main award because he managed one more assist. Uruguay's Sebastian Gallegos and Switzerland's Haris Seferovic also finished the tournament with five goals apiece. Yuri Nikiforov scored a joint-best five goals for Russia at the 1987 tournament, including one in the final as his team beat Nigeria on penalties – but FIFA awarded the Golden Shoe to Ivory Coast's Moussa Traore, who also hit five but for a lower-scoring side. The Soviet Union scored 21 overall, to the Ivory Coast's nine.

GOALS FLO

Apart from Cesc Fabregas, the only other man to have won both the Golden Ball and the Golden Shoe is France's **Florent Sinama-Pongolle**, whose nine goals in 2001 set a tournament record for one player. His tally included two hat-tricks in the opening round. Unlike Fabregas, Sinama-Pongolle also ended the final on the winning side. The team goalscoring record is held by Spain, who struck 22 times on their way to third place in 1997.

SEOUL SURVIVOR

The final of the 2007 tournament was the first to be hosted by a former FIFA World Cup venue – the 68,476-capacity Seoul FIFA World Cup Stadium in South Korea's capital, which had been built for the 2002 FIFA World Cup. The game was watched by a crowd of 36,125, a tournament record. The 2007 event was the first to feature 24 teams instead of 16, and was won by Nigeria – after Spain missed all three of their spot-kicks in a penalty shoot-out.

TAKING WING

Nigeria's youth side, the "Golden Eaglets", became the first African nation to win a FIFA tournament when they triumphed at the inaugural Under-16 FIFA World Cup in 1985 (it became an Under-17 event in 1991). Their opening goal in the final against West Germany was scored by striker Jonathan Akpoborie, who would go on to play for German clubs Stuttgart and Wolfsburg.

GOOD AND BAD BOY BOJAN

Barcelona star **Bojan Krkic** quickly went from hero to villain in the final moments of Spain's semi-final victory over Ghana in 2007 – he scored his team's winner with four minutes of extra-time remaining, but was then sent off for a second yellow-card offence just before the final whistle. His expulsion meant he was suspended for the final, which Spain lost on penalties to Nigeria.

GOLDEN HAUL

West Germany's Marcel Witeczek is the only person to finish top scorer at both a FIFA Under-16 World Championship and the Under-20 version of the event. The Polish-born striker hit eight goals at the 1985 Under-16 tournament, followed by seven more at the Under-20 championship two years later. Brazil's Adriano – a different Adriano to the one who later played for the senior side and Serie A club Internazionale – came closest to equalling the feat: he won the Golden Shoe, for top scorer, after scoring four goals at the 1991 FIFA Under-17 World Cup, then the Golden Ball, for best player, at the Under-20 event in 1993.

FAB FABREGAS

Spain's **Cesc Fabregas** joined Florent Sinama-Pongolle as only two players to win both the Golden Shoe, for top scorer, and the Golden Ball, for best player, at a FIFA Under-17 World Cup. He took both prizes after scoring five goals at the 2003 tournament, despite losing the final to Brazil. He and team-mate David Silva would later be part of the senior Spanish team that won the 2008 European Championship and, two years later, the FIFA World Cup in South Africa. Fabregas, born in Arenys de Mar on 4 May 1987, left Barcelona for Arsenal a month after the 2003 tournament, where he later became club captain.

TOURNAMENT TOP SCORERS

Year	Player	Goals
1985	Marcel Witeczek (West Germany)	8
1987	Moussa Traore (Ivory Coast)	5
	Yuri Nikiforov (USSR)	5
1989	Khaled Jasem (Bahrain)	3
	Fode Camara (Guinea)	3
	Gil (Portugal)	3
	Tulipa (Portugal)	3
	Khalid Al Roaihi (Saudi Arabia)	3
1991	Adriano (Brazil)	4
1993	Wilson Oruma (Nigeria)	6
1995	Daniel Allsopp (Australia)	5
	Mohamed Al Kathiri (Oman)	5
1997	David (Spain)	7
1999	Ishmael Addo (Ghana)	7
2001	Florent Sinama-Pongolle (France)	9
2003	Carlos Hidalgo (Colombia)	5
	Manuel Curto (Portugal)	5
	Cesc Fabregas (Spain)	5
2005	Carlos Vela (Mexico)	5
2007	Macauley Chrisantus (Nigeria)	7
2009	Borja (Spain)	5
	Sani Emmanuel (Nigeria)	5
	Sebastian Gallegos (Uruguay)	5
	Haris Seferovic (Switzerland)	5

LITTLE ITALY

The 1991 tournament was originally scheduled to take place in Ecuador, but a cholera outbreak in the country meant it was switched to Italy instead – though played in much smaller venues than those that had been used for the previous year's senior FIFA World Cup in the country. The 1991 tournament was the first to be open to Under-17s – the first three had been known as the FIFA U-16 World Cup.

EVER–PRESENT AMERICA

While Brazil and Nigeria have enjoyed the most success in the FIFA U-17 World Cup, with three triumphs each, the only country to take part in all 12 competitions is the United States – their best finish was fourth in 1999.

SWISS SURPRISE

Switzerland were the unexpected winners in 2009, in their first-ever appearance at the tournament. Their 1-0 win over favourites Nigeria in the final, thanks to a Haris Seferovic goal, prevented the Africans from becoming only the second country to retain the trophy. Swiss goalkeeper Benjamin Siegrist, who conceded only four goals in seven games, was given the Golden Glove prize for best goalkeeper. Nigerian preparations for the finals had been disrupted when 15 of their players were found to be over-age and had to be dropped from the squad.

HOSTS AND FINAL RESULTS

(Host country)

1985 (China) Nigeria 2 West Germany 0

1987 (Canada) USSR 1 Nigeria 1
(aet: USSR win 4-2 on penalties)

1989 (Scotland) Saudi Arabia 2 Scotland 2
(aet: Saudi Arabia win 5-4 on penalties)

1991 (Italy) Ghana 1 Spain 0

1993 (Japan) Nigeria 2 Ghana 1

1995 (Ecuador) Ghana 3 Brazil 2

1997 (Egypt) Brazil 2 Ghana 1

1999 (New Zealand) Brazil 0 Australia 0
(aet: Brazil win 8-7 on penalties)

2001 (Trinidad & Tobago) France 3 Nigeria 0

2003 (Finland) Brazil 1 Spain 0

2005 (Peru) Mexico 3 Brazil 0

2007 (South Korea) Nigeria 0 Spain 0
(aet: Nigeria win 3-0 on penalties)

2009 (Nigeria) Switzerland 1 Nigeria 0

FIFA CONFEDERATIONS CUP

The FIFA Confederations Cup has assumed numerous guises over the years. In 1992 and 1995 it was played in Saudi Arabia and featured a collection of continental champions. From 1997 to 2003 FIFA staged a tournament every two years. The tournament was played in its current format for the first time in Germany in 2005. It is now celebrated throughout the football world as the Championship of Champions.

OVERALL TOP SCORERS

1	Cuauhtemoc Blanco (Mexico)	9
=	Ronaldinho (Brazil)	9
3	Romario (Brazil)	7
=	Adriano (Brazil)	7
5	Marzouq Al-Otaibi	6
6	Alex (Brazil)	5
=	John Aloisi (Australia)	5
=	Luis Fabiano (Brazi)	5
=	Vladimir Smicer (Czech Rep.)	5
=	Robert Pires (France)	5

FAB'S FIVE

Brazil's victory over the United States in the 2009 final made them the first country to complete a hat-trick of FIFA Confederations Cup triumphs, following success in 1997 and 2005. But they did it the hard way, needing to come back from two goals down at half-time before winning 3–2 – thanks to a late goal from captain and centre-back Lucio. Their other two were struck by forward **Luis Fabiano**, who ended as tournament top scorer with five goals overall. His team-mate Kaka was voted best player, with Luis Fabiano second and America's Clint Dempsey third.

TOURNAMENT TOP SCORERS

1992 Gabriel Batistuta (Argentina), Bruce Murray (USA) 2
1995 Luis Garcia (Mexico) 3
1997 Romario (Brazil) 7
1999 Ronaldinho (Brazil), Cuauhtemoc Blanco (Mexico), Marzouq Al-Otaibi (Saudi Arabia) 6
2001 Shaun Murphy (Australia), Eric Carriere (France), Robert Pires (France), Patrick Vieira (France), Sylvain Wiltord (France), Takayuki Suzuki (Japan), Hwang Sun-Hong (South Korea) 2
2003 Thierry Henry (France) 4
2005 Adriano (Brazil) 5
2009 Luis Fabiano (Brazil) 5

FIT FOR A KING

Before being rebranded as the FIFA Confederations Cup, a tournament bringing together the continental champions of the world was known as the King Fahd Cup and was hosted in Saudi Arabia. Copa America holders Argentina reached both finals, beating their hosts in the first in 1992 thanks to goals by Leonardo Rodriguez, Claudio Caniggia and Diego Simeone. Only four teams took part in the 1992 event, with the United States and the Ivory Coast also represented, but world champions Germany and European champions Holland did not participate. In 1995, a six-team version was won by European champions Denmark, when goals from Michael Laudrup and Peter Rasmussen were enough to see off Argentina in the final in Riyadh.

TRIPLE CROWNS

Two countries have held a clean sweep hat-trick of titles at one time. Brazil's FIFA Confederations Cup triumph in December 1997 came six months after they were crowned South American champions, in the Copa America – and while still reigning world champions, after winning the 1994 FIFA World Cup. Patrick Vieira's golden-goal winner for France in the final of the FIFA Confederations Cup 2001 meant they emulated Brazil's feat, having won the FIFA World Cup in 1998 and the European Championship in 2000.

DIFFERENT BALL GAMES

The 2009 hosts South Africa had to amend their plans for staging matches when building work on Port Elizabeth's Nelson Mandela Bay Stadium fell behind schedule – leaving the games shared between Ellis Park Stadium in Johannesburg, Loftus Versfeld Stadium in Pretoria, Free State Stadium in Bloemfontein and Royal Bafokeng Stadium in Rustenburg. The venues also hosted rugby union matches for the British Lions' tour of South Africa in June 2009, though at least nine days separated any rugby and football games in the same stadium.

THREE APIECE

Brazil's Romario holds the record for the most goals scored in a single FIFA Confederations Cup – seven, in five games, as his country took the title for the first time in 1997. His tally included three in the 6-0 final win over Australia – but he had to share the hat-trick glory: the rest of the goals were claimed by his strike-partner Ronaldo.

UNEVEN DISTRIBUTION

Both Saudi Arabia's **Marzouk Al-Otaibi** and Brazil's Ronaldinho were on the scoresheet in their sides' 1999 semi-final, when Brazil won 8-2 – the most goals ever scored in one FIFA Confederations Cup match. Al-Otaibi got two and Ronaldinho hit three, in a match that was even at 2-2 after half an hour.

SCREENS BLANKED

There was controversy over Brazil's dramatic last-gasp win over Egypt in the first round of the 2009 tournament. Their 4-3 win came courtesy of a stoppage-time penalty by Kaka – though English referee Howard Webb had initially signalled for a corner, instead of handball by Egyptian defender Ahmed al-Muhammadi. He then changed his mind, pointing to the spot and sending off al-Muhammadi. The Egyptians later claimed he changed his mind due to information from video replays, and FIFA president Sepp Blatter announced TV monitors would now be banned from the side of the pitch.

CLINT MAKES AMERICA'S DAY

The United States' surprise run to the 2009 final included a shock semi-final win over Spain that ended the European champions' long unbeaten run. Heading into the match, Spain had won a record 15 international matches in a row – and gone 35 successive games unbeaten, a tally shared with Brazil. But their hopes of a record 36th match without defeat were ruined by goals from US striker Jozy Altidore and winger **Clint Dempsey**. The result put the Americans into the final of a FIFA men's senior competition for the first time.

SHARED SADNESS

The 2003 tournament was overshadowed by the tragic death of Cameroon's 28-year-old midfielder **Marc-Vivien Foe**, who collapsed on the Lyon pitch after suffering a heart attack 73 minutes into his country's semi-final win against Colombia. After Thierry Henry scored France's golden-goal winner against Cameroon in the final, he dedicated his goal to Foe, who played much of his club career in the French championship. When the trophy was presented at the Stade de France in Paris, it was jointly lifted by the captains of both teams – Marcel Desailly for France and Rigobert Song for Cameroon.

FIFA CONFEDERATIONS CUP HOSTS AND FINAL RESULTS

1997　(Host country: Saudi Arabia) Brazil 6 Argentina 0
1999　(Mexico) Mexico 4 Brazil 3
2001　(South Korea and Japan) France 1 Japan 0
2003　(France) France 1 Cameroon 0
　　　(aet: France win on golden goal)
2005　(Germany) Brazil 4 Argentina 1
2009　(South Africa) Brazil 3 United States 2

FIFA CLUB WORLD CUP

As is the case with the FIFA Confederations Cup, the FIFA Club World Cup has been played in many different formats since 1960, when Real Madrid defeated Peñarol. In its current guise, the competition pits the champion clubs from all six continents against each other and has been staged on an annual basis, in Japan, since 2005. In 2009 the tournament was staged in Abu Dhabi for the first time.

SAINT PEDRO

Pedro Rodriguez – known simply as "Pedro", or sometimes "Pedrito" – looked like he might be on his way out of Barcelona before Josep Guardiola's appointment as manager in summer 2008, but went on to make history with the club the following year. Pedro – born in Tenerife on 28 July 1987 – managed to score in an unprecedented six different competitions: Spain's domestic La Liga and Copa del Rey, the country's Super Cup, the UEFA Champions League, the UEFA European Super Cup and the FIFA Club World Cup. The last of these feats was achieved in the Club World Cup semi-final against Mexico's Atlante, but his contribution in the final was even more significant – his 89th-minute goal cancelled out Estudiantes' first-half lead, paving the way for Lionel Messi's extra-time winner.

OVERALL NATIONAL RECORD

9	Argentina
7	Italy
6	Brazil, Uruguay
5	Spain
3	Germany, Holland
2	Portugal
1	England, Paraguay, Yugoslavia

SEVEN UP

Despite Al-Ahly's defeat to Adelaide United in the 2009 fifth-place play-off, the game was a landmark for four of the Egyptian club's players: Mohamed Aboutrika, Wael Gomaa, **Shady Mohamed** and Hossam Ashour were all playing in a FIFA Club World Cup match for a seventh time. They passed the six-match record previously held by Brazilian goalkeeper Dida, who played in the tournament for Corinthians (2000) and AC Milan (2007).

SIX APPEAL

Barcelona's triumph in 2009 made them the first club to lift six different major trophies in one calendar year: the FIFA Club World Cup, the UEFA Champions League, the UEFA European Super Cup, and a Spanish hat-trick of La Liga, Copa del Rey and Super Cup. This made their trophy cabinet one cup heavier than Liverpool's in 2001, when Gerard Houllier's men won the FA Cup, League Cup and Charity Shield in England and the UEFA Cup and Super Cup in Europe.

UAE O.K.

The 2009 tournament was the first of the "new" FIFA Club World Cup events to take place outside Japan – in the United Arab Emirates state of Abu Dhabi, where a repeat is scheduled in December 2010. Two stadia shared the workload – the **Al Jazira Mohammed bin Zayed Stadium**, which hosted the opening game between Ah-Ahli and Auckland City among others, and the 60,000-capacity Sheikh Zayed Stadium, the setting for the final. The UAE saw off rival bids from Australia and Japan to secure hosting rights for the December 2010 event. But the competition is due to return to Japan in 2011 and 2012.

SWITCHING SYSTEMS

From 1960 until 1968, the Intercontinental Cup was settled, not on aggregate scores, but by using a system of two points for a win and one for a draw. This meant a third, deciding match was needed in 1961, 1963, 1964 and 1967. No team that had not been worse off on aggregate after the first two legs had gone on to win the third match, though before losing their play-off 1-0 to Argentina's Racing Club in 1967, Celtic would have won the two-legged tie if aggregate scores and away goals counted. The Scottish side won their home leg 1-0, before losing 2-1 away. From 1980 onwards, the annual event was a one-off match staged in Japan.

FIGURE OF EIGHT

Manchester United's 5-3 win over Gamba Osaka in the semi-final of the FIFA Club World Cup in 2008 was the highest-scoring single game in the history of the competition in all its forms – bettering the 5-2 victory over Benfica by a Santos team featuring Pele in 1962. Even more amazingly, all but two of the goals in the Manchester United–Gamba game were scored in the final 16 minutes, plus stoppage-time. United were leading 2-0 with 74 minutes gone, before a burst of goals – including two by substitute Wayne Rooney – at both ends. Manchester United became the first team to score five goals in the FIFA Club World Cup's revised format.

LONG–DISTANCE, LONG–RUNNING RIVALRY

The precursor to the modern FIFA Club World Cup was the Intercontinental Cup, also known informally as the World Club Cup and/ or the Europe–South America Cup, which pitted the champions of Europe and South America against each other. Representatives of UEFA and CONMEBOL contested the event from 1960 to 2004, but now all continental federations send at least one club to an expanded Club World Cup organized and endorsed by the world federation, FIFA. The original final, in 1960, was between Spain's Real Madrid and Uruguay's Penarol. After a goalless draw in the rain in Montevideo, Real triumphed 5-1 at their own stadium in Madrid – including three goals scored in the first eight minutes, two of them by Ferenc Puskas. The two clubs are among five sharing the record for Intercontinental Cup triumphs, with three victories apiece – the others being Argentina's Boca Juniors, Uruguay's Nacional and AC Milan of Italy. Milan are the only one of these clubs to have added a FIFA Club World Cup to their tally, as the championship was first contested in 2000 (in Brazil) before it was swallowed up by the Intercontinental Cup and was instituted on an annual basis.

SUCCESS IN PHASES

Since FIFA introduced its own, expanded Club World Cup in 2000, with representatives from all the world's continental football federations, Brazilian sides have the best overall record – with Corinthians the first winners. Carlo Ancelotti's AC Milan finally broke the Brazilian stranglehold in 2007, when the trophy was lifted by club captain Paolo Maldini, who had appeared for Milan – alongside Alessandro Costacurta – in five Intercontinental Cup showdowns between 1989 and 2003.

COACHING CONSISTENCY

Carlos Bianchi is the only man to have won the world club title three times as coach – lifting the Intercontinental Cup with Velez Sarsfield in 1994 and Boca Juniors in 2000 and 2003. Two Uruguayans have won the world title both as player and coach – Luis Cubilla and Juan Mugica, who were team-mates when Nacional beat Greek side Panathinaikos in the 1971 final. Midfielder Cubilla had already won the trophy with Penarol in 1961, and coached Paraguay's Olimpia Asuncion to glory in 1979. Mugica was the winning manager the following year, again with Nacional.

FIFA CLUB WORLD CUP FINALS (2000–09)

2000	Corinthians (Brazil) 0 Vasco da Gama (Brazil) 0 (aet: Corinthians win 4-3 on penalties)
2005	Sao Paulo (Brazil) 1 Liverpool (England) 0
2006	Internacional (Brazil) 1 Barcelona (Spain) 0
2007	AC Milan (Italy) 4 Boca Juniors (Argentina) 2
2008	Manchester United (England) 1 LDU Quito (Ecuador) 0
2009	Barcelona (Spain) 2 Estudiantes (Argentina) 1 (aet)

INTERCONTINENTAL CUP TRIUMPHS (1960–2004)

3 wins: Real Madrid, Spain (1960, 1998, 2002); Penarol, Uruguay (1961, 1966, 1982); AC Milan, Italy (1969, 1989, 1990); Nacional, Uruguay (1971, 1988, 1988); Boca Juniors, Argentina (1977, 2000, 2003).

2 wins: Santos, Brazil (1962, 1963); Internazionale, Italy (1964, 1965); Ajax, Holland (1972, 1995); Independiente, Argentina (1973, 1984); Bayern Munich, West Germany/Germany (1976, 2001); Juventus, Italy (1985, 1996); Porto, Portugal (1987, 2004); Sao Paulo, Brazil (1992, 1993).

1 win: Racing Club, Argentina (1967); Estudiantes, Argentina (1968); Feyenoord, Holland (1970); Atletico Madrid, Spain (1974); Olimpia Asuncion, Paraguay (1979); Flamengo, Brazil (1981); Gremio, Brazil (1983); River Plate, Argentina (1986); Red Star Belgrade, Yugoslavia (1991); Velez Sarsfield, Argentina (1994); Borussia Dortmund, Germany (1997); **Manchester United**, England (1999).

MEN'S OLYMPIC FOOTBALL TOURNAMENT

First played at the 1900 Olympic Games in Paris, although not recognized by FIFA as an official tournament until the 1908 Games in London, the men's Olympic football tournament was played strictly in accordance with the Games' strong amateur tradition until 1984, when professionals were allowed to play for the first time. Since then, the competition has provided countries with an opportunity to hand their rising young stars an invaluable taste of tournament football under the glare of the world media spotlight.

HOW REFRESHING

Argentina's 1-0 victory over Nigeria in the 2008 final at Beijing's Bird's Nest Stadium had to be interrupted twice, so both sets of players – including Lionel Messi, Juan Roman Riquelme, Javier Mascherano and Sergio Aguero – could be offered water to help them cope with the oppressive 42°C (107°F) midday heat. Messi set up Angel Di Maria for the only goal of the game in the 58th minute.

MEN'S OLYMPIC FOOTBALL FINALS

1896 Not played
1900 (Paris, France)
Gold: Upton Park FC (GB) Silver: USFSA XI (France) Bronze: Universite Libre de Bruxelles (Belgium) (only two exhibition matches played)
1904 (St Louis, US)
Gold: Galt FC (Canada) Silver: Christian Brothers College (US) Bronze: St Rose Parish (US) (only five exhibition matches played)
1908 (London, England)
Great Britain 2 Denmark 0 (Bronze: Holland)
1912 (Stockholm, Sweden)
Great Britain 4 Denmark 2 (Bronze: Holland)
1916 Not played
1920 (Antwerp, Belgium)
Belgium 2 Czechoslovakia 0 (Silver: Spain, Bronze: Holland)
1924 (Paris, France)
Uruguay 3 Switzerland 0 (Bronze: Sweden)
1928 (Amsterdam, Holland)
Uruguay 1 Argentina 1; Uruguay 2 Argentina 1 (Bronze: Italy)
1932 Not played
1936 (Berlin, Germany) Italy 2 Austria 1 (aet) (Bronze: Norway)
1940 Not played
1944 Not played
1948 (London, England) Sweden 3 Yugoslavia 1 (Bronze: Denmark)
1952 (Helsinki, Finland) Hungary 2 Yugoslavia 0 (Bronze: Sweden)
1956 (Melbourne, Australia) USSR 1 Yugoslavia 0 (Bronze: Bulgaria)
1960 (Rome, Italy) Yugoslavia 3 Denmark 1 (Bronze: Hungary)
1964 (Tokyo, Japan) Hungary 2 Czechoslovakia 1 (Bronze: Germany)
1968 (Mexico City, Mexico) Hungary 4 Bulgaria 1 (Bronze: Japan)
1972 (Munich, West Germany) Poland 2 Hungary 1 (Bronze: USSR/East Germany)
1976 (Montreal, Canada) East Germany 3 Poland 1 (Bronze: USSR)
1980 (Moscow, USSR) Czechoslovakia 1 East Germany 0 (Bronze: USSR)
1984 (Los Angeles, USA) France 2 Brazil 0 (Bronze: Yugoslavia)
1988 (Seoul, South Korea) USSR 2 Brazil 1 (Bronze: West Germany)
1992 (Barcelona, Spain) Spain 3 Poland 2 (Bronze: Ghana)
1996 (Atlanta, USA) Nigeria 3 Argentina 2 (Bronze: Brazil)
2000 (Sydney, Australia) Cameroon 2 Spain 2 (**Cameroon win** 5-3 on penalties) (Bronze: Chile)
2004 (Athens, Greece) Argentina 1 Paraguay 0 (Bronze: Italy)
2008 (Beijing, China) **Argentina 1 Nigeria 0** (Bronze: Brazil)

SHARE AND SHARE ALIKE

The bronze medal was shared at the 1972 Olympic Games in Munich, when the play-off between defeated semi-finalists East Germany and the Soviet Union ended 2-2 after extra-time. East Germany had been 2-0 down after half an hour.

FIFA WOMEN'S WORLD CUP™

The first FIFA Women's World Cup finals were held in China in 1991. Twelve teams, divided into three groups of four, took part, with the top two in each group, plus the two "best losers" going through to the knockout quarter-finals. The tournament was expanded in 1999 to include 16 teams, divided into four groups of four, with the top two in each group progressing to the quarter-finals. That is the current format, although an expansion of the tournament to 24 teams is still under consideration.

FINALS SHOOT–OUT DRAMA

The 1999 clash between the USA and China was the only final in FIFA Women's World Cup history settled by a shoot-out. The losing Chinese had previously been involved in the first shoot-out – in the quarter-finals in 1995, when they beat Sweden 4-3 on penalties after a 0-0 draw. The 1999 third-place game was also settled by a shoot-out, with Brazil pipping Norway 5-4 after a 0-0 draw. These are the only three shoot-outs since the tournament began in 1991.

HAVELANGE'S DREAM COMES TRUE

The FIFA Women's World Cup was the brainchild of former FIFA president **Joao Havelange**. The tournament began as an experimental competition in 1991 and has expanded in size and importance ever since. The success of the 1999 finals in the United States was a turning point for the tournament, which now attracts big crowds and worldwide TV coverage. The USA and Norway – countries in which football (soccer) is one of the most popular girls' sports – dominated the early competitions. The Americans won the inaugural competition and the 1999 tournament. Norway lifted the trophy in 1995. Germany became the dominant force in the new century, winning the trophy in 2003 and retaining it in 2007. The recent emergence of challengers such as Brazil, China and Sweden underlined the worldwide spread and appeal of the women's game.

US LEAD GAMES TALLY

The USA have played the most games in the finals – 30. They have also recorded the most wins – 24. They have drawn three games and lost three. Germany are the next most successful team. They have played 28, won 20, drawn three and lost five. Norway have also played 28 matches, won 19, drawn two and lost seven.

FIFA WOMEN'S WORLD CUP™ FINALS

Year	Venue	Winners	Runners-up	Score
1991	Ghuangzhou	USA	Norway	2-1
1995	Stockholm	Norway	Germany	2-0
1999	Los Angeles	USA	China	0-0
	USA won 5-4 in penalty shoot-out			
2003	Los Angeles	Germany	Sweden	2-1 (aet)
2007	Shanghai	Germany	Brazil	2-0

THIRD–PLACE PLAY–OFF MATCHES

Year	Venue	Winners	Losers	Score
1991	Guangzhou	Sweden	Germany	4-0
1995	Gavle	USA	China	2-0
1999	Los Angeles	Brazil	Norway	0-0
	Brazil won 5-4 in penalty shoot-out			
2003	Los Angeles	USA	Canada	3-1
2007	Shanghai	USA	Norway	4-1

US CELEBRATE FIRST ACHIEVEMENT

The USA's victory in the inaugural FIFA Women's World Cup in 1991 made them the first USA team to win a world football title. The USA men's best performance came when they reached the semi-finals in 1930, losing 6-1 to Argentina.

FOUR GAIN DOUBLE MEDALS

Four of the USA's 1991 winners were in the team that beat China on penalties in the 1999 final: **Mia Hamm** (right), Michelle Akers, Kristine Lilly and Julie Foudy.

WINNERS KEEP SQUAD TOGETHER

Six Germany players appeared in their 2003 and 2007 final wins: **Kerstin Stegemann**, Birgit Prinz, Renate Lingor, Ariane Hingst and Kerstin Garefrekes started both games, while Martina Muller came on as a substitute both times.

AUSTRALIA, GHANA LEAD ON REDS

Only two teams have had more than one player sent off in the finals: Australia's Sonia Gegenhuber was red-carded in their 5-0 defeat by Denmark in 1995; and Alicia Ferguson was sent off in 1999, in the second minute of Australia's 3-1 defeat by China. Ghana are the other side to have two players dismissed. Both came at the 1999 finals: Barikisu Tettey-Quao was red-carded in the 1-1 draw against Australia; and Regina Ansah was sent off in the 7-0 defeat by China.

GERMANS SET DEFENSIVE RECORD

In 2007, Germany became the first team to make a successful defence of the FIFA Women's World Cup. They also set another record. They went through the tournament – six games and 540 minutes – without conceding a single goal. As a result, their goalkeeper Nadine Angerer overhauled Italy keeper Walter Zenga's record of 517 minutes unbeaten in the 1990 men's finals. The last player to score against the Germans was Sweden's **Hanna Ljungberg**, who scored in the 41st minute of the 2003 final.

LA FINALE BEATS THEM ALL

The 1999 finals in the USA were the best attended of the five tournaments to date. A total of 3,687,069 spectators watched the matches, at an average of 24,913 per game. The final, between hosts USA and China – at the Rose Bowl, Los Angeles on 10 July – drew 90,185 spectators, a world record for a women's match. The programme that day also included the third-place play-off between Brazil and Norway.

TOP TEAMS

Country	Winners	Runners-up	Third
Germany	2	1	-
US	2	-	3
Norway	1	1	-
Brazil	-	1	1
Sweden	-	1	1
China	-	1	-

TOP TEAM SCORERS

1991:	USA	25
1995:	Norway	23
1999:	China	19
2003:	Germany	25
2007:	Germany	21

TOP ALL-TIME TEAM SCORERS

1	USA	85
2	Germany	84
3	Norway	75
4	China	48
5	Brazil	46

THE FIRST GAME

The first-ever game in the FIFA Women's World Cup finals was hosts China's 4-0 win over Norway at Guangzhou on 16 November 1991. A 65,000 crowd watched the game.

THE REGULAR EIGHT

Eight teams have played in all five finals tournaments – the USA, Germany, Norway, Brazil, China, Japan, Nigeria and Sweden.

NORWAY POST LONGEST WIN RUN

Norway, winners in 1995, hold the record for the most consecutive matchtime wins in the finals – ten. Their run started with an 8-0 win over Nigeria on 6 June 1995 and continued until 30 June 1999 when they beat Sweden 3-1 in the quarter-finals. It ended when they lost 5-0 to China in the semi-finals on 4 July.

CHAMPIONS RUN UP 11

The biggest victory margin in the finals was **Germany**'s 11-0 win over Argentina in Shanghai on 10 September 2007. Argentina keeper Vanina Correa punched a Melanie Behringer corner into her own net after 12 minutes. Birgit Prinz and Sandra Smisek scored hat-tricks, with Germany's other goals coming from Renate Lingor (2), Behringer and Kerstin Garefrekes.

UNBEATEN CHINA SENT HOME

In 1999, China became the only team to go through the finals without losing a match, yet go home empty-handed. The Chinese won their group games, 2-1 against Sweden, 7-0 against Ghana and 3-1 against Australia. They beat Russia 2-0 in the quarter-finals and Norway 5-0 in the semi-finals, but they lost on penalties to the USA in the final after a 0-0 draw.

FIFTEEN ON TARGET FOR NORWAY

Norway hold the record for scoring in the most consecutive games – 15. They began their sequence with a 4-0 win over New Zealand on 19 November 1991 and ended it with a 3-1 win over Sweden in the quarter-finals on 30 June 1999.

THE LOWEST CROWD...

The lowest attendance for any match at the finals came on 8 June 1995, when only 250 spectators watched the 3-3 draw between Canada and Nigeria at Helsingborg.

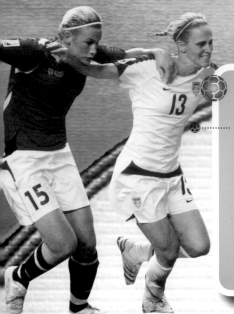

LILLY KEEPS SETTING RECORDS

Kristine Lilly is the only player to have appeared in five finals tournaments. She has played a record 340 games for the USA and scored 129 goals. She is also the oldest scorer in finals history – she was 36 years, 62 days when she netted the third in the USA's 3-0 quarter-final win over England at Tianjin on 22 September 2007.

QUICKEST RED AND YELLOW

The record for the fastest red card is held by Australia's Alicia Ferguson, who was sent off in the second minute of their 3-1 defeat by China in New York on 26 June 1999. North Korea's Ri Hyang Ok received the quickest yellow card, in the first minute of their 2-1 defeat by Nigeria in Los Angeles on 20 June 1999.

THE FASTEST GOAL

Lena Videkull of Sweden netted the fastest goal in finals history when she scored after 30 seconds in their 8-0 win over Japan at Foshan on 19 November 1991. Canada's **Melissa Tancredi** struck the second-fastest goal – after 37 seconds – in their 2-2 draw with Australia in Chengdu on 20 September 2007.

NORDBY THE LONG–DISTANCE KEEPER

Norway goalkeeper Bente Nordby is the only other player to have gone to five FIFA Women's World Cup tournaments. She was a squad member in 1991, but did not play any games. Four years later, she conceded only one goal in six matches as Norway won the trophy. She retired from the national team in January 2008, after making 172 appearances.

DANILOVA THE YOUNGEST SCORER

The youngest scorer at the finals was Russia's Elena Danilova. She was 16 years 96 days when she scored her country's only goal in the 2003 quarter-final against Germany at Portland on 2 October. The Germans scored seven in reply.

MORACE HITS FIRST HAT–TRICK

Carolina Morace of Italy scored the first hat-trick in finals history when she netted the last three goals in Italy's 5-0 win over Taiwan at Jiangmen on 17 November 1991.

HOT SHOT AKERS SETS THE STANDARD

US forward Michelle Akers (born in Santa Clara on 1 February 1966) hold the record for the most goals scored in a single finals tournament – ten in 1991. She also set a record for the most goals scored in one match, with five in the USA's 7-0 quarter-final win over Taiwan at Foshan on 24 November 1991. Akers grabbed both goals in the USA's 2-1 victory in the final, including their 78th-minute winner. Judges voted her as FIFA's Women's Player of the 20th Century.

THE FASTEST SUBSTITUTIONS

The fastest substitutions in finals history were both timed at six minutes. Taiwan's defender Liu Hsiu Mei was subbed by reserve goalkeeper Li Chyn Hong in their 2-0 win over Nigeria in Jiangmen on 21 November 1991. Li replaced No. 1 keeper Lin Hui Fang, who had been sent off. Therese Lundin subbed for the injured Hanna Ljungberg, also after six minutes, in Sweden's 2-0 win over Ghana at Chicago on 26 June 1999.

NEW STARS DOMINATE THE FINALS

The FIFA Women's World Cup has been dominated by a series of great players. American attackers Michelle Akers and Carin Jennings starred in the opening tournament in 1991. Playmaker **Hege Riise** and top scorer Ann-Kristin led Norway to victory four years later. Another American great, Mia Hamm, was at the top of her form when the USA triumphed for a second time in 1999. That tournament marked the emergence of the best-ever Chinese player, Sun Wen, who finished joint top scorer and won the Player of the Tournament award. Birgit Prinz of Germany was Player of the Tournament and top scorer when Germany won for the first time in 2003. The Brazilian forward, Marta, matched that feat in 2007, though, unlike Prinz, she found herself on the losing side in the final. Hamm, Prinz and Marta are the only winners of FIFA Women's Player of the Year award, introduced in 2001. Hamm took the prize in 2001 and 2002. Prinz won it in 2003, 2004 and 2005. Marta came top of the voting list in 2006, 2007, 2008 and 2009.

MOST FINALS APPEARANCES (BY TOURNAMENTS)

5   Kristine Lilly (US – 1991, 1995, 1999, 2003, 2007)
4   Bente Nordby (Norway – 1995, 1999, 2003, 2007)
     Joy Fawcett (US – 1991, 1995, 1999, 2003)
     Julie Foudy (US – 1991, 1995, 1999, 2003)
     Mia Hamm (US – 1991, 1995, 1999, 2003)
     Hege Riise (Norway – 1991, 1995, 1999, 2003)
     Sun Wen (China – 1991, 1995, 1999, 2003)
     Bettina Wiegmann (Germany – 1991, 1995, 1999, 2003)
     Formiga (Brazil – 1995, 1999, 2003, 2007)
     Katia (Brazil – 1995, 1999, 2003, 2007)
     Tania (Brazil – 1995, 1999, 2003, 2007)
     Sandra Minnert (Germany – 1995, 1999, 2003, 2007)
     Birgit Prinz (Germany – 1995, 1999, 2003, 2007)
     Sandra Smisek (Germany – 1995, 1999, 2003, 2007)
     Maureen Mmadu (Nigeria – 1995, 1999, 2003, 2007)
     Andrea Neil (Canada – 1995, 1999, 2003, 2007)
     Cheryl Salisbury (Australia – 1995, 1999, 2003, 2007)
     Homare Sawa (Japan – 1995, 1999, 2003, 2007)
     Briana Scurry (US – 1995, 1999, 2003, 2007)

SUN RATTLES THE MEN

In 1999, Shanghai-born **Sun Wen** became the first woman player ever to be nominated for the Asian Footballer of the Year award, following her performances in China's run to the 1999 FIFA Women's World Cup final. Three years later, she won the Internet poll for FIFA's Women's Player of the 20th Century.

PRINZ SEIZES FINALS CHANCE

In 2007, Birgit Prinz became the first player to appear in three FIFA Women's World Cup finals. She was also the youngest player to appear in a FIFA Women's World Cup final. The Germany forward was 17 years 336 days when she started in the 2-0 defeat by Norway in 1995. Team-mate Sandra Smisek was just 14 days older. The oldest finalist was Sweden's Kristin Bengtsson, who was 33 years 273 days when her side lost to Germany in the 2003 final.

MARTA'S FINAL AGONY

Brazil's **Marta** may have been the star of the 2007 tournament, but she was heartbroken in the final after Germany goalkeeper Nadine Angerer saved her penalty that would have put Brazil level. Germany won the match 2-0.

FIFA WOMEN'S WORLD CUP™ PLAYER OF THE TOURNAMENT

Year	Venue	Winner
1991	China	Carin Jennings (USA)
1995	Sweden	Hege Riise (Norway)
1999	USA	Sun Wen (China)
2003	USA	Birgit Prinz (Germany)
2007	China	Marta (Brazil)

FIFA WOMEN'S WORLD CUP™ FINALS TOP SCORER

1991	Michelle Akers (USA)	10
1995	Ann-Kristin Aarones (Norway)	6
1999	Sissi (Brazil)	7
2003	Birgit Prinz (Germany)	7
2007	Marta (Brazil)	7

ALL-TIME TOP SCORERS

1	Birgit Prinz (Germany)	14
2	Michelle Akers (USA)	12
3	Sun Wen (China)	11
=	Bettina Wiegmann (Germany)	
5	Ann-Kristin Aarones (Norway)	10
=	Marta (Brazil)	
=	Heidi Mohr (Germany)	
8	Linda Medalen (Norway)	9
=	Hege Riise (Norway)	
=	Abby Wambach (USA)	

FIFA WOMEN'S WORLD CUP™ WINNING CAPTAINS

1991	April Heinrichs (USA)
1995	Heidi Store (Norway)
1999	Carla Overbeck (USA)
2003	Bettina Wiegmann (Germany)
2007	Birgit Prinz (Germany)

MOST FINALS APPEARANCES (BY GAMES)

30	Kristine Lilly (USA)
24	Julie Foudy (USA)
23	Mia Hamm (USA)
22	Bente Nordby (Norway)
	Birgit Prinz (Germany)
	Hege Riise (Norway)
	Bettina Wiegmann (Germany)

THE FIRST SENDING OFF

Taiwan goalkeeper Lin Hui Fang was the first player to be sent off in finals history. She was red-carded after six minutes of Taiwan's 2-0 win over Nigeria in Jiangmen on 21 November 1991.

OTHER WOMEN'S TOURNAMENTS

"GOLDEN GOAL" NORWAY

Norway are the only team to have won Olympic gold thanks to a "golden goal". In the 2000 final, Dagny Melgren scored their winner 12 minutes into extra-time, to beat the USA 3-2. That came as sweet revenge for the Norwegians, who had lost their 1996 semi-final to the Americans after **Shannon MacMillan**'s golden goal.

WOMEN'S OLYMPIC FINALS

Year	Venue	Winners	Runners-up	Score
1996	Atlanta	USA	China	2-1
2000	Sydney	Norway	USA	3-2
	Norway won with a golden goal			
2004	Athens	USA	Brazil	2-1 (aet)
2008	Beijing	USA	Brazil	1-0 (aet)

THIRD-PLACE PLAY-OFFS

Year	Venue	Winners	Losers	Score
1996	Atlanta	Norway	Brazil	2-0
2000	Sydney	Germany	Brazil	2-0
2004	Athens	Germany	Sweden	1-0
2008	Beijing	Germany	Japan	2-0

MEDALLISTS

Country	Gold	Silver	Bronze
US	3	1	-
Norway	1	-	1
Brazil	-	2	-
China	-	1	-
Germany	-	-	3

WOMEN'S OLYMPIC TEAM TOP SCORERS

1996: Norway   12
2000: USA   9
2004: Brazil   15
2008: USA   12

WOMEN'S OLYMPIC INDIVIDUAL TOP SCORERS

1996: Ann-Kristin Aarones (Norway)
Linda Medalen (Norway)
Pretinha (Brazil)   4
2000: Sun Wen (China)   4
2004: Cristiane (Brazil)
Birgit Prinz (Germany)   5
2008: Cristiane (Brazil)   5

CRISTIANE'S TREBLE DOUBLE

Brazil striker **Cristiane** is the only player to score two hat-tricks in FIFA Olympic history. She netted three in a 7-0 win over hosts Greece in 2004 and added another treble in a 3-1 win over Nigeria in Beijing four years later. Birgit Prinz is the only other hat-trick scorer, with four goals against China in 2004.

US DOMINATE OLYMPIC GOLDS

The USA have dominated the Olympic football tournament since it was introduced at the 1996 Games in Atlanta. They have won three gold medals and finished runners-up in the other final. Norway and China were the Americans' early challengers, with Brazil and FIFA Women's World Cup holders Germany proving their toughest rivals in the past two Olympics (2004 and 2008). The tournament has rapidly grown in popularity, attracting record crowds at the 2008 Olympic Games in Beijing. FIFA have added two worldwide competitions for younger teams, too. The FIFA U-20 Women's World Cup was staged for the first time in 2000 and the first edition of the Under-17 event followed in 2008. Once more, the USA have been prominent, though they have faced a strong challenge from North Korea in recent years.

GERMANS CHALK UP BIGGEST WIN

Germany hold the record for the biggest win in the Olympic finals. They beat China 8-0 at Patras on 11 August 2004, with Birgit Prinz scoring four times. The Germans' other goals came from Pia Wunderlich, Renate Lingor, Conny Pohlers and Martina Muller.

PRINZ ALWAYS ON TARGET

Germany forward **Birgit Prinz** is the only player to have scored in all four Olympic finals tournaments. Prinz is the joint overall leading scorer, along with Brazil's Cristiane. Both have ten goals. Next in the scoring list are two Brazilians, Pretinha (8) and Marta (6).

OLDEST, YOUNGEST PLAYERS

The oldest player in Olympic women's finals history was the Brazil goalkeeper Meg, when she appeared in the third-place play-off against Norway on 1 August 1996, aged 40 years 212 days. The youngest was also a Brazilian, Daniela, who made her finals debut against Sweden on 13 September 2000, aged 16 years 244 days.

LOOKING FOR A NEW ENGLAND

England's female footballers were unluckily denied a place in the 2008 Olympic tournament in China. Their performance at the 2007 Women's World Cup would have been enough for the third and final qualifying spot allocated to Europe. But they missed out because England, Scotland, Wales and Northern Ireland do not compete individually at the Olympics, but collectively as Great Britain. Their place instead went to Sweden, who beat Denmark in a qualifying play-off. Similar rules meant England had also been barred from competing in 1996 in Atlanta, with Brazil going forward instead. Qualification in 1996 was based on the eight best performers at the previous year's Women's World Cup, which meant there were no representatives from Africa or Oceania. But FIFA amended their rules so a British team can play at the Olympics in London 2012.

FIFA U–20 WOMEN'S WORLD CUP

FINALS

Year	Venue	Winner	Runners-up	Score
2002	Edmonton	USA	Canada	1-0 (aet)
2004	Bangkok	Germany	Chile	2-0
2006	Moscow	North Korea	China	5-0
2008	Santiago	USA	North Korea	2-1

TOP SCORERS

2002	Christine Sinclair (Canada)	10
2004	Brittany Timko (Canada)	7
2006	Ma Xiaoxu (China),	
	Kim Song Hui (North Korea)	5
2008	Sydney LeRoux (USA)	5

FIFA U–17 WOMEN'S WORLD CUP

FINAL

Year	Venue	Winner	Runners-up	Score
2008	Auckland	North Korea	USA	2-1 (aet)

TOP SCORERS

6	Dzsenifer Marozsan (Germany)
5	Vicki Di Martino (USA)
4	Jon Myong Hwa (North Korea)
	Courtney Verloop (USA)
	Chinatsu Kira (Japan)
	Natsuki Kishikawa (Japan)

GERMANY IN COMMAND

Germany won the UEFA Women's Championship for the seventh time in 10 tournaments when they thrashed England 6-2 in the 2009 final. **Inka Grings** took her top-scoring status to six goals with two in the final in Helsinki's Olympic Stadium. Karen Carney and Kelly Smith scored for England, lining up in their first final in 25 years. Birgit Prinz, twice, Melanie Behringer and Kim Kulig also scored for Germany. The beaten semi-finalists were Holland and Norway.

ADDING A YEAR

The Women's Under-19 World Championship was first held in 2002, then again in 2004, before a rule change led to it being renamed the Women's Under-20 World Championship in 2006. Germany were lined up to stage the 2010 tournament, in July and August 2010, with four stadiums – at Augsburg, Bielefeld, Bochum and Dresden – with capacities above 30,000 and high hopes of becoming the first country to lift the trophy as hosts.

US SUNK BY KOREAN SUB

Substitute Jang Hyon Sun hit North Korea's 113th-minute winner to beat the USA in the first Under-17 final, in Auckland, on 16 November 2008. The USA went ahead in the second minute when Korean keeper Hong Myong Hui deflected a long throw into her own net. Kim Un Hyang headed a 76th-minute equalizer to force extra-time. Germany beat England 3-0 in the third-place play-off, with goals by Inka Wesely, Turid Knaak and Lynn Mester.

KIM GRABS ONLY HAT–TRICK

North Korea's **Kim Song Hui** netted the only hat-trick in the history of the FIFA U-20 Women's World Cup finals, in their 5-0 win over China on 3 September 2006. Jo Yun Mi and Kil Son Hui scored the other goals.

SINCLAIR HITS FIVE

Christine Sinclair of Canada holds the record for the most goals scored in the Under-20 finals (ten). She also holds the record for the most goals in one game. She netted five in Canada's 6-2 quarter-final win over England at Edmonton on 25 August 2002.

One of football's biggest social events is the FIFA World Player Gala at which FIFA rewards a range of achievements in the international game over the previous 12 months. Pride of place, of course, goes to the World Player of the Year awards, presented in 2009 by president Sepp Blatter to the top women's player, Marta of Brazil, and to the top men's player, Argentina's Lionel Messi.

FIFA PLAYER OF THE YEAR 2009

LIONEL MESSI

Cristiano Ronaldo and **Lionel Messi** having emerged as the two finest footballers in the world game, it seems only fair play that both have been acclaimed officially as FIFA Player of the Year – Ronaldo in 2008, Messi 12 months later. Messi became the 11th winner from Spain's La Liga, and Barcelona's seventh, while Ronaldo – then at Manchester United, before his move to Real Madrid – had been the first player from the English Premier League to lift the award since its inception in 1991 (when Germany's Lothar Matthaus became the first winner). FIFA polls its votes from the managers and captains of the world's national teams. They are asked to vote for their top three players, but cannot vote for anyone from the national association under whose jurisdiction they operate. The votes were cast in Messi's favour to an unprecedented degree in 2009, following his leading role in Barcelona's remarkable 2008–09 treble. He topped the ballot on 1,073 points, with Ronaldo a distant second on 352. Ronaldo's consolation was in receiving the first FIFA Puskas Award for "most beautiful goal" for his long-range UEFA Champions League quarter-final strike against Portugal's FC Porto. But Messi's prize was icing on the cake, after helping Barcelona sweep up the Spanish league and cup titles, as well as the UEFA Champions League. Messi scored the second of Barcelona's two goals in the European final against Ronaldo's Manchester United, somehow eluding centre-back Rio Ferdinand and looping a header over lofty goalkeeper Edwin Van der Sar. Bearing in mind his dazzling dribbling and ferocious shooting, few would have expected Messi to mark the occasion with a headed goal – after all, one of the reasons he left Argentina for Barcelona at the age of 12 was the Spanish club's promise to fund his growth-hormone treatment. Despite making a slow start with Argentina's senior national side, Messi quickly proved a prolific goal-scorer and goal-creator at Barcelona, whom he had helped to three league titles, four domestic cup trophies, two UEFA Champions League triumphs plus UEFA European Super Cup and FIFA Club World Cup success for good measure. He also won Olympic gold with Argentina in 2008, having been winning captain, top scorer and player of the tournament at the FIFA Under-20 Cup three years earlier. Not bad for someone still aged only 22.

PREVIOUS WINNERS

1991 Lothar Matthaus (Germany)
1992 Marco van Basten (Netherlands)
1993 Roberto Baggio (Italy)
1994 Romario (Brazil)
1995 George Weah (Liberia)
1996 Ronaldo (Brazil)
1997 Ronaldo (Brazil)
1998 Zinedine Zidane (France)
1999 Rivaldo (Brazil)
2000 Zinedine Zidane (France)
2001 Luis Figo (Portugal)
2002 Ronaldo (Brazil)
2003 Zinedine Zidane (France)
2004 Ronaldinho (Brazil)
2005 Ronaldinho (Brazil)
2006 Fabio Cannavaro (Italy)
2007 Kaka (Brazil)
2008 Cristiano Ronaldo (Portugal)
2009 Lionel Messi (Argentina)

MARTA

Marta of Brazil, FIFA Women's Player of the Year four times in a row and previously placed third and second, is one of the greatest women players of all time. Born on 19 February 1986, Marta Vieira da Silva has won a string of team awards and personal prizes. She won the Golden Ball as best player and the Golden Boot as seven-goal top scorer at the 2007 Women's FIFA World Cup and was a silver medal winner with Brazil at both the 2004 and 2008 Olympic Games, in Athens and Beijing respectively. Marta has twice been a winner at the Pan-American Games and was voted the best player at the 2004 FIFA Under-19 Women's World Championships in which she scored six goals. At the age of 14 Marta's teenaged footballing talents took her 1,200 miles south from Dois Riachos, Alagoas, where she was born and brought up, to Rio de Janeiro, where she startled coaches and other players with her attacking skill for Vasco da Gama and Sao Martins. In 2004, she transferred to Swedish club Umea, with whom she won four league titles and one domestic cup before moving on to Los Angeles Sol in the new Women's Professional Soccer championship in the United States in early 2009. Later the same year, she went on loan to Brazil's Santos and spearheaded them to glory in both the Copa Libertadores and the Copa do Brasil.

PREVIOUS WINNERS

2001 Mia Hamm (United States)
2002 Mia Hamm (United States)
2003 Birgit Prinz (Germany)
2004 Birgit Prinz (Germany)
2005 Birgit Prinz (Germany)
2006 Marta (Brazil)
2007 Marta (Brazil)
2008 Marta (Brazil)
2009 Marta (Brazil)

OTHER FIFA AWARDS

In conjunction with the FIFA World Player of the Year awards (for both men and women), and tournament-specific prizes for best player, top scorer and top goalkeeper, in recent years the game's governing body has handed out other prizes at its end-of-year gala: the presidential award, the fair play award, a development prize, and recognition to the best rankings mover of the year and the team of the year.

1991
Fair Play award: Real Federacion Espanola de Futbol (Spanish FA), Jorginho (Brazil)

1992
Fair Play award: Union Royale Belge des Societes de Football Association

1993
Fair Play award: Nandor Hidgekuti (Hungary)*, Football Association of Zambia
Top Team of the Year: Germany
Best Mover of the Year: Colombia
*award presented posthumously

1994
Top Team of the Year: Brazil
Best Mover of the Year: Croatia

1995
Fair Play award: Jacques Glassmann (France)
Top Team of the Year: Brazil
Best Mover of the Year: Jamaica

1996
Fair Play award: George Weah (Liberia)
Top Team of the Year: Brazil
Best Mover of the Year: South Africa

1997
Fair Play award: Irish spectators at the FIFA World Cup preliminary match versus Belgium, Jozef Zovinec (Slovak amateur player), Julie Foudy (United States)
Top Team of the Year: Brazil
Best Mover of the Year: Yugoslavia

1998
Fair Play award: National associations of Iran, the United States and Northern Ireland
Top Team of the Year: Brazil
Best Mover of the Year: Croatia

1999
Fair Play award: New Zealand football community
Top Team of the Year: Brazil
Best Mover of the Year: Slovenia

2000
Fair Play award: Lucas Radebe (South Africa)
Top Team of the Year: Holland
Best Mover of the Year: Nigeria

2001
Presidential award Marvin Lee (Trinidad)*
Fair Play award: Paolo Di Canio (Italy)
Top Team of the Year: Honduras
Best Mover of the Year: Costa Rica
*award presented posthumously

2002
Presidential award: Parminder Nagra (England)
Fair Play award: Football communities of Japan and Korea Republic
Top Team of the Year: Brazil
Best Mover of the Year: Senegal

2003
Presidential award: Iraqi football community
Fair Play award: Fans of Celtic FC (Scotland)
Top Team of the Year: Brazil
Best Mover of the Year: Bahrain

2004
Presidential award: Haiti
Fair Play award: Confederacao Brasileira de Futebol
Top Team of the Year: Brazil
Best Mover of the Year: China PR
Interactive World Player: Thiago Carrico de Azevedo (Brazil)

2005
Presidential award: Anders Frisk (Sweden)
Fair Play award: Football community of Iquitos (Peru)
Top Team of the Year: Brazil
Best Mover of the Year: Ghana
Interactive World Player: Chris Bullard (England)

2006
Presidential award: Giacinto Facchetti (Italy)*
Fair Play award: Fans of the 2006 FIFA World Cup
Top Team of the Year: Brazil
Best Mover of the Year: Italy
Interactive World Player: Andries Smit (Holland)
*award presented posthumously

2007
Presidential award: Pele (Brazil)
Fair Play award: FC Barcelona (Spain)
Top Team of the Year: Argentina
Best Mover of the Year: Mozambique

2008
Presidential award: Women's football (presented to the United States women's team)
Fair Play award: Armenia, Turkey
Development award: Palestine
Interactive World Player: Alfonso Ramos (Spain)
Top Team of the Year: Spain
Best Mover of the Year: Spain

2009
Presidential award: Queen Rania Al Abdullah of Jordan [co-chair of 1Goal: Education for All]
Fair Play Award: Sir Bobby Robson (England)*
Development prize: Chinese Football Association
Interactive World Player: Bruce Grannec (France)
Top Team of the Year: Spain
*award presented posthumously

Note: The FIFA Fair Play award was instituted in 1987 and, before its inauguration into the annual gala, was made as follows:
1987: Fans of Dundee United (Scotland)
1988: Frank Ordenewitz (Germany) and spectators at the Olympic football tournament in Seoul
1989: Spectators of Trinidad & Tobago
1990: Gary Lineker (England)

NEW AWARDS FOR 2009
FIFA Ferenc Puskas Award (outstanding goal):
Cristiano Ronaldo (Manchester United v Porto)

FIFA/FIFpro World XI:
Iker Casillas (Spain), Dani Alves (Brazil), Nemanja Vidic (Serbia), John Terry (England), Patrice Evra (France), Andres Iniesta (Spain), Xavi (Spain), Steven Gerrard (England), Cristiano Ronaldo (Portugal), Fernando Torres (Spain), Lionel Messi (Argentina)

FIFA/COCA-COLA WORLD RANKINGS 2010

FIFA's world rankings system was launched in August 1993 and computes a regular statistical image of the rise and fall of the fortunes alike of the FIFA World Cup finals giants and the qualifying-round fallers. The system, simplified in 2005–06, is based on results in international A matches and takes into consideration match status, goals scored, strength of the opposition and regional balance. The rankings are issued every month.

Spain took over as the world's top team after the country won the 2010 FIFA World Cup. Europe's champions became the first country to lose their opening game of a FIFA World Cup finals and still win the tournament.

FIFA/COCA-COLA WORLD RANKINGS 2010

The status Spain secured with their 1-0 victory over Holland in the 2010 FIFA World Cup Final in Soccer City, Johannesburg, was underlined by their regaining of top spot in the subsequent FIFA/Coca-Cola World Rankings. This was the third time they had gone top since the rankings' creation. The first time was in July 2008 after their UEFA European Championship success. A year later Brazil toppled them by winning the FIFA Confederations Cup in South Africa. Brazil slipped to fourth place after their quarter-final loss at the 2010 FIFA World Cup to Holland. who sat in third place, just behind Germany. A decline in the value of past results, over the previous four years, is also taken into account.

RANKINGS (July 2010)

Pos.	Country	Points
1	Spain	1883
2	Netherlands	1659
3	Brazil	1536
4	Germany	1464
5	Argentina	1289
6	Uruguay	1152
7	England	1125
8	Portugal	1062
9	Egypt	1053
10	Chile	988
11	Italy	982
12	Greece	975
13	USA	969
13	Serbia	969
15	Croatia	968
16	Paraguay	961
17	Russia	956
18	Switzerland	940
19	Slovenia	917
20	Australia	911
21	France	890
22	Norway	878
23	Ghana	874
24	Mexico	872
25	Ukraine	870
26	Côte d'Ivoire	843
27	Slovakia	829
28	Turkey	810
29	Denmark	785
30	Nigeria	773
31	Czech Republic	769
32	Japan	768
33	Algeria	759
34	Gabon	755

Pos.	Country	Points
35	Sweden	747
36	Republic of Ireland	734
37	Israel	733
38	Peru	726
39	Colombia	725
40	Cameroon	710
41	Scotland	699
42	Romania	697
43	Bulgaria	672
44	Korea Republic	660
45	Burkina Faso	646
46	Honduras	644
47	Venezuela	592
48	Belgium	589
49	Costa Rica	584
50	Latvia	579
51	Finland	576
52	Lithuania	571
53	Bolivia	570
54	New Zealand	557
55	Mali	548
56	Poland	547
57	Bosnia-Herzegovina	546
58	Ecuador	545
59	Northern Ireland	540
60	Austria	536
61	Benin	535
62	Hungary	534
63	Cyprus	523
64	Iran	522
65	Tunisia	519
66	South Africa	504
66	FYR Macedonia	504
68	Saudi Arabia	471

Pos.	Country	Points
69	Bahrain	460
70	Uganda	457
71	Albania	455
72	Montenegro	448
73	Zambia	446
74	Malawi	425
75	Togo	421
76	Trinidad and Tobago	405
77	Belarus	403
78	China PR	393
79	Iceland	385
80	Mozambique	377
81	Oman	374
82	Morocco	371
83	Jamaica	368
84	Wales	366
85	Kuwait	365
86	Angola	356
87	Uzbekistan	352
88	United Arab Emirates	351
89	Moldova	350
90	El Salvador	343
91	Senegal	338
92	Syria	334
93	Botswana	331
94	Panama	323
95	Estonia	321
96	Armenia	318
96	Libya	318
98	Qatar	300
98	Jordan	300
100	Canada	295
101	Guinea	286
102	Gambia	285

Pos.	Country	Points	Pos.	Country	Points	Pos.	Country	Points
103	Korea DPR	284	138	Indonesia	141	173	Somalia	39
104	Iraq	276	139	Sierra Leone	130	173	Laos	39
105	Thailand	273	140	Liechtenstein	126	173	Cayman Islands	39
106	Azerbaijan	266	141	Burundi	125	176	Samoa	38
107	Congo	263	142	Malaysia	124	177	Mauritius	37
108	Cape Verde Islands	261	143	Myanmar	122	177	Seychelles	37
109	Yemen	248	144	Madagascar	121	179	Bahamas	34
110	Zimbabwe	238	145	Maldives	117	180	Dominica	33
111	Georgia	237	146	Ethiopia	115	180	Cambodia	33
112	Tanzania	235	147	St. Kitts & Nevis	110	182	Mongolia	32
113	Rwanda	233	147	Niger	110	182	Belize	32
114	Cuba	215	147	Equatorial Guinea	110	182	Turks &Caicos Islands	32
115	Kenya	210	150	Netherlands Antilles	108	185	Dominican Republic	26
116	Luxembourg	209	151	Lebanon	106	186	Tonga	23
117	Faroe Islands	206	152	Malta	105	187	Brunei Darussalam	21
118	Guatemala	204	153	Bangladesh	104	188	St. Lucia	19
119	Namibia	203	154	Lesotho	101	188	Guinea-Bissau	19
119	Guyana	203	155	Sri Lanka	96	188	Tahiti	19
121	Singapore	198	156	Nepal	94	191	Djibouti	18
121	Sudan	198	156	Liberia	94	191	British Virgin Islands	18
123	Suriname	187	158	Eritrea	92	193	Guam	17
124	Congo DR	185	159	Bermuda	91	193	Afghanistan	17
124	Chad	185	160	St. Vincent & Grenadines	87	193	Cook Islands	17
126	Kazakhstan	184	161	Nicaragua	86	196	Macau	12
127	Vietnam	179	162	New Caledonia	82	197	Aruba	11
128	Barbados	174	163	Pakistan	75	198	Bhutan	9
129	Antigua & Barbuda	168	163	Vanuatu	75	199	US Virgin Islands	5
130	Haiti	167	165	Kyrgyzstan	74	200	Timor-Leste	4
130	Fiji	167	166	Chinese Taipei	69	201	Andorra	2
132	India	160	167	Philippines	67	202	San Marino	0
133	Grenada	158	168	Mauritania	62	202	Anguilla	0
134	Swaziland	155	169	Solomon Islands	60	202	Montserrat	0
135	Hong Kong	152	170	Puerto Rico	52	202	American Samoa	0
136	Turkmenistan	150	171	Palestine	48	202	Central African Republic	0
137	Tajikistan	144	172	Comoros	43	202	Papua New Guinea	0

INDEX

Aboutrika, Mohamed 215, 224
Abramovich, Roman 122
AC Milan 79, 81, 88, 89, 97, 128, 153, 225
Achiou, Hocine 210
Adamache, Stere 43
Adelaide United 224
Adiyiah, Dominic 218, 219
Advocaat, Dick 97
AFC 165 173, 179, 180, 181
Africa Cup of Nations 164, 165, 166, 208
  1957 213, 214
  1959 215
  1962 214
  1968 212
  1970 215
  1974 212
  1978 214
  1980 215
  1992 210
  1994 213
  1996 210
  1998 215
  2002 213
  2004 210
  2004 211
  2006 210, 215
  2010 208, 210, 211, 213, 214, 215
  2012 211
  2014 211
  finals 214
  most appearances 211
  most tournaments 212
  most wins 211
  penalty shoot-outs 215
  top scorers 212, 213
  winning coaches 215
African Football Confederation see AFC
African Footballer of the Year 166, 213
Aghahowa, Julius 169
Aguero, Sergio 147, 219, 226
Aguinaga, Alex 205
Aguirre, Javier 17, 185
Ah-Ahly 224
Ajax 78, 79, 83
Akers, Michelle 236, 238
Akpoborie, Jonathan 220
Akwa 168
Al Abdullah of Jordan, Queen Rania 247
Albania 198
Al-Baski, Ali 165
Alberto, Julio 93
Alcock, Charles 61
Aldair 202
Al-Deayea, Mohamed 176, 185
Algeria 162, 163, 165, 208, 210, 214
Al-Ghesheyan, Fahad 174
Al-Jabar, Sami 176, 174, 177
Al-Jahani, Mahmoud 165
Al-Johar, Nasser 178
Almeida, Hugo 117
Al-Muhammadi, Ahmed 223
Aloisi, John 172, 173
Alonso, Norberto 147
Alonso, Xabi 55, 83
Al-Otaibi, Marzouk 223
Altafini, Jose 153
Altidore, Jozy 223
Altitude problems 157
Alvarez, Leonel 205
Alvim, Daniel 206
Amarilla, Raul Vicente 158
Amaya, Ivan 229
American Samoa 22, 181
Amin, Fuad 174
Amodu, Shaibu 214
Amsterdam ArenA 79
Amunike, Emmanuel 227
Anastasi, Pietro 194

Anastopoulos, Nikos 107
Ancelotti, Carlo 225
Anderlecht 97
Anderssen, Daniel 196
Anderssen, Patrik 196
Andersson, Kennet 128, 174
Andorra 143, 193
Andrade, Jose 227
Anelka, Nicolas 69, 196
Angelillo, Antonio Valentin 200, 203
Angerer, Nadine 239
Angola 211
Ann-Kristin 238
Ansah, Regina 237
Antic, Radi 127
Arab Nations Cup 165
Aragones, Luis 91, 107, 197
Archundia, Benito 47
Ardiles, Osvaldo 147, 148
Arena, Bruce 186
Argentina 18, 25, 26, 27, 33, 34, 42, 43, 45, 48, 54, 55, 144, 146-9, 167, 189, 200, 204, 205, 206, 207, 218, 219, 222, 226, 227, 228, 237, 244
  v Brazil 14
  v Colombia 148
  v Czechoslovakia 148
  v Ecuador 146, 203
  v England 64, 148
  v France 147
  v Greece 149
  v Jamaica 149
  v Nigeria 147
  v Peru 149
  records 147
  squad numbering 147
  top caps 149
  top scorers 148
  v Uruguay 147, 148
  youngest captain 149
Aristazabal, Victor 156, 203
Armenia 139
Arsenal 132
Arsenijevic, Milorad 127
Arshavin, Andrei 123
Ashour, Hossam 224
Asia Coach of the Year 178
Asian Cup 178, 179
Asian Footballer of the Year 176, 177
Asian Nations Cup **1964** 139
Asparukhov, Georgi 98
Astafjevs, Vitalijs 140
Ateya, Raafat 213
Athletic Bilbao 91, 94
Attendances 50-51
Augusto, Jose 117
Australia 22, 172-3, 175, 178, 179, 180, 181, 223, 237, 238
Austria 30, 73, 140, 142, 228
Auxerre 71
Avetisyan, Arsen 141
Ayala, Milner 203
Ayala, Roberto 149, 227
Ayew, Andre 15
Azerbaijan 139
Azteca Stadium 52

Baggio, Roberto 40, 43, 54, 84
Bagheri, Karim 175
Bahr, Walter 187
Bahrain 20, 175, 181
Bakhramov, Tofik 46
Balcazar, Tomas 185
Bale, Gareth 137
Ballack, Michael 38, 167, 192
Ballon d'Or 135
Banks, Gordon 39
Barassi, Ottorino 84
Barcelona 16, 92, 95, 224, 229, 230, 244

Baros, Milan 103
Barron, Andy 181
Barthez, Fabien 41, 42, 43, 67, 70
Basile, Alfio 149
Bassiouny, Abdel Hamid 23
Batista, Jose 28, 48
Batistuta, Gabriel 149, 204
Batres, Carlos 46, 55
Batteux, Albert 70
Battle of Santiago 158
Batty, David 55
Baxter, Jim 125
Bayern Munich 72, 74, 75, 77
Beasley, DaMarcus 186, 187
Beausejour, Jean 156
Beckenbauer, Franz 36, 72, 74, 76, 77, 78
Beckham, David 60, 62, 64, 186, 188
Beenhakker, Leo 114
Behrami, Valon 130
Behringer, Melanie 241
Belarus 139
Belgium 42, 96-97, 103, 180, 194, 195, 196, 198, 199, 227
  v Costa Rica 153
  v Egypt 223
  v Holland 150
  v Italy 150, 152
  v Ivory Coast 153
  leading World Cup scorers 152
  v Poland 152
  records 151
  v Saudi Arabia 223
  v Scotland 150
  top caps 152
  top scorers 152
  v United States 222
Bellamy, Craig 137
Bellone, Bruno 195
Belqola, Said 164
Ben Suwed, Ahmed 165
Bene, Ferenc 229
Benfica 117, 225
Bengtsson, Kristin 239
Bento, Paulo 197
Berbatov, Dimitar 98
Bergkamp, Dennis 80
Bergomi, Giuseppe 37, 39, 40, 87
Bernaus, Marc 143
Best, George 110
Bianchi, Carlos 225
Bican, Josef 142
Bicycle kick 152
Bierhoff, Oliver 73, 196
Biggest crowds 198
Biggest wins
  Copa America 203
  Croatia 100
  England 60, 61
  European Championship 192, 195
  Germany 76
  Holland 83
  FIFA World Cup 31, 181
  UEFA 143
  Wales 137
Biggest defeats
  Holland 83
  Scotland 125
  UEFA 143
  Wales 137
Bilic, Slaven 69, 100
Bingham, Billy 111
Blanc, Laurent 67, 69
Blanchflower, Danny 110
Blanco, Cuauhtemoc 32, 184, 222
Blatter, Joseph S. 28, 223, 230, 242
Blokhin, Oleg 135
Blue Stars FC 230
Blue Stars FIFA Youth Cup 230
Boateng, Jerome 167
Boateng, Kevin-Prince 167
Boca Juniors 146, 225, 230
Bohemia and Moravia 142
Bolatti, Mario 147
Boli, Basile 71
Bolic, Elvir 140
Bolivia 156, 157, 202, 203, 205, 206
Boniek, Zbigniew 115
Bordeaux 69

Borghetti, Jared 184
Borja,220, 221
Boruc, Artur 114
Borussia Dortmund 102, 130
Bosnia-Herzegovina 139, 140
Bossis, Maxime 54
Botagofo 150
Botswana 168
Bouazizi, Riadh 163
Boulahrouz, Khalid 39
Boumnijel, Ali 162
Bozhkov, Stefan 98
Bradley, Bob 34, 186, 187
Bradley, Michael 34, 187
Brandts, Ernie 36
Brazil 12, 13, 18, 21, 25, 26, 27, 28, 29, 30, 30, 43, 44, 45, 47, 49, 49, 49, 51, 54, 90, 144, 150-53, 156, 169, 175, 200, 202, 203, 205, 207, 216, 218, 219, 221, 222, 223, 227, 231, 232, 236, 237, 238, 239, 240, 241, 245
  v Costa Rica 153
  v Egypt 223
  v Holland 150
  v Italy 150, 152
  v Ivory Coast 153
  leading World Cup scorers 152
  v Poland 152
  records 151
  v Saudi Arabia 223
  v Scotland 150
  top caps 152
  top scorers 152
  v United States 222
Bresciano, Marco 172
Brighton & Hove Albion 133
British Home Championship 56, 111, 124, 125, 137
Brolin, Tomas 128
Bronze Shoe 32
Brookes, Ed 119
Brown, Bobby 125
Bruckner, Karel 103
Brussels International Supporters Award 110
Buffon, Gianluigi 39, 41, 42, 88, 141, 227
Bujsaim, Ali 39
Bulgaria 22, 98-99, 107, 129, 213
Bullard, Chris 233
Buncol, Andrzej 115
Burns, Tommy 125
Burruchaga, Jorge 148
Bury 133
Butragueno, Emilio 93, 95
Bwalya, Kalusha 22, 169
Byong Ju, Chong 22

Cabanas, Salvador 158
CAF 164, 208
Cafu 36, 48, 152
Cagliari 87
Cagliuri, Paul 186
Cahill, Tim 173
Camara, Henri 168
Camataru, Rodion 121
Cambiasso, Esteban 149
Cameroon 48, 166, 167, 174, 180, 208, 210, 211, 212, 213, 215, 215, 223, 229
Canada 25, 185, 188, 237, 238, 241
Canedo, Estadio Guillermo 52
Caniggia, Claudio 39, 222
Caniza, Denis 159
Cannavaro, Fabio 84, 86, 87, 88, 227
Cantona, Eric 71, 232
Capdeville, Georges 46

Capello, Fabio 17, 64, 65
Caps 60
Carbajal, Antonio 37, 40, 184
Carbonero, Sara 42
Cardozo, Jose 158
Cardozo, Oscar 40, 55, 157
Carew, John 113
Carey, Johnny 119
Carlos, Roberto 153, 227
Carney, Karen 241
Carragher, Jamie 55, 64, 167
Carrasso, Cedric 69
Carvalho, Ricardo 47
Casillas, Iker 12, 40, 42, 55, 90, 92
Cech, Petr 102
Celtic 225
Central European International Cup 140
Cesar, Bostjan 139
Cesar, Julio 43
Ceulemans, Jan 97
Chanov, Viacheslav 41
Chanov, Viktor 41
Chapuisat, Pierre-Albert 130
Chapuisat, Stephane 130
Charisteas, Angelos 106
Charles, John 137
Charlton Athletic 169
Charlton, Jack 118, 119
Charlton, Jack 118, 119
Chelsea 122, 229
Chiellini, Giorgio 86
Chilavert, Jose Luis 158
Chile 47, 49, 156, 157, 158, 159, 187, 203, 204, 207
  v Honduras 156
  v Italy 158
  v Paraguay 159
  v Soviet Union 156
  top caps 157
  top scorers 157
  v Uruguay 157, 159
  v Yugoslavia 1567
China 44, 175, 178, 179, 236, 237, 238, 241, 247
Chislenko, Igor 47
Chyn Hong, Li 238
Ciolek, Wlodzimierz 115
Clairfontaine 71
Clean sheets 43, 130
Club Brugge 97
Cmikiewicz, Leslaw 38
Cole, Andy 62
Collins, John 125
Collovati, Fulvio 194
Colombia 156, 158,
Colombia 158, 159, 179, 181, 185, 203, 205, 223
Coluna, Mario 117
Commonwealth of Independent States 123, 134 see also Russia, Soviet Union
CONCACAF 182-3, 185, 189
Conceicao, Flavio 202
Congo DR 208
CONMEBOL 155, 156, 225
Copa America 56, 146, 148, 151, 154, 156, 200, 222, 223
  1916 204
  1917 202, 204
  1919 202
  1942 202
  1949 205
  1953 203
  1957 200, 203
  1963 206
  1975 203
  1997 202, 223
  2001 203
  2004 205
  2007 200, 207
  biggest wins 203
  hosts 202, 203

longest match 202
most appearances 204
most goals 204, 205
most red cards 207
own goals 204
red cards 207
winners 202, 203
winning coaches 206, 207
Copa Libertadores 157, 225
Cordoba, Ivan 156
Cordoba, Oscar 159, 203
Corinthians 225
Correa, Vanina 237
Costa Rica 44, 175, 188, 189
Costa, Jorge 218
Costa, Rui 218
Costacurta, Alessandro 225
Costinha 39
Crespo, Hernan 32, 227
Crespo, Pedro 232
Cristiane 240
Croatia 100-01, 126, 139, 141, 173, 189, 192
Croke Park 118
Crouch, Peter 37, 62
Cruyff, Johan 78, 79, 80, 81, 82
CSKA Sofia 98, 99
Cuba 189, 231
Cubilla, Luis 225
Cubillas, Teofilo 158
Cufre, Leandro 28, 48
Custers, Theo 42
Cyprus 142
Czech Republic/ Czechoslovakia 42, 49, 55, 92, 102-3, 107, 139, 142, 143, 190, 192, 194, 195, 196, 227, 229

Da Silva, Leonidas 152
Daei, Ali 23, 175, 177
Dahlin, Martin 128
Dalglish, Kenny 124
Daniela 241
Danilova, Elena 238
David, Mario 158
De Azevado, Thiago Carrico 233
De Boer, Frank 81, 196
De Boer, Ronald 81, 196
De Brito, Valdemar 41
De Jong, Nigel 83
De Leon, Julio Cesar 189
De Macedo, Evaristo 205
De Neve, Eddy 82
Deco 39
Dedic, Zlatko 138
Defoe, Jermain 61, 63
Del Bosque, Vicente 27
Delhasse, Guy 97
Dellas, Traianos 195
Demirel, Volkan 132
Dempsey, Clint 187, 222, 223
Denilson 38, 202
Denmark 104-5, 107, 141, 174, 192, 194, 195, 222, 227, 228, 229
Derwall, Jupp 77
Desailly, Marcel 68, 69, 71, 164, 223
Deschamps, Didier 68, 69, 71
Dhouib, Mokhtar 163
Di Maria, Angel 147, 226
Di Stefano, Alfredo 93
Diarra, Boubacar 165
Dida 224
Didi 36, 45
Didulica, Joey 173
Dienst, Gottfried 46
Dietz, Bernd 197
Djalminha 202
Dodds, Billy 125
Doherty, Peter 111
Doll, Thomas 72

Domenech, Raymond 67, 69, 70, 71
Domenghini, Angelo 194
Domergue, Jean-Francois 195
Donovan, Landon 186, 187
Doo Ik, Pak 177, 178
Dorner, Hans-Jurgen 73
Dos Santos, Giovani 15, 185
Dos Santos, Jonathan 185
Douglas, Jimmy 43
Drogba, Didier 167
Duckadam, Helmuth 120
Dudek, Jerzy 114
Dujkovic, Ratomir 167
Dukla Prague 103
Duk-Yung, Hong 40, 175
Dumitrescu, Ilie 120
Dunga 17, 38, 151, 202, 219
Durban 53
Dutch East Indies 27, 177 see also Indonesia
Dynamo Kiev 134, 135
Dynamo Tbilisi 143
Dynamo Zagreb 101
Dzajic, Dragan 126

Earliest booking 48
Earliest sending off 48
East Germany 192, 226 see also Germany
East Timor 179
East Timor 231
Eckel, Horst 23
Ecuador 157, 159, 202, 205
Edmundo 202
Eduardo 100
Egypt 21, 162, 164, 165, 175, 208, 210, 213, 213, 214, 218
v Algeria 162
most caps 213
v Sweden 165
El Salvador 24, 30, 42, 156, 188
El-Attar, Mohamed Diab 213
El-Gohary, Mahoud 215
Elizondo, Horacio 47
Elkjaer, Preben 141
Ellis Park 53
Ellis, Arthur 198
Emmanuel, Sani 220
Endeladze, Zviad 141
England 18, 20, 24, 25, 26, 27, 28, 30, 33, 34, 43, 45, 47, 54, 55, 60–65, 91, 129, 163, 187, 189, 190, 192, 193, 197, 234, 241
v Algeria 61
v Argentina 64
v Australia 62
v Austria 62
biggest wins 60, 61
biggest defeats 61
v Brazil 61
v Croatia 62
v Denmark 61
v France 193
v Germany 61
v Hungary 61, 64
v Ireland 60, 64
v Italy 65
managers 65
v Moldova 62
v Northern Ireland 63
oldest debut 62
oldest players 61, 62
oldest scorer 62
v Portugal 60
v Republic of Ireland 61, 64
v San Marino 64
v Scotland 60, 61, 62, 64, 65
v Serbia & Montenegro 64
v Slovakia 62
v Slovenia 63
v Spain 64
tallest and shortest 62
top caps 63
top scorers 63
v USA 61
v Uruguay 61
v Wales 64
youngest hat-trick 62
youngest player 62
youngest scorer 62
v Yugoslavia 60
Enrique, Luis 38, 49
Equatorial Guinea 208, 211
Eredivisie 16

Eriksen, Christian 105
Eriksson, Sven Goran 45, 62, 129, 185, 214
Erlingmark, Magnus 129
Escobar, Andres 159
Estonia 139, 140, 143
Estudiantes 224
Ethiopia 212, 213
Eto'o, Samuel 167, 212, 213, 229
Europe 58
European Cup 86, 88, 89, 120, 192, 196, 225, 230
see also UEFA Champions League
European Cup-Winners' Cup 89
European Footballer of the Year 99, 103, 123
European Golden Boot 121
Eusebio 32, 116, 117, 141
Evra, Patrice 67

Fabiano, Luis 153, 222
Fabianski, Lukasz 114
Fabregas, Cesc 93, 220, 221
Facchetti, Giacinto 87
Fadrhonc, Frantisek 79
Falcao (Futsal) 231
Falcao (FIFA World Cup) 150
Fan Fests 51
Faroe Islands 193
Fastest goal 23, 132, 196
Fastest hat-tricks 23
Fastest red card 28
Fastest substitutions 37
Fathy, Ahmad 165
Fawzi, Abdelrahman 162
FC Basel 230
FC Sierre 230
FC Zurich 230
Fenerbahce 132,1 33
Feola, Vicente 151
Ferencvaros 109
Ferguson, Alicia 237, 238
Fernandes, Gelson 131
Fernandez, Luis 195
Fernandez, Matias 158
Ferrari, Giovanni 36, 89
Ferrer, Albert 230
Fewest goals average 31
Fewest goals conceded 28
Fewest goals scored 28, 30
Feyenoord 79, 83, 177
Field, Edgar 64
FIFA 130, 167, 181, 225
FIFA Awards 246–7
FIFA Beach Soccer World Cup 232
FIFA Club World Cup 129, 216, 224–5 see also FIFA Intercontinental Cup
FIFA Confederations Cup 56, 146, 151, 216, 222–3
FIFA Futsal World Cup 231
FIFA Interactive World Cup 233
FIFA Intercontinental Cup 225 see also FIFA Club World Cup
FIFA Player of the Year 117, 169, 242, 244
FIFA Women's Player of the Year 238, 242, 245
FIFA Women's Under-17 World Championship 241
FIFA Women's Under-19 World Championship 241
FIFA Women's Under-20 World Championship 241
FIFA Women's World Cup 50, 234
1991 234, 236, 237, 238
1995 50, 234, 237, 238
1999 50, 236, 237, 238
2003 238
2007 237, 238
fastest booking 238
fastest goal 238
fastest sending off 238, 239
fastest substitution 238
finals 236
finals captains 239
leading scorers 239
most appearances 239
oldest player 239
penalty shoot-outs 236
player of the tournament 239

records 239
smallest crowd 237
third-place playoffs 236
top scorers 237, 238
top teams 237
youngest player 239
youngest scorer 238
FIFA World Cup 6, 8, 10, 12–55, 56, 67, 73, 75, 84, 85, 139, 150, 186, 188, 189, 222, 223
1930 8, 27, 33, 45, 52, 120, 126, 127, 147, 148, 154, 182, 185, 186, 189, 200, 227, 236
1934 24, 30, 73, 76, 83, 85, 89, 103, 130, 139, 142, 148, 155, 162, 163, 175, 186
1938 73, 77, 83, 84, 89, 103, 109, 113, 114, 129, 130, 131, 142, 152, 156, 175, 177, 189
1950 26, 51, 52, 127, 129, 132, 154, 187, 205
1954 29, 30, 61, 72, 73, 77, 108, 109, 130, 131, 132, 175, 185, 190
1958 29, 580, 70, 110, 111, 128, 129, 136, 139, 150, 151, 152, 153, 203, 205
1962 47, 49, 103, 123, 126, 151, 152, 153, 156, 158, 203
1966 28, 30, 33, 47, 63, 75, 84, 99, 109, 116, 117, 131, 141, 151, 152, 177
1970 29, 43, 47, 48, 75, 76, 139, 151, 152, 162, 179, 182, 184, 185, 188
1974 49, 72, 74, 78, 79, 80, 82, 83, 84, 114, 115, 117, 124, 134, 154, 156, 158, 173, 174, 180, 189, 212
1978 26, 33, 34, 42, 45, 47, 71, 79, 80, 83, 84, 124, 125, 146, 147, 148, 158, 163
1982 42, 54, 66, 84, 85, 86, 91, 110, 111, 114, 115, 147, 150, 156, 180, 181, 188, 215
1986 28, 32, 33, 43, 49, 91, 93, 96, 97, 98, 104, 105, 109, 110, 111, 117, 141, 146, 163, 167, 182, 184, 185, 219
1990 26, 31, 43, 48, 54, 72, 75, 84, 88, 118, 121, 143, 148, 155, 158, 176, 179, 181, 186, 187, 188, 215
1994 22, 30, 31, 48, 49, 50, 54, 80, 98, 99, 107, 113, 120, 123, 128, 129, 134, 146, 150, 151, 156, 158, 159, 163, 166, 167, 174, 177, 185, 187, 213, 218, 219, 223
1998 26, 31, 48, 66, 68, 69, 70, 71, 87, 88, 100, 101, 105, 112, 120, 123, 125, 127, 141, 150, 153, 159, 164, 166, 167, 172, 176, 177, 178, 179, 180, 184, 185, 187, 189, 223
2002 21, 29, 31, 38, 53, 82, 91, 94, 96, 115, 118, 128, 129, 132, 140, 150, 151, 153, 155, 159, 170, 175, 176, 178, 179, 185, 186, 187, 188, 220
2006 26, 27, 30, 34, 38, 47, 48, 54, 55, 69, 71, 83, 84, 88, 92, 102, 127, 128, 129, 130, 131, 134, 135, 139, 149, 155, 162, 166, 167, 172, 173, 177, 179, 185, 186, 187, 188
2010 6, 8, 10, 12–17, 26, 27, 28, 31, 32, 33, 34, 38, 42, 43, 44, 46, 47, 49, 50, 53, 54, 55, 56, 61, 63, 64, 67, 68, 69, 71, 73, 74, 76, 77, 79, 83, 84, 85, 86, 88, 90, 92, 93, 94, 95, 104, 105, 106, 107, 117, 127, 130, 131, 132, 133, 140, 141, 142, 146, 147, 149, 151, 153, 154, 155, 156,

157, 159, 160, 162, 163, 166, 167, 173, 174, 176, 178, 179, 180, 181, 185, 186, 187, 188, 189, 208, 214, 221, 248, 251
2014 200
biggest wins 31, 181
Fair Play 90
fastest booking 93
fastest goals 132
fastest goals 132
fastest substitutions 87
final referees 46
first sending off 120
Golden Boot 75, 99, 101, 103, 148, 158, 218
hat-tricks 149
highest crowd 178
lowest crowd 120, 178
most bookings 83
most clean sheets 130
most goals 167, 176, 181
most substituted player 75
most venues 91
most wins 29
opening matches 150
penalty kicks 185
penalty shoot-outs 120, 121, 128, 134, 157, 178
qualifiers 20–25, 119
rankings 13
red cards 130, 162, 173
referees 164
sendings off see FIFA World Cup red cards
shortest career 129
substitutes 105
Team of the Tournament 132
youngest coach 147
youngest players 105
FIFA World U-17 Championship 168, 216, 220–21
FIFA World U-20 Championship 117, 147, 169, 216, 218–9
FIFA/Coca-Cola World Rankings 94, 248–51
Figueroa, Flias 158
Figo, Luis 116, 218
Filho, Estadio Jornalista Mario 52
Filho, Romualdo Arppi 49
Finland 142
Firmani, Eddie 169
Ho, Tore Andre 112
Flowers, Ron 193
Fluminense 150, 157
Foe, Marc-Vivien 223
Fontaine, Just 29, 33, 70, 149
Football War 24
Foreign coaches 44
Forlan, Diego 14, 15, 54, 154
Forlan, Pablo 154
Foudy, Julie 237
France 18, 22, 25, 26, 27, 28, 29, 45, 48, 54, 55, 66–71, 164, 166, 167, 176, 194, 195, 196, 197, 197, 220, 223, 227, 229, 232
v Belgium 195
v Brazil 66, 68, 164
v Croatia 69
v Denmark 195
first manager 70
v Hungary 71
v Italy 69, 166
list of managers 70
v Mexico 67
v Portugal 195
v Republic of Ireland 68
v South Africa 67
v Spain 195 top caps 68
top goals 68
v Uruguay 67
Franklin 231
Frei, Alexander 130, 131
Friedel, Brad 40, 186, 187
Friedrich, Arne 77
Friedrich, Manuel 192
Frossi, Annibale 228
Fuchs, Gottfried 76, 229
Furino, Giuseppe 89

Gabon 208, 211, 212
Gaetjens, Joe 187
Galatasaray 132, 133
Galba, Karol 48
Galindo, Placido 48, 120

Gallegos, Sebastian 220
Gamba Osaka 225
Gambia 215
Gamper, Hans 95
Gancarczyk, Seweryn 138
Garay, Juan Gardeazabal 46
Garcia, Luis 204
Garefrekes, Kerstin 237
Garrincha 18, 33, 36, 49, 92, 150
Gattuso, Gennaro 88
Gedo 212, 214
Genenhuber, Sonia 237
Georgia 138, 139, 143
Geovani 219
Germany/West Germany 13, 15, 16, 18, 21, 27, 29, 30, 45, 54, 55, 72–7, 163, 167, 169, 170, 190, 192, 193, 194, 196, 196, 197, 199, 219, 220, 221, 222, 227, 229, 234, 237, , 236, 237, 238, 239, 240, 241
see also East Germany
v Albania 192
v Argentina 73, 74, 75, 77
v Australia 73, 74
v Belgium 73
biggest win 76
v Bulgaria 77
v Czech Republic 73
v East Germany 73
v England 73, 75, 193
v Ghana 167, 169
v Holland 73
v Hungary 73, 77
v Northern Ireland 192
v Poland 74
v Russia 76
v Saarland 77
v San Marino 75
v Saudi Arabia 75
v Soviet Union 73, 195
v Spain 73, 74
v Switzerland 73
top caps, E Germany 73
top caps, Germany 75
top goals, E Germany 73
top goals, Germany 74, 75
v Turkey 199
v Uruguay 76
Gerrard, Steven 55, 61, 130, 131
Ghana 15, 54, 167, 168, 169, 208, 210, 214, 215, 218, 219, 227, 229, 237, 238
v Germany 167, 169
Ghezzal, Abdelkader 16
Ghommidh, Nejib 163
Giggs, Ryan 136
Giles, Johnny 119
Gilmar 36
Giresse, Alain 195
Given, Shay 118, 119
Givens, Don 119
Goalless draws 31
Godfather, The 98
Golden Boot 34, 117, 218
Golden Glove 42
Golden goals 73, 132, 196, 240
Golden Shoe 32 see also Golden Boot
Gomaa, Wael 224
Gomes, Nuno 197
Gomez, Hector Rivadavia 155
Gonella, Sergio 46
Gonzalez, Mark 131, 159
Gorlukovich, Sergei 48, 93
Gorski, Kazimierz 115
Gottinger, Richard 23
Goycochea, Sergio 39, 54
Grannec, Bruce 233
Grant, Avram 139
Grasshopper Club 130, 230
Great Britain 227
Greaves, Jimmy 105
Greece 44, 106–7, 175, 195, 196, 198
v Argentina 107
v Czechoslovakia 107
colours 106
v England 106
v Nigeria 107
v South Korea 107
v Spain 107
top caps 106, 107
top scorers 106
v Ukraine 107

Green, Robert 14, 61, 187
Greenwell, Jack 206
Gren, Gunnar 39, 128
Grindheim, Christian 112
Grings, Inka 241
Grosics, Gyula 73
Gualtieri, Davide 23
Guam 175
Guardiola, Josep 224, 230
Guatemala 231
Gudjohnsen, Arnor 140
Gudjohnsen, Eidur 140
Guerin, Robert 67
Gullit, Ruud 81
Gyan, Asamoah 15, 47, 155

Haan, Arie 79, 80
Haffey, Frank 125
Hagi, Gheorghe 120, 121
Haiti 189
Half Man Half Biscuit 103
Halilhodzic, Vahid 214
Hamad, Adnan 178
Hamburg 75, 177
Hamm, Mia 236, 238
Hampden Park 64, 125
Handanovic, Jasmin 141
Handanovic, Samir 141
Hansen, Carl 105
Happel, Ernst 45, 79
Harte, Ian 40
Hassan, Ahmed 213
Havelange, Joao 20, 236
Healy, David 111
Heitinga, Johnny 17
Henry, Thierry 25, 37, 68, 71, 223
Herberger, Sepp 72, 73, 77
Herbert, Ricki 17, 181
Hermann, Heinz 131
Hernandez Jr, Javier 185
Hernandez Sr, Javier 185
Hernandez, Luis 184
Hertha Berlin 177
Heskey, Emile 61, 64
Hewie, John 169
Hickersberger, Josef 193
Hidalgo, Michel 67
Hiddink, Guus 122, 123, 173, 178, 179
Hierro, Fernando 91, 93
Highest attendance 50
Higuain, Gonzalo 34
Higuita, Rene 158, 203
Hingst, Ariane 237
Hitzfeld, Ottmar 131
Hitzlsperger, Thomas 192
Hoddle, Glenn 62, 64
Hodge, Steve 37
Hoeness, Uli 80, 193
Hogan, Jimmy 108
Holland 12, 16, 21, 26, 28, 39, 45, 47, 49, 78 83, 167, 179, 193, 194, 196, 197, 198, 198, 199, 222, 227, 241
v Argentina 78, 82, 83
v Australia 79
v Belgium 79, 82
biggest defeat 83
biggest win 83
v Brazil 82
v Denmark 83
v Czechoslovakia 194
v England 79, 83
v Finland 83
v Germany 79, 82
v Italy 83
v Norway 83
v Portugal 83
v Republic of Ireland 82, 193
v Spain 79, 83
v South Korea 115
v Soviet Union 79, 82
top caps 80
top scorers 81
Holman, Brett 173
Honda, Keisuke 174
Honduras 24, 55, 156, 188, 189
Hong Kong 179
Hosting rights 53
Hruska, Zdenek 42
Hsui Mei, Liu 238
Hui Fang, Lin 238, 239
Hungary 17, 29, 30, 42, 92, 108–9, 177, 197, 229
Hurst, Geoff 33, 63

Hurtado, Ivan 22, 159
Hyang Ok, Ri 238
Hyon Sun, Jang 241

Ibrahimovic, Zlatan 129
Iceland 140
IFK Gothenburg 129
Ilic, Sasa 173
Ilyin, Anatoly 197
India 49
Indonesia 139 see Dutch East
    Indies
Iniesta, Andres 15, 32
Inileyev, Rauf 178
Intercontinental Cup 147
Internazionale 86, 87, 149,
    192, 196
Internet 199, 233
Inzaghi, Filippo 86
Iran 175, 178
Iraq 165, 178, 181
Irmatov, Ravshan 47
Israel 25, 139, 142, 179, 181
Italian Job, The 198
Italy 18, 24, 25, 26, 27, 28,
    29, 30, 43, 48, 54, 55,
    84–9, 153, 169, 180, 189,
    190, 193, 194, 195, 198,
    203, 227, 228, 238
    v Argentina 84
    v Cameroon 85
    v Germany 85
    v New Zealand 85
    v Paraguay 85, 88
    v Peru 85
    v Poland 85
    records 85
    v Slovakia 85
    v Soviet Union 87
    v Spain 85
    top caps 86
    top goals 86
    v Turkey 193
    v Yugoslavia 84, 87, 194
Ivanov, Valentin 39
Ivory Coast 167, 208, 210,
    212, 214, 220, 222

J-League 16
Jacquet, Aime 68, 70
Jaidi, Rahdi 163
Jairzinho 29
Jamaica 189
James, David 14, 61
James, Leighton 137
Jansen, John 194
Jansen, Wim 80
Japan 12, 21, 31, 53, 170, 174,
    175, 176, 177, 178, 179,
    181, 189, 227, 237, 238
    v Argentina 178
    v Cameroon 178
    v Denmark 174
    v Paraguay 174, 178
    v Saudi Arabia 178
    top caps 175
    top scorers 175
    v Tunisia 178
    v Turkey 178
Jennings, Carin 238
Jennings, Pat 110
Ji-Sung, Park 176, 177
Johannesburg 53, 56
Johnston, Sam 111
Jones, Bryn 137
Jones, Cliff 137
Jones, Cobi 186
Jones, Ivor 137
Jones, Ken 137
Jongbloed, Jan 39, 80
Jonni, Maurice 47
Joo-Sung, Kim 177
Jorgensen, Martin104
Jovanovic, Milan 13
Juan 153
Jules Rimet Trophy 67, 151
Jung-Hwan, Ahn 176
Jung-Moo, Huh 17
Jurion, Jef 97
Juventus 27, 66, 86, 89,
    137, 146

Kaabi, Ali 163
Kadlec, Michal 196
Kadlec, Miroslav 196
Kahn, Oliver 41
Kaka 16, 17, 150, 153, 222,
    223, 230
Kaladze, Kakha 138

Kana-Biyik, Andre 48
Kanchelskis, Andrei 134
Karembeu, Christian 71, 176
Karhan, Miroslav 140
Karimi, Ali 175
Katanec, Srecko 140
Kato 232
Kazakhstan 139, 179
Kazim-Richards, Colin 133
Keane, Robbie 119
Keane, Roy 118
Keegan, Kevin 62
Keita, Seydou 211
Keller, Kasey 186
Keller, Tore 129
Kelly, Gary 82
Kempes, Mario 33, 34, 148
Kenya 210
Kenyon, James 137
Kewell, Harry 173
Khedira, Sami 76
Khune, Itumeleng 42
Kilbane, Kevin 118
King Fahd Cup 222 see also
    FIFA Confederations Cup
Kingdome 25
Kirichenko, Dmitri 196
Kirsten, Ulf 73
Kkhairi, Abderrazak 163
Klasnic, Ivan 101
Klein, Abraham 47
Klinsmann, Jurgen 35, 77
Klose, Miroslav 15, 32, 75,
    158, 192
Kluivert, Patrick 82, 193
Knaak, Turid 241
Kobierski, Stanislaus 73
Kocsis, Sandor 33, 108, 149
Koeman, Erwin 108
Kohut, Vilmos 177
Koller, Jan 102
Komano, Yuichi 12, 178
Kompany, Vincent 97
Kopa, Raymond 66, 67, 70
Koren, Robert 142
Kostadinov, Emil 22, 99
Kotkov, Nikolai 98
Kovac, Niko 101
Kovac, Robert 101
Krahn, Annike 234
Kranjcar, Niko 101
Kranjcar, Zlatko 101
Krkic, Bojan 220
Krol, Ruud 79, 80, 82
Kubala, Ladislav 92
Kucukandonyadis, Lefter 38
Kuffour, Samuel 168, 229
Kuhn, Jakob 131
Kulig, Kim 241
Kusto, Marek 114
Kuszczak, Tomasz 114
Kuwait 44
Kuzmanovic, Zdravko 127
Kyrgyzstan 139, 179

Lampard, Frank 55, 62
Lansdowne Road 118
Laos 164
Larsson, Henrik 128
Latest booking 48
Latest red card 48
Latest sending off 48
Lato, Grzegorz 42, 114, 115
Latvia 139, 140, 142
Laudrup, Brian 105
Laudrup, Michael 105, 222
Laurent, Lucien 8
Law, Denis 124
Lazio 86
LDU Quito 157
Le Guen, Paul 166
Leao, Emerson 39
Leeds United 119
Leekens, Georges 97
Lehmann, Jens 55, 102
Lemerre, Roger 71
Leonardo 207
Letchkov, Yordan 99
Leweck, Alphonse 139
Lewis, John 227
Liberia 169, 215
Libya 164, 165, 211
Liechtenstein 142
Liedholm, Nils 128,1 29
Liedson 117
Liga, La 16, 95
Ligue 1 – 16, 95
Lillo, Eduardo 233
Lilly, Kristine 236

Lineker, Gary 33, 34, 133
Lingor, Renate 237
Lippi, Marcello 27, 71, 84, 85
Lithuania 139, 142, 143
Liverpool 86, 224
Livingstone, Sergio 204
Lizarazu, Bixente 69
Llunga, Mwepu 49
Lodeiro, Nicolas 16
Loftus Versfeld 53
Longest suspensions 38
Lorenzo, Giuseppe 89
Low, Joachim 73, 76
Lowest attendance 50
Lucio 222
Lugano, Diego 251
Lukovic, Aleksandar 17
Lunberg, Hanna 238
Lundin, Therese 238
Luxembourg 139
Lyon 69

Mabhida Stadium, Moses 53
Macau 179
Macedonia 139, 140, 141, 143,
    173, 193
McBride, Brian 186, 187
McCarthy, Benni 168
McCarthy, Mick 118
McClaren, Steve 64, 65
McCoist, Ally 141
McFadden, James 124
MacMillan, Shannon 240
Maddison, Richard 203
Madjer 232
Madsen, Ole 192
Mahdavikia, Mehdi 177
Maier, Sepp 75, 102
Majidi, Farhad 175
Malawi 168
Malaysia 218
Maldini, Cesare 45, 88
Maldini, Paolo 39, 88, 225
Maldives 175
Mali 165, 211, 213
Malmo 129
Malta 142, 192
Mamam, Souleymane 23
Manchester City 143
Manchester United 23, 117,
    119, 132, 177, 225
Mandela Stadium, Nelson 53
Mandela, Nelson 166, 210
Mao 232
Maracana Stadium 50, 51, 52
Maradona, Diego 17, 38,
    43, 146, 147, 148, 149,
    157, 219
Marchegiani, Luca 40
Marchena, Carlos 92
Marchetti, Federico 88
Marini, Giampiero 48
Marquez, Rafael 184
Marschall, Olaf 72
Marta 238, 239, 240, 242, 245
Martin, Con 119
Martino, Gerardo 159
Martins, Obafemi 169
Marumo, Modiri 168
Masantonio, Herminio 203
Mascherano, Javier 147,
    207, 226
Maschio, Humberto 200, 203
Masek, Vaclav 31
Masopust, Josef 103
Maspoli, Roque 154
Materazzi, Marco 47, 48
Matthaus, Lothar 36, 37, 39,
    40, 74, 75, 154, 163, 197
Matthews, Stanley 61, 62
Maurice, Michael 186
Mauritius 211
Mazzola, Sandro 89
Mazzola, Valentino 89
Mbombela Stadium 53
Meazza, Giuseppe 36, 85, 89
Meazza, Stadio Giuseppe 89
Medina, Napoleon 202
Meg 241
Meier, Urs 38
Meireles, Raul 117
Melgren, Dagny 240
Mellberg, Olof 128
Melo, Felipe 43, 49
Mendez, Norberto 204, 205
Mendibil, Jose Maria Ortiz
    de 46
Menotti, Cesar Luis 33, 45,
    148

Meola, Tony 42
Mervezzi, Juan 205
Messi, Lionel 149, 167, 219,
    224, 226, 242, 244
Mester, Lynn 241
Metsu, Bruno 45
Mexico 16, 24, 44, 150, 163,
    182, 184–5, 188, 189, 205
    v Argentina 184, 185
    v Brazil 188
    v Bulgaria 185
    v Czechoslovakia 185
    v France 185
    v Germany 184, 185
    v Holland 184
    v Honduras 185
    v Italy 185
    records 184
    v South Korea 184
    top caps 184
    top scorers 184
    v United States 185
Mexico City 52
Michel, Henri 167, 214
Michels, Rinus 78, 79, 80, 82
Middelboe, Nils 105, 229
Mikhailov, Borislav 98, 99
Mikhtarski, Petar 129
Milla, Roger 15, 31, 36, 166
Miller, Charles 151
Milosevic, Savo 126
Milutinovic, Bora 44, 167, 175
Mitchell, Sagar 137
Miura, Kazu 23
MLS 187
Mogaladi, Michael 168
Mohamed, Shady 224
Mohamed, Peter 53
Mokhtar, Mahmoud 163
Moldova 139
Monalisa, Luisito 37, 148
Monti, Luisito 37, 148
Monumental, El 146
Moore, Bobby 62, 63
Moore, Paddy 119
Mora, Luis Ricardo Guevara
    42
Morace, Carolina 238
Moran, Ruben 39
Moreno, Jose 205
Moreno, Jose Manuel 146
Moreno, Manuel 203
Moreno, Rafael 95
Morientes, Fernando 93
Mori, Damian 172
Morocco 21, 162, 163, 165,
    167, 208, 229
Morten, Alexander 62
Mortensen, Stan 109
Most bookings, 38, 48, 49
Most capped players 140, 141,
    158, 185
Most clean sheets 90
Most goals 30, 31, 141, 192,
    193, 158, 204, 205
Most matches coached 45
Most red cards 48, 39, 194,
    207
Most substitute appearances
    38
Most substituted player 75
Most wins, coach 44
Mpenza, Emile 196
Mpenza, Mbo 196
Mugica, Juan 225
Muller, Gerd 33, 35, 74, 114,
    149, 193, 195
Muller, Martina 237
Muller, Thomas 14, 15, 33,
    34, 73, 74
Mullery, Alan 60
Munaron, Jacques 42
Mundialito 154
Munich air disaster 23
Musial, Adam 115
Mutu, Adrian 120
Myong Hui, Hong 241
Myong-Won, Kim 179
Myrie, Roy 188
Myung-Bo, Hong 175

Nacional 225
Nakamura, Shunsuke 177
Nakata, Hidetoshi 176, 177
Nancy 66
Nasazzi, Jose 14, 227, 206
NASL 187
Natia, Natia 181
Ndaye, Mulamba 212

Nedved, Pavel 103
Neeskens, Johan 79, 80,
    82, 194
Nehoda, Jan 194
Neill, Lucas 173
Nejedly, Oldrich 103
Nelsen, Ryan 251
Nelspruit 53
Nemeth, Szilard 141
Nerz, Otto 76
Nesta, Alessandro 37, 87
Netolicka, Jaroslav 194
Netto, Igor 47, 123
Netzer, Gunter 193
Neuer, Manuel 40
Neville, Gary 64, 196
Neville, Phil 64, 196
New Caledonia 180
New Zealand 20, 138, 156,
    175, 179, 180, 181, 251
Nielsen, Richard Moller 105
Nielsen, Sophus 229
Nielsen, Torkil 193
Nigeria 44, 168, 169, 213, 214,
    219, 220, 221, 226, 227,
    237, 238, 239
Nikiforov, Yuri 220
Nikolaidis, Nikos 106
Nisot, Fernand 97
Nkono, Thomas 213
Nordahl, Bertil 129
Nordahl, Gunnar 128, 129
Nordahl, Knut 129
Nordby, Bente 238
Nordic Championship 129
Normcharoen, Vilard 232
North Africa 162–5
North Korea 167, 175, 176,
    177, 178, 179, 238, 241
Montenegro 139
North Yemen 165
Northern Ireland 25, 27,
    110–111, 119, 192
    v England 111
    v Germany 192
    v Luxembourg 111
    v Spain 111, 192
    top caps 110, 111
    top scorers 111
Norway 112–13, 227, 236,
    237, 238, 240, 241
Novikov, Aleksandre 218
Nyasulu, Philip 168
Nyberg, Arne 129
Nzigou, Chiva Star 212

Oceania 179, 180–81
Octopus 17
Ognenovski, Sasa 173
Oivella, Fernando 91
Okada, Takeshi 178
Okazaki, Shinji 174
Okocha, Jay Jay 169
Oldest captain 43
Oldest coach 44
Oldest goalscorers 22
Oldest players 23, 36, 39
Oldest referee 46
Olimpia Asuncion 129, 225
Olimpico, Stadio 52
Olisadebe, Emmanuel 115
Oliveira, Carlos 189
Olmeta, Pascal 232
Olsen, Egil 112, 113
Olsen, Morten 17, 104
Olympiastadion, Berlin 52
Olympic Games 52, 56, 98,
    103, 105, 109, 113, 114,
    115, 122, 123, 128, 129,
    140, 143, 147, 154, 168,
    169, 178, 213, 216, 226–9
    finals 226
    penalty shoot-outs 229
    top scorers 228, 229
Olympic Games Women
    234, 240–41
Olympic Stadium, Helsinki
    142
Olympic Stadium, Kiev 135
Omam-Biyik, Francois 48
Oman 164, 165
Ono, Shinji 177
Onopko, Viktor 123, 134
Orsi, Raimundo 148
Osim, Ivica 178
Oval, The 64, 65
Owairan, Saeed 174, 177
Owen, Michael 37, 61, 63,
    64
Own goals 64, 138

Pagliuca, Gianluca 40
Palacios, Edwin 189
Palacios, Jerry 189
Palacios, Johnny 189
Palacios, Milton 189
Palacios, Wilson 189
Palermo, Martin 148, 149
Palestine 163, 175
Palmer, Carl Erik 22
Panama 188
Panathinaikos 225
Pancev, Darko 141, 193
Pandev, Goran 140
Panenka, Antonin 102
Pantelic, Ilja 194
Paraguay 12, 31, 55, 157,
    157–9, 189, 203, 207
Parreira, Carlos Alberto 44
Passarella, Daniel 146
Patenaude, Bert 35, 186
Paul the Octopus 17
Pauleta 72
Pavlyuchenko, Roman 122
Pavon, Carlos 188
Pearce, Stuart 55
Pecnik, Nejc 138
Pedersen, Morten Gamst 112
Pele 18, 31, 35, 36, 39, 126,
    150, 152, 186, 187, 205,
    219
Penalty shoot-outs 21, 31, 26,
    39, 54–5, 72, 83, 84, 91,
    94, 132, 133, 172, 194, 210,
    218, 220, 229, 231, 236
Penarol 225
Penev, Dimitar 98
Pentland, Fred 91
Pereda, Jesus 196
Perez, Diego 15
Perrotta, Simone 133
Peru 42, 45, 120, 156, 158,
    203, 206, 207
Peruzzi, Angelo 86
Petit, Manu 71
Petric, Mladen 132
Petrone, Pedro 204, 229
Petrov, Stilian 98
Peyroteo 116
Pfaff, Jean-Marie 42
Pichichi 95
Piendibene, Jose 204
Pimenta, Ademar 152
Pinto, Joao 218
Pires, Robert 222, 227
Piriz, Juan Emilio 207
Planicka, Frantisek 41
Platini, Michel 66, 67, 195
PlayStation® 233
Poborsky, Karel 102
Podolski, Lukas 15, 192
Pokou, Laurent 212, 213
Poland 30, 114–15, 138, 163,
    179, 189
Poll, Graham 38, 173
Pollak, Jaroslav 194
Polokwane 53
Popescu, Gheorghe 120
Popescu, Gica 120
Port Elizabeth 53
Portugal 39, 44, 54, 116–17,
    141, 163, 167, 179, 194,
    195, 197, 218, 219,
    232
Prandelli, Marcello 89
Premier League 16
Pretinha 240
Pretoria 53
Preud'homme, Michel 96
Prinz, Birgit 237, 238, 239,
    240, 241
Prosinecki, Robert 37
PSV Eindhoven 173, 179, 196
Puc, Antonic 103
Puhl, Sandor 49
Pula 231
Puskas, Ferenc 64, 108,
    109, 225
Puyol, Carles 16, 95
Puzach, Anatoli 39

Qatar 219
Queiroz, Carlos 117, 218
Quiniou, Joel 47
Quiroga, Ramon 42

Racing Club 225
Radoman, Miroslav 125
Raducioiu, Florin 120
Rahn, Helmut 73

Rainea, Nicolae 49
Rajevac, Milovan 127, 167
Ramos, Alfonso 233
Ramsey, Sir Alf 64, 65
Rappan, Karl 131
Rasmussen, Peter 222
Rasunda Stadium 50
Raul 91, 93
Ravelli, Andreas 129
Ravelli, Thomas 128, 129
Raynor, George 129
Reader, George 46, 47
Real Madrid 27, 91, 93, 94, 95, 117, 153, 196, 225
Rebrov, Serhiy 135
Red Star Belgrade 126
Redknapp, Jamie 158
Referees 46–7
Rehhagel, Otto 44, 106, 107
Reid, Winston 180
Reim, Martin 140
Reims 70
Rekdal, Kjetil 112
Rensenbrink, Rob 80, 83
Rep, Johnny 80
Republic of Ireland 22, 25, 54, 118–19, 192, 193
  v Belgium 119
  v England 118, 119
  v France 118
  v Holland 193
  top caps 119
  top scorers 119
  v Turkey 119
  v United States 119
Revie, Don 64
Reyna, Claudio 186, 187
Ribbeck, Erich 77
Rica Raducanu 43
Ricardo 39, 54
Richards, Sir Viv 23
Ricken, Lars 130
Riise, Hege 238
Rimet, Jules 8, 27, 67
Rio de Janeiro 50, 51, 52
Riquelme, Juan Roman 226
Riva, Gigi 87, 194
River Plate 146
Roa, Carlos 48
Robben, Arjen 16, 28, 32, 37, 49
Robertinho 232
Roberto 232
Roberto, Ze 202
Robson, Bobby 247
Robson, Bryan 37, 43, 133, 163
Rodriguez, Leonardo 222
Rodriguez, Pedro 224
Rodriguez, Rodolfo 154
Rojas, Eladio 156
Roma 86
Romania 43, 120–21, 189
Romano, Angel 205
Romario 202, 223
Romerito 158
Rommedahl, Dennis 104
Ronaldinho 18, 223
Ronaldo 18, 32, 33, 35, 150, 153, 202, 223, 227
Ronaldo, Cristiano 117, 167, 247
Rooney, Wayne 47, 62, 197, 225
Rosas, Manuel 185
Rose Bowl 50, 52
Rosetta, Virginio 89
Ross, Diana 54
Rossi, Giuseppe 228
Rossi, Paolo 32, 33, 86, 150
Roux, Guy 71
Rubin Kazan 135
Rueda, Reinaldo 189
Ruffier, Stephane 69
Rummenigge, Karl-Heinz 38, 74
Rush, Ian 136
Russia 122–3, 134, 139, 173, 196, 220, 229, 231, 237, 238 see also Soviet Union
Rustu, Recber 41, 132
Rydell, Sven 129

Saadane, Rabah 163
Saarland 23, 45, 77
St-Denis 68
St-Etienne 66
Salapu, Nicky 181
Salas, Marcelo 158, 159

Salem, Abdel Aziz 164
Salenko, Oleg 134, 218
Salinas, Julio 91
Salpingidis, Dimitrios 107
Sammer, Matthias 72, 74
Sampdoria 89
San Marino 138, 142, 192, 193
San Siro 89
Sanchez, Erwin 156
Sanchez, Leonel 158
Sand, Ebbe 105
Santana, Tele 150
Santini, Jacques 71
Santos 152, 225
Santos, Djalma 36
Santos, Francileudo 165
Santos, Nilton 36, 39
Santrac, Slobodan 127
Sao Paulo 230
Sarosi, Gyorgy 177
Sastre, Fernand 66
Saudi Arabia 44
Saudi Arabia 48
Saudi Arabia 163
Saudi Arabia 174–8, 222, 223
Saviola, Javier 219
Scarone, Hector 154, 205, 227
Schmeichel, Peter 83, 104, 105, 194
Schneider, Bernd 192
Scholz, Heiko 72
Schon, Helmut 45, 76, 77
Schumacher, Harald 39, 54, 55
Schurpf, Pascal 230
Schuster, Dirk 72
Schwarzer, Mark 172
Schweinsteiger, Bastian 192
Scifo, Enzo 196
Scolari, Luiz Felipe 44
Scotland 24, 25, 27, 124–5, 169, 180
Seedorf, Clarence 81
Seeler, Uwe 75
Seferovic, Haris 220, 221
Selva, Andy 138
Semak, Sergei 122
Seman, Stanislav 42
Semih Senturk 133
Sendings off 38, 39, 49 see also Red cards
Senegal 45, 246
Serbia 13, 126–7, 139, 173
Serebrianikov, Viktor 39
Sergio, Paulo 232
Seric, Anthony 173
Serie A 16, 84, 89
Shakira 6, 167
Shalamanov, Alexsandar 99
Shaqiri, Xherdan 230
Sheffield United 133
Shehata, Hassan 215
Sherbakov, Sergei 218
Shesternev, Albert 195
Shevchenko, Andriy 134, 135
Shilton, Peter 39, 43
Shovkovskyi, Oleksandr 134
Siegenthaler, Urs 55
Siegrist, Benjamin 221
Silva, Dario 155
Silva, David 221
Silver goals 195
Silver Shoe 32
Simao Sabrosa 116, 117
Simeone, Diego 222
Simic, Dario 101
Simoes, Antonio 117
Simon, Jacques 48
Simons, Timmy 96
Simunic, Josip 38, 173
Sinama-Pongolle, Florent 220
Sinclair, Christine 241
Sindelar, Matthias 140
Sivori, Omar 146, 200, 203
Sivuha, Yuri 218
Six, Didier 54
Slovakia 138–41, 143
Slovenia 138–42, 163
Smeltz, Shane 181
Smisek, Sandra 237
Smit, Andries 233
Smith, John 64
Smith, Kelly 241
Smith, Walter 126
Smolarek, Wlodzimierz 115
Sneijder, Wesley 14, 34, 49, 79, 80, 167
Soccer City 8, 10, 13, 17, 50, 53, 56

Socorro, Hector 189
Socrates 150
Solomon Islands 20
Sonck, Wesley 96
Song Billong, Alexandre 166
Song Hui, Kim 241
Song, Rigobert 37, 48, 166, 212, 223
South Africa 6, 8, 10, 12, 16, 21, 24, 42, 44, 56, 167, 169, 210, 212, 214
South America 144
South American Footballer of the Year 158
South Korea 21, 31, 34, 53, 156, 170, 174–9
Southall, Neville 136
Soviet Union 47, 91, 122, 123, 134, 135, 139, 156, 169, 190, 193, 194, 195, 197, 198, 218, 219, 226 see also Russia, Ukraine
Spain 8, 13, 14, 16, 18, 21, 24, 26, 27, 27, 28, 30, 32, 42, 47, 54, 55, 58, 90–95, 187, 190, 192, 194, 195, 196, 199, 220, 221, 223, 227, 229, 231, 232, 248
  v Belgium 91
  v Brazil 93
  v Chile 93
  colours 28
  v England 91, 94
  v Germany 95
  v Greece 92
  v Holland 92
  v Honduras 93
  v Italy 91
  main stadiums 95
  records 91
  v Malta 192
  v Republic of Ireland 94
  v Saudi Arabia 92
  v Soviet Union 91, 194
  major tournaments 91
  top caps 92
  top scorers 92, 93
  youngest player 92
Srna, Darijo 101
Stabile, Guillermo 33, 35, 206
Stade de France 68
Stankovic, Dejan 127
Staunton, Steve 118
Steaua Bucharest 120, 121
Siegemann, Kerstin 237
Steiner, Karel 227
Stekelenburg, Maarten 155
Stewart, Earnie 186
Stockholm 50
Stoichkov, Hristo 99
Stojkovic, Nenad 233
Streltsov, Eduard 122
Stromsik, Karel 42
Suarez, Claudio 185, 205
Suarez, Luis 42, 93, 155, 190, 196
Sub-Saharan Africa 166–9
Substitutes 105
Substitutions 22, 23
Sudan 139, 208, 213
Suker, Davor 101, 141, 192
Sukur, Hakan 31, 132
Superga disaster 89
Suurbier, Wim 80, 82
Svenssen, Thorbjorn 113
Svensson, Anders 128
Svensson, Karl-Oskar 129
Sweden 13, 22, 45, 47, 128–9, 139, 189, 227, 236, 237, 238, 241
Swiss Bolt defence 131
Switzerland 28, 30, 130–31, 139, 197, 220, 221
Szarmach, Andrzej 114

Tabarez, Oscar Washington 155
Tae-Se, Jong 176
Tahiti 180, 218
Taiwan 178, 179, 238, 239
Tajikistan 139, 175, 179
Tancredi, Melissa 238
Tanzania 21
Tasfaout, Abdelhafid 165
Tassotti, Mauro 38, 49
Taylor, David 141
Taylor, MacDonald 23
Taylor, Maik 111
Taylor, Peter 64

Team America 187
Teixeira, Alex 218
Terim, Fatih 133
Tettey-Quao, Barikisu 237
Tevez, Carlos 158, 228
Thom, Andreas 72
Thomas, Clive 47
Thompson, Archie 22, 181
Thorstvedt, Erik 113
Thunderstorm 199
Thuram, Lilian 69, 71
Thys, Guy 97
Tiago 117, 231
Tim 156
Tobias, Manoel 231
Tobin, Alex 172
Togo 214
Toldi, Geza 177
Toldo, Francesco 83
Toledo, Lido 153
Tomaszewski, Jan 40
Tonga 2, 181
Torino 89
Torosidis, Vasileios 107
Torrado, Gerrado 184
Torres, Fernando 92, 190
Torres, Jose 117
Toshack, John 137
Total Football 82
Tottenham Hotspur 63, 110, 135, 137, 148, 189
Toure, Kolo 167
Toure, Yaya 167
Tovey, Neil 219
Trabelsi, Hatem 163
Tramutola, Juan Jose 45, 147
Traore, Moussa 220
Trappatoni, Giovanni 88
Trappeniers, Jan 97
Trezeguet, David 54, 69, 71
Trinidad & Tobago 137, 189
Trobbiani, Marco 148
Troussier, Philippe 178
Tshabalala, Siphiwe 16
Tuncay Sanli 132
Tunisia 21, 162, 163, 165, 177, 210, 214
Turkemenistan 178
Turkey 24, 26, 31, 132–3, 139, 163, 170, 173, 175, 193
Turkmenistan 139, 179
Tymoschuk, Anatoliy 134
Udinese 141

UEFA 66, 130, 179, 190, 225
UEFA Champions League 27, 130, 132, 224, 225, 244
UEFA Cup 89, 129, 132, 133, 224
UEFA European Championship 27, 55, 66, 67, 68, 69, 73, 90, 91, 190, 222
  1960 91, 122, 123, 126, 192, 197, 198
  1964 91, 93, 109, 193, 196, 198
  1968 84, 87, 126, 192, 194, 195, 198
  1972 72, 73, 74, 193, 195, 198
  1976 102, 194
  1980 72, 96, 97, 107, 194, 197
  1984 116, 192, 194, 195, 196, 197
  1988 78, 79, 81 82, 118, 196, 197, 198
  1992 104, 105, 128, 192, 193, 194, 197
  1996 72, 73, 74, 91, 100, 101, 123, 196, 197
  2000 68, 69, 83, 96, 121, 196, 197, 198, 199, 223
  2004 69, 92, 103, 106, 107, 130, 142, 195, 196
  2008 91, 92, 94, 95, 100, 114, 122, 123, 130, 131, 132, 133, 192, 196, 197, 199, 221
  2012 114, 115, 135, 137, 198
  champions 195
  biggest crowd 198
  biggest wins 195
  hosts 198
  most games 197
  most goals 195, 196, 197
  penalty shoot-outs 194
  qualifiers 192–93
  qualifying playoff 193

youngest player 197
UEFA Women's Championship 234, 241
Ukraine 134–5, 138, 139, 218
  see also CIS, Soviet Union
  v Italy 134, 135
  records 134
  v Saudi Arabia 135
  v Switzerland 135
  top caps 135
  top scorers 135
Un Hyang, Kim 241
United Arab Emirates 20, 44
United States 24, 25, 42, 43, 44, 162, 163, 185, 186–7, 188, 189, 205, 221, 222, 223, 234, 236, 237, 238, 239, 240
Upson, Matthew 61
Upton Park FC 227
Uruguay 8, 12, 14, 15, 16, 18, 20, 21, 26, 27, 28, 47, 51, 52, 54, 98, 144, 147, 154–5, 200, 202, 203, 204, 205, 206, 207, 220, 227, 229, 232, 251
  v Argentina 154, 155
  v Australia 155
  v Brazil 154
  v Chile 157
  v Costa Rica 147, 155
  v Germany 154
  v Ghana 155
  v Australia 155
  top caps 155
  top scorers 154
Utjesenovic, Doug 173
Uzbekistan 139, 178, 179

Valderrama, Carlos 205
Valeiro, Roberto 232
Valeron, Juan Carlos 94
Van Basten, Marco 79, 81, 83
Van Bommel, Mark 37, 80
Van Bronckhorst, Giovanni 15, 38, 39, 79
Van den Buys, Stan 130
Van der Kerkhof, Rene 80
Van der Sar, Edwin 83
Van Gaal, Louis 82
Van Hanegem, Wim 194
Van Marwijk, Bert 12, 78, 80, 83
Van Nistelrooy, Ruud 81
Vandereycken, Rene 97
Vanuatu 181
Vasquez, Sergio 157
Vava 33, 36
Velez Sarsfield 225
Venables, Terry 62, 64
Venezuela 203, 207
Vennegoor of Hesselink, Jan 38
Vercauteren, Franky 97
Videkull, Lena 238
Vidic, Nemanja 127
Vidinic, Blagoje 45
Vieira, Patrick 68, 71, 223, 227
Vieri, Christian 173
Vieri, Max 173
Vilfort, Kim 194
Villa, David 14, 30, 33, 55, 93
Villa, Ricardo 148
Villalonga, Jose 91
Villar, Justo 55
Villar, Justo 55
Vittek, Robert 141
Vogts, Berti 74, 76, 125
Voller, Rudi 76, 77
Vonlanthen, Johan 197
Vutsov, Ivan 98
Vuvuzela 167

Waddle, Chris 55
Wagner, Theodor 30
Wajoka, Pierre 180
Walcott, Theo 62
Walden, Fanny 62
Walden, Harold 228
Wales 25, 27, 136–7, 139
  biggest defeat 137
  biggest win 137
  v Brazil 137
  v England 137
  v Estonia 136
  v Ireland 137
  v Northern Ireland 136
  v Scotland 137
  top caps 137

top scorers 137
  v Trinidad & Tobago 137
  v Turkey 136
Wallis and Futana 181
Wanchope, Paulo 188
Warnken, Alberto 48
Weah, George 169, 246
Webb, Howard 17, 47, 223
Weiss, Vladimir I 143
Weiss, Vladimir II 17, 143
Weiss, Vladimir III 143
Wembley 52, 64, 65
Wen, Sun 238, 239
Wesely, Inka 241
West Germany see Germany
West Ham United 63, 135
Wetterstrom, Gustav 129
Whiteside, Norman 36, 111
Whitmore, Theodore 189
Wilimowski, Ernest 114
Wilkins, Ray 43, 163
Wilkinson, Howard 62
Williams, Bert 187
Williams, Mark 210
Wilson, Andy 125
Wimbledon 112, 113
Wimmer, Herbert 195
Winterbottom, Walter 65
Witeczek, Marcel 221
Wodz, Dariusz 72
Wolfsburg 86
Wolstenholme, Kenneth 33
Wolverhampton Wanderers 63
Women's football 234–41
Woodward, Vivian 228
World Club Cup 225 see also FIFA Club World Cup
Wright, Billy 63, 109, 113

Xavi 26, 229
Xavier, Abel 197, 218

Yahia, Antar 162
Yashin Award, Lev 96
Yashin, Lev 41, 123
Yatabare, Mustapha 211
Yekini, Rashidi 213
Yellow card 22
Youngest captain 42
Youngest goalkeeper 42
Youngest players 23, 36, 39, 97, 197
Youngest referee 46
Youngest sending off 48
Young-Pyo, Lee 177
Yugoslavia 45, 139, 174, 190, 193, 194, 195, 212 see also Serbia
  v Italy 194
  v Zaire 117
Yuran, Serei 134

Zagallo, Mario 36
Zagorakis, Theodoros 106
Zahovic, Zlatko 140
Zaire 45, 49, 212
Zaki, Amr 165
Zalgiris Vilnius 143
Zaluska, Lukas 114
Zambia 22, 169
Zambrotta, Gianluca 84
Zamora, Ricardo 41, 94
Zamorano, Ivan 159
Zand, Mahmoud 165
Zanetti, Javier 149
Zarate, Mauro 147
Zarraonaindia, Telmo 95
Zdrilic, David 22
Zenga, Walter 26, 39, 88
Zico 47, 150, 152, 158, 178
Zidane, Zinedine 38, 47, 48, 66, 67, 68, 69, 71, 102, 166
Zito 36
Zizinho 205
Zmuda, Wladyslaw 114
Zoff, Dino 39, 40
Zokora, Didier 167, 168
Zsengeller, Gyula 177
Zsolt, Istvan 47
Zuberbuhler, Pascal 39, 130
Zubizarreta, Andoni 92

ABOUT THE AUTHOR

Keir Radnedge has been covering football for more than 40 years. He has written countless books on the subject, from tournament guides to comprehensive encyclopedias, aimed at all ages. His journalism career included the *Daily Mail* for 20 years, as well as the *Guardian* and other national newspapers and magazines in the UK and abroad. He is a former editor of *World Soccer,* generally recognized as the premier English-language magazine on global football. In addition to his writing, Keir has been a regular analyst for BBC radio and television, Sky Sports and the American cable news channel CNN. He also edited a tournament newspaper at the FIFA World Cup tournaments of 1982, 1986 and 1990. He has also scripted video reviews of numerous international football tournaments. He is also the London-based editor of SportsFeatures.com, the football and Olympic news website.